THE FUTURE *of* ETHICS

THE FUTURE
of
ETHICS

SUSTAINABILITY, SOCIAL JUSTICE, AND
RELIGIOUS CREATIVITY

WILLIS JENKINS

Georgetown University Press
Washington, DC

Library of Congress Cataloging-in-Publication Data

Jenkins, Willis.
  The future of ethics : sustainability, social justice, and religious creativity / Willis Jenkins.
    pages cm
  Includes bibliographical references and index.
  ISBN 978-1-62616-017-0 (pbk. : alk. paper)
  1. Christian ethics. 2. Religious ethics. 3. Human ecology—Religious aspects—Christianity. 4. Human ecology—Religious aspects. 5. Christianity and justice. 6. Religion and justice. I. Title.
  BJ1251.J373 2013
  241—dc23

2013002931

♾ This book is printed on recycled, acid-free paper meeting the requirements of the American National Standard for Permanence in Paper for Printed Library Materials.

15 14 13   9 8 7 6 5 4 3 2
First printing

Printed in the United States of America

Contents

Preface

This book depicts how emerging problems of human power challenge ethical inquiry and it tries to suggest the sort of moral creativity that opens possibilities of meaningful response to those challenges. It does not offer predictions or blueprints, despite what the title may suggest. It rather develops multidisciplinary inquiry into concrete problems that arise as human and ecological systems hybridize and change, searching for resources to cope with those changes and, to some extent, take responsibility for them.

Initially I set out to write a different kind of book. After a first book on theology and environmental ethics, I thought I should try to apply the theory to practice. Students had pressed me to say what difference ecotheologies make for confronting particular problems, and colleagues in other disciplines wanted to know how I think theology matters to processes of cultural change. So I set out to describe how grammars of belief could generate satisfactory responses to representative problems of human power like: climate change, human poverty, biodiversity loss, and chemical exposures. My idea was to show how ethics interprets the relevant disciplines (economics, social theory, environmental sciences) within a general theological account of sustainability.

Two things happened to me. First, working on each concrete problem changed my understanding of its practical challenge and of the concepts I had to interpret it. Paying closer attention to the fields of knowledge interpreting each problem, and to innovative projects using theological and cultural inheritances to confront them, shifted how I think about doing religious ethics. The experience of working on those problems and with those projects nudged me away from a notion of social ethics as putting ideas into practice and toward a view in which ideas and practices form inherited patterns of life that agents can redeploy to confront new challenges. This book depicts the tasks of ethics when understood as a form of critical participation in how reform projects adapt their traditions to respond to overwhelming problems. Religious ethics, I argue, should focus less on constructing and applying religious worldviews and more on inviting, tutoring, and pressuring moral communities to make better use of their inheritances.

The second thing that happened to me was that I became a parent. Simeon was born in the midst of writing this book, and the experience of pregnancy and parenthood drive its concerns. Writing a book on the ethics of overwhelming problems matters differently when one is writing for the world of one's own child. Not only did I pay more acute attention to research on how chemicals accumulate in uterine tissues and to the risks of atmospheric changes fifty years from now, I also searched for creative responses that seemed to bear potential for change. Confronting a series of problems so overwhelming that they foster a whole genre of collapse literature, I felt compelled to find and write alongside live pledges of practical hope. In the face of problems that would disinherit the future—diminishing migrations, embittered injustice, impoverishing markets, deluded moralities—I came to orient my task as teacher and parent on finding sustaining graces.

That task would be impossible without Rebekah Menning, who parents gracefully and has been supportive of me in more ways than I can name. In researching this book I visited communities in South Africa and Ecuador, and tried to learn from several transnational projects, which was made possible by a Conant Grant from the Episcopal Church Center. The shifting ideas in this book were forged through presentations given at Boston College, Centro des Estudios Teologicos, the College of William & Mary, Harvard Divinity School, Michigan State University, Oregon State University, Pacific Lutheran University, the Society of Christian Ethics, the Spring Institute on Lived Theology, the University of Montana, and the University of Virginia. I am especially indebted to Jim Childress and Chuck Mathewes for believing in this project and organizing occasions to discuss it. Mary Evelyn Tucker and John Grim have been extraordinary and patient tutors. My colleagues in ethics at Yale—Jennifer Herdt, Gene Outka, Fred Simmons, and Emilie Townes—encouraged and criticized in just the right measures. Coteaching with Os Schmitz instructed me in what ethics must do in order to make a difference for the everyday work of ecological scientists.

Many other friends and colleagues offered crucial gifts of reading, including: Sarah Azaransky, David Barr, Sofia Betancourt, Stephen Blackmer, Jonathan Cannon, Elizabeth Gerle, Sarah Fredericks, Laura Hartman, Tim Hartman, Christina McRorie, Stephen Macekura, Christopher Morck, Kathleen Deane Moore, Kevin O'Brien, Peter Paris, Travis Pickell, Kathryn Salisbury, and Gretel Van Wieren. I wish also to thank the helpful reviewers from Georgetown University Press, and especially Richard Brown. The meticulous care of Andrew Forsyth corrected many errors. Publication was assisted by the Frederick W. Hilles Publication Fund of Yale University.

As this book goes to press I am moving back to the University of Virginia to join an exciting initiative in the environmental humanities. I go in keen recognition of my debt to the remarkable students at Yale Divinity School and the Yale School of Forestry and Environmental Studies who have shaped this project by their yearning to work well in a daunting world.

Ethics in the Anthropocene

✦

Ethics seems imperiled by unprecedented problems. The accelerating expansion of human power generates problems that exceed the competency
of our laws, our institutions, and even our concepts. What does justice mean
for climate change, a problem in which humans from many nations, traditions, and generations find themselves collectively responsible for how a
planetary system will function over centuries? The ethics of climate change
is more complicated than applying received norms to novel objects because,
as philosopher Hans Jonas puts it, "the qualitatively novel nature of certain
of our actions has opened up a whole new dimension of ethical relevance
for which there is no precedent in the standards and canons of ethics."[1]
Received ideas of justice do not anticipate moral agency exercised cumulatively across generational time, aggregately through ecological systems, and
nonintentionally over evolutionary futures. Climate change involves dimensions of human action without precedent in our traditions and institutions
of justice.

Yet even as they overwhelm capacities of moral response, problems like
climate change press ethics into the center of public life. "If the great new
fact of our time is that cumulative human activity has the power to affect all
life in fundamental and unprecedented ways," writes religious ethicist Larry
Rasmussen, then "this means the ascendancy of ethics for our era, as an utterly practical affair."[2] The rising significance of human action within basic
systems of life means that every social project and political decision—from
economic policy to health care to zoning codes—carries fundamental ethical questions. What must we sustain, and why? The powers that imperil ethics also make it unavoidable.

The atmospheric chemist Paul Crutzen calls this planetary condition
of human power the "anthropocene," a new geological epoch characterized
by pervasive human influence throughout earth's systems.[3] Consider that

most of earth's flowing fresh water has been dammed, impounding gigatons of sediment. The terraform power to reengineer watersheds already leaves a lasting stratigraphic legacy for future geologists. It may also leave clues about the demise of this civilization, for those dams accelerate the sinking of urban deltas, cause the disappearance of riparian life, and in the long run will not last as long as the rivers they seek to control. Similar power and peril lie in the nitrogen cycle. Humans now fix more nitrogen than all other ecological processes combined. Accelerating the nitrogen cycle drives agricultural productivity but also creates eutrophication ("dead zones") in every major body of water, with unknown consequences for the future of marine life. Climate change represents the anthropocene condition most dramatically: the human energy economy is shifting how the planet regulates solar energy. To reflect the pervasive influence of humanity, some scientists have begun remapping earth's biomes as "anthromes," in recognition that most of the planet's habitats are now "human systems with natural ecosystems embedded within them."[4] In a sense, humanity has become earth's habitat.

It is not unprecedented for a species to transform the biosphere. Upstart bacteria did it several billion years ago, radically remaking the atmosphere and banishing previously dominant species. It is unprecedented that a species should do so knowingly, worrying over the changes it makes, wondering if it imperils the systems on which life depends, if it acts badly, if it risks its hopes for the future. Never before (we think) has a species understood that its story was renarrating life, and asked itself if it was telling the story well. The anthropocene is an epoch of ethics because it is an epoch of dominion by a moral species. The duration and meaning of this epoch will depend on whether humanity can, in the face of unprecedented problems, sustain its capacities of moral response. The future of humanity, and so of life in the anthropocene, depends on the future of ethics—which stands in jeopardy.

Ethics is in jeopardy not because the rise of human power is necessarily evil and destructive. Ethics is imperiled by the difficulties of interpreting and taking responsibility for the complex and ambiguous story of humanity's social intelligence growing into a geophysical force. The problems of human power overwhelm ethics because they arise from rapidly hybridizing social and environmental systems. A problem like climate change forces humans to recognize responsibilities for managing earth systems as influential participants. "Management" is a controversial metaphor, risking complicity with arrogance, mastery, and colonization. This book investigates other metaphors of responsibility, but it accepts the basic reality of power behind the managerial metaphor: humanity already exercises responsibility for how earth systems function. However fragile and temporary, human dominion is planetary fact. "Most aspects of the structure and functioning of Earth's ecosystems," say leading ecologists, "cannot be understood without accounting for the strong, often dominant influence of humanity."[5] How earth's ecosystems will function in the future therefore depends on the character and responsibility of human societies. Whether humans create stronger forms of global cooperation, how we reconcile ideals of freedom and justice, if we overcome extreme poverty—all will make a difference for how rivers flow, which plants grow, and what the temperature will be. So will our obtuseness and passivity, our injustice to one another, our selfishness and greed for power. Recognizing anthropocene power acknowledges that managing earth systems as influential participants means learning to manage ourselves. Do we know how to do that? Can we be taught?

Our ethical traditions seem incompetent to the trouble our powers create. For most of human history, explains religious ethicist William Schweiker, "human actions reached only so far into the future, at most a generation, and had effects only on others who were relatively near to me. The scope of responsibility was delimited by the extent of human power." Now that human powers have become "titanic," ethics must find a way to generate corresponding dimensions of responsibility.[6] Ethics seems unprepared to address human action as a globalizing aggregate that influences systems through dispersed, cumulative, nonintentional effects. The very powers that make ethics an imperative global conversation also undermine cultural capabilities to have an adequate conversation. Ethics must help humanity imagine and construct new forms of responsibilities, or, in the failure to do so, face the portents of collapse.

That is the general challenge of sustainability and it would be daunting on its own. However, the same powers also generate new dimensions of social injustice. Humanity's planetary power does not distribute well among human individuals. At the outset of the anthropocene epoch many humans struggle to live. Two billion humans lives in extreme poverty, about one in five children lives in chronic hunger, and about one in four persons live without access to safe water. The difficulty here is not simply that ethics faces two axes of crisis, one made by ecological powers and the other by social powers. Planetary structures of moral agency elide distinctions between ecological and social problems. How the world confronts poverty affects biodiversity loss, and how it responds to climate change affects protection of human rights. Distinguishing social and environmental problems obfuscates the moral task, so ethics must invent ways to confront the hybrid problems of integrating systems.

Deepening the challenge, ethics must address planetary problems and global injustice in conditions of moral pluralism and cultural conflict. The planet faces increasingly shared problems but its many moral cultures do not interpret them by a common story or even a shared sense of responsibility. The globalizing forces that Peter Singer observes obliterating moral distance to create "one world" are the same forces that Schweiker observes causing new moral conflicts, thus creating "a time of many worlds."[7] We live simultaneously in "one world" and "many worlds." Ethics must find a way to develop new and shared responsibilities among a pluralist and alienated human family. How to construct a global ethic from many moral worlds?

Ethics is formal reflection on cultural repertories of response to important human challenges. Ethics is at risk because practices and concepts that sustain the moral agency of humanity are at risk. The rise of anthropocene power generates problems that seem to overwhelm our repertories of response. Over the first chapters of this book I explain how those problems are "unprecedented," "planetary," and "wicked." Do not let those adjectives distract from the basic challenge I am illustrating: ethical reflection helps drive adaptive change even when uncertain about what to do, while lacking satisfactory concepts, and without shared traditions. Amidst fears of cultural collapse, ethics must help generate new possibilities of moral agency.

THE COSMOLOGICAL TEMPTATION

This book pursues an unconventional way of approaching those challenges. It is almost conventional wisdom that unprecedented challenges require religious and ethical thinkers to narrate a new story or retrieve a forgotten moral vision in order to reorient humanity's moral consciousness. Jonas, Rasmussen, Schweiker, and Singer each propose a new moral worldview within which to make sense of the problems of sustainability and social justice. In contrast, I attempt to do ethics in the context of reform projects that are trying to make their moral inheritances support adaptive patterns of action. That means beginning from concrete problems and doing ethics with imperfect concepts and incompetent communities in anticipation that the work of responding to problems can fire the moral imagination, improve our concepts, and make communities more competent to meet their challenges.

Reckoning with anthropocene power and unprecedented problems can tempt ethicists to dwell in moral cosmology, proposing foundational metaphors and symbols by which agents could better interpret the world of human responsibility. That approach, I worry, draws ethical attention away from concrete problems, scientific learning, pluralist negotiations, and the dynamics of cultural change. Religious ethics is especially vulnerable to the cosmological temptation because it assigns such an important role to beliefs and because it often imagines that professional moralists take the lead in reforming those beliefs. In my view, however, religious ethics holds promise for confronting unprecedented problems not because it possesses a special kind of moral resource (values, beliefs, worldviews) but because it works within traditions that are constantly being renegotiated and redeployed in order to meet new contextual demands. Cultural change mimics evolutionary change, I think, in that it adapts what it receives, working with the material it has to meet new challenges. The inventive work of transforming human behavior remains path-dependent, contingent on how we use our moral inheritances to meet contextual challenges. Because they self-consciously nurture distinctive ways of living a moral life, religious communities have strong incentives to develop and test the creativity that sustains that exercise.

Religious ethicists sometimes overestimate the practical importance of religious beliefs and cultural worldviews while underestimating the moral creativity in religious reform projects. Creeds do not straightforwardly produce problems like climate change or human impoverishment, and trying to modify the cognitive structure of belief is not an obviously effective way of modifying human behavior. The relationship between the structures of moral consciousness and patterns of social behavior seems more reflexive. No worldview or belief arrives into moral action without already having taken leave from embodied, socialized ways of living. There is more explanation for the problems we face than that we are failing to live up to our beliefs or that our worldviews are corrupt. Both of those things are continually true, but problems like climate change do not reduce to justice trespassed or nature violated. A significant part of their challenge lies in the way that they exceed the competence of our practices of justice and confound our views of nature. While continuing to criticize and interrogate background beliefs as part of the process, ethics must expand the scope and capacity of our moral repertories. It needs the sort of cultural creativity that incorporates new dimensions of moral action within concrete ways of cultivating a human life.

Agents can learn new moral competencies, I argue, by participating in projects that use their inheritances to create new responsibilities for unexpected problems. At least when confronting problems that require expanded moral competencies, the formal discipline of ethics should collaborate in those generative reform processes. If that approach seems too irenic and provisional for urgent crises like climate change, I submit that it is also the cultural ground for the deep moral learning that any adequate sustainability ethic needs. Adaptive moral learning is not as inexorable as the powers for which it tries to take responsibility, nor as easy as proposing to start different traditions or tell ourselves better myths. Ethics lies at risk of what moral communities manage to invent.

I explain and defend that strategy of ethics in chapters on theology and culture, global ethics, and the ethics of ecological management (chapters 2–4). The book exemplifies its method by opening with a concrete problem and reckoning with the apparent difficulty of response. Chapter 1 investigates why climate change seems to overwhelm ethics and then considers several strategies of religious response, each incompetent to the moral challenge. Readers of environmental books accustomed to an opening catalog of woe that functions to motivate support for its recommendations should keep in mind that this opening chapter functions differently. By explaining the moral complexity of climate change, I establish the unavoidable public roles for ethical reflection and illustrate how ethics can participate in interdisciplinary projects of adaptive learning. Descriptive serves to depict how the problem overwhelms moral agency and what adequate response would entail. Describing the uncertainties and perverse conflicts presented by the problem helps explain why climate change makes our moral traditions appear incompetent. Yet ethics can begin from that incompetence, I argue, when reform projects take their incompetence as a demand to create new possibilities from their inherited traditions. Then ethics can work from the tactics moral communities devise to sustain the possibility of a moral life in the face of problems that would defeat it.

My approach is pluralist and nonfoundationalist in that it does not suppose that the world needs to share a common faith or worldview in order to cooperate in confronting shared problems. Insofar as gathering all humanity in one shared belief has been a special emphasis of Christian evangelism, I argue that religious ethics should not be methodologically "Christian" in that way. The world does not necessarily need a shared metaphysics of nature or creation story in order to conform to climate change. It needs practical capacities of responsibility and cooperation. Those capacities of response might be forged from within and across all sorts of traditions as agents recognize new demands in new problems and invent new possibilities of cultural action from their inheritances. The generic belief claims of religious traditions matter less than the possibilities of moral agency opened by particular communities making their traditions face unprecedented problems.

Beliefs, worldviews, and cosmologies matter, in this view, in the ways that particular communities use them to support possibilities of response. My particularist and pluralist approach intentionally opens space for constructive argument in many other religious scenes. Religious creativity is always particular and contextual, so throughout the book I work with Christian projects and make constructive theological arguments. I do so in order to depict one moral tradition undergoing change as it is variously redeployed and renegotiated, and for the wider freedom one has to make constructive proposals as a participant within one's own tradition.[8] At times I show the reader, as if outside the tradition, how some Christian predicament illustrates a general challenge or role for religious creativity; at other times I write as if inside the tradition, showing the reader how to work constructively with religious creativity. Conducting the project this way invites participants in other moral traditions to undertake similar work. Letting Christian ethics host the interdisciplinary dialogues in this book does not mean to imply the centrality of Christianity; it rather uses its predicament and potential as an example of the sort of religious and moral transformation needed within many traditions. For example, the opening chapter establishes the peril to ethics by illustrating how climate change imperils Christianity. Christian ethics is formal reflection on Christianity as a way of life, but as planetary powers begin to exceed practices of love or render uncertain the meaning of justice, Christian ways of life offer little material through which ethicists can interpret climate change. The challenge to Christian ethics, then, lies in finding or inventing the practices that sustain possibilities for living the faith amidst anthropocene powers. Insofar as those practices overcome features of problems that would defeat moral agency, they will matter to wider publics looking for analogies of adaptation.

PROPHETIC PRAGMATISM

This project is made possible by the emergence of the field of religion and ecology, which has established the significance of religion and culture for any adequate understanding of sustainability problems. Because of that work, this book can proceed without dwelling on the novelty of addressing ecological problems from religious ethics. This project is also shaped by methodological tensions within religion and ecology. Some critics, worried that the field is too normative, too belief-focused or tradition-centered, have called for scholarship more attentive to particular communities and changing cultural expressions of religiosity. Other critics, worried that the field tends to treat injustice abstractly and secondarily, have called for scholarship more attentive to social power and ecological violence. In the crosscurrents of those tensions, I realized that my own first book in the field was vulnerable to both worries: focused on structures of belief, it remained abstract from particular problems of power. Attempting to articulate how theological traditions matter for problems like climate change pressed me to forge a different approach in the field. Doing so has made me rethink how I understand the role of ethics in complex social problems, the cultural function of religious arguments, and the tasks of Christian ethics in confronting new dynamics of power and violence.[9]

This book takes a broadly pragmatic approach to religious ethics. It starts from concrete problems and works with the ideas and practices generated from reform projects attempting to address them. It investigates how projects use their beliefs and practices to simultaneously sustain and revise some tradition of life by creating new opportunities for meaningful moral agency in the face of overwhelming problems. By interpreting those projects in light of the disciplinary arguments surrounding the problems they address, it intends to test and improve their experimentation. On this approach, ethics is a form of collaboration in the processes of moral and cultural transformation that makes agents become competent to the problems they face.

The tensions built into this approach create a dialectical structure to most of my chapters. I explain the complexity of a problem from several disciplinary perspectives in light of how some reform project has begun to address it. I investigate how that reform project uses and adapts its moral resources, and then gather a host of critical questions about its trajectory of moral change. Critique comes dialogically, attempting to constructively push a reform trajectory in order to enhance its ability to open concrete opportunities for meaningful agency. Planetary problems and global crises lend themselves to sweeping critiques, and when religious ethics faces ecological and economic problems it often runs long on critique, short on constructive possibility. While often compelling, cosmological critiques pose a practical trade-off: they make our inherited moral world seem incapable of facing difficult problems. In my view, cosmological critiques defeat the ethical task before it begins. I want to explore how far new possibilities of agency can be opened within received worlds by learning from problems how to use our traditions differently—with the view that using traditions differently is how they are changed. As each chapter tests the limits of those dialogical tensions, it also tests possibilities of hope. The dialectical style asks readers to judge those possibilities within the tension between available avenues of action and the deep demands of a problem.

The book makes a cumulative argument about how to do ethics amidst overwhelming problems, but it is written so that each chapter stands on its own, since some readers may care about the conversation in a particular chapter while indifferent to the cumulative argument. Particular chapters interpret and attempt to improve the interdisciplinary conversations happening within global ethics, political ecology and human rights, climate change, intergenerational ethics, the economics of sustainability, and the ethics of ecological management. Participants in those conversations should feel free to read just the relevant chapter, for each chapter was in fact first written for the interdisciplinary area it addresses.

I hope to persuade religious ethicists that they should read the whole book, including sections that do not seem directly religious, because each chapter exemplifies my argument about how to do ethics so as to sustain its future. Ethics cannot start by responding to problems, but must participate in the interpretation and construction of problems, which requires attending to climate science, models of poverty, and the economics of discounting. Ethics cannot be a disciplinary operation performed by specialists after some problem is posed; it must be a capacity of practical reasoning cultivated within interdisciplinary research struggling to interpret and frame emerging problems. I offer theological and methodological reasons for religious scholars to care about those conversations, and attempt to introduce them in ways that invite further and better contributions from religious ethics.

The sensibility and method of this book might be designated as a form of prophetic pragmatism since it seeks cultural transformation through critical participation in reform processes. It broadly inhabits the spirit of Cornel West's account of prophetic pragmatism, which privileges "emancipatory social experimentalism" in order to face collective experiences of disaster by working with inherited traditions to cultivate "tragic action with revolutionary intent, usually reformist consequences, and always visionary outlook."[10] However, various chapters deploy the term "pragmatic" in distinct ways, and it may be helpful to the reader to have them differentiated here at the start. First, by developing an ethic from interdisciplinary descriptions of problems, I follow C. S. Peirce's supposition that problems properly give rise to doubts and uncertainties that drive intellectual learning.[11] Developing ethics for new problems may rightly begin from moral uncertainty, I hold, rather than the applied certainty one might expect from a religious ethicist. For example, chapter 1 elaborates the practical challenges of climate change in order to cast doubt on the ability of Christian tradition to respond adequately. Sowing the right doubts may be crucial for cultivating moral learning.

Beginning from unprecedented problems means beginning from interpretation of how contexts mediate demands for moral change. Chapter 2 considers what it means for ethics to begin from reality by reconsidering the initial question that H. R. Niebuhr set for social ethics: what is going on? I argue that Christian ethics should interpret what is going on from the cultural strategies deployed by theological projects, as they respond to the demands of their situation. By holding that the meaning of moral beliefs and practices lies in the patterns of action they support, I focus on how reform projects make their moral inheritances capable of doing new things in order to face new problems. As opposed to a view of ethical change that focuses on cognitive worldviews, I argue that ethics needs a pragmatic view of culture in which morality is learned in bodies, carried by practices, and formed into repertories that teach agents how to see and solve problems. Reading sociologists Pierre Bourdieu and Ann Swidler with theologians Kathryn Tanner and Graham Ward, I argue that the work of Christian social ethics should not be understood as application of a Christian worldview but as a style of cultural response to problems that mediate properly theological demands.

Focusing on particular projects abjures common metaethical foundations in favor of organizing ad hoc pluralist cooperation. In chapter 3 I defend a way of doing global ethics "from below," as a reflection on shared projects rather than establishment of shared foundations. A pragmatic approach to global ethics prevents moral pluralism from becoming intractable "religious" conflict. Listening to liberation theologians, my approach locates ethics as a form of participation in the work of communities struggling to overcome some defeating problem. Chapters 5–7 illustrate how my prophetic pragmatism differs from liberation theology, even while maintaining its epistemic commitment to begin ethics from participation in political reform projects from the margins. One key difference is that my prophetic pragmatism does not offer an interpretation of the meaning of the Christian gospel. This book is not a sufficient theory of Christian ethics; it rather demonstrates how communities make their interpretations of the gospel meet the demands of new problems and explains why that makes a difference to interdisciplinary and cross-cultural cooperation.

In chapter 4 I critically engage the school of "environmental pragmatism" and the emergence of "sustainability science," in order to explore how ethics, science, and other disciplines might collaborate in addressing difficult problems. The chapter criticizes separation of natural sciences from moral humanities and explores what it might look like to conduct ethics within science-based social learning. I consider the prospects of an adaptive management framework for organizing collaboration, while arguing that collaboration needs the sort of inventive moral imagination often cultivated in religious communities. That argument introduces two liabilities of a pragmatic approach to sustainability: obtuseness to social power and weakness before hegemonic ideologies.

Chapters 5, 6, and 7 test the limits of the pragmatic experiment in three different sets of problems. Chapter 5 addresses the ecological mediation of political violence by working with environmental justice responses to chemical distributions. It traces how concepts and practices of justice, especially human rights, are shifting as environmental justice projects deploy them to meet new problems. It explains why cosmological approaches have missed ecological flows of racism, and also why liberationist ethics seems to need the cosmological imagination. Chapter 6 interprets trajectories of human and biological impoverishment within the dominance of the human economy, asking: what are the prospects for a practical economic ethic within globalizing market relations? I show how Christian ethics can open constructive possibilities by focusing on the two fundamental problems of impoverishment, considering their relation within several distinct economies of human desire. Chapter 7, on intergenerational ethics, asks how to pursue a pragmatic approach in the absence of any meaningful reform projects. Explaining how intergenerational relations are already shaped by unexamined moral futures, it closes the book with a stark meditation on the peril of the book's pragmatist experiment. Perhaps the most a pragmatist ethic can hope to achieve is to sustain the capacity of the future to forgive us for our failures.

Each chapter shows how religious ethics can intensify the tension between feasible reform and deep cultural change by interpreting problems as demands for moral transformation. I explain the Christian form of this approach as prophetic theological pragmatism, developed in the spirit of Cornel West and remembered in the legacies of Martin Luther King and Dietrich Bonhoeffer. My view exceeds some usual pragmatist constraints, including even what West seems willing to say, in that I hold that faith in a transformative God appropriately drives moral creativity. I do not claim that moral creativity requires faith in God or the transcendent, but I do demonstrate why ethicists might expect extraordinary moral creativity from communities that believe that in facing their problems they give answer to a transcendent and transforming God. Working from those projects allows my account to offer what pragmatism usually lacks: a way to begin from the problems of the world as it is, yet still expect deep transformation. It also excludes two common senses of pragmatism. While ironic and constructivist, it obviously refuses the naturalist prohibition on theology found in the pessimistic irony of Richard Rorty and the antireligious constructivism of Philip Kitcher. Both seem willfully obtuse to how traditions of transcendence generate irony and drive moral change.[12] It also resists senses of pragmatism as instrumentalist support for a science-based "war against nature" (as in the words of William James).[13] Pragmatic thought does not necessarily buoy the eagerness of those ready to take the crises of anthropocene power as occasion to reengineer earth systems or grasp the reins of evolution. I argue for a more chastened and adaptive form of responsibility, in which humans must manage earth for their own learning and ongoing moral transformation.

So this book represents an odd sort of pragmatism: particularist in its attention to traditions, theological in its constructive mode, pluralist in its modest assumption of particularist contributions to global projects, irenic in its hope for adaptive cultural change, fallibilist and ironic in its wariness of human power. Whether this approach should rightly be called pragmatic may remain an open question. Defending some account of pragmatism is not finally my aim; illustrating how moral communities open ways of practical hope from the midst of overwhelming problems is.

SUSTAINABILITY, SOCIAL JUSTICE, AND SUSTAINING ETHICS

I need to say a word about the concepts this book uses to organize its project. I take "sustainability" and "social justice" as sites of plural debate over how humanity can take responsibility for its powers and order them in a way acceptable across moral worlds. This book's point is not to promote sustainability and social justice as important values or good ideas. It rather treats those concepts as broad discursive sites that host a pluralist conversation about what recently powerful humans should sustain and how to rightly order those powers. It uses the conversation around them to improve disciplinary connections among the environmental sciences, political theory, economics, philosophy, and religious studies, without attempting to synthesize those fields of knowledge into a grand theory of sustainability and social justice. Instead, it gathers and evaluates the state of conversation in several problems and projects. As part of the emergence of what universities have begun calling environmental humanities and sustainability sciences, this project attempts to cultivate the intellectual ecotones made necessary by flows of power that move beyond the limits of our disciplines.

Sustainability is a remarkably absorptive and malleable concept, admitting of many incompatible ideologies and rivalrous projects. This book does not argue that it enjoys any intrinsic advantage over other integrating concepts, such as resilience, subsistence, stewardship, common good, or eco-justice. I work with "sustainability" because of its discursive success; in just a few decades the concept of sustainability has become a live site of argument and experimentation for responding to unprecedented social problems. Its very thinness as a normative concept permits this pluralist exchange and public use, and just so invites theological engagement. For better or worse, a significant part of the conversation of ethics happens under the rubric of sustainability, where theorists, scientists, and policymakers try to work out the human condition in response to rapid change. Rather than argue over the metaphor, better to enter the conversation and work to improve it. (In chapter 3, I explain the emergence of sustainability discourse and its competing theories.)

"Social justice" refers to normative reflection on patterns and institutions of mutual relation. In Christian ethics, "social justice" has for more than a century served as a summary referent to reflection on how the tradition of Jesus interprets the forms and institutions that shape human relations to one another. It has been particularly focused on economic impoverishment, political violence, and social oppression. Its use in this book implies a commitment to maintain that focus on impoverishment and injustice while considering the grand questions of sustainability. Some would argue that social justice is one component of sustainability and others the converse. I keep the two terms separate in gesture to the integrating task of ethics in a hybridizing world. Amidst complexity that tempts us to conjunctive shortcuts ("eco-justice") and misleading conflations ("sustainable development"), it seems better to distinguish what has until now named separate streams of normative reflection.

Both concepts start from acknowledgment of human power as a moral fact. They do not offer much ground for celebrating or lamenting that fact; they begin from a commitment to confront the problems arising as human power reshapes social and ecological relations. They are moral concepts for managing the problems of a humanizing earth, which makes their scope so mundane and limited that some religious ethicists find their frame insufficiently cosmic or theological. However, even as concepts for making this transient moment of human power merely less short and violent than it might otherwise be, their scope is tremendous. Earth's life systems are shaped by the desires of ten billion humans, its surfaces terraformed by their dwellings, its atmosphere made in the exhale of their fossil-fuel energy economy, and is inhabited only by the creatures that can habituate to what an anthropocene epoch affords them. The ideas of sustainability and social justice start from acknowledgment that our ways of life are already remaking the world and ask: what are we now sustaining? Can we learn to sustain whatever beauty, justice, love, wildness, truth, wealth, otherness, and sacredness sustain the human spirit? Can we sustain the practices that teach and transform us?

The task of "sustainability and social justice" for religious ethics does not then lie in supporting those two ideas with religious ones, as if to lend religious support to secular projects to save us from ourselves. Some notions of sustainability carry bad salvation stories. Sustainability cannot mean sustaining this world of injustice and domination, this economy of impoverishment, these sacrificing powers. Some aspects of our world *should* collapse, and some powers we must stop sustaining. The task for religious ethics lies in demonstrating how the faith of its communities generates practical answers to the question that all humanity faces: what must we sustain and why?

NOTES

1. Hans Jonas, *The Imperative of Responsibility: In Search of an Ethics for the Technological Age* (Chicago: University of Chicago Press, 1984), 1.

2. Larry L. Rasmussen, *Earth Community, Earth Ethics* (Maryknoll, NY: Orbis, 1996), 5.

3. For the original proposal, see P. J. Crutzen and E. Stoermer, "The Anthropocene," *Global Change Newsletter* 41, no. 1 (2000). The notion behind Crutzen's term follows other proposals for naming the rise of industrial humanity into an evolutionary force. Two influential contributions include Teilhard de Chardin's account of human power transforming the biosphere into a "noosphere" and Thomas Berry's description of a civilizational transition into the "ecozoic era." I use "anthropocene" to refer to the emergent condition of human power because, for now, it has the greatest interdisciplinary currency. For an overview, see Jan Zalasiewicz et al., "The New World of the Anthropocene," *Environmental Science & Technology* 44, no. 7 (2010). Important developments in the integration of the idea include P. J. Crutzen, "Geology of Mankind," *Nature* 415, no. 6867 (2002); W. Steffen, P. J. Crutzen, and J. R. McNeill, "The Anthropocene: Are Humans Now Overwhelming the Great Forces of Nature?" *AMBIO: A Journal of the Human Environment* 36, no. 8 (2007); J. Zalasiewicz et al., "The Anthropocene: A New Epoch of Geological Time?" *Philosophical Transactions of the Royal Society A: Mathematical, Physical and Engineering Sciences* 369, no. 1938 (2011); W. Steffen et al., "The Anthropocene: From Global Change to Planetary Stewardship," *AMBIO: A Journal of the Human Environment* (2011).

4. Erle C. Ellis and Navin Ramankutty, "Putting People in the Map: Anthropogenic Biomes of the World," *Frontiers of Ecology and Environment* 6, no. 8 (2008): 445.

5. See Peter M. Vitousek et al., "Human Domination of Earth's Ecosystems," *Science* 277, no. 5325 (1997): 494.

6. William Schweiker, *Responsibility and Christian Ethics* (Cambridge: Cambridge University Press, 1995), 190.

7. Peter Singer, *One World: The Ethics of Globalization* (New Haven, CT: Yale University Press, 2002); William Schweiker, *Theological Ethics and Global Dynamics: In the Time of Many Worlds* (Malden, MA: Blackwell, 2004).

8. Christianity is itself many traditions, of course, and this book makes no attempt to be representative. The theological ideas and projects that appear within the book I chose because they were relevant and creative, not because I think they best represent the faith. Engagement is ad hoc, working with projects and perspectives useful to the field around a problem. The unique aggravations of membership in the Episcopal Church and citizenship in the United States shape my inquiries. The latter is especially

important: throughout the book I self-consciously write as a participant in North American power and religiosity.

9. I explain some of those tensions and rethinking in Willis Jenkins, "After Lynn White: Religious Ethics and Environmental Problems," *Journal of Religious Ethics* 37, no. 2 (2009); Willis Jenkins, "Religion and Ecology: A Review Essay on the Field," *Journal of the American Academy of Religion* 77, no. 1 (2009): 187–97; Willis Jenkins and Christopher Chapple, "Religion and Environment," *Annual Review of Environment and Resources* 36 (2011): 441–63. For more perspectives on the field of religion and ecology, see the excellent collection of essays in Whitney Bauman et al., eds., *Inherited Land: The Changing Grounds of Religion and Ecology* (Eugene, OR: Wipf and Stock, 2011).

10. Cornel West, *The American Evasion of Philosophy: A Genealogy of Pragmatism* (Madison: University of Wisconsin Press, 1989), 214, 229.

11. Charles Sanders Peirce, "The Fixation of Belief" [1877], in *Pragmatism: A Reader*, ed. Louis Menand (New York: Random House, 1997).

12. Richard Rorty, *Contingency, Irony, and Solidarity* (New York: Cambridge University Press, 1989); Philip Kitcher, *The Ethical Project* (Cambridge, MA: Harvard University Press, 2011).

13. William James, *The Moral Equivalent of War* (New York: American Association for International Conciliation, 1910).

CHAPTER ONE

Atmospheric Powers:
Climate Change and Moral Incompetence

✦

God keeps faith with the created world forever. God upholds the cause of the oppressed and gives food to the hungry. The Lord sets free the prisoners, gives sight to the blind, lifts up those who are bowed down, and loves the righteous. God sustains.

Ps. 146:6–9

Climate change exemplifies the challenge to ethics posed by humanity's sudden planetary powers. Burning carbon for energy is not intrinsically wrong; our bodies use oxygen from the atmosphere to burn the carbon in our food for energy and then exhale carbon dioxide. Yet as the metabolism of humanity expands with the industrialization of carbon-burning technologies, so do its moral implications. Everyday actions as mundane as cooking breakfast become geopolitical acts, moral in significance and nearly mythic in scope. Burning carbon fuels has begun to generate strange new moral relations. Nations project power across global space and over generational time through their energy policies, yet without reflection on their fairness or prudence. Market commerce affects the temperature of the air and salinity of the oceans, yet economics remains ecologically indifferent. Individual actions participate in diffuse, indirect, and cumulative networks of agency for which we yet lack the concepts for understanding our responsibility. Making breakfast alters conditions of life around earth, as the exhale from ten thousand power plants influences the planet's thermal metabolism. Humanity has accidentally begun to manage planetary ecological systems, and we lack cooperation or even criteria for doing so well.

Ethics seems overwhelmed by climate change. None of our inherited moral traditions anticipate practical responsibilities for managing the sky, nor construct institutions of justice to discipline power across cultures and generations, nor imagine harming and loving neighbors through diffuse ecological flows. Adequate responses to climate change elude us in part because atmospheric powers outstrip the capacities of our inherited traditions for interpreting them. Insofar as the problem requires moral competencies that we lack, climatic change reveals humanity as ill adapted to the conditions of life that its powers are making.

This is the greatest peril of climate change: that the accidental powers of humanity generate problems that exceed our moral imagination and defeat our abilities to take responsibility. Insofar as atmospheric powers escape the bounds of justice or make talk of loving neighbors unintelligible, they disinherit cultures of the concepts and practices that sustain a way of being human. Climate change thus poses more than a technical problem of managing emissions, more than an economic problem of allocating costs and benefits, and more than a political problem of negotiating international treaties. It poses a cultural problem that calls into question our ability to keep sustaining our humanity in the face of unprecedented powers. The rise of "sustainability" as a global moral concept captures an intuition about the basic challenge posed by problems like climate change: can societies sustain the conditions in which their virtues and concepts make sense? Can they sustain what is worth loving and honoring?

Climate change is not the sort of problem that can be solved. It presents new and enduring relations of human power and thus new and enduring questions of responsibility. Even when nations finally agree on a comprehensive climate treaty, the problem of climate change will not go away. Ongoing responsibility for a planetary system, with all the relations and conflicts that involved, will then have just begun. The ethics of climate change therefore includes much more than evaluating policies and motivating action; it entails helping moral communities develop capabilities to take responsibility for the relations and powers in which they live.

While climate change is an unprecedented problem, that kind of adaptive ethical task is perennial to periods of social change. The discipline of social ethics, in fact, formed in response to the rise of industrial powers in a previous century. "The social problem," as it was then called, stood for the challenge of creating responsibility for the new social relations imposed by steam-driven economic powers—between labor and capital, state and citizen, individual and market. Then too it seemed that ethics had become impossible in the face of accelerating global change. Then too fatalist ideologies taught that love and justice were irrelevant to laws of economic power. The world still lives under clouds of the industrial revolution and has not entirely left behind those fatalist materialisms, but the most cataclysmic threats to a decent civilization were averted (or at least deferred) by a series of projects that expanded moral responsibilities. "Social justice," a nineteenth-century innovation, came to name a series of humanizing responses to industrial economic powers, and it remains a summary category for critical reflection on the relation of persons and political economy.

How the world conducts its atmospheric experiment amid poverty and inequality will renegotiate the meaning of justice. Some climate policies would intensify resource capture by the powerful; others would assign equal rights to atmospheric space. Either way, the atmosphere has become a political arena in which justice is being renegotiated. The converse is also true: projects for social justice affect the climate. Efforts to overcome poverty and promote democracy affect the chemical composition of the atmosphere. Our ideas of justice now alter the planet's temperature. It is an open question whether we can make our ideas of justice bear responsibility for that fact.

This book holds that the moral uncertainty created by unprecedented problems can, if squarely faced, generate practical inventiveness that begins to make moral cultures more competent to meet their challenges. This chapter illustrates the argument by analyzing how various features of climate change seem to overwhelm possibilities of moral agency. Understanding why a problem defeats ethical response or seems invisible to everyday life teaches us what sort of practical creativity would begin to make a culture more competent. The discussions here of climate science and political conflict therefore do more than set the stage for ethics; interpreting the difficulty and demands of a problem is a key ethical task itself. As I explain troublesome features of the problem, I also set tasks taken up by subsequent chapters (intergenerational obligations, global ethics, a theory of ecological management) and demonstrate a method for approaching other problems (chemical toxins, world poverty, biodiversity loss).

This approach to ethics may seem unusual, so the chapter opens with a short argument for why religious ethics should begin from incompetence and uncertainty, and then illustrates what that means in particular for Christian ethics. Section 2 ("Reality after the End of Nature") interprets the difficulties of description and section 3 ("A Perfect Moral Storm") analyzes features of the problem that generate conflict and frustrate response. Those two sections do not try to motivate action by cataloguing woe, as other descriptive introductions to essays on climate ethics often do. They explain ambivalent and perverse features of reality that seem to defeat practical response. The fourth section ("Christ and Climate Change") then depicts several Christian strategies of practical response. Each strategy appears obviously unsatisfactory, but my argument orients readers to look for their trajectory of moral creativity. Insofar as they begin to meet overwhelming features of the problem, they begin to create ways to sustain some practice of Christian life in the midst of unprecedented relations and powers.

Starting with the problem of climate change and the creativity of incompetent responses illustrates the general argument of the book: to confront problems that imperil it, ethics should work with projects that open possibilities of moral agency. Doing so hardly guarantees adequate responses. Some problems may too far exceed the potential of our traditions or the possibilities of pluralist cooperation. The jeopardy of ethics here represents portents of cultural collapse. Evading ethics, however, leaves the blind exercise of power to answer for us what should be sustained. Even now the apparatus of human power probes for more carbon fuel beneath every land and ocean, ignoring wars or starting new ones. Oil-fueled power fractures bedrock to extract natural gas, which it burns to refine tar sands into more oil, which it scrapes away boreal forests to find. "Coal carries coal," observed Ralph Waldo Emerson, "by rail and by boat, to make Canada as warm as Calcutta, and with its comfort brings its industrial power." Those words now communicate in a way that Emerson did not imagine (making Canada as warm as Calcutta), and in a way that intensifies what he did: oil quarries oil to sustain a culture of power and wealth.[1]

Confronting climate change as a moral problem makes societies take responsibility for what they are already sustaining. Sustainability, I argue over this book, must not mean sustaining this world of injustice, domination, and impoverishment. Some aspects of our world *should* collapse. The task for Christian ethics lies in demonstrating whether and how it can sustain the hopes for love and justice carried by its practice of life in the midst of atmospheric powers. Every moral tradition faces a similar challenge: can its members sustain their practice of life in ways that bear responsibility for the relations in which they now live?

INCOMPETENCE AND UNCERTAINTY IN RELIGIOUS TRADITIONS

Anthropogenic changes on a planetary scale force cultures to reconsider their interpretations of the human role in earth, their symbols of nature and value, their narratives of progress and purpose. Because religious traditions curate worldviews and grand stories of human purpose, they seem central to that reconsideration. Ethicists sometimes approach an overwhelming problem like climate change, therefore, by reconsidering the cosmology of major traditions. Yet religions are always more and different than their formal beliefs about the world, because they are carried by practitioners who constantly reuse their traditions in creative ways in order to meet the problems of everyday life. Cultural action seems underdetermined by worldviews and narratives. How we cook breakfast is as much a contingent historical product, a practice made by following inherited paths, as it is the consequence of beliefs about God and nature. How we make sense of and adapt cooking breakfast in the time of climate change depends on how we use our traditions to invent new possibilities of action.

This book therefore argues for a more pragmatic way of thinking about the task of religious ethics and its role in adaptive social change. I start from climate change, rather than beliefs about creation or moral world-views, in order to illustrate how ethics can develop its tasks from attention to concrete problems and critical engagement with initial reform projects. Those efforts are chronically inadequate, but good reform projects make that chronic inadequacy a source of normative creativity, expanding the competence of their traditions through innovative ways of practicing their meaning.

Religious ethics, in this view, can begin from concrete problems, un-certain traditions, and incompetent communities. That may seem odd. In the face of overwhelming crises and chronic conflict, it might seem that religious ethics should assert definite moral foundations. However, moral uncertainty is an inherent part of what makes climate change a difficult prob-lem. Like many other sustainability problems, it is a structurally "wicked problem," in that what would count as a solution is ecologically and cultur-ally indeterminate.[2] Styles of response that imply that there is some definite solution that would dissolve the crisis, if only the world would do what is obviously right, obscure the fundamental character of the problem. There is no response that can dissolve the problem by reverting earth systems to a state in which humanity has insignificant influence. Human responsibility for how atmospheric systems function is a condition of life that will exist for generations to come. The most important ethical question is how moral communities will adapt to that condition by sustaining possibilities of acting justly and responsibly.

The task for religious ethics in climate change, then, does not lie in sup-plying moral certainty. To turn an inchoate crisis into a real problem, ethics needs to make complexity and uncertainty drive innovation and ferment in moral traditions. That task has sometimes been occluded by the need to confront misuses of scientific uncertainty. Climate science does involve un-certainties, which I discuss, but the greatest uncertainty in climate change is moral: how will humanity respond to its atmospheric powers? Moral uncer-tainty bears acutely on religious traditions. Because traditions conserve sto-ries and cultivate practices that interpret the meaning of life, new problems that appear to outstrip their practical competence pose a crisis of authority.

The meaning carried by a tradition's way of life is jeopardized until its participants create a way to extend its interpretation to a new domain. When
it finds itself incompetent to a changing context, religious traditions need
reform projects capable of generating new possibilities of action that can be
recognized by its members as legitimate interpretations.

Traditions endure by producing change. They are not static repositories
of beliefs and symbols, but embodied patterns of life, the meaning of which
is carried through ongoing response to contextual challenges. Religious traditions host contested processes of negotiation over the meaning of those
patterns and the legitimacy of new contextual responses. Over the long
run, traditions sustain meaning for their members only if they make possible a pattern of living in the midst of new existential, social, or political
problems. At the heart of live religious traditions, then, is something like
a sustainability logic by which the tradition reproduces the authority and
intelligibility of its way of life for a changing world.[3]

For a problem in which meaningful action frustrates the practical imagination, religious processes of inventing and authorizing new ways of living a
tradition can be especially important. If a religious tradition can develop new
capacities of responsibility while sustaining some thick practice of life, then
societies might hope to meet overwhelming problems while still preserving the central commitments that sustain a sense of humanity. If they cannot, their inability to overcome their incompetence may betoken a broader
cultural collapse.[4] The peril and promise is especially acute for Christianity,
whose North Atlantic traditions have developed with the industrial powers
that drive climate change. If North Atlantic Christianity cannot generate an
adequate climate ethic, then perhaps its traditions have been corrupted or
exhausted by atmospheric powers. If so, the fact that a major moral tradition of industrial societies can no longer sustain adaptive change may betoken the cultural exhaustion of those societies. Some Christian thinkers, as
we will shortly see, welcome that exhaustion as the collapse of Babylon, the
coming of the end of the North's empire, of human domination over earth,
and of the industrial captivity of Christianity.

My own view is more moderate and more difficult. Atmospheric powers form an unexpected and strange empire, made as much by accident as by
intentional project. Despite the indefensible bullying of the United States,
the violence to democracy done by fossil-fuel corporations, and the dishon-
esty built into high-carbon lifestyles, climate change does not reduce to evil
action. It is a cumulative, unintended outcome of generations of everyday
life across the planet. The causes of its harms are multiple, indirect, and
dispersed through time and space. It has no definite solution, but rather imposes a chronic condition of responsibility for a dynamic planetary system.

Reducing a structurally wicked problem to a case of moral wicked-ness would evade the most difficult questions. Wrong and ignorant actions certainly contribute to climate change, but its crisis lies in the difficulty of creating meaningful and adequate forms of responsibility. How might humanity collectively modify its influence within the world's atmospheric system? What commitments would allow a pluralist world to cooperate? How to allocate responsibilities across relations of injustice and resentment, for multiple generations of humans, in respect for today's poor and the future of other species? If religious ethics avoids reckoning with those questions by supposing that the failures to this point are entirely attributable to evil, it refuses the most difficult aspect of responsibility: the struggle to create social practices and political communities capable of answering those questions.

Religious traditions are always ambiguous, used in various ways by various communities. What matters for climate ethics is how particular faith communities deploy their traditions in order to sustain their practices of faith in the midst of atmospheric powers. For Christian ethics, then, what matters most is how communities respond to the way climate change renders uncertain their practices of following Jesus. What does love of enemies mean when enmity is mediated by nonlinear ecological systems? How to follow the liberating savior when an everyday commute is part of an accidental empire? The way that Christian communities respond to atmospheric powers will determines the meaning of their practices of love and justice, their faith in a reconciling God. How Christian communities respond to climate change, in other words, will make the future of Christian ethics. "It is now becoming clear that climate change concerns more than an ethical issue," acknowledges the South African Council of Churches; "it is also a matter where the content and significance of the Christian faith are at stake."[5] The content of Christian faith is at stake here because the problem goes beyond merely failing to practice one's beliefs; the problem jeopardizes the intelligibility of the concepts and practices by which members of the tradition understand their beliefs.

Religious traditions, I am arguing, are at risk of the practical creativity of their adherents. Theology is at risk of ethics here, in the sense that how Christian communities make sense of climate change will interpret who Jesus Christ is for them in an era of atmospheric powers. Of course theology is always at risk of what Christian communities actually do; the "grammar" of Christian faith always depends on how "speakers" actually use the "language."[6] Here that risk intensifies in the uncertainty of how Christian communities will use their language to interpret climate change. What love and justice will come to mean for life in the era of climate change depends on innovations that make those concepts work through its unanticipated anomalies and conditions. Those innovations will become authoritative insofar as adherents recognize them as coherent interpretations of the tradition, and insofar as they adopt them as authentic ways of speaking the faith.

While uncertain and risky, this pragmatic approach offers hope for overcoming the alienation of moral experience from an overwhelming problem by working from the practices through which a tradition begins to overcome its incompetence.[7] A religious ethic for climate change should not begin from a posture of sure criticism of the world's failings, but rather from the risk to its own tradition. For Christian ethics, confessing moral uncertainty opens new possibilities of living the faith by asking how God acts for the world of atmospheric power by summoning people into concrete relations of love and justice. Meaningful Christian responsibility happens, then, not as the application of ideals from the Christian life to a problem at hand, but *as that life itself*.

A Christian climate ethic should begin, then, by analyzing how the problem alienates the practice of Christian life from reality. For any tradition, a practical gap between a new problem and its repertories of response should press it to expand its ethical competencies. If Christian communities experience that practical gap as confrontation by God, who continues to call persons into relations of love and justice (as I argue in chapter 2 that they should), then they have extraordinary pressure to expand the competency of love and justice. The Lutheran document, *God, Creation, and Climate Change*, opens with H. Richard Niebuhr's initiating question for Christian ethics: "what is going on?"[8] Niebuhr thought that the social problems of the industrial era situated persons in complex webs of relations and action for which received ethical frameworks were inadequate. An account of responsibility, proposed Niebuhr, must begin from a renewed interpretation of reality, integrating empirical description and moral interpretation, so that agents understand the relations in which they are involved, and can discern how God may be confronting them through those relations.[9] In the following sections I interpret the conflicts, uncertainties, and perversions that corrupt Christian ethics. Recognizing how it renders uncertain and incompetent their practice of life, communities may begin to create practices in which it becomes possible to give answer to God for atmospheric powers.

REALITY AFTER THE END OF NATURE

Interpreting "what is going on" with the climate entails making sense of cultural and scientific uncertainties about changing ecological systems. Talk about uncertainty is often manufactured to delay political processes and defer responsible action, so let me state from the outset that any honest description of climate change depicts this basic reality: as long as humans emit greenhouse gases (GHGs) faster than earth's forests and oceans can sink them then atmospheric concentrations of those gases will rise, affecting multiple planetary systems. Stabilizing atmospheric concentrations at any level requires eventually reducing humanity's net GHG additions to zero.

The practical form of that responsibility depends on how climate change is interpreted as a moral problem. It is therefore important for any account to show how it integrates empirical research and ethical judgments. How climate change engenders practical responsibilities depends on evaluative interpretations of how atmospheric systems interact with social systems. Ethical decisions cannot wait until the facts about nature are established because cultural and evaluative factors arise in the act of describing nature.

In fact, the term "nature" may not be much help in understanding the problem. Climate change destabilizes cultural ideas of nature that have been used (especially in North American environmentalism) to interpret the reality of other ecological problems. Seeing nature as stable, balanced, autonomous, and other to humanity makes anthropogenic climate factors appear as unnatural interference and (therefore) wrongful violation. That way of interpreting climate change represents the problem as a post-moral reality, implying a responsibility to reestablish conditions in which (that idea of) nature again makes sense. Nature as untouched other cannot make sense of pervasive human influence in ecological communities—which is precisely the anthropocene condition. Yet the loss of that idea of nature often appears as the fundamental cultural crisis that climate critics have in mind. Bill McKibben titled one of the first books on global warming *The End of Nature* in order to convey his worry that humanity's atmospheric powers denaturalize earth (call it "Eaarth" now). McKibben relies on readers assuming that moral peril lies in the loss of nature undefiled by human touch. His 350.org movement sometimes seems to use the 350ppm (parts per million of carbon dioxide) threshold as a numerical proxy for the natural, past which lies interference and violation.[10]

Now maybe "nature" in that sense was never a reliable concept for describing reality. Maybe, as Bruno Latour puts it, "we have never been modern" in that way, but rather always live with and in hybridized natures.[11] Maybe the idea of untouched nature, and the environmentalist ideology that goes with it, is a peculiarly North American construct.[12] Either way ("after" or "without" nature), climate change escapes interpretive frameworks that would make interference with nature the moral focus, for it depicts humans participating in a global system as both determinant and dependent. As a result, it is not then obvious why the fact of anthropogenic factors in the planet's climate system presents an ethical problem. If humans have always been making natures, what is wrong with an atmosphere remade by humanity?[13]

Interference with nature is not itself the problem with climate change; the problem lies in the risks that human influence poses to sustaining goods. The United Nations Framework Convention on Climate Change (UNFCCC)—the treaty adopted in 1992 by most nations (including the United States and China)—stipulates that nations must cooperate to "prevent dangerous anthropogenic interference with the climate system."[14] Unless human participation in a planetary system is intrinsically wrong, the important questions concern when and how the human factors become "dangerous," and what constitutes danger.[15]

The most robust institutional process for tracking human and climate interactions is currently the Intergovernmental Panel on Climate Change (IPCC), which was established by the United Nations in 1989 to gather research from around the world, submit it to peer review, and communicate it to the global public. Its periodic Assessment Reports represent a consensus update on climate science. Critics charge that the IPCC makes unreliable descriptive claims, that it distorts research to support political claims, and that it exceeds its mandate by interpreting the ethical claims of its scientific findings. Some of that criticism seems manufactured to suppress political action, but some of it demonstrates that establishing the reality of climate change involves natural science and moral culture in awkward relations. Scientific research is indispensable for approaching the reality of climate change, but interpreting that reality requires cultural facilities that exceed what science can do. Ethics and policy cannot simply "follow science" in deciding what to do about climate change because aspects of the descriptive task are irreducibly evaluative.

Because descriptions of climate change involve moral culture in ecological science, they create hazards for scientists. IPCC-involved scientists have sometimes—especially when frustrated with chronic indifference to the implications of their work—adopted forms of moral interpretation and political advocacy that exceed the mandate of their research. However, they have been drawn into those functions because of a failure of moral culture; the evaluative tasks have largely been left to scientists to perform. Major audits of the IPCC have made recommendations for more transparent governance, clearer communication about uncertainty, and more cautious behavior around political advocacy. Yet those audits also confirmed the basic reality established by IPCC research: anthropogenic emissions are influencing earth's climate system in ways that carry significant social and ecological risks.[16]

Climate change becomes dangerous when the magnitude and pace of its changes exceeds the capacity of social and ecological systems to adapt, thus degrading sustaining goods.[17] In order to describe it as a problem, then, we need to (1) understand why and how systems are changing, (2) correlate those changes with impacts on sustaining goods, and (3) predict how adaptive human responses could protect those goods. I explain the ethics of each task and then (4) observe attempts to evade ethics altogether.

Why Is the Climate Warming?

"Warming of the climate system is unequivocal." Decades of observation show that global average temperatures are rising, and that, consistent with temperature rise, ice cover is retreating while average sea level is rising. Temperatures in the Northern Hemisphere during the late twentieth century were likely "the highest in at least the past 1300 years," and the warming has already begun to affect basic biological rhythms like leaf unfolding, animal migrations, and reproductive cycles.[18] On this there is no doubt: the climate system is steadily absorbing more thermal energy in ways that affect systems of life.

Why is the atmosphere absorbing more thermal energy? The best explanation is that human energy emissions have increased the concentration of greenhouse gases. There has long been a coherent theory to expect sensitivity of global temperatures to a carbon-intensive energy economy. As early as 1890 Svante Arrhenius calculated that increased carbon dioxide would enhance the planet's natural greenhouse effect.[19] Since then carbon dioxide has risen from a preindustrial value of 280ppm to 400ppm. It continues to rise about 2ppm/year. Methane concentration has more than doubled over the same span. Concentrations of both gases far exceed the range of variation found for those two gases over the previous 650,000 years.[20] So there is a strong explanatory theory and just the empirical record one would expect to find: increased concentration of GHGs and a planetary warming trend.

The IPCC reports show the steady development of consensus that the warming trend is caused by radiative forcing from anthropogenic emissions. Each Assessment Report has communicated greater confidence on anthropogenic causes of warming and less likelihood of another explanation. Year by year the empirical research, including many tests of alternative hypotheses for the change, make a null hypothesis about human influence on the atmosphere increasingly implausible.[21]

There are uncertainties about the precise influence of specific gases on temperature change. Different gases persist in the atmosphere for different periods and the interaction of their various radiative impacts is not fully understood. Aerosol emissions have a negative impact on temperature, but the magnitude is not clear. (Some forms of air pollution have a cooling effect.) Complicating measurements of temperature sensitivity, the volume of carbon that forests and oceans sink each year is difficult to measure and seems to be changing. Those uncertainties make it difficult to precisely correlate a volume of greenhouse gas emissions to a specific temperature change. The IPCC's mean estimate of climate sensitivity is that a doubling of atmospheric carbon dioxide equivalent concentration (from preindustrial 280ppm to 560ppm) would lead to a 3C (degrees Celsius) rise in temperature, although it could be as low as 1.5C or higher than 4.5C.[22]

Those are not the sort of uncertainties that warrant deferred action. On the contrary, the important scientific disagreements here concern how climate functions under different conditions of human influence.[23] The most significant variable in this unplanned experiment is not how temperature responds to GHG emissions, but how human societies will take responsibility for the temperature changes. The ethics of climate change, in other words, is the chief uncertainty in our understanding of it. That is not the sort of uncertainty that can be reduced by waiting for clearer data, or by, as Stephen Gardiner puts it, "insisting that it be turned into a more respectable form of problem."[24] Delaying response for more research at this point misunderstands the character of the problem. For complex human-ecological systems, uncertainty is not a condition that can be defeated in advance of human action. It is part of the reality under investigation, such that research must be conducted within actions to take responsibility for it.

Meanwhile, each year humanity adds about forty gigatons of carbon dioxide to the atmosphere. Transferring carbon from underground into the sky in such quantities has consequences. Earth has already begun to warm and, even if the skyward flow of carbon ceased today, would continue to do so for a very long time. The rate and magnitude, as well as the permanence of change are all significant. John Houghton observes that the rate "is probably faster than the global average temperature has changed at any time over the past 10,000 years." Because the difference between an ice age and a warm period is about six degrees, Houghton describes the magnitude as "from one third to a whole ice age in terms of the degree of climate change."[25] Irreversible changes are already underway and their impacts will appear over centuries.[26]

What Are Its Impacts?

The next task in describing climate change as a moral reality is to correlate ecological changes with impacts on important goods. Here the science depends on predictive modeling of how systems will function, so its descriptive confidence decreases. But the cumulative picture of likely impacts portrays an array of risks to the social and ecological systems that sustain basic goods of human life and many other forms of life.

For one important example, sea level rise is difficult to predict precisely, but long-term measurement shows a general rise since the nineteenth century of about 200mm with the rate accelerating over recent decades.[27] Seas are probably going to rise at least an additional half-meter over the coming century and even with mitigation of GHG emissions, are likely to rise a full meter by 2100. Including feedback from accelerated ice sheet melting, projections go above two meters (six feet), and without any emissions reduction range toward the catastrophic (four meters) and diluvian (ten meters!) by 2300.[28] Even on the low side of that range, those sea levels mean the end of existence for some island nations, some of which have thus begun to seek relocation for their populations. They threaten delta nations (like Bangladesh) with massive displacement and suggest major infrastructure vulnerabilities for coastal cities.

Sea-level rise is just one example. Climate modeling predicts significant impacts in almost every sector of life, including agricultural stress, water shortages, and increased disease spread. How should societies evaluate those impacts? The difference between a rise of 2C and 4C over the coming century may represent the difference between the capacity for grain agriculture maintained or lost in some regions, or the difference between an extinction event of one quarter of life's species and one in which more than half of species are lost. "Impact" may be the wrong metaphor for changes that would necessitate a different form of human society altogether, but the World Bank has begun to consider how to help societies meet the impacts of 4C warming.[29]

Interpreting risks of climate change becomes thornier if impacts become feedbacks into processes of change. For example, a 3C rise within the century might cause terrestrial ecosystems to stop sinking carbon and become instead a net carbon source, thus accelerating global warming. While it is difficult to pinpoint the precise thresholds, at some point impacts can cause the collapse of sustaining ecological functions and a rapid "tipping" from one kind of ecological community into another. Some critics think that the IPCC underestimates the probability of tipping points and feedback loops, and some science suggests that, due to deferred responsibility and continued fossil-fuel investment, 4C warming may happen by the end of this century.[30]

Again, these are not the sort of scientific uncertainties that can be defeated by deferring responsibility in hope of obtaining clearer data. Understanding how climate change impacts sustaining systems depends on how humanity responds to apparent risks. While some responses are obvious, like moving island peoples as their lands disappear, others depend on how humanity weighs the goods at risk. Consider species extinctions. Half of the kinds of currently living creatures now depend for their existence as much on human capacities of social adaptation as on their own capacity for biological adaptation. Climate impacts are already extinguishing some species and displacing others.[31] Some might survive if humanity reduces its emissions. Some might survive if societies manage habitats differently. How societies respond depends on whether they interpret that reality minimally, as a risk to the resilience of systems that produce important social goods; more extensively, as a diminishment of earth's beauty and creativity; or strongly, as a violation of the existence rights of other species.

Thus the reflexivity of ecology and ethics in the anthropocene condition: human activity changes global ecology, and the ideas that humanity uses to interpret the impact of those changes shapes both the future of life's adaptation as well as the future of humanity's interpretation of itself. The future of earthly life is bound to the future of ethics.

What Should Be Our Objective?

It would be convenient if climate science could uncontroversially establish the objective for responsible human action, but there are two obstacles. First, it is easier to offer a causal explanation, from human emissions to atmospheric concentrations to planetary temperature to systemic impacts, than it is to reason back the other way in an attempt to establish an emissions target that would avoid a particular impact. The climate system is not reversibly linear in that way. Its performance under future emissions scenarios is difficult to precisely predict, which makes setting a policy objective difficult.

Second, deciding which impacts are too dangerous or unbearable is finally a cultural decision involving many values and knowledges. British Prime Minister Tony Blair once declared that science should determine what concentration "is self-evidently too much." Yet what appears as a high-minded commitment to "follow science" actually abdicates the role of political societies in producing the necessary knowledge "with science."[32] Deciding how to respond to climate change is not simply a matter of following the science, because action requires gathering the scientific, economic, political, and ethical criteria into integrated assessments that make practical reasoning possible.

Nature supplies no simple standard. Over its geological history earth has seen various climate regimes, some with utterly different compositions of atmospheric gas. Human vulnerability does, however, offer some comparative standards. Everything civilizations know about growing food and building societies developed within a relatively stable global climate, in which carbon dioxide made up 280ppm of the atmosphere. "If humanity wishes to preserve a planet similar to that on which civilization developed and to which life on earth is adapted," write James Hansen and colleagues, "paleoclimate evidence and ongoing climate change suggest that CO_2 will need to be reduced to at most 350ppm, but likely less than that."[33] Philosopher Simon Caney proposes another measure: "Dangerous climate change should be interpreted as climate change that systematically undermines the widespread enjoyment of human rights."[34] In other words, our most important commitments should drive climate action objectives.

Deciding whether to set a climate objective in reference to a broad survival target (preserving a similar planet), or a dictum of justice (prevent human rights violations), or a norm of efficiency (balanced costs and benefits) generates a range of warranted goals. The 350ppm target has a strong chance of keeping the global average temperature rise above preindustrial levels to less than 2C. Yet it would also require immediate energy contraction, near zero emissions within decades, and probably a program of intentional carbon removal (a.k.a., geoengineering). If that project impeded development rights of the poor or undermined political participation, then a human rights standard might push the objective higher than 350ppm. IPCC scenarios suggest the world has an even chance of keeping temperature rise to near 2C with stabilization as high as 450ppm.[35] That target would also require costly action—emissions would need to peak very soon and within a few decades drop 80% below year 2000 emissions—but it might pose less threat to the energy activity of developing populations. Attempting to balance the costs of climate action with avoided risks, the Stern Report recommends an even higher target range of 450–550ppm.[36]

Stabilizing carbon dioxide at 550pm makes it more likely that global average temperature would rise 3C. In that range, human systems are likely to face food and water shortages and greater coastal flooding, while ecological systems would suffer double the species extinctions and higher probabilities of tipping into another state. Those might be acceptable impacts when their costs are generalized and assessed against economic systems. A higher view of the moral significance of other species or the integrity of ecological systems, however, would make even 2C seem irresponsible. For example, the *People's Agreement of Cochabamba* calls for returning carbon concentrations to 300ppm, or to preindustrial levels. That level would be impossible to sustain within anything like the current global economy. The Cochabamba statement calls for deep structural transformation of civilization, away from capitalist globalization and toward democratic ecological membership. [37]

Deciding among climate objectives thus makes a moral choice for a future world and for a path of human life. The 2C target has been endorsed in the Conference of Parties process. It also seems to be the target most often used by climate scientists to organize research, and is often the objective assumed by philosophers writing on climate ethics. That convergence among climate negotiators, scientists, and philosophers is important because any objective must combine political interpretation of feasible action, scientific projections, and moral evaluation of impacts. 2C thus seems to represent a convergent judgment about the envelope of climatic change within which societies have the best chance of sustaining important forms of human life. That judgment may shift over time as humanity begins taking action and better understands the problem. It may then reconsider what it holds important. Any objective must be revisable in light of ecological and cultural feedback. 2C, 350ppm, and other popular threshold designations should not be treated as natural boundaries. Significant danger lies on either side and much remains uncertain about how human and environmental systems will adapt.

Climate science does supply one absolute standard: whatever objective humanity eventually adopts, maintaining it requires that human emissions eventually match the level of earth's sequestration capacity. As long as emissions exceed sinks, humanity keeps adding to the stock of GHGs in the atmosphere. Because there does not appear any way to bring human emissions to net zero without significant decarbonization of the energy economy before the end of the century, any reasonable objective carries daunting tasks of social transformation. Meanwhile, deferred action and continued investment in fossil-fuel energy are making futures that no one can justify and few except petro-capitalists want.

Evading Ethics

My point in this section has been that the reality of climate change cannot be established apart from ethical decisions. I close this section by naming three ways that societies try to evade ethics. The first is what many politicians are currently doing: calling for more scientific certainty about climate change as a way to defer those daunting tasks of social transformation. That creates a vicious cycle of uncertainty, asking for more science before considering action, while the most important uncertainty remains whether and how humans will take responsibility. Scientists sometimes abet that vicious cycle by failing to engage the humanities in descriptions of climate reality, feeding the misimpression that the important uncertainties can be addressed by more science.[38] Energy companies have been happy to defer political accountability by funding research on uncertainty, all the while redoubling their investments in fossil fuels.

Second, some proposals for emergency geoengineering try to evade ethics by skipping the challenges of creating political cooperation in favor of a program of scientific control of the atmosphere. Even were some technology to make it possible to control the climate without otherwise changing human energy behavior, geoengineering, apart from a human conversation about shared responsibilities, would simply inscribe into the atmosphere unresolved questions about human power. Who decides, pays for, and conducts geoengineering? For what objectives and whose interests? How to politically mandate something that affects every creature of earth and binds future generations to its decisions? The questions raised by geoengineering encounter the same social and moral challenges as mitigation and adaptation. Geoengineering does not offer a way around ethical difficulties; it just shifts them to another location.[39]

That does not mean that geoengineering is intrinsically wrong. Paul Crutzen, the atmospheric chemist who popularized the term "anthropocene," points out that humans already manage the climate. The point of any climate policy is to do so intentionally and responsibly. Geoengineering could include, as ecologist Thomas Lovejoy proposes, a program of global ecosystem restoration in order to restore and protect earth's carbon sinks.[40] Yet there remains a hazard of ethical evasion in schemes to engineer the climate, especially in those like Crutzen's proposal to disperse sulfur into the stratosphere in order to deflect incoming solar energy.[41] The prospect of a technological fix makes it more likely that societies will sidestep important questions about cooperative responsibility for human power. The appearance of geoengineering options may corrupt the process of developing the ethical competencies needed to responsibly implement them.[42] The metaphor of "engineering" can offer the illusion that science can save humanity from the need to become responsible, and could even function to let climate change license enhanced human domination of earth.

Third, in their urgency to get to the tasks of allocating responsibilities and facilitating cooperation, ethicists themselves sometimes shortcut the role of the humanities in interpreting climate change. Because of frustrating political delays and religious skepticism, Christian ethicists have often focused on underscoring the fact of human responsibility pictured in climate science. Ecumenical consensus on that point undermines the respectability of using Christian ideas in climate denial. However, as Ernst Conradie observes, much Christian discussion of climate change gathers the relevant

science and then leaves off at baptizing its basic finding of human responsibility.[43] But climate science does not need religious communities to authorize that basic finding; it needs moral communities to invent ways to
meaningfully respond. Christian ethics, like other moral traditions, struggles to interpret climate change because it struggles to create possibilities
of meaningful action.

A PERFECT MORAL STORM

This section explains features of the problem that frustrate meaningful action and cooperative response, in order to illustrate what a practical climate
ethic must overcome. By doing so, I do not mean to imply that changing
human behavior on a global scale just awaits a better moral argument. I
agree with economist William Nordhaus that ethics on its own cannot solve
climate change; "it is unrealistic to hope that major reductions in emissions
can be achieved only by hope, trust, responsible citizenship, environmental
ethics, or guilt."[44] Any ethic with a modicum of realism about individual
and national interests would concur, and support an arrangement of justice
with coercive measures, such as the carbon price Nordhaus seeks. But it is
also unrealistic to suppose that a carbon tax, or any other form of mutual
coercion, could be imposed *without* the social hope, mutual trust, and responsible citizenship that a shared sense of justice makes possible. Collective
action on climate change depends on all the relevant participants agreeing
to govern themselves according to principles they agree are fair—but that
sort of ethical agreement is elusive.

Why is there uncertainty about fairness? At first glance climate change
seems a matter of "kindergarten ethics:" polluters should clean up their own
mess and everyone should have equal shares in shared resources.[45] People in
industrialized nations have taken more than their share of atmospheric space
and caused a mess in the process. So, as any child can see, fairness requires
that they bear the burden of responsibility for making the situation right.
The "polluter pays principle" observes equal respect for all persons by holding each accountable to the consequences of her action, assigning burdens
according to an agent's causal role in creating the problem.[46] Flouting this
principle displaces justice with the arbitrary inequalities of bullying.

Climate change is more complicated than kindergarten, however. Instead of clear harms caused by discrete actions of definite agents, its impacts
are the indirect, cumulative outcome of human action aggregated across
space and time. Carbon dioxide emission counts as pollution only because
of the stock of GHGs emitted by past generations, who themselves did not
understand the damage they would eventually cause. Contemporary agents

thus inherit a stock of atmospheric gases that transforms previously neutral acts (turning on a light) into morally charged decisions. It is not intrinsically unjust or mess-making to illuminate one's home with electricity generated by burning a carbon fuel. The act becomes implicated in injustice only because it participates in a web of trillions of similar acts that have an aggregate influence on a planetary ecological system.

Moreover, contemporary agents are born into an infrastructure that organizes everyday life such that most pursuits of normal ends cannot avoid participating in production of the problem. For problems involving indirect, cumulative, and aggregate outcomes of injustice, argues Iris Marion Young, ethics must learn to construct justice without perfect liability or even the idea of complicity. When injustice is the outcome of the social relations that connect agents pursuing acceptable interests, then justice must take shape as responsibility for the systems through which we belong to each other.[47] That does not absolve persons born into high-carbon societies, but rather tutors the shape of our responsibility. How can justice reflect such contextual contingency, causal dispersion, accumulating privilege, and global participation?

The complexity here must not obscure a basic portrait of causal responsibility. Henry Shue has been especially persistent in keeping these features before the eyes of justice. Humanity faces a climate problem because "nations and firms have behaved as if each of them had an unlimited and unshakable entitlement to discharge any amount of greenhouse gases that it was convenient to release."[48] The consequences impose burdens on nations that contributed little to the problem, harm people too marginal to have benefitted from the action and too poor to adapt to it, and create adversity for future generations.[49] When the powerful refuse to stop harming others, then they must be shown that the rights of others are at stake and that "there is no God-given right to burn fossil fuel and live highly consumptive lives."[50] Shue is undoubtedly right that much of the moral impasse over climate change can be explained by the blunt refusal of the powerful to acknowledge claims of mutual respect within the human family.

Nonetheless, the complexity of moral agency involved in climate change seems to overwhelm efforts to establish shared principles of fairness. Notice how Shue finds himself addressing multiple kinds of agents: nations, corporations, economic classes, generations, and individuals. Just establishing the relevant moral agents seems complicated, let alone their mutual responsibilities.

Climate change is a "perfect moral storm," writes Stephen Gardiner, because several features, each difficult in itself, combine to defeat ethical understanding. Gardiner identifies global, intergenerational, and theoretical "storms" that distort interpretation of the problem and, in combination, corrupt abilities to take responsibility for it.[51] Working from Gardiner's framework of three storms and adding radical inequality as a fourth, the following section will explain obstacles that any ethic must begin to overcome in order to make agents competent to climate change.

Global Unfairness

Climate change takes the form of a global commons problem. A shared resource (the carbon sink of the atmosphere) is being degraded by overuse at the hands of many agents, for each of whom, in the absence of mutual coercion, it seems rational to continue overusing the resource. Any adequate climate strategy must manage the commons by limiting entitlements to use the atmosphere and by allocating bearers and beneficiaries of adaptation burdens. In the Framework Convention, nations agree to seek global cooperation "for the benefit of present and future generations of humankind, on the basis of equity and in accordance with their common but differentiated responsibilities and respective capabilities."[52] Each point is miserably contested: nations disagree on (1) how to assess the costs of climate impacts, (2) how equity differentiates responsibilities, and (3) what obligations accrue with capabilities. Understanding the political disagreements as ethical disagreement about the shape of justice in a dispersed planetary web of action explains impediments to (4) the formation of a global ethic. While debates over fairness involve arguments between major frameworks of moral philosophy, especially utilitarian and rights-based approaches, they do not fail because of meta-ethical differences.[53] They fail because the interests at stake distribute perversely along global inequalities, making the demands of justice appear differently according to context.[54]

Disagreement on how to value impacts.
The costs of climate change distribute with perverse unfairness. Many populations with low historic emissions face some of the worst impacts, while some industrialized peoples may face only moderate consequences. Kenya emits a very small percentage of GHGs, but faces severe stresses to agriculture and water availability. Kenyan negotiators thus tend to value potential impacts highly and favor a robust policy. The United States emits a greater share of GHGs than Kenya, is more economically dependent on a carbon fuel economy, and faces less severe costs from climate impacts. So the US values impacts less expensively, making the up-front costs of action seem more costly. According to one US view of fairness, those nations for which cooperating has higher costs than benefits should be compensated to participate in an international agreement by those with lower costs than benefits.[55]

That seems repugnant to those people facing the worst predicaments. Peoples of Oceania and of the Arctic who have done almost nothing to alter the planet's climate nonetheless find their continued existence threatened. If the largest emitters do nothing to reduce their emissions, consequent sea level rises could make low-lying islands uninhabitable and Arctic temperature increases could melt an ancient way of life. Even when survival is not at stake, the distributional effects of climate change generally impact poor persons more severely than the wealthy simply because poverty often makes one more vulnerable to the negative impacts of climate change. Because relative wealth seems to lead some to ignore or undervalue the costs of climate change to others, some philosophers frame costs as harms, so that their imposition by the powerful constitutes a human rights violation.[56] In this view, climate change is a planetary environmental justice issue because ecological benefits and harms flow along unfair lines of power and vulnerability.

There are also costs to ecological communities, and here lies another asymmetry: at least a third of life on earth faces risk of extinction while humanity debates relative costliness to its way of life. Can justice evaluate impacts, beyond the human family, to the whole membership of life? Practical interpretation of harm and change amid multiple ecological scales seems difficult, but ignoring impacts on other creatures and on earth itself, simply because we do not seem competent to evaluate them, would let obtuseness decide fairness.[57]

Disagreement on how to fairly differentiate responsibilities.
One key question in interpreting fair allocation of responsibilities is whether and how historic emissions generate contemporary responsibilities. The "polluter pays principle" follows the intuitive sense of fairness that agents should bear burdens of responsibility in proportion to their contribution to the problem. Fair accounting for the historic emissions of industrialized nations would require them to pay for adaptive measures while undertaking great reductions, even while the emissions of other nations still grow. Unequal responsibility for mitigating and adapting redresses unfair advantages previously taken by industrialized nations. There are two moral moments to the principle, one of sharing and one of repairing. First, industrialized peoples have used their share of atmospheric space and have a duty to make way for others to have their turn. Second, industrialized peoples are largely at fault in making a problem and have corrective duties to remedy the situation and perhaps compensate victims.

Critics counter that most original polluters are no longer alive, so the actual polluters would not be the ones paying. Instead, those citizens born into an energy economy they did not choose are asked to shoulder the burden of transforming that economy while also paying for actions they themselves did not commit. It is no longer polluters paying, but beneficiaries. For current beneficiaries to have a corrective justice duty to citizens in nations that developed later, one would have to demonstrate that their benefit also harmed others.[58] Critics of historic accountability argue that the global economic development fueled by those emissions generally benefitted the world, so there is no harm to remedy.[59] Those less impressed by market globalization are also unimpressed by that argument. The World Council of Churches (WCC) has consistently interpreted climate change as a result of an unjust global economy. If globalization is neocolonial domination, then historic accountability for emissions is but one aspect of serial injustice. WCC documents appeal to the concept of ecological debt to make the case that climate change is made by "historical and current resource plundering."[60] Debates over global economic inequality are so long-standing and embittered that they generate a moral storm of their own, so I will return to consider ecological debt within a separate section on radical inequality.

At stake in debates over "polluter pays" are disagreements over intentionality and responsibility. Should agents be held accountable for actions that they could not know would lead to bad consequences? The appeal to ignorance becomes moot for emissions after 1992, when the UNFCCC signaled worldwide recognition of serious consequences from anthropogenic climate change. However, the motivation for appealing to ignorance may reveal important differences of perspective on the relative goodness or badness of the past century. Consider Peter Singer's judgment: "since the wealth of the developed nations is inextricably tied to their prodigious use of carbon fuels . . . it is a small step from here to the conclusion that the present global distribution of wealth is the result of a wrongful expropriation by a small fraction of the world's population of a resource that belongs to all human beings."[61] Accepting "polluter pays" may imply responsibility for centuries of criminal wrongdoing, which early industrializing nations are reluctant to accept. Again, historic principles for allocating responsibility turn on interpretations of contemporary inequality—to which we must return.

A related controversy lies in refusals to accept responsibilities that occur through participation in a social membership (a state usually, but perhaps a people, culture, or religious community). Some philosophers reject historic criteria for differentiating responsibility by rejecting an enduring collective identity. It seems hard to take that objection as more than disingenuous evasion of the implications of national memberships that most people acknowledge, even when critical of their nation's policies. However, Simon Caney explains universalist grounds to respect the objection: any individualist cosmopolitanism that makes equal respect of all persons its criterion of fairness resists the collectivist cosmopolitanism implied in a historical principle that lumps people into national groups.[62] A global climate ethic based on justice among persons, rather than fairness among states, might then have reason to forego historic criteria of fault in order to develop climate responsibilities from individual rights.

A climate ethic focused on fairness among states may obscure duties and claims among individuals, including those arising from inequalities within states. Aside from questions of fault, a rights-based account of fairness assigns wealthier people obligations to prevent the lives of poor persons from falling below a minimal threshold of dignity. No matter who caused the problem, with this approach inequalities in power and vulnerability bear several implications for allocating responsibilities. Duties to not harm others imply that the wealthy should contract their emissions while promoting increased energy use by the very poor. If the poor are denied access to the atmospheric commons in order to protect its uses by the wealthy, then atmospheric powers become colonial powers.[63] Even among those living high-carbon lives, however, burdens of change also distribute unevenly. Contracting GHG emissions may be devastating to those employed by fossil-fuel industries, even while it is a boon to new energy economies. Within and beyond states, fair allocation must account for structural inequalities in the burdens of change.[64]

Disagreement over how obligations accrue with increasing capabilities.
Opportunities to respond also distribute with global variation, some of it perverse. Three capabilities matter most here, one held by citizens of wealthy economies, another by citizens in rapidly developing economies, and another by citizens in nations with ecological resources that function as significant carbon sinks. If obligation accrues with economic capability, then wealthy citizens and wealthy nations bear greater burdens because of their greater capacity to absorb the costs of climate action.[65]

If obligation accrues with efficiency, then rapidly developing nations have a different kind of capability. Several populous nations with historically low emissions but growing energy economies have unique opportunities to reduce GHG emissions by investing now. Brazil, India, and China will be the greatest aggregate GHG emitters in the coming decades. Because they are making infrastructure investments now, these countries can avoid future emissions at a lower economic and political cost than developed nations can. If these nations fail to limit their emissions growth, the world faces little hope of stabilizing emissions.

If obligation accrues with ecological resources, then citizens of countries with significant forest cover possess capabilities to caretake an important carbon sink. The Democratic Republic of Congo (DRC)—despite its

poverty and despite its causal innocence in the problem—may have an obligation to protect its forests in light of the role they play in sequestering
carbon.

The three cases become progressively controversial in light of the historic and continuing emissions of developed nations. To what extent can
the United States (20 tons of CO_2 per capita) ask China (5 tons per capita)
or the DRC (almost zero) to bear greater burdens in light of their capabilities? Rarely do parties make a direct claim on poor countries not to exploit
their resources, but carbon exchange mechanisms may incentivize poorer
societies to forego forest exploitation. They are controversial for just that
reason, as critics worry that assigning responsibility by ecological capacity perpetuates structural inequality between the powerful and the weak,
allowing the former to use climate change to dispossess the latter of their
lands.[66]

Creating global agreement.
By treating disagreements over fair responsibility as moral debates over the
shape of global justice, rather than stark conflicts of sovereign self-interest,
ethics makes a cosmopolitan claim: that moral respect for all persons on the
planet is possible and imperative. Creating an effective global climate agreement based on fairness is crucial to solving a commons problem in a way
that respects the moral dignity of all persons. If the way forward into the
world of atmospheric powers is made by sheer bullying, by taking and wast-
ing earth's atmosphere according to mere might, then the moral agency of
everyone is eroded.

The political failure of climate negotiations thus suggests two tasks for
global ethics (further explained in chapter 3). First, within nations whose
citizens resist claims from outside its borders, ethicists must work to help
agents recognize their membership in the planetary relations made by climate change. Second, climate ethics should address itself to agents other
than states. States are recalcitrant cosmopolitan actors, but their negotiations are not the only form of action on climate change. Fixating on the
UNFCCC process can in fact dampen other forms of global civic friendship. Any plausible account of global climate justice needs projects that take
shape across boundaries of nation, class, and culture in order develop responsibilities within the relations that produce the problem.

Intergenerational Deferral

A second "storm" combines with features of the first, intensifying both.
Moral agency in climate change is dispersed temporally as well as spatially:
causes and effects are separated over time, again with perverse asymmetry.
The most serious effects of climate change will fall on future generations,

while action taken now to mitigate those effects will have only minimal consequence for decades. Due to the stock of atmospheric GHGs put in the atmosphere by previous generations and the energy infrastructure left to us, the current generation faces significant costs in order to avoid negative consequences for future generations. If those costs compete with social spending on contemporary poverty, then persons today may suffer so that the vulnerable of tomorrow do not suffer more. Of course that is a false choice since most societies seem unwilling to invest in either overcoming poverty or meeting climate change. But the tension poses a question about how to think about social justice and intergenerational obligations.

That question must be answered in a context liable to moral corruption. Past generations are not present to be held accountable for their actions, while future generations have no political voice, so the present generation must decide justice while facing a strong incentive to defer the question to the next generation. That disincentive structure stays the same for each generation: as it rises into agency it inherits incentives to defer action to the next generation.[67] It falls to the generation taking or failing to take responsibility in the years 2010–2035 to make especially fateful decisions about futures, for we have inherited atmospheric stocks of GHGs that have just begun to cause temperature rises and we still have before us opportunities to contain the rise. The window of opportunity for moral agency is narrowing; as GHGs accumulate, possible futures close down and minimal thresholds of change become more costly to protect.

The global commons problem thus has an odd temporal dimension: the sink must be allotted over time as well as distributed among present users. One way to conceptualize allotments over time is to consider a total amount of GHGs humanity can emit over a period of time and still stay within an upper bound of temperature rise. If that amount were one trillion tons over a two-hundred year period (as one study calculates), then a great deal has been spent by previous generations, leaving a limited amount to allot among today's peoples and future generations. What principles should guide how that allotment is allocated?[68] For now the question is being answered by fossil fuel companies, who have massive incentives to sell all the underground reserves they have without regard for the future.

Consider six major proposals for allocating the atmospheric commons by some principle of responsibility. (1) A realist "grandfathering" approach starts with unequal uses of the atmosphere from a point in time (1990 in the Kyoto Protocol), and assesses percentage reductions over subsequent decades. (2) A historic equity view takes the opposite view of contemporary inequality, arguing that developed nations have already consumed their share of atmospheric space and must contract to make atmospheric room for future development of other nations. (3) An egalitarian principle supports equal per capita shares of the total commons available each year, regardless of citizen location, based on a declining annual limit set by some overall objective (say, 2 degrees C). Personal emissions beyond that share might incur a fee or penalty. (3b) To function well over time, the shares might be allocated to nations based on a future projection of population, thus incentivizing demographic stability, and a declining annual ceiling based on a target GHG stabilization, with the intent to incentivize innovation and spread costs over generations. (3c) Individual shares might be tradeable, allowing markets to reallocate the initial annual entitlements. On this scheme, individuals could receive an annual dividend from a fund generated by major emitters paying for the use of their share.[69] (4) A human rights approach, worried that a declining ceiling and entitlement market could deprive the poor and future generations of emissions shares needed for basic needs, would guarantee all persons, now and in the future, a minimum entitlement, regardless of its implications for the target concentration.[70] (5) A greenhouse development rights approach restores a target concentration, structuring contraction and convergence over time according to a "responsibility-capacity index" as the basis for a progressive climate tax.[71] (6) A final view measures equity from the relative marginal costs of reductions among parties, with a view to reducing the carbon intensity of economies while maintaining capital wealth for the future.

Which proposal seems most fair depends on how one interprets the convergence of global and intergenerational "storms" of climate change. A weak moral sense of obligation to future generations allows stronger priority for contemporary social need, which usually functions (but need not) as a priority for contemporary profits. A strong sense of obligation to the future may constrain intragenerational claims of justice. Deciding for a climate policy thus shapes the meaning of social justice operating across different scales of vulnerability.

James Martin-Schramm's *Climate Justice* is one of the few projects in Christian ethics to directly address the awkwardness of apparent tensions between today's poor and future generations. Martin-Schramm identifies basic norms of ecojustice, from which he develops subsidiary policy guidelines and criteria, endorsing features of the historic equity approach and the human rights approach that seek fairness and feasibility across time. Yet his policy recommendations, cast with an eye toward North American political viability, seem still vulnerable to corruption by lack of accountability. If the present is, as Shue argues, "inflicting adversity" on future generations, then the modesty of a $5/ton carbon tax does not seem to escape Gardiner's charge that a token climate policy "provides each generation with the cover under which it can seem to be taking the issue seriously . . . when really it is simply exploiting its temporal position."[72] How can any practice of justice overcome a temporal structure so liable to moral corruption?

The problem of intergenerational ethics is so important for the meaning of sustainability, and so challenging for the moral priority of the poor in Christian ethics, that I return to take it up at length in chapter 7. Deciding obligations to the future comes close to the basic question of sustainability, forcing deliberation over what goods to sustain and what sort of world we are making. Industrial societies may be so lacking the temporal imagination to bear that responsibility, I argue there, that the most important contribution of Christian communities may lie in sustaining the capacity of future generations to forgive us. The bleakness of that argument points to a third storm.

Theoretical Ineptitude

The global and intergenerational features of climate change so flummox available ethical concepts that Gardiner identifies a third storm: theoretical ineptitude to answer the moral questions it raises. Along lines similar to my account of ethical incompetence, Gardiner thinks that our ethical concepts are "poorly adapted" for answering those questions. Like mine, his account holds that our concepts are not hopelessly corrupt or the genetic origin of our troubles; "we are currently 'inept,' in the (nonpejorative) sense of lacking the skills and basic competence for the task."[73] Cognitive science attests to that ineptitude by suggesting that several aspects of climate change frustrate moral cognition. Our brains are not adapted to problems with such abstract causation, inherent uncertainty, and extensive scales of time and space.[74] Neither are our concepts. Ethics needs, then, the sort of analyses of frustration and commitments to act in the face of defeating storms that can develop in agents the moral skills to become more competent to the problems we face.

Others are less irenic about prospects for overcoming what Mary Midgley calls a "conceptual emergency." Perhaps adequate action on climate change first requires a deep change in consciousness. Midgley proposes a Gaian framework.[75] A number of Christian eco-theologians have argued that modern humanity seems to have lost the capacity to listen to creation, which must be remedied for any meaningful climate action. Churches of indigenous peoples have been especially insistent on this point: any climate action developed from within an individualist anthropocentric cosmology will be hopelessly inadequate. Rightly interpreting the reality of climate change, they claim, requires a theological facility for hearing "the cry of Mother Earth" in the indicators of climate change.[76]

Yet there is a danger to intensifying the theoretical storm in this kind of critique. Consider Michael Northcott's argument that "climate change represents a challenge not only to energy-led consumerism and unfettered capitalism . . . but to the epistemological and ontological foundations of modern liberalism."[77] If interpreting climate change requires rethinking epistemology and ontology, that seems to underscore the cultural impossibility of generating responsible agency. Sallie McFague's *New Climate for Theology*, although different in theological school and style, nonetheless shares the paradoxical weakness of strong conceptual criticism. McFague argues that responding to climate change requires reconstructing ideas of God and humanity that permit ecologically violent societies.[78] However, if the first step to taking responsibility for climate is reconstructing anthropology or renouncing modern epistemology, then responsibility will always be deferred, waiting for cultural conversion to a better worldview. That is precisely how the theoretical storm works to defeat practical responsibility: by paralyzing action before the ineptitude of our ideas for interpreting our problems.

This book argues that the best way to meet a conceptual emergency is to work with what we have to create practices through which we learn how to make our concepts do new things. Instead of constructing alternative cosmologies from the start, it expects that moral consciousness shifts as agents use their inheritances, and collaborate with others using their own inheritances, to create possibilities of moral action in the face of overwhelming problems. I offer theological and sociological defense of that view in the next chapter, and then illustrate the role that cosmological criticism (including indigenous perspectives) still must play as I develop its implications for science-based management in chapter 4.

Radical Inequality

A fourth feature of climate change merits independent consideration. Debate over climate change takes place in conditions of radical inequality: there are resources enough to support the basic needs of all, but many do not have enough to survive, while some have much more than others.[79] In a global society in which about twenty percent of people live without electricity, climate ethics confronts a problem made by a power-rich energy economy that nonetheless leaves many persons powerless. The contemporary span of inequality in human power is unprecedented. In terms of access to energy for work, the difference between today's powerful and powerless is greater than that between a pharaoh and his slave laborer, or between a medieval king and his serfs. Moreover, the real deprivation across that span is staggering: one person of every eight lives hungry to the point of undernourishment.[80] Attempts to develop shared responsibility for climate change are frustrated by (1) the way climate impacts increase inequalities, (2) the corrupting effect of political inequality on international negotiations, and (3) contrasting views of the relation of globalization to inequality.

First, climate impacts tend to distribute perversely across inequalities, falling more severely on the poor, indigenous peoples, future generations, and other species. In each case, social vulnerability leads to increased climate vulnerability. That corrupts possibilities of cooperative action because inequalities between developed and developing nations, between wealthy and poor classes, between North and South, and between humanity and the rest of earth drive different interpretations of what a decent response entails.

Second, background global inequality compromises the fairness of climate negotiations. For any agreement to be fair, its process must include adequate participation for all parties, reasons for agreement other than coercive threat, and trustworthy reporting among parties. Yet powerful countries, especially the United States, manipulate climate negotiations by negotiating with coercive economic threats and by sending huge delegations that control information and distort participation. The unfair negotiating by a powerful state illustrates a problem for fairness across vulnerability: inequality in representation corrupts the possibility of fair accounting for the powers driving climate change.

Third, interpretations of justice follow such poisoned experiences of inequality. Debates over climate fairness, argue J. Timmons Roberts and Bradley Parks, are often driven by different beliefs about the relative fairness of global economic inequality. "The experience of poorer nations in the world economy . . . has reinforced a worldview and a set of causal beliefs that are at odds with those of wealthy nations; this has bred generalized mistrust and polarized expectations about how to proceed on climate issues." So deep-seated is this mistrust, they argue, that negotiations will never be able to produce shared responsibilities without at least acknowledging the historic and structural inequalities which give rise to divergent interpretations of justice.[81] Inequality drives noncooperation because it leads to alternative views of reality that support divergent senses of justice.

Consider starkly different views of historic responsibility and ecological debt. The idea of ecological debt organizes several related claims about the way global markets drive inequality: (1) that northern energy consumption has been accelerated by northern capture of southern resources, beginning from the colonial period; (2) that southern financial debt servicing perpetuates inequality and shapes southern communities into conformity with economic practices that undervalue environments and the future; (3) that southern financial debt should be canceled in recognition that southerners are greater creditors of northern ecological debt; (4) that northern "structural adjustment" to a more fair, less consumptive economy should be the focus of climate responsibilities, not southern acceptance of emission quotas.[82] Indigenous peoples often use ecological debt to present their climate vulnerability as continuation of a long history of colonial devastation. Working from that perspective, Christian theologians from indigenous communities may demand that ethical response to climate change must begin with deep economic and cultural transformation away from colonizing structures. That might include admitting fault for unjust seizures and recognizing ecological degradation as a form of genocide.[83]

Those with less malign views of the production of global inequality consider fairness in cooperation quite differently. Working from recognition that inequality creates a disincentive for wealthy industrialized nations to act, especially if coupled with charges of historical culpability, Martino Traxler proposes that responsibilities should be allocated on the forward-looking basis of "fair chore division," so that each state bears an equally burdensome share of responsibility.[84] That treats inequality as a morally indifferent obstacle to cooperation. Even ethicists with a keener sense of global economic injustice may reject "polluter pays" because it seems to criminalize certain histories. Richard Miller thus wants a "fair teamwork" model that looks for relatively equal sacrifices without judging the historic emission of the developed world as unjust.[85] Iris Marion Young similarly rejects liability for historic injustice, while arguing that those who benefit from and contribute to structural processes that keep creating injustice have a responsibility to change them. In Young's account, however, an account of ecological debt as historic injustice may help illuminate how present structures have evolved and why they continue to harm the vulnerable, and so where they most need change.[86]

For a practically minded ethicist in a northern institution, the differences between ecological debt and forward-looking responsibility generate uncomfortable questions about how my relative position in a radically unequal world economy shapes my perspective on climate justice. If the forces driving climate change are the same forces increasing global inequalities, then any meaningful response must reckon with global economic powers. In chapter 6 I take up debates over the global market in relation to human poverty and the earth's economy. For now I observe that, in the midst of disagreement and resentment across global inequalities, developing shared responsibilities at least requires agents who collaborate across alienating boundaries and develop trust across conflicting accounts of reality.

CHRIST AND CLIMATE CHANGE

The realities of climate change explained in the last two sections depict a problem that puts Christian ethics at risk by demonstrating a gap between human power and the tradition's moral capabilities of interpretation and practice. That gap is difficult to close because perverse features of the problem (its four "storms") defeat attempts to respond. For Christian ethics, that should shift the question from Christianity's perspective on whether and why climate change is a moral problem toward how to sustain the practices of Christian life in the world of that problem.

More important than a church's statements on climate change is how it enacts its faith within the world of atmospheric powers.[87] Insofar as faith communities suppose that God addresses them through that world, and within the relations and structures changing it, they should interpret their inability to enact responsibility for climate change as a gap between how they live the faith and how God would have them live. If they find themselves incompetent to love neighbors, do justice, or worship God well, then they face pressure to invent ways for central practices of their tradition to begin to answer for the world in which they live. Insofar as they fail to give answer, they fail to interpret how God acts for the world of atmospheric powers, fail to open possibilities of moral agency, and so leave the tradition's way of life in peril of moral collapse.[88]

Turning to religion does not obviously help humanity's predicament. Adding religious pressure to a host of other divisive features might just deepen disagreements and further corrupt possibilities of responsibility. Religious communities might make the moral storm worse by representing conflicts as foundational culture wars. Religious ethics makes an interesting difference, I think, only insofar as it demonstrates possibilities of agency that overcome features of the problem that defeat moral response. For Christian ethics, that means finding or inventing ways of enacting the faith that transform the everyday relations that produce climate change, or that interpret its intergenerational challenge, or that work across global divisions of enmity and inequality. Much depends, then, on how a project or community opens a strategy of action within the culture of atmospheric powers. In the style of H. Richard Niebuhr's *Christ and Culture*, consider five ways of construing the relation of Christ and climate change, making for five ideal types of Christian climate action.[89]

Avoidance Strategies

Some faith communities use Christian ideas to deny that a problem exists. Avoidance strategies, to use Pierre Bourdieu's term, protect a pattern of cultural action (a "habitus") by refusing to recognize any problem for which it does not already carry the principle of a solution.[90] Avoidance counts as a response to climate change because it deploys theological tradition to delegitimize a problem that (the community implicitly thinks) would challenge its way of life. So denialism is a strategic cultural response to a perceived threat.

Christian denialism is not as widespread as its loudness in North American culture would make it seem. The leadership of most Christian memberships recognize climate change as an important problem. There are statements from Popes John Paul II and Benedict XVI; from the Ecumenical Patriarch of the Eastern Orthodox churches; from nearly every mainline Protestant church; and from many Evangelical institutions, including the Southern Baptist Convention, the National Association of Evangelicals, and World Vision.[91] When the reality of climate change is attested by church councils in every major tradition on every continent (not to mention the joint campaign of the Reverends Pat Robertson and Al Sharpton), ecumenical consensus undermines the respectability of Christian climate denial.

Nonetheless, despite what the official leadership may say, some religiously conservative groups do deny that climate change is happening. They are aided by explicit production of a denialist strategy within institutions such as the Acton Institute and the Cornwall Alliance. This strategy uses the idea of climate change to cultivate theological resistance to what it sees as the moral corruptions of environmentalist culture. Climate change becomes the symbol of a conflict between fundamental worldviews, perhaps even an item of belief in a competing green religion.[92] In this strategy, Christ rescues the faithful from a corrupting culture that would use climate change to demean human dignity in the use of creation, perhaps by luring people into false pieties toward earth. Concerns about climate change and ecological sustainability, its proponents argue, "are rooted, ultimately, in the loss of faith in God."[93] Denying climate realities sustains a practice of faith.

However rationally this strategy protects a pattern of life, denials of climate change are deadly for Christian faith. Using theology to deny the moral significance of atmospheric powers does worse than distract public debate and make religion look silly; denial adopts a nihilist view toward its own tradition by supposing that Christian faith cannot confront the emergence of atmospheric powers—except by denying that they could cause problems. When a community reacts to a new problem by denying that it exists, the community implies that its tradition cannot generate possibilities of moral agency adequate to changing conditions. Avoidance is the paroxysm of a tradition that has lost its ability to improvise, that gives up interpreting reality for defending one peculiar (North American, energy-intensive) way of life.

Unable to shape Christians for faithful life in the time of climate change, its last tactic is to bet Christian faith on the nonexistence of some reality. Static incompetence foretells collapse.

Still worse for a tradition of faith, avoidance may imply that the entanglement of Christian life with fossil-fuel culture must be defended because a community sees no way to distinguish the way of life in Jesus from a privileged idea of the American way of life. Climate deniers are overwhelmingly conservative white men—a group that has disproportionately held power in the industrial economy, and which has the most incentive to dismiss challenges to it.[94] When a theological community deploys Christian theology to defend its privilege by denying climate change, it ridicules the faith, not the science.

Explicit denialism is, however, only the flashiest form of an avoidance strategy. The implicit, everyday denialism of those well-informed about climate science but unchanged in daily habit seems more obdurate and more important. Kari Norgaard's ethnography of implicit denial among Norwegians argues that nonresponse to climate change is produced not by mistaken knowledge or missing values, but by cultural practices in which "those qualities are acutely present but actively muted in order to protect individual identity and sense of empowerment and to maintain culturally produced conceptions of reality." Everyday denial among those who understand and worry about climate change is socially organized by cultural practices that protect the innocence of privilege. Overcoming avoidance, her account concludes, does not require better information but a deeper moral imagination, developed by using cultural inheritances to engage reality.[95]

Apocalyptic Strategies

Apocalyptic strategies focus on the moral imagination, deploying theology to interpret climate change as an event of massive cultural transition. Two senses of apocalyptic appear here: the imminent catastrophism in urgent warnings about the worst consequences of climate change, and the symbolic interpretation of the present in light of a revealed future.[96] The first kind of apocalyptic is seen in predictions of civilizational collapse amid runaway climate change. The second kind attempts to open space for cultural transformation by interpreting the world in terms of its future in God. The latter is closer to the function of biblical apocalyptic, says Stefan Skrimshire, because "its essential feature is the radical openness of the future, and its invitation to see in the days to come an imperative for resistance even beyond the tipping point of climate salvation."[97] One way to interpret the future of atmospheric powers is by inscribing everyday life into terms of the archetypal empires of the biblical world. Barbara Rossing thus presents "our unsustainable system of carbon consumption" as the Rome of our time, "imposing a new kind of climate slavery on the world's poorest nations and on future generations."[98] By depicting high-carbon culture within the fate of Rome or Babylon, an apocalyptic strategy undermines the normalcy of high-carbon patterns of life. By radically separating the way of life in Jesus from the American way of life, it opens space for actions that treat fossil-fuel culture as an empire passing away before the coming Kingdom of Christ. It summons Christians to, as Carol Robb puts it, leave the Kingdom of Oil and look for the Kingdom of God.[99] Apocalyptic strategies thus make climate change a scene in which to seek the irruptive, transforming coming of God.

Northcott brings the two senses of apocalyptic together, by inscribing a warning of imminent ecological collapse into a scriptural warning about God's judgment on empires. "Just as Jeremiah reads the fall of the House of David . . . as divine judgment on the imperial ambitions of David's successor kings, so . . . the threatened ecological collapse of industrial civilization . . . can be traced to an imperious refusal of biopolitical limits." The consequent catastrophe mediates divine condemnation of industrial capitalism: "Global warming is the earth's judgment on the global market empire."[100]

The power of Northcott's interpretation also shows the peril of an apocalyptic strategy. Climate change already overwhelms the moral imagination; further symbolic saturation may not help unless one can specify what it concretely means to resist Babylon or to leave the Kingdom of Oil. Trying to imagine resistance to the diffuse, metaphoric "empire" of energy infrastructure may reproduce helplessness. Without producing definite ways of participating in the coming transformation, an apocalyptic strategy may perversely underwrite quiescence before the habits that sustain today's fossil-fuel empire. Or, by affirming a systemic crisis in civilization, its strategy might license massive emergency measures to confront climate change without regard to other moral commitments—overriding human rights to cut emissions, for example, or unilaterally engineering the atmosphere back to 350ppm.

How an apocalyptic strategy functions depends in part on the relative social power of those using it. Deployed by the powerless, an apocalyptic strategy can interrupt inertia by unmasking the reality maintained by those who have stakes in the present energy economy as false, weak, and already beginning to collapse.[101] In conditions of theoretical ineptitude, when we seem to lack the concepts we need, it fires the imagination to look beyond our inheritances. (Chapter 7 further explores this role for apocalyptic thinking in intergenerational ethics.) Even then, apocalyptic remains a risky strategy because the excess of its imagination beyond practical participation can work against meaningful moral agency. The excess in apocalyptic thus shares the nihilist peril in an avoidance strategy: if humanity's atmospheric agency signifies an evil empire, then taking real responsibility for it seems superfluous. Apocalyptic hearkening for the world coming after climate change might then amount to cultural wistfulness for the world before climate change. When justice and love no longer seem possible, apocalyptic imagines the world in which the meaning of Christ was possible and will be again.

Advocacy Strategies

Political advocacy strategies mobilize Christian moral resources to support realistic measures of policy response. This approach informs many church statements and ecumenical councils, including those of the World Council of Churches, the US Conference of Catholic Bishops, and the Latin American Council of Churches. A Church World Service survey in fact reports that issuing policy statements is the most common form of climate action in its member denominations.[102] This strategy deploys theology as an evaluative tool to interpret policy options, with a view toward cultivating both parochial and public support for definite political action toward responsibility for climate change.

In a political advocacy strategy, Christ usually appears as the teaching rabbi whose vision calls for justice to neighbors and reconciliation of enemies. The task for theological ethics is to produce principles and guidelines grounded in that basic moral vision that can offer directions to policy responses. Exemplary of this strategy is Martin-Schramm's *Climate Justice*. The leading concept in several global church processes, "climate justice" projects interpret, reiterate, and expand prophetic commitments to social justice amidst global ecological change. Martin-Schramm explains how those commitments cohere toward feasible policy avenues for which Christians can advocate.[103]

The weaknesses of an advocacy strategy lie in its realism. By focusing on policy opportunities for state action, a prophetic strategy may lose the cultural imagination in apocalyptic and avoidance strategies. If Christ's teaching of justice reduces to Christian voters' support for a moderate carbon tax, then the culture-transforming power of Christian faith seems weak. If, on the other hand, it demands that humans cease participating in fossil-fuel culture, it seems either distant from feasible policy or apocalyptically hopeful (and thus a different sort of strategy). That tension between practical reform and deep transformation recurs throughout this book, and I take it up directly in chapter 4. My appeals for a pragmatic approach do not want to constrain ethics to what appears feasible; they want the sort of practical reforms that drive cultural transformation.

That tension appears in the WCC's work on climate justice. Documents from WCC processes endorse equal emission entitlements, the polluter pays principle, compensation for historic emissions, recognition of ecological debt, the precautionary principle, priority for the poor, rights for future generations, responsibilities proportioned to capabilities, and an obligation to return the atmosphere to 350ppm.[104] Now, it is certainly no mark against a church's witness that the world finds its demands infeasible. When political demands express the counterimagination of those on the underside of atmospheric powers, and if they are so extraordinary that they force re-imagining an entire way of life, then they begin to exercise the interruptive power of an apocalyptic strategy. Yet here lies the ambivalence of the WCC's position: because it deploys this strong witness to call for definite political action by other social bodies, the transformation of Christian life recedes from scrutiny. After making onerous concrete demands on the global public in the name of Christian churches, the WCC documents offer only vague suggestions for the life of its own membership. Its account of climate justice is directed at state action, but describes the practices of justice in no particular church. So the WCC admonishes the world to do better in its negotiations by a demanding measure of justice, without pointing to any concrete form of justice in the life of its own communities.

The result is an account of climate justice that seems impossible apart from a political order transformed beyond what even Christian communities can enact and image. It recalls Northcott's interpretation of climate change within Jeremiah's judgment: atmospheric powers must collapse before justice becomes imaginable. But it is not yet clear that prophetic justice means civilizational collapse. The South African Council of Churches makes a point of saying that the world faces the task of Josiah, not of Jeremiah: there is still time to initiate concrete reforms, to vindicate hope in justice.[105] If so, Christian communities who would witness to justice have an obligation to offer enactments or icons of what they mean.

Missional Strategies

Missional strategies characterize projects that use climate change as an occasion to reconfigure Christian practice. These include climate-focused initiatives such as carbon tithes, adaptive community development projects, church-networked sequestration projects, as well as characteristic acts of faith self-consciously performed in the cultural space of climate change—such as experiments in prayer, worship, and scriptural study. A National Council of Churches study of the impact of climate change on its members' ministries found that the problem threatened nearly every social mission program, implying that every aspect of church ministry would need to respond.[106] Evangelical strategies have been particularly focused on love in a time of climate change, framing climate change as a practical challenge to following the command of Jesus to love neighbors.[107]

These projects are inevitably inadequate. Consider, for example, World Vision's attempt to extend its mission of poverty relief to meet climate change by starting a carbon sequestration project in Ethiopia, to be registered under the Kyoto Protocol's Clean Development Mechanism.[108] It is an innovative expansion of Christian mission, but nowhere does its literature address unequal uses of atmospheric space or gesture toward global injustice. Generated by a global North mission agency without a word of confession or acceptance of responsibility, its offsetting project is liable to the criticism that it provides cheap moral cover for northern overconsumption. It is vulnerable, however, only because it actually hazards a practical response. The project therefore ventures a chance to better learn the meaning of neighbor-love as it makes itself accountable to the moral storms of climate change.

Other missional projects may stimulate that learning. For example, the Latin American Council of Churches (CLAI) gathers churches from multiple sides of social conflict for dialogue and mutual commitment. When it has gathered communities alienated by different perspectives on climate justice, global South participants have questioned mission projects that fail to appreciate southern Christian witness against structural injustice. Sequestration and clean development projects may leave untouched cultural logics of domination and trajectories of unsustainable development. CLAI's reconciliation mission might then deepen efforts like those of World Vision's project by pressing them to reflect theologically and socially across multiple contextual relations.

Missional strategies work by summoning Christian and other communities into definite relations through which moral agency can be cultivated. Timothy Gorringe calls the efforts to build just and resilient communities a contemporary form of ark building. The time for prophecy is gone, writes Gorringe; the waters are rising and it is the time for projects of rescue.[109] The Christ of this strategy bears the risk of incarnation, opening the body of God through specific hazards of love in order to open a way to God and neighbor. Missional projects can offer promise for overcoming the defeating features of climate change insofar as their experiments cross boundaries of social conflict, moral disagreement, and political power in order to create practical projects that enact faithful possibilities of solidarity and responsibility. Like most mission projects, they risk the awkwardness of outreach and complicity with dominant cultural and political powers. Yet opening the practice of faith to those risks opens a theological community to concretely learn from its participation in the world.

Survival Strategies

A network of indigenous peoples' Christian churches has developed a response to climate change arising from the broader struggles of indigenous peoples everywhere to maintain their existence. As communities of a double inheritance (Christian belief and indigenous cosmovision) seeking political recognition from outsiders, they deploy resources from multiple moral traditions in order to depict climate change as another chapter in an ongoing history of genocide and to generate corresponding practices of political justice. Specifically, they redeploy Christian theology, indigenous cosmology, and human rights in order to articulate an indigenous political subject long victimized by colonial violence and yet endowed with a special vocation to speak for earth. Because their own histories with colonial violence are also the histories of the industrial powers driving climate change, the survival tactics of indigenous peoples force dominant cultures to reckon with their histories of violence.[110]

Articulating a common indigenous identity in peril of climate change can give voice to yearnings for cultural transformation shared by nonindigenous people. While often self-conscious of the essentializing danger in lumping together the diversity of many peoples, theologians help construct a common Mother Earth cosmology and global indigenous identity in order to represent shared vulnerabilities to the ecological violence of dominant cultures.[111] Maria Chavez Quispe thus writes that, "in this context of an articulation space, we indigenous peoples are not [only] a minority to be protected with international laws but revolutionary spaces in which alternatives to the current system of life are generated."[112] George Tinker suggests that indigenous quests for survival of a way of life with a particular land convey a warning about the unsustainability of white settler culture and offers wisdom about how they must change for their own survival.[113]

One way this strategy transforms culture is by redeploying Christian theologies of creation that were used to warrant the colonization of indigenous peoples. Europeans drew on biblical tropes of stewardship, fall, and redemption to narrate their imperial expansion as a Christianizing project. By reworking theologies of creation through indigenous cosmologies, indigenous theologians establish their own special vocation to be caretakers of creation and restore its voice.[114] Earth comes to voice in the Christ of a survival strategy, the cosmic liberator in whose suffering lies the future of creation. The groans of Mother Earth become the groans of the crucified

Christ, whose body, in the time of climate change, is an indigenous body.[115] By mobilizing theological traditions that were used to warrant conquest, indigenous theologians decouple Christian creation theology from the high-carbon capitalism primarily responsible for contemporary climate change. Climate justice thus becomes a project to break from colonial exploitation in theology and political ecology.

A survival strategy that depends on a planetary indigenous subject and works from its victimization raises worries about essentialism and about identity politics. Anticolonial race politics in service of an ecological debt approach to climate change seems likely to retrench the bitterness that corrupts possibilities of cooperation in a world of radical inequality. However, while it remains to be seen how the indigenous climate justice project will develop, this strategy bears potential to function as a politics that seeks a decent future without forgetting colonial violence simply because it is unthinkable or impractical. Pairing claims for indigenous sovereignty with ecological debt makes any future-oriented politics of sustainability remember that the past history of anthropocene powers is marked by criminal genocide and ecological pillage. In other words, the indigenous survival strategy may meet the "storm" of radical inequality by showing how to transform an awful history into a possible future in ways other than simply forgetting the past. Practical wisdom for a shared future on a planet of human domination requires attending to what has been lost and to successful tactics of biocultural survival, even in the face of overwhelming challenges.[116]

Tactical Theology

The point of that brief heuristic was to show that any ethical strategy must make its tradition open a strategy of cultural action in order to confront climate change. In the next chapter I work with legacies of Niebuhr on religion and culture in order to defend the theological significance of developing cultural tactics to meet unprecedented problems. Regarding climate change, it seems to me that a decent strategy of Christian ethics needs aspects of each of those five strategies. Ethics needs the risk of missional creativity with the imaginative power offered by apocalyptic and the realist political governance sought by advocacy. It also must acknowledge what the avoidance strategy and the survival strategy recognize (in different ways): that climate change threatens the collapse of some cultural ways of life.

It is easy to disapprove of climate change but harder to concretely meet its challenge. Projects that show how Christian moral practices might take meaningful shape within the world of climate change begin to exhibit the sort of social and ecological relations within which responsibility for atmospheric powers begins to become possible. Churches with global communions (like the Catholic, Anglican, Orthodox, World Reformed, and World Lutheran memberships) have a unique opportunity here. Theological communities that organize themselves across South and North and across gaps of wealth and energy use can cultivate unique possibilities of moral agency. (Membership across generations and across species remains a practical challenge to the ecclesial imagination.) Real prospects for justice in the world of climate change depend on movements that can build solidarity across the alienating features of the problem, and so begin to generate moral learning within relationships of responsibility. In chapter 3, I develop that role for religious projects in global ethics, arguing that cross-boundary projects can help sustain generative arguments that make minimal norms for cooperation—such as the norm of sustainability—capable of hosting global deliberation over planetary problems.

Consider, for example, Vatican City's carbon offsets. When in 2007 it offset its GHG emissions for the year, the Vatican undertook a practical form of responsibility for the social and ecological costs of its energy use. By doing so it stimulated debate over whether and how market mechanisms are appropriate devices for managing responses to climate change. Offsets have been criticized as "moral indulgences"—a provocative charge in the Vatican case—that allow the powerful to purchase permissions to pollute. Offsets might allow the wealthy to control ecological resources of the poor and moralize private ownership of the atmosphere. So an important debate about responsibility for climate change is enjoined within the space of a specific practice, from which everyone interested in the problem can learn. On one hand, any realistic account of climate responses must include some way of setting a price on carbon in order to reshape economic behavior; prices teach humans the moves of atmospheric finitude. On the other hand, market mechanisms might reinforce a commodifying worldview at the root of the crisis; pricing carbon teaches humans that even the atmosphere can be bought and sold.[117]

That controversy surfaces a basic tension for the ethics of sustainability: is it about solving problems with the tools at hand or about changing cultures with new visions? Chapter 4 takes up the tension between pragmatic management and deep cultural transformation in order to argue that, under the right conditions, it can be both. Science-based adaptive management needs the sort of moral creativity and cosmological reflection that religious tactics can cultivate. Because any action by the Vatican carries a thick moral theology, when it ventures the meaning of that theology in an offsetting project its action makes carbon regulation schemes a site of reflection on natural order, social justice, and moral anthropology. However inadequate or wrongheaded, projects like offsetting offer a theological practice that can gather scientists, economists, religionists, and others into the kinds of arguments through which cultures learn from their most difficult problems.

Other tactics for responding to climate change might be more appropriate. Indigenous and global South churches seem right when they reject proposals for market-based reforms without structural changes to the current northern way of life. Their rights-based protest combines the "indulgences" charge with a neocolonial warning: global inequalities allow the powerful North to pay a modest fee for continuing to live an exploitative way of life, and gain control over southern forests in the process. The appropriate response to such biopolitical power is noncooperation, including divestment from fossil fuel companies and the nurture of grassroots political resistance, of the sort represented at the World Peoples Summit on Climate Change. Starting from the problem of toxic exposures, in chapter 5 I follow the basic insight of environmental justice projects: ecological change mediates political power, and because human bodies are ecological bodies, pollution is a form of political violence. When the indigenous climate justice projects make human rights confront the political violence mediated by atmospheric systems, it begins to shift the sort of person protected by rights and open a wider ecology of justice.

That argument forces any practical attempt to bear carbon costs to reckon with the history and trajectory of the global economy. Whatever their specific causes, anthropocene problems, like climate change and biodiversity loss, basically represent the massive footprint of humanity within earth's economy. Chapter 6 considers economic growth within Christian practices for educating desire away from impoverishment and toward real wealth. Some Christian communities have undertaken "carbon fasts" as a form of contemporary asceticism. Others develop "food sovereignty" networks that divest from commodity markets and cultivate landscapes of justice. Projects like that hardly alter global capitalism, but they do open spaces in which to reconsider purposes of economy and the real meaning of wealth. Undertaken as practices of faith, they can reorient desire.

Tactical responses to climate change can drive theological learning and sustain the possibility of Christianity as a meaningful practice of life. Projects like carbon fasts and farmers' markets, when undertaken as attempts to love creation or do justice or follow Jesus, become practices through which a theological community learns what those commitments may mean for a problem that threatens to overwhelm its moral world. Over the next few chapters, I explain how ethics should work to make such projects into dynamic sites of theological, social, and ecological learning. Insofar as they become sites of practical cultural invention, those tactics can sustain the resource our world seems most in danger of exhausting—hope.

In the face of overwhelming problems with depressing trajectories and entrenched powers, projects that sustain the central concepts of some practice of life also sustain hope that our moral capacities are not yet overwhelmed by the world we have made. Theological communities may play a unique cultural role here because their loyalty to a vision of life with God can give them the courage and imagination to break from inherited cultural patterns in search for other ways to bear responsibility for reality before God.

Confession may be one of the most important practices that Christian communities have for sustaining faith into the uncertain future being made by climate change. The South African Council of Churches has offered an exemplary confession in both senses. First, locating itself within a storied legacy of South African professions of belief in the midst of social evil, it renews the church's faith in Jesus Christ. In the era of climate change, it says, that means renewing faithfulness to creation. The need for renewal implies the need for the second form of confession—repentance from sin.[118] As with apartheid, the guilt of beneficiaries and the resentment of the oppressed could harden possibilities of practical cooperation over climate change. We face a similar need now, says one of its drafters: those who benefit from the global energy economy must confess their guilt—not in order to accept personal judgment, but in order to bear the responsibility of solidarity with those that economy harms.[119]

Practicing confession of sin frees persons to undertake forms of responsibility even within relations of guilt, resentment, complicity, and injustice. Christians in the United States must go first in confessing our guilt, for we find ourselves enmeshed in a dishonest political ecology. We should confess that we experience climate change as a kind of judgment from God, who calls us away from folly and toward justice. In that way, God's judgment sustains us. Confession cannot be facile, however; it must reckon with the complexity of the problem by seeking to bear responsibility for structures of power from which we cannot easily escape and in which we continue to participate. Confessions accompanied by campaigns to divest from fossil-fuel corporations, for example, attempt to open a way of turning from folly. The point of repentance in such projects cannot be spiritual purity, however; they must function for the practical imagination, to aid discernment in how one is called to bear burdens for the sake of a world that we are implicated in harming. "The ultimate question for responsible people to ask," wrote Dietrich Bonhoeffer in the midst of a morally impossible situation, "is not how to extricate themselves heroically from the affair, but how the coming generation is to live."[120] Chapter 7 argues that our most important obligation to future generations may be passing on practices of confession and love through which the future might forgive us. Those confessions mean nothing, however, apart from tactics that attempt to give answer for the world we are making, that invent possibilities of responsibility.

The point of all these tactics, from purchasing offsets to confessing sin, is to make it possible for a membership to live its faith in answer to the God who sustains, who keeps faith with creation, who liberates the oppressed. Tactical theology learns that sustenance by inventing ways to participate in how God reconciles the alienated, sets free the captives, and overcomes our self-destruction. The many little projects, from councils and confessions to sequestration projects and liturgical prayers, interpret how God acts to transform and redeem the anthropocene earth, and create ways to participate in it. All of those tactics involve ethical controversy; they appear practically insufficient, ideologically narrow, or theologically thin. The obvious inadequacy of Christian response to climate change, I am arguing, illustrates the peril it poses to Christianity as a way of life. However, because those ventures exist as concrete hazards of faith, by attempting to make a way in the face of unprecedented problems Christian ethics can start from incompetence in anticipation that faith can drive further innovation and deeper faithfulness.

CONCLUSION

This chapter has introduced a pragmatic approach to emerging problems of human power by interpreting the task of religious ethics in the face of climate change. Climate change defeats effective political and cultural response because its several "moral storms" conspire to defeat cooperation and responsibility. Global conflict, intergenerational asymmetry, conceptual ineptitude, and radical inequality seem to confound adequate responses. Ethical response depends on inventive practices that meet those several alienations of practical action. Religious ethics participates in that invention by critically engaging the tactical attempts to make the practices of some traditions answer the world made by atmospheric powers. Christian ethics should begin work on climate change, then, by looking for how theological projects sustain the meaning of their practices of faith, by making them bear responsibility for problems that would overwhelm them.

Why would Christian responses matter to a planetary problem involving many other moral worlds? Chapter 3 explains the role of particularist reform movements within the tasks of a global sustainability ethic for a pluralist world. Chapter 4 then shows how religious creativity matters for sustainability sciences. First, however, I must defend the theological coherence of this overall approach, which is unusual in religious ethics and might seem instrumentalist toward the faith of Christians. So in the next chapter I offer a theological interpretation of cultural change, explaining why ongoing cultural invention in the face of new social problems is a central practice of faith.

NOTES

1. From the essay, "Wealth," in *Essays and Lectures* (New York: Literary Classics of the United States, 1983), 990.

2. The term "wicked problems" comes from H. W. J. Rittel and M. M. Webber, "Dilemmas in a General Theory of Planning," *Policy Sciences* 4, no. 2 (1973), discussed further in chapter 4.

3. My view of religious traditions is informed by the account of traditions as arguments that sustain the concepts they need to hold an argument in Alasdair MacIntyre, *Whose Justice? Which Rationality?* (Notre Dame, IN: University of Notre Dame Press, 1988); by the pragmatic discursive practices in Jeffrey Stout, *Democracy and Tradition* (Princeton: Princeton University Press, 2004); by the embodied material flows in Manuel Vasquez, *More Than Belief: A Materialist Theory of Religion* (New York: Oxford University Press, 2011); and by the account of Islamic jurisprudence as schooling in the logic of authoritative reform in Wael Hallaq, *Authority, Continuity, and Change in Islamic Law* (Cambridge: Cambridge University Press, 2001). I will explain in the next chapter how those several views cohere in an account of Christian ethics as a tradition of generating reform.

4. See S. Bergmann and D. Gerten, *Religion and Dangerous Environmental Change: Transdisciplinary Perspectives on the Ethics of Climate and Sustainability* (Berlin: Lit Verlag, 2010).

5. South African Council of Churches, *Climate Change: A Challenge to the Churches* (Marshalltown, 2009), 45.

6. Those metaphors and the following sentences allude to George Lindbeck, *The Nature of Doctrine: Religion and Theology in a Postliberal Age* (Louisville, KY: Westminster John Knox Press, 1984).

7. On moral alienation and social hope see Sarah Amsler, "Bringing Hope to Crisis: Critical Thinking, Ethical Action and Social Change," in *Future Ethics: Climate Change and Apocalyptic Imagination*, Stefan Skrimshire, ed. (London: Continuum, 2010).

8. Karen L. Bloomquist, *God, Creation, and Climate Change: A Resource for Reflection and Discussion* (Geneva: The Lutheran World Federation, 2009).

9. H. Richard Niebuhr, *The Responsible Self: An Essay in Christian Moral Philosophy* (New York: Harper and Row, 1963; Louisville, KY: Wesminster John Knox Press, 1999).

10. Bill McKibben, *The End of Nature* (New York: Random House, 1989); Bill McKibben, *Eaarth: Making a Life on a Tough New Planet* (New York: Henry Holt, 2010).

11. Bruno Latour, *We Have Never Been Modern*, Catherine Porter, trans. (Cambridge, MA: Harvard University Press, 1993).

12. William Cronon, "The Trouble with Wilderness; or, Getting Back to the Wrong Nature," in *Uncommon Ground: Rethinking the Human Place in Nature*, William Cronon, ed. (New York: W. W. Norton, 1996).

13. For discussion of "the end of nature" discourse and uneasiness with new responsibilities, see Allen Thompson, "Responsibility for the End of Nature: Or, How I Learned to Stop Worrying and Love Global Warming," *Ethics and the Environment*, 14.1 (2009): 79–99.

14. UNFCCC, Article 2; May 9, 1992, S. Treaty Doc. No. 102–38, 1771 U.N.T.S. 107.

15. S. Dessai et al., "Defining and Experiencing Dangerous Climate Change," *Climatic Change* 64, no. 1–2 (2004): 11–25.

16. H. T. Shapiro et al., "Climate Change Assessments: Review of the Processes and Procedures of the IPCC" (Amsterdam: InterAcademy Council, 2010); N. Oreskes, "Beyond the Ivory Tower: The Scientific Consensus on Climate Change," *Science* 306, no. 5702 (2004); W. Anderegg, J. W. Prall, J. Harold, and S. Schneider, "Expert Credibility in Climate Change," *Proceedings of the National Academy of Sciences* 107, no. 27 (2010): 12107–09.

17. See Michael E. Mann, "Defining Dangerous Anthropogenic Interference," *Proceedings of the National Academy of Sciences* 106, no. 11 (2009).

18. R. K. Pachauri and A. Reisinger, eds., *Climate Change 2007: Synthesis Report* (Cambridge: IPCC, 2007), section 1.1–2.

19. For description of early climate research, see Mike Hulme, *Why We Disagree about Climate Change: Understanding Controversy, Inaction and Opportunity* (Cambridge: Cambridge University Press, 2009), 42–60.

20. Pachauri and Reisinger, *2007 Synthesis Report* 2.2.

21. R. T. Watson and D. L. Albritton, eds., *Climate Change 2001: Synthesis Report* (Cambridge: IPCC, 2001). 2.10–2.15; S. Solomon, ed. *Climate Change 2007: The Physical Science Basis* (Cambridge: IPCC, 2007), section 9.2. See section 9.7 for a summary of anthropogenic evidence.

22. "Carbon dioxide equivalent" or "CO_2e" attempts to combine the various radiative forcing impacts (positive and negative) of various gases into one measure, using the radiative impact of carbon dioxide as a common unit. For now the equivalent number is about the same as the carbon dioxide number alone because the negative radiative effect of aerosols nearly washes the positive effect of other gases (like methane). That will change over time, making the CO_2e the measure of enduring importance, but for simplicity in this section I discuss concentrations of CO_2. See John Houghton, *Global Warming: The Complete Briefing*, 4th ed. (Cambridge: Cambridge University Press, 2009), 142–49, 313.

23. M. Oppenheimer et al., "Climate Change: The Limits of Consensus," *Science* 317, no. 5844 (2007); W. J. Burroughs, *Climate Change: A Multidisciplinary Approach* (Cambridge: Cambridge University Press, 2007), 336–41.

24. Stephen Gardiner, "Ethics and Global Climate Change," *Ethics* 114, no. 3 (2004): 565.

25. Houghton, *Global Warming*, 13, 143–44.

26. S. Solomon et al., "Irreversible Climate Change due to Carbon Dioxide Emissions," *Proceedings of the National Academy of Sciences* 106, no. 6 (2009). For visual perspective on the spatial volume of emissions, see http://carbonquilt.org/visualiser.

27. J. A. Church and N. J. White, "Sea-Level Rise from the Late 19th to the Early 21st Century," *Surveys in Geophysics* 32, no. 4–5 (2011).

28. Houghton, *Global Warming*, 176–87; Martin Vermeer and Stefan Rahmstorf, "Global Sea Level Linked to Global Temperature," *Proceedings of the National Academy of Sciences* 106, no. 51 (2009); Robert Kopp et al., "Probabilistic Assessment of Sea Level during the Last Interglacial Stage," *Nature* 462 (2009): 863–68.

29. World Bank, *Turn Down the Heat: Why a 4°C Warmer World Must Be Avoided* (Washington, DC, 2012). For more on impacts see M. L. Parry, ed., *Climate Change 2007: Impacts, Adaptation and Vulnerability* (Cambridge: IPCC, 2007).

30. Timothy M. Lenton et al., "Tipping Elements in the Earth's Climate System," *Proceedings of the National Academy of Sciences* 105, no. 6 (2008). On resilience and global change, see C. S. Holling, "The Resilience of Terrestrial Ecosystems: Local Surprise and Global Change," *Sustainable Development of the Biosphere*, no. 10 (1986). On the likelihood of 4°C increase in global temperature, see Richard Betts et al., "When Could Global Warming Reach 4°C?" *Philosophical Transactions of the Royal Society A* 369, no. 1934 (2011): 67–84.

31. C. Parmesan and G. Yohe, "A Globally Coherent Fingerprint of Climate Change Impacts across Natural Systems," *Nature* 421, no. 6918 (2003).

32. Quoted in Hulme, *Why We Disagree*, 102–3.

33. J. Hansen et al., "Target Atmospheric CO_2: Where Should Humanity Aim?" *Open Atmospheric Science Journal* 2, no. 15 (2008).

34. Simon Caney, "Climate Change, Human Rights, and Moral Thresholds," in *Climate Ethics: Essential Readings*, Stephen Gardiner et al., eds. (New York: Oxford University Press, 2010), 172.

35. N. Nakicenovic and Rob Swart, eds., *Special Report on Emissions Scenarios* (Cambridge: IPCC, 2000), section D.18. Those scenarios list the concentration in CO_2e (see n.21).

36. Nicholas Stern, *The Economics of Climate Change: The Stern Review* (Cambridge: Cambridge University Press, 2006).

37. *People's Agreement of Cochabamba*, World People's Conference on Climate Change and the Rights of Mother Earth, April 22, 2010.

38. See Mike Hulme, "Meet the Humanities," *Nature Climate Change* 1 (2011): 177–79.

39. For the argument in favor see David G. Victor et al., "The Geoengineering Option," *Foreign Affairs* 64 (2009). For the history see James Rodger Fleming, *Fixing the Sky: The Checkered History of Weather and Climate Control* (New York: Columbia University Press, 2010).

40. Thomas Lovejoy, "Geo-Engineering Can Help Save the Planet," *New York Times*, June 10, 2011.

41. P. J. Crutzen, "Albedo Enhancement by Stratospheric Sulfur Injections: A Contribution to Resolve a Policy Dilemma?" *Climatic Change* 77, no. 3 (2006).

42. See the helpful discussion in Stephen Gardiner, *A Perfect Moral Storm: The Ethical Tragedy of Climate Change* (New York: Oxford University Press, 2011), chap. 10.

43. Ernst M. Conradie, "Climate Change and the Church: Some Reflections from the South African Context," *The Ecumenical Review* 62, no. 2 (2010): 7–9.

44. William D. Nordhaus, *A Question of Balance: Weighing the Options on Global Warming Policies* (New Haven, CT: Yale University Press, 2008), 20.

45. J. Timmons Roberts and Bradly C. Parks, *A Climate of Injustice: Global Inequality, North-South Politics, and Climate Policy* (Cambridge, MA: MIT Press, 2006), 135.

46. Henry Shue, "Global Environment and International Inequality," *International Affairs* 75, no. 3 (1999).

47. Iris Marion Young, *Responsibility for Justice* (New York: Oxford University Press, 2011).

48. Henry Shue, "Subsistence Emissions and Luxury Emissions," *Law and Policy* 15, no. 1 (1993): 49.

49. Henry Shue, "Deadly Delays, Saving Opportunities: Creating a More Dangerous World?" in *Climate Ethics: Essential Readings*, Stephen Gardiner et al., eds. (New York: Oxford University Press, 2010); Shue, "Global Environment and International Inequality."

50. Henry Shue, "Climate," in *A Companion to Environmental Philosophy*, Dale Jamieson, ed. (Oxford: Blackwell, 2003), 454.

51. Gardiner, *A Perfect Moral Storm*.

52. UNFCCC, Article 3.

53. See J. Ikeme, "Equity, Environmental Justice and Sustainability: Incomplete Approaches in Climate Change Politics," *Global Environmental Change* 13, no. 3 (2003).

54. See M. R. Kamminga, "The Ethics of Climate Politics: Four Modes of Moral Discourse," *Environmental Politics* 17, no. 4 (2008); Hulme, *Why We Disagree*.

55. E. A. Posner and C. R. Sunstein, "Climate Change Justice," *Georgetown Law Journal* 96 (2007). Gardiner calls this the "polluters get paid principle" in *A Perfect Moral Storm*, 323.

56. Caney, "Climate Change, Human Rights, and Moral Thresholds"; Shue, "Global Environment and International Inequality."

57. See Clare Palmer, "Does Nature Matter? The Place of the Nonhuman in the Ethics of Climate Change," in *The Ethics of Global Climate Change*, Denis Arnold, ed. (New York: Cambridge University Press, 2011).

58. Simon Caney, "Cosmopolitan Justice, Responsibility, and Global Climate Change," *Leiden Journal of International Law* 18, no. 4 (2006): 753–60.

59. Posner and Sunstein, "Climate Change Justice," 1593–94.

60. "Statement on Eco-justice and Ecological Debt," World Council of Churches (February 9, 2009).

61. Peter Singer, *One World: The Ethics of Globalization* (New Haven, CT: Yale University Press, 2002), 31.

62. Caney, "Cosmopolitan Justice."

63. Anil Agarwal and Sunita Narain (New Delhi: Centre for Science and Environment, 1991).

64. J. Paavola and W. N. Adger, "Fair Adaptation to Climate Change," *Ecological Economics* 56, no. 4 (2006); Paul Baer, "Greenhouse Development Rights: A Framework for Climate Protection That Is 'More Fair' than Equal Per Capita Emissions Rights," in *Climate Ethics: Essential Readings*, Stephen Gardiner et al., eds. (New York: Oxford University Press, 2010); Richard W. Miller, *Globalizing Justice: The Ethics of Poverty and Power* (New York: Oxford University Press, 2010), chap. 4.

65. Caney, "Cosmopolitan Justice."

66. Joan Martinez-Alier, "Ecological Debt and Property Rights on Carbon Sinks and Reservoirs," *Capitalism, Nature, Socialism* 13, no. 1(2002); Chukwumerije Okereke and Kate Dooley, "Principles of Justice in Proposals and Policy Approaches to Avoided Deforestation: Towards a Post-Kyoto Climate Agreement," *Global Environmental Change* 20, no. 1 (2010); K. Birrell, L. Godden, and M. Tehan, "Climate Change and REDD+: Property as a Prism for Conceiving Indigenous Peoples' Engagement," *Journal of Human Rights and the Environment* 3, no. 2 (2012).

67. Gardiner, *Perfect Moral Storm*, chaps. 5–6.

68. M. Meinshausen et al., "Greenhouse-Gas Emission Targets for Limiting Global Warming to 2°C," *Nature* 458, no. 7242 (2009); Henry Shue, "Human Rights, Climate Change, and the Trillionth Ton," in *The Ethics of Global Climate Change*, Denis Arnold, ed. (New York: Cambridge University Press, 2011).

69. Singer, *One World: The Ethics of Globalization*, chap. 2.

70. Shue, "Subsistence Emissions and Luxury Emissions."

71. Baer, "Greenhouse Development Rights."

72. Shue, "Deadly Delays," 150; Gardiner, *Perfect Moral Storm*, 48. For Martin-Schramm's policy recommendations, see *Climate Justice,* 105f.

73. Gardiner, *Perfect Moral Storm*, 214, 41.

74. E. M. Markowitz and A. F. Shariff, "Climate Change and Moral Judgement," *Nature Climate Change* 2, no. 4 (2012).

75. Mary Midgley, "Individualism and the Concept of Gaia," in *How Might We Live? Global Ethics in the New Century*, Ken Booth, Tim Dunne, and Michael Cox, eds. (New York: Cambridge University Press, 2001).

76. See "Joint Declaration of Indigenous Churches," World Council of Churches (May 21, 2009); "Cambio Climatico: Declaracion ecumenica," Latin American Council of Churches (April 22, 2010).

77. Michael S. Northcott, *A Moral Climate: The Ethics of Global Warming* (Maryknoll, NY: Orbis Books, 2007), 179.

78. Sallie McFague, *A New Climate for Theology: God, the World, and Global Warming* (Minneapolis: Fortress Press, 2008).

79. The concept "radical inequality" comes from Thomas Nagel, "Poverty and Food: Why Charity Is Not Enough," in *Food Policy: The Responsibility of the United States in Life and Death Choices*, Peter Brown and Henry Shue, eds. (New York: Free Press, 1977), 54–62.

80. Energy access figures are updated by the International Energy Association (http://www.iea.org); hunger figures by the Food and Agricultural Organization of the United Nations (http://www.fao.org).

81. Roberts and Parks, *A Climate of Injustice: Global Inequality, North-South Politics, and Climate Policy*, 8.

82. See J. Rice, "North-South Relations and the Ecological Debt: Asserting a Counter-Hegemonic Discourse," *Critical Sociology* 35, no. 2 (2009); Juan Martínez-Alier, *The Environmentalism of the Poor: A Study of Ecological Conflicts and Valuation* (Cheltenham, UK: Edward Elgar Publishing, 2002), viii–xx, 213–14, 230–33.

83. María Chávez Quispe, "Transformative Spirituality for a Transformed World: Contributions from the Indigenous Perspective," *International Review of Mission* 98, no. 2 (2009); George Tinker, *American Indian Liberation: A Theology of Sovereignty* (Maryknoll, NY: Orbis, 2008).

84. Martino Traxler, "Fair Chore Division for Climate Change," *Social Theory and Practice* 28, no. 1 (2002).

85. Miller, *Globalizing Justice*, chap. 4.

86. Young, *Responsibility for Justice*, chap. 7.

87. See Ernst Conradie, *The Church and Climate Change* (Pietermaritzburg, South Africa: Cluster Publications, 2008), 10–11.

88. For a complementary view on practical theological responses to the anxiety caused by the moral wickedness of climate change, see Byron Smith "Doom, Gloom, and Empty Tombs: Climate Change and Fear," *Studies in Christian Ethics* 24 (2011): 77–92.

89. H. Richard Niebuhr, *Christ and Culture* (New York: Harper, 1951). Compare with the different and quite helpful heuristic in Mike Hulme, "The Four Meanings of Climate Change," in *Future Ethics: Climate Change and Apocalyptic Imagination*, Stefan Skrimshire, ed. (New York: Continuum, 2010). I owe thanks to Richard Herron for research supporting my typology.

90. Pierre Bourdieu, *The Logic of Practice*, Richard Nice, trans. (Stanford, CA: Stanford University Press, 1990), 52–65. I further discuss Bourdieu and theological strategies in chapter 2.

91. See Katharine Wilkinson, *Between God and Green: How Evangelicals Are Cultivating a Middle Ground on Climate Change* (New York: Oxford University Press, 2012).

92. See the film *Resisting the Green Dragon* (2009), produced by the Cornwall Alliance.

93. Calvin Beisner et al., "A Call to Truth, Prudence and Protection of the Poor: An Evangelical Response to Global Warming" (Burke, VA: Cornwall Alliance, 2006), 3. See also Wylie Carr et al., "The Faithful Skeptics: Evangelical Religious Beliefs and Perceptions of Climate Change," *Journal for the Study of Religion, Nature, and Culture* 6, no. 3 (2012): 276–99.

94. Aaron McRight and Riley Dunlap, "Cool Dudes: The Denial of Climate Change among Conservative White Males in the United States," *Global Environmental Change* 21, no. 4 (2011): 1163–72.

95. Kari Norgaard, *Climate Change, Emotions, and Everyday Life* (Cambridge: MIT Press, 2011), 207.

96. Stefan Skrimshire, "What Are We Waiting For? Climate Change and the Narrative of Apocalypse," in *Religion and Dangerous Environmental Change: Transdisciplinary Perspectives*, Sigurd Bergmann, ed. (Berlin: LIT Verlag, 2010). See also Stefan Skrimshire, ed., *Future Ethics: Climate Change and Apocalyptic Imagination* (New York, Continuum, 2010).

97. Skrimshire, "What Are We Waiting For?" 206.

98. B. Rossing, "God Laments with Us: Climate Change, Apocalypse and the Urgent Kairos Moment," *The Ecumenical Review* 62, no. 2 (2010): 125.

99. Carol S. Robb, *Wind, Sun, Soil, Spirit: Biblical Ethics and Climate Change* (Minneapolis: Fortress, 2010), 146–47.

100. Northcott, *Moral Climate*, 5–7.

101. See Robin Lovin, *Christian Realism and the New Realities* (New York: Cambridge University Press, 2008), 33–37.

102. Church World Service, *Briefing Paper: CWS Survey: Members' Work on Climate Change* (2008).

103. Martin-Schramm, *Climate Justice*.

104. "Moving beyond Kyoto with Equity, Justice, and Solidarity," World Council of Churches (October 11, 2004); "Statement on Eco-justice and Ecological Debt," World Council of Churches, (February 9, 2009).

105. SACC, *Climate Change*, 57.

106. National Council of Churches, *Climate and Church: How Global Climate Change Will Impact Core Church Ministries* (Washington, DC, 2008), 11.

107. Dorothy Boorse et al., *Loving the Least of These: Addressing a Changing Environment* (National Association of Evangelicals, 2011); "Climate Change: An Evangelical Call to Action" (Washington, DC, 2006).

108. Descriptions of the Humbo Natural Regeneration Project can be found on websites of World Vision International (http://www.wvi.org) and the Carbon Finance Unit of the World Bank (http://www.wbcarbonfinance.org).

109. Timothy Gorringe, "On Building an Ark: The Global Emergency and the Limits of Moral Exhortation," *Studies in Christian Ethics* 24 (2011): 23–34.

110. "Joint Declaration of Indigenous Churches," World Council of Churches, May 21, 2009; "Cambio Climatico: Declaracion ecumenica," Cochabamba, April 22, 2010 (signed by the Higher Andean Ecumenical Institute of Theology, among others). On the broader movement see http://www.indigenousclimate.org/.

111. M. R. Dove, "Indigenous People and Environmental Politics," *Annual Review of Anthropology* 35 (2006); A. A. Doolittle, "The Politics of Indigeneity: Indigenous Strategies for Inclusion in Climate Change Negotiations," *Conservation and Society* 8, no. 4 (2010).

112. Quispe, "Transformative Spirituality for a Transformed World: Contributions from the Indigenous Perspective," 247.

113. Tinker, *American Indian Liberation: A Theology of Sovereignty*.

114. See Tore Johnsen, "Listen to the Voice of Nature: Indigenous Perspectives," in *God, Creation, and Climate Change: Spiritual and Ethical Perspectives* (Geneva: Lutheran World Federation, 2009), 101–14; Dina Ludeña Cebrián, "The Sources and Resources of Our Indigenous Theology," *The Ecumenical Review* 62, no. 4 (2010). María Chávez Quispe, "Land as Mother: An Indigenous-Theology Perspective," in *Creation and Salvation: A Companion on Recent Theological Movements*, Ernst Conradie, ed. (Zurich: LIT Verlag, 2012).

115. Those themes are worked out in Leonardo Boff, *Cry of the Earth, Cry of the Poor* (Maryknoll, NY: Orbis Books, 1997).

116. I am here interpreting ecological debt through the treatment of reparations for slavery in Lawrie Balfour, "Reparations *After* Identity Politics," *Political Theory* 33, no. 6 (2005): 768–811.

117. For a description of offsetting as "outsourcing of an obligation," see Michael Sandel, *What Money Can't Buy: The Moral Limits of Markets* (New York: Farrar, Strauss, & Giroux, 2012), 75. For the argument on which the charge is made, see Robert Goodin, "Selling Environmental Indulgences," *Kyklos* 47, no. 4 (1994). The indulgence charge takes another turn in this case, as the offsets were not purchased but rather donated to the church, making it unclear how the Vatican actually understands its responsibility. The donating company hoped its gift would win it attention in the offset market, but by April 2010 they had failed to plant the trees and the Vatican was threatening to sue. For more on the ethics of offsetting, see Martin-Schramm, *Climate Justice*, 126; against the whole idea, see Michael Northcott, "The Concealments of Carbon Markets and the Publicity of Love in a Time of Climate Change," *International Journal of Public Theology* 4, no. 3 (2010).

118. SACC, *Climate Change*, 26–29, 51–58.

119. Conradie, *The Church and Climate Change*, 80–91.

120. Dietrich Bonhoeffer, *Letters and Papers from Prison*, Eberhard Bethge, ed. (New York: Collier Books, 1972), 7 (translation altered).

CHAPTER TWO

Christian Ethics and
Unprecedented Problems

❖

*God's demands are not overwhelming because whatever comes from God over-
comes the world. And this is what overcomes the world: our faith.*

1 John 5:3–4

Climate change represents the challenge that anthropocene powers pose to
Christian ethics. Unprecedented social and ecological relations threaten to
overwhelm capacities of theological response, rendering practices of faith
incompetent to their world. If loving neighbors, for example, becomes uncertain within emerging planetary relations, then Christian communities
begin to lose a central practice through which they interpret themselves
and their world in relation to God. In order to sustain their faith, Christian
communities must create ways for love to overcome the storms that would
defeat it. Like other moral traditions, Christianity must generate ways to
sustain the meaning of its way of life in changing conditions—or face collapse. It must invent ways for love to overcome the world of climate change
or concede to atmospheric powers the defeat of a moral life shaped around
love. So how do theological communities adapt the practice of faith?

A popular view of Christian social ethics supposes that its task is to apply
theological ideals to social problems. Christian engagement with society, in
this view, starts from fundamental moral values and then works deductively
toward concrete situations. When Paul Ramsey introduced his *Basic Christian Ethics* he opened with that common sense: "before there can be a Christian social ethic, understanding of the fundamental moral perspective of
the Christian must be deepened and clarified."[1] The ethicist, on his account,
should first establish a fundamental Christian worldview and then work toward applying it to particular problems. This book opened in a different
way, starting from the particular problem of climate change and appealing

to creative reform projects. My approach shares some of the sensibilities of Traci West's *Disruptive Christian Ethics*: skeptical that communities need professional ethicists to clarify their worldview before they can begin acting on their problems, committed to working with the moral knowledges that reform projects are already producing, and focused on empowering moral agency to meet problems through conversation across disciplines and confrontation across boundaries.[2]

Between "basic" and "disruptive" ways of doing Christian ethics there exists an important choice in practical strategy. What role should social problems and grassroots projects play in shaping the tasks of a religious ethic? By emphasizing "inventive" and "tactical" dimensions of religious ethics, I have signaled an approach that grants high significance to problems and projects. Those emphases align with liberationist claims that moral theory should arise from the margins of power, within communities working to overcome oppression and poverty. With regard to a problem like climate change, however, doing ethics from grassroots struggles may not always be possible. In the last chapter I explained how the "unprecedented" scope and "wicked" features of climate change frustrate meaningful action. When responses are either missing or tactically inadequate to the scale and complexity of the problem, then it might seem better for ethicists to approach climate change by reconstructing a tradition's "fundamental moral perspective," in order to offer communities new interpretations of their basic worldview.

Confronting climate change thus presses a methodological question about how to do religious ethics in conditions of moral incompetence. This chapter defends a pragmatic strategy by offering reasons from theology and social theory to suppose that traditions of faith are sustained through practical responses to social problems. Differentiating this approach from what I call a "cosmological strategy," I argue that Christian ethics tends to drift away from concrete problems and communities when it assumes that social change begins by changing worldviews, and when it considers the church as a kind of culture with its own worldview. My theocentric pragmatism explains how new problems drive theological production, and why Christian ethics can begin from what is already going on in communities, even when their projects and concepts remain incompetent to the problems they want to face.

Religious ethicists tend to be suspicious of pragmatism for (at least) three reasons. First, problem-based moral reasoning can be crudely instrumentalist toward religious traditions. If an ethicist deploys whatever "moral resource" appears convenient toward the sort of solution that (she already knows) the situation requires, then the moral meaning of a tradition reduces to its use in some extrinsic project. Second, cultural emergencies seem to call for revolutionary change, not plodding reformism. Adaptive incrementalism can seem supine to social injustice and complicit with ecological catastrophe, undermining the authority of a tradition to call for deep conversion. Third, pragmatist contentment with pluralism seems to imply moral relativism, while action on planetary problems seems to require a global consensus, if not a universal foundation.[3] A pragmatic strategy of religious ethics must then show how response to social problems is itself a religious practice, how reform projects bear promise for deep cultural change, and how a particularist approach matters to the tasks of global ethics.

This chapter establishes the first point within Christian ethics. I explain how the struggle to invent practical responses to overwhelming social problems is a struggle to give faithful answer to God for the world and so should be understood as a proper theological exercise. Ethical work within another religious tradition would, of course, establish that point differently, showing how response to social problems can be understood as a religious practice on its own terms and by its own logic. The Christian theological argument of this chapter therefore illustrates an internal task that may look quite different within other traditions. Subsequent chapters explain how a pragmatic strategy of religious ethics can negotiate moral pluralism in global ethics (chapter 3) and develop culture-transforming collaboration with the ecological sciences (chapter 4). Integrating the moral humanities into science-based management of sustainability problems and forging practical collaborations across alienating borders, I argue there, needs a mode of ethical engagement that begins from concrete problems.

My task in this chapter is to establish that working from problems in Christian ethics is not merely more effective but also more theological. In the end I retain important roles for argument over worldviews and ontologies and hold that cosmological and pragmatic strategies complement one another. However, because the pragmatic approach is regarded with suspicion, both within the field of religion and ecology as well as within theological ethics, I take time to differentiate and defend it. In order to interpret overwhelming problems within a faith that "overcomes the world," I argue, Christian ethics should imagine the practice of faith less in terms of a worldview with ideals ready to apply and more in terms of a movement constantly trying to open possibilities of living the tradition of Jesus in unexpected conditions.

SOCIAL PROBLEMS IN THEOLOGICAL ETHICS

Christian social ethics emerged as a distinct field in the late nineteenth century in response to "the social problem" created by emerging industrial powers. Economic dislocation, class conflict, and urban poverty drew attention to new structures of human relation being made by industrial capitalism. Attending to the political production of human misery, Christian social ethics made structures of relation susceptible to theological criticism. One important line of criticism refuted the social Darwinisms that counseled economic indifference to human suffering. Another criticism interpreted conflicts between labor and capital within an account of the Kingdom of God. By making the social problem a theological problem, Christian ethics made society a subject of God's concern for justice. So Christian ethics helped invent "social justice"—an adaptation that extended the competency of justice to industrial forms of relation.[4]

Ernst Troeltsch's *Social Teaching of the Christian Churches* (1911) was hugely influential in shaping the task of Christian social ethics. By showing how different historical traditions had generated contextual expressions of Christian sociality, Troeltsch demonstrated that the ethos of Christianity could develop in new ways to address modern problems. The ongoing task of Christian communities, Troeltsch thought, is to bring their faith into social existence in new and unexpected contexts. Industrial society made major traditions of Christian life seem incompetent, but creative responses like the social gospel movement bear promise of revitalized expression. The future of civilization, Troeltsch worried, depends on the success of reform communities achieving a social expression that extends a Christian ethos to industrial powers.[5]

At the beginning of the twenty-first century, Christian ethics seems to find itself in a similar situation. The planetary economy of human power is transforming structures of human relation, making new problems of dislocation, conflict, and impoverishment. Once again reductive ideologies try to suppress cultural impulses to civilize those relations, and once again the ethical task includes rejecting fatalist indifference to human suffering and (this time) ecological loss. At stake, it seems, is the future of human civilization. "Sustainability" is now a summary keyword for its complex of problems—for "the social problem" expanded to planetary scale and ecological depth.

The task facing Christian social ethics is therefore analogous to the one Troeltsch saw, only now more complex. For, as we saw in the last chapter with climate change, ethics must address the enduring conflicts of social injustice within humanity's growing conflict with ecological systems. Those tensions cannot be resolved by conjunctions like "eco-justice;" they must be reconstructed by inventing practices that bring the Christian ethos to expression within all the relations within which agents now live. As Troeltsch put it, new moral teachings must be developed "out of the inner impulse of Christian thought, and out of its vital expression at the present time."[6] A century later, the task of Christian social ethics remains constant: to discover vital expressions of Christian life that meet the needs of societies imperiled by their own powers.

Unless the whole idea of a Christian social ethic is a mistake. Stanley Hauerwas and John Milbank, in their distinct styles, condemn the notion that Christianity should worry over the problems caused by a corrupt civilization's fragmentation. Why should Christians care about sustaining modern cultures of power? To the contrary, argue Hauerwas and Milbank, theology must refuse to serve a civilization that views religion as a moral instrument useful for safeguarding its power. Faith is not a "resource" for sustaining industrial power. Christianity does not have a social ethic, says Hauerwas, it *is* a social ethic.[7] Theology does not *relate to* social theory, writes Milbank, it *is* its own social theory.[8] Both attack the very idea of "Christian ethics and social problems" by deconstructing the notion that Christianity is a religious aspect of culture and arguing that it is better understood as a unique culture of its own. Christianity need not accept the problems of modern power as its own; it should rather interpret them as symptoms of another culture's alienation from God and creation. If Christian social ethics has a task, it is to help the church to continue being the church by sustaining its own unique sociality.[9]

In their view, Troeltsch formalized a standing temptation for the church to accept responsibility for social problems and thereby surrender its own social existence. Christian social ethics has largely been the literature of yield to that temptation. Especially in the responsibility ethics of H. Richard Niebuhr, Milbank and Hauerwas see plans for the church to cease being Christian. The mistake lies in assuming that social problems pose real theological challenges. This book's opening chapter exemplifies their fear: beginning a Christian ethic by acknowledging theological incompetence before a problem of industrial powers seems to allow those powers to interpret what Christian practices must mean, and implies that the church should be measured by its effectiveness in the world.

Their critique of the very idea of a Christian social ethic must be taken seriously. Milbank and Hauerwas force any ethic, and especially a project constructed like this book, to defend its account of "problems." Why is climate change a real problem for Christian ethics, rather than just another symptom of the world's violence? Why is practical response to it a theological responsibility, rather than a capitulation to power?

Social problems become theological problems when Christian communities receive them as challenges to their practice of faith. When problems seem to mediate transformative demands from God they become the scene of a theological exercise to open new ways of living the faith. In the late nineteenth century, Christian reform projects made structural poverty a theological problem that challenged proclamation of good news to the poor. Christian socialism and the social gospel opened new ways of proclaiming good news amidst economic powers threatening to overwhelm that practice of faith. The problems of atmospheric powers await analogous adaptations of Christian moral agency.

My argument depends on a different relation of Christianity and culture than the one Milbank and Hauerwas seem to have in mind. Instead of narrating a separate Christian culture with its own worldview and language, in which the world's problems seem distracting and compromising, I argue that Christian social ethics arises from missional projects that bear and respond to the world's problems as their own. Doing so, Christian ethics does not sanction industrial powers or submit to market relations; it rather opens those powers and relations to different uses by inventing ways to live faithfully within them. By bearing responsibility for emerging problems of human power, the church learns to sustain the practices that carry its faith—loving enemies and neighbors, asking and granting forgiveness, witnessing to justice, and proclaiming good news for the poor. In other words, the church sustains its unique sociality precisely by taking seriously the world's problems.

I therefore take a less dim view of Christian social ethics over the past century and in fact develop my argument in conversation with H. Richard Niebuhr's responsibility ethics. The Christian social reform projects that emerged over the twentieth century were hardly aporetic losses of church; on the contrary, missional reform movements kept opening possibilities of Christian practice by theologically confronting social problems. The Catholic Worker Movement, for example, demonstrates that ways of love and justice have been opened amidst political and economic powers that would make those concepts almost unintelligible. Catholic Worker hospitality has been an important guarantor of the meaningfulness of neighbor-love within industrial economies. Critical theological interpretations of social structures rely on communities that sustain the credibility of Christian moral thought, by making practices of faith possible within structures of relation that would seem to defeat possibilities of acting in the way of Jesus.

Christian social ethics developed alongside a practical response to social problems. The Protestant social gospel developed alongside labor struggles and in settlement houses. Catholic social thought developed in response to class conflict and in Catholic Worker houses. A half century of liberationist initiatives have expanded and intensified those legacies. Liberation projects have exhibited a particular genius for making social problems into theological problems by locating interpretation of God's action within struggles to overcome exploitation and poverty. Jon Sobrino completes the logic of that genius in his revision of Cyprian's dictum ("outside the church there is no salvation") to proclaim "outside the poor there is no salvation." That is to say, outside confrontation with poverty, there is no church, no practice of faith, no meaningful talk of salvation.[10] My argument shares the liberationist commitment to locate theological meaning within practices of response to the world's wounds.

I do not mean to romanticize. Christian social projects sometimes mobilize "Christian values" to govern cultures as if that were the special prerogative of the Christian religion. Troeltsch looked for a new Christian social philosophy because he thought that the ethos of the Christian religion must play a central role in sustaining western civilization.[11] Troeltsch thought Christianity *could* perform that role because he followed Max Weber's view of the relation of ethos and society. With a different view of how religious ethics matters for moral culture and how culture matters in confronting social problems, ethicists would take a different view of the task of Christian social ethics. Later in the chapter I offer a view of religion and culture that situates Christian projects in a more pluralist and fluid setting.

Nor do I mean to diminish the role of theology. Christian social projects sometimes substitute moral earnestness for critical interpretation. Starting from problems and practices does not mean that theology mutely serves "action." The social gospel movement is often remembered as an example of the risk that theological communities might let some notion of social needs determine the meaning of God and salvation. Social gospel advocates could all too easily talk of correlating Christian teachings with economic principles and of realizing Christian ideals through political institutions. By overdetermining theology with its earnestness on the issues of the day, the social gospel movement could baptize nationalist and ethnocentric impulses as divine movements.[12] Most worrisome, its initially strong account of social transformation was prone to dilution into an empty liberalism of social progress, which was the target of H. Richard Niebuhr's famous epigraph: "A God without wrath brought men without sin into a kingdom without judgment through the ministrations of a Christ without a cross."[13]

Yet those cautions do not vitiate the idea of Christian ethics as a social project. Niebuhr does not dispute the idea of social salvation but rather laments its desuetude. Christianity's social expression loses its ability to make a cultural difference when it collapses faith in a transformative God into the romance of a movement. When the needs of a social moment overdetermine the church's task, Christianity's dynamism for cultural reform calcifies into an inert institution of cultural sanction. Niebuhr was not shy about naming where in church history were pillars of salt. If the kingdom of God is really salvation and is really social, thought Niebuhr, then its faith should produce a dynamic, tactical engagement with its world. Church forms as a "grand strategy of life under the kingdom of God."[14]

Later in the chapter I question the ideas of "Christ and culture" that shaped Niebuhr's strategy for theologically framing social problems. I contest his idea of culture, however, in order to intensify the generative tension of church and social problems that he made conditional to Christian ethics. The "church's social teaching," according to Niebuhr, is shaped by how an inventive community constructs faithful responses to its context. Describing the church as "the organic movement of those who have been 'called out' and 'sent,'" Niebuhr looks for it as "the social expression of the movement of life toward its true goal" in the God who creates and redeems.[15] Niebuhr thus sought to preserve the central tension of Christian social ethics with a pragmatic sensibility to test Christianity by its social expression and a theological insistence that meaningful expression happens through faith in a transformative God.

I think Niebuhr was right about the "strategic" character of Christian sociality, and in this chapter describe two basic strategies of Christian social ethics. The difference between them turns on key assumptions about how religion functions in cultural change and how social problems matter for theological communities. *A cosmological strategy* uses theological discourse to critically interpret cultural worldviews, on the notion that such interpretations can illuminate the significance of social problems in an agent's moral imagination. *A pragmatic strategy* attends to how Christian reform projects already use theological discourse to interpret practical problems, on the notion that such interpretations form part of how social problems drive moral change. The former focuses on worldviews as the patterns of meaning behind action. The latter focuses on practices as the patterns of action that carry and change meaning.

Both strategies appear in the legacy of H. Richard Niebuhr, which I show in order to avoid drawing the distinction between them too sharply by illustrating how the two strategies differently treat central tensions in a common body of work. My point in this exercise is not to defend Niebuhr's own version of responsibility ethics, nor do I mean to impose a Protestant style for Christian ethics in general. Using Niebuhr allows a common angle of approach for sketching two complementary methods for addressing social problems. Ethicists working in Catholic social thought or Eastern Orthodox theology would sketch them differently, but I think they would recognize this outline of methodologies. While departing from Niebuhr's account of responsibility at many points, this exercise nonetheless follows his sensibility that ethics should begin in interpretation of how moral agents are situated within social relations and structures of power. His orienting question, "what is going on?" makes contextual interpretation central to Christian ethics.[16] Indeed Niebuhr's most important legacy for Christian social ethics may lie in the field's subsequent focus on interpreting relations and powers, and its enduring interest in how those religious interpretations figure in cultural dynamics.[17]

These two strategies represent two general ways of thinking about the relation of Christian ethics and social problems. They do not correspond to normative frameworks, confessional settings, or theological traditions; they offer no taxonomy of the field. They differentiate two broad ways of thinking about how problems shape the task of Christian ethics.[18] Because they also correspond to analogous debates within global ethics and sustainability science (the subjects of the next two chapters), the play of this argument within Christian ethics matters for how one interprets other fields and the role of religious ethics within them.

THE STRATEGY OF MORAL COSMOLOGY

A cosmological strategy creates an imaginative field for moral agency by using theological beliefs and symbols to interpret social reality and its problems from a Christian point of view. Niebuhr called his approach "Christian moral philosophy," and seemed to understand it as countercultural religious interpretation of social problems. "The great religions in general, and Christianity in particular . . . make their impact on us by calling into question our whole conception of what is fitting." Religions do that "by questioning our picture of the context into which we now fit our actions."[19] Reinterpreting pictures of reality with Christian beliefs and symbols allows the ethicist to redescribe the field of moral action. The ethicist thus confronts social problems by investigating the cultural imaginary in which they appear and by uncovering the reality-shaping goals and values that have led to a crisis. She can then propose alternative moral symbols by which to reshape the worldview through which agents determine fitting action.[20]

William Schweiker demonstrates rigorous pursuit of a cosmological strategy as he develops his own ethic of responsibility for planetary problems. He presents his two books on the subject as "Christian moral philosophy" in Niebuhr's sense.[21] "What is at issue most basically is how we 'picture' or imagine the moral space of life."[22] Schweiker introduces *Responsibility and Christian Ethics* by describing the ethical task as interpretation of a technological extension of human power that threatens to "overwhelm moral reason."[23] His *Theological Ethics and Global Dynamics* intensifies the situation:

"Nothing so much characterizes the age of globality as the fantastic, even terrifying, expansion of the human capacity to respond to, shape, and even create reality, that is, the explosive growth of human power . . . a power that increasingly is beyond our capacities or desire to control and orient."[24] Writing with David Klemm on *Religion and the Human Future*, Schweiker characterizes this as the age of "overhumanization." The task for religious ethics is then to construct value symbols that can guide hyperbolic powers while abstaining from a "hypertheism" that would govern powers by absolutizing a particular view of the divine. Ethics must picture the moral space of globalizing power while recognizing that its problems bring many moral worlds into conflict.[25]

To meet those tasks Schweiker works in two steps. He first shows how to use Christian symbols to rescue moral reason from titanic powers. The symbols of God, creation, and Christ's love call into question a cultural obsession with power while still valuing the significance of power within finite lives.[26] Agents living in an era of overhumanization need the capacity to imagine "endangerment to the entire life system." Explicating reality with Christian interpretive symbols invites moral agents to revise the interpretation of power and peril within their worldview, for the sake of better orienting their action. Then secondly, because not all find Christian symbols acceptable, Schweiker offers metatraditional reflection on what his reinterpretation of those symbols accomplishes. He proposes "integrity of life before God" as an ideal norm that gathers and regulates the illuminative claims of particular cultural symbols. It names the summary claim on the humanist imagination and grounds an imperative of responsibility.[27]

Other religious ethicists working on the problems of anthropocene power may work with different interpretive symbols and propose different summary claims, but they share a sense of their strategic task: ethics criticizes visions of reality. For several ethicists, that shared task is made possible by the cultural theory of Clifford Geertz. What makes an ethic "religious," affirms John Reeder, is its critical engagement with pictures of fundamental reality.[28] What makes an ethic "Christian," as Douglas Ottati puts it, is "the reflective attempt to articulate a Christian worldview in the service of the life of faith." Proposals for practical action lie implicit in the content of its worldview. "We need a picture of things in relation to God if we are to know how to interact with them."[29] Focused on the symbolic imagination of moral consciousness, Gibson Winter affirms that "ideology furnishes the subject matter of religious social ethics."[30] So we have visual metaphors for a foundational relation between religious ethics and social problems: some picture, worldview, vision, or image creates the symbolic background that grounds and orients practical action.

Those metaphors indicate the practical trade-off in this strategy of religious ethics: beginning from a worldview and working toward application abstracts ethics from concrete problems. Schweiker's compelling description of titanic powers seems likely to include climate change and his references to disempowerment seem likely to include human rights violations, but he hardly mentions those problems, except as symptoms of a deficient moral consciousness. While he clearly intends to help public discussion of social problems, his interpretive work requires only a very general notion of global threats. More particular engagement with a problem like climate change is not required by his approach because the bedrock of response lies in the metaethical sediments of myth and metaphor. That assumption limits the relevant range of interdisciplinary exchange because all the important ethical work happens at the level of moral ontology. Schweiker thus stays close to moral philosophy while remaining aloof from the environmental and social sciences, and distant from the organic creativity of reform projects.

Two important examples from within this strategy complicate that description. Sallie McFague's book on climate change shows how acutely a cosmological approach can apply itself to a specific problem, and is not aloof from the relevant sciences. Interrogating the metaphors that mediate cultural behavior, she approaches climate change by critiquing the deficient cosmological ideas that she thinks permit and produce its emergence. In order to reform the dysfunctional vision of the human place in earth that she thinks underwrites anthropogenic climate change, McFague develops alternative metaphors of God and nature.[31]

Still, the particular problem seems overdetermined by the task of cosmological interpretation, as if climate change were a direct manifestation of mental metaphors and religious symbols. Because all the important moral work happens within worldviews, the particular practices of responsive projects can seem derivative and secondary, while concrete features of the problem have little bearing on what those projects should do. Generating practices of responsibility for climate change awaits the new landscape of agency made possible by a better moral imagination.

Emilie Townes shows how closely a cosmological strategy can cleave to concrete embodiments of reality and how interdisciplinary its work can be. Writing self-consciously in H. R. Niebuhr's mode of cultural interpretation, her *Womanist Ethics and the Cultural Production of Evil* develops an account of the "fantastic hegemonic imagination" that weaves racism, sexism, militarism, and classism into the fabric of everyday life. She reads history, literature, and cultural theory as avenues of "getting into the interior worlds of structural evil itself," seeking to show how social evil is maintained not only by ideologies, but "by more heuristic forces that emerge from the imagination as emotion, intuition, and yearning."[32] Townes brings readers into that interior imaginative world by tracing the cultural production of figural stereotypes that come to function as fantastic, deadly images. For example, she traces the role of the Mammy figure—the devoted, asexual, rotund Negro matriarch of plantation myth—from antebellum narratives to blackface minstrel shows to early baking-product advertising campaigns to Aunt Jemima syrup. Uncovering the charged, "fantastic" connections of an everyday grocery item, Townes begins to make visible a cultural imaginary embodied and implicit in everyday interactions. Historicist and pluralist in method, Townes shows a nonfoundationalist variety of the cosmological strategy that avoids abstract deductivism by describing the moral visions carried and reproduced through material culture.

Townes exhibits both the power and the risk of a cosmological strategy. On the one hand, deep cultural transformation seems to require this investigation into the interior worlds of evil in order to open critical space between everyday life and the ghostly haunts that shape our inhabitation of it. On the other hand, her account of the cultural production of evil seems so fantastic and hegemonic—plantation ideologies reproduced by a maple syrup container—that it almost overwhelms everyday practices of resistance. Apart from the intellectual work of criticizing the social production of evil, how can agents open spaces for freedom? There seems little opportunity for practical moral agency to appropriate, redirect, and reinvent the world that they inhabit.

Townes's work cautions would-be reformers not to move too quickly to adaptive solutions. She wants moral agents to pay close interpretive attention to the cultural landscape that produces the problems on which ethicists work—including the imaginaries that shape how we identify and frame "problems." The work of Schweiker, McFague, and Townes addresses what James Gustafson approvingly calls "global questions"—investigations into how views of human nature, social structures, and moral values cohere into a prevailing ethos.[33] Such investigations maintain the spirit of Christian social reform, says Gustafson, but with a more sophisticated account of the meta-ethical work required to generate meaningful change. The drawback to this strategy, Gustafson admits, is the difficulty of identifying points for practical action: "given the socialization processes of culture and society, it is difficult to apprehend what the points of explicit activity would be to which one could turn one's reforming zeal."[34] A cosmological reception of social problems cannot easily solve that difficulty, and Gustafson must leave the point with a discomfiting exhortation for ethicists to maintain an agnostic interest in cultural reform along with their focus on the big questions.

Gustafson's caution likely stems from continued embarrassment with aggressive reform optimism, which reappears with each new movement in the zeal of social activists who have a plan to change the world in this generation. Gustafson is therefore suspicious of strategies of practical reason that make too much of problems and projects.[35] However, the civilization-threatening problems of planetary human power that interest Schweiker and McFague seem to beg for a clearer account of how the work of religious ethics participates in adaptive social change. Precisely because climate change threatens to overwhelm the moral imagination, organizing the task of religious ethics around the interpretation of worldviews can underscore the impossibility of any cooperative action until agents adopt a more satisfactory worldview. That seems to involve an unlikely three-step process of social change: first, religious ethicists or other cultural producers articulate a revised moral worldview and, second, they successfully persuade many individuals to adopt it. Only then does ethics come to the task of negotiating concrete applications. In relation to climate change, the chronic deferral of practical action in that approach feeds the accumulating wickedness of the problem—inability to act becomes part of what paralyzes productive ethical deliberations.

A cosmological strategy risks that long interval of ideological debate in order to achieve the deep cultural transformation that it holds necessary to address problems whose roots lie in moral consciousness. If architectonic ideas drive the emergence of climate change, if dominant worldviews corrupt interpretation of reality, then religious ethics cannot turn to addressing climate change until it critically revises the foundations of moral imagination. No adequate response to discrete "social problems," Townes shows, can avoid confronting the cultural production of evil.

Criticism of Christianity's role in the cultural production of anthropocentrism is especially influential for how Christian ethics approaches sustainability problems. Lynn White's argument that "The Historical Roots of our Ecologic Crisis" lie in religious cosmology—specifically in the dualist worldview of western Christianity—provoked a debate that has shaped work in several fields. Even when disputed in fact, White's claim that Christian belief generated the modern ecological crisis has been methodologically influential for how theorists think ethics matters for environmental problems. "What people do about their ecology depends on what they think about themselves in relation to things around them," writes White.[36] Problems like climate change, in this view, are symptoms of a crisis in worldview, and must be addressed at that metaethical level. The fields of religion and ecology, Christian ecotheology, and environmental ethics have often followed that assumption: adequately addressing environmental problems requires constructing a new value theory, reclaiming a doctrine of creation, or telling a different narrative. My own *Ecologies of Grace* follows that assumption by treating visions of salvation as the background of environmental behavior. The method: first establish a basic moral vision, then see about applying it to particular problems. (Of course I never got around to any problems in that book—so secondary and derivative seemed the task of application.)[37]

Christian ethics participates in cultural reform, in this strategy, in much the way that Gustafson describes: through interpretive criticism that can alter dominant pictures of reality. Gustafson's own critique of anthropocentrism questions religious tendencies to suppose that God and nature stand in service of human benefit, and so casts doubt on a corresponding modern assumption that nature must serve human interests. What happens to ethics, Gustafson asks, if humanity "is rightly related not only to other persons, not only to social institutions and their relations to each other, but to the elements of nitrogen, oxygen, and carbon . . . to the world of plants and animals, and even to the inanimate features of our planet?"[38] Recognizing our limits and vulnerability, thinks Gustafson, would shift the moral perspective in a way that would allow better interpretation of planetary ecological relations, and, finally, more fitting responses to the problems arising within those relations.

An ethicist might, of course, pursue a cosmological strategy without subscribing to a view that global problems represent cultural catastrophe. Max Stackhouse follows the Weberian view "that in the dominant structures of social, political, and economic life, religious themes that were worked out over centuries have been plowed into the very fabric of the common life." Ethicists "cannot understand the globalizing forces if we do not grasp the ways in which these ideas are derived directly from biblical and Christian religious resources." Stackhouse, however, evaluates global social conditions more approvingly than most Christian ethicists, so he thinks that the religious roots of those conditions do not need revision as much as reinforcement. Globalizing social forces bear promise for humanity, thinks Stackhouse, and will continue to do so as long as they are guided by the religious worldview which first generated them.[39] "If the Christian traditions that have shaped so much of the spiritual and social life of our contemporary world are not to fade into oblivion, bringing an utter collapse of civil society, a renewal of Christian ethics as it bears on economic life is necessary."[40] In a view similar to that of Troeltsch in his era, Stackhouse thinks that global sustainability needs renewal of Christian social thought. Stackhouse has a much sunnier interpretation of both inherited Christian cosmology and global society than the other ethicists in this section, but he follows a similar strategic aim: to supply a theological picture of reality that helps agents rightly interpret new social relations.

My point in this section has been to identify one distinctive approach to concrete problems in religious ethics. A cosmological strategy approaches social problems through interpretation of cultural worldviews. It addresses problems indirectly by confronting the metaphors, symbols, and stories that shape an agent's perception of her world. Through this strategy, Christian ethics sustains possibilities of moral agency in the face of unprecedented problems, by using imaginative resources to reinterpret worldviews and thus alter the pictures of reality by which persons orient their action.

THE STRATEGY OF THEOCENTRIC PRAGMATISM

A pragmatic strategy works in the other direction, from confronting problems toward rethinking reality. Practical action, in this strategy, does not await the outcome of interpretation; it is itself a site of interpretive production. Rather than supposing that the most important moral resources of a religious tradition are the symbols and metaphors that an ethicist might use to illuminate general conditions of human life, or to criticize the roots of a cultural ethos, a pragmatic strategy supposes that its most important resources are the tactics generated by communities using their traditions to confront new problems. Those tactics cultivate opportunities for moral agency to bear responsibility for unprecedented problems, and thereby permit moral agents to sustain the meaning of life carried by their tradition of faith.

I introduce this strategy also within the legacy of H. R. Niebuhr in order to avoid overdrawing the divergence between the two methods, each of which an ethicist might deploy in different contexts. I also want to illustrate how much of the difference between strategies depends on how one conceives of the relation between Christian ethicist and Christian community, and of the relation between Christian community and wider society. In an essay on the "responsibility of the church for society," Niebuhr appeals to the church as "the sensitive and responsive part in every society and mankind as a whole . . . the pioneer part of society that responds to God on behalf of the whole society." Analogous to the way natural science specializes in responding to the rationality of the world and artists in responding to its beauty, says Niebuhr, the church is a community of prophetic specialists, taking the lead in responding to injustice and idolatry. The church "pioneers" in developing and enacting practical forms of responsibility for the relations and powers of a society. "It is the first to repent for the sins of a society and it repents on behalf of all," beginning with concrete efforts to realize justice in its own communities, thus creating new practices of being church before God.[41] By invoking a responsive, missional sense of church, Niebuhr points Christian ethics toward the practices of faith communities struggling for faithfulness in an overwhelming world.[42]

That sense of a constant struggle for faithfulness makes the actual practices of Christian communities come nearer the center of Christian ethics. Ethics in a cosmological strategy often overlooks the organic creativity of faith-based movements for social change. When religious ethics organizes around transforming worldviews, its task belongs primarily to professional interpreters who work with symbols and texts. Even when church is celebrated as the source of Christian sociality, attention to what specific churches or faith-based projects do is muted because their actions remain derivative of the first task (the cosmological task). I opened this chapter with Traci West contesting the notion that Christian communities await the specialized knowledge of great moral thinkers. Interpretation of social problems is more accountable to how agents are already responding to their world, she argues, when done in collaboration with what she calls "community sources." West takes the example of racial justice initiatives in relation to the legacies of Reinhold Niebuhr and Martin Luther King. According to some commentators, the elder Niebuhr's realist theory of justice was the decisive influence on Martin Luther King, who in turn guided the movement with successful ideas of power, pride, and political prospect.[43]

If we think of ethics this way, with Reinhold Niebuhr as the genius behind King's thought, and King as the genius of a movement, says West, "it conceals the multiple actors and innovators in the moral dramas of history, and reinforces the supremacy of whites in our understanding of how moral knowledge is generated." West points to a Harlem network of projects bubbling with social creativity and strategic innovation—just blocks away from where Niebuhr wrote. The Harlem Housewives League analyzed the economic flows of Harlem and devised some of the first targeted boycotts in the country, while the Harlem YWCA cultivated a social space free from white hegemony in order to develop black culture and black pride. Interpretive actions like those, says West, show areas where Reinhold Niebuhr's theories of power and pride would have been improved by attending to how the communities around him used those moral resources. West is pressing a methodological claim: "this Christian social ethics work of critical reflection and social confrontation can never be adequately carried out as a solitary journey but must be waged within and through some form of Christian faith community."[44]

West develops a self-consciously liberationist approach with the characteristic epistemological claims: that theological, ethical, and social analyses follow the practices of those suffering the world's evil and struggling for liberation from it. A pragmatic strategy aligns with claims that privilege the contextual practices of communities attempting to overcome some problem.[45] It differs from some liberation theologies in its openness to how communities may understand what it means to overcome. "Liberation" does not always function here as a final claim about God's action or the meaning of Christian life. A pragmatic strategy begins interpretation of God's action more sparely: by supposing that Christian ethics should interpret social problems in relation to communities already creating live strategies of response. Recall H. R. Niebuhr's description of the church as an organic movement, continually seeking strategies by which to give social expression to the mission of God. Over the past half century some of the most dynamic movements to confront social powers have been liberationist, but in the next half century they might understand themselves and God's action differently. Where reform projects meet new problems in ways that sustain or open possibilities of faithful response to God, they present the object of a Christian social ethic: a venture of response that interprets the events of the world in terms of how God is acting through them.

Creative theological thinking, observes Mary McClintock Fulkerson, arises from the scene of a wound; it is "generated by a sometimes inchoate sense that something *must* be addressed."[46] A pragmatic strategy considers problems as goads to creative responses in Christian communities. Fulkerson writes in ethnographic description of a particular church, but her metaphor of wound holds, I think, for a general role that social problems can play in eliciting moral production across theological communities. It may not be clear how exactly to respond to a refugee crisis, or to global hunger, or to climate change; but each problem carries a demand. Each wounds Christian life, the credibility of which would diminish if no response were forthcoming. A pragmatic strategy supposes that the most interesting theological production is driven by confrontation with the most overwhelming problems.

The role for the professional ethicist, according to this strategy, is to critically participate in some project of response, interpreting and evaluating how it functions in meeting some problem's demand. Academically trained ethicists can cultivate and critique these initial responses by seeking to make them more competent to the problems they face and more adept with the traditions they deploy. Ethicists need not remain loyal to a project if they find it hopelessly incompetent. They may try to convince a community that its current tactic misuses its tradition or misunderstands its context and persuade them to adopt alternative tactics, perhaps by claiming their tradition differently or by borrowing from other communities and traditions. "Competence" here means a capability to address wounds that demand response from a community of faith in a way that sustains or improves the community's understanding of itself before God. That is no simple task of matching a tradition's resources to contextual need because how a community responds is likely to reframe the problem and its ostensible demands, as well as to renegotiate the meaning of its tradition. A pragmatic strategy expects those interpretive shifts and makes it one task of religious ethics to describe and evaluate them.

"The church" in this strategy appears not as the community of a certain worldview, story, or identity. It is rather more like a social movement or a mission project, constantly seeking to open possibilities of response to God amidst difficult and changing conditions. In this strategy the metaphors for the relation between theological traditions and social problems are more dialogical than visual: confronting, answering, responding. Christian symbol and narrative remain important interpretive resources, but this strategy emphasizes their tactical function. They are not available as a stock of symbols and values, from which a master technician might construct a new worldview. They appear within the patterns of action by which a community interprets and addresses its world. Christian ethics should therefore work from those practices, relentlessly criticizing them in order to make them more productive, more capable of facing the problems they seek to address. A pragmatic strategy supposes that the most interesting ethical production happens within the tactics of live moral communities because those tactics enable a community to keep cultivating the sort of moral agents who can understand themselves and so give answer to God amid *and for* emergent powers and unprecedented problems.

But how then to account for the inert dullness of most self-advertised churches? The North American churches of the twentieth century have not always been so "pioneer" in addressing social problems. More often they have been laggard and dim, using religious thought as a refuge from thinking about social problems. What passes for "prophetic" in North American churches often means showing up in vestments at rallies organized by others. H. Richard Niebuhr helps here because his image of an innovative moral community, responsive to social evils through practices of inward critique and outward witness, need not describe the empirical reality of ecclesial institutions in order to depict an ethical function that characterizes the notion of "church" at the center of this strategy. This church exists by the act of taking responsibility for an overwhelming world, by which it participates in God's responsibility for the world. The fundamental moral community for Christian ethics, this suggests, may not be a group explicitly shaped for the maintenance of a Christian identity or worldview, but might rather be an association of shared practice formed by attempts to respond to the world's wounds, as before God.

My point here is that with a pragmatic strategy, Christian social ethics can start from adaptive projects because theological production and social interpretation happen within them. Martin Luther King's interpretation of the civil rights movement offers an important example of how formal theological reflection can arise from tactical actions, and can then contribute to those practices to make them more productive, more competent, and more faithful. King saw in the actions of those willing to risk their bodies for the sake of political solidarity a glimpse of what Christian love might mean. As he preached that practice as Christ's love in action, he cultivated a resource implicit in the movement: the Christian symbol of agape as a tactic for overcoming racism. Now, maybe appealing to agape was politically imprudent in the face of white violence, or maybe it was too strained an extension of the tradition's thought on love. Critics have made both claims. The inquiry of Christian ethics can begin from how the movement community used love as a tactic for responding to a social wound and then test and perhaps improve that tactic through critical engagement.

Does that imply that agape might come to mean anything that a community's problems need it to mean? Which is to ask: what makes a pragmatic strategy meaningfully theological? According to one view of pragmatism, social needs *should* determine the task of religious ethics, which should try to supply reform projects with cultural tools that help a broad political community meet its challenges. "Our task," writes Jeffrey Stout, "like Thomas Aquinas's, Thomas Jefferson's, and Martin Luther King's, is to take the many parts of a complicated social and conceptual inheritance and stitch them together into a pattern that meets the needs of the moment." Stout depicts that taking and stitching with the metaphor of "bricolage," and his description fits King's genius for borrowing from multiple moral traditions in order to organize a broad coalition of democratic reform. In Stout's pragmatism, King was a skilled moral entrepreneur, fitting religious resources to the needs of social reform.[47]

However, Gustafson and others worry that this sort of pragmatism represents the worst legacy of the American social gospel: a crude instrumentalism that puts God and religion in the service of moral ventures already determined by whatever society thinks it needs. In this view, there is eventually nothing interestingly Christian about a pragmatic ethic.[48] Christian ethicists from a variety of perspectives have similar worries. John Yoder objects to Stout that "there is nothing in bricolage worth dying for."[49] Hauerwas complains that "something has gone terribly wrong in the linking of charity with effectiveness. For while it is certainly true that the Gospel is a social gospel . . . by the world's standard Christ was ineffective."[50] If the content of Christian love reduces to its use-value for some situation, then the apparent demands of a political moment determine the meaning of life in Jesus. Perhaps a pragmatic Christian ethic becomes merely a sensitive reading of social science with theological glosses.[51]

Those objections worry that a pragmatic strategy compromises the basis for a distinctively Christian ethic. But tactical uses of religious traditions do not necessarily reduce religious meaning to social efficacy—and they would not work if they did. H. R. Niebuhr observes that religion only works instrumentally if its members do not in fact view their faith in instrumental terms, but take it as the proper object of their ultimate loyalty.[52] For bricolage to be effective, then, it must be understood as a theological practice, such that taking and knitting cultural resources to meet the needs of a moment is an important way of living and keeping the faith. For King, tactical confrontations with white violence were practices through which a community could learn what Christ's love means precisely because he had faith that God was (effectively) loving the world through the tactics of the civil rights movement. If by the world's standard Christ was ineffective that does not make it a theological principle that love should not seek success by its own standard. Jesus did not lay down his life for the method of bricolage, true; but he did creatively adapt a religious lexicon in combination with other political and cultural inheritances in order to open new possibilities of love.

Creative responses to social problems can become occasions in which a community decides what is going on in its world by deciding how to answer for it to God. This problem-driven process of development in Christian ethics accommodates Alasdair MacIntyre's account of how traditions work. MacIntyre describes traditions developing through internal arguments about their orienting sense of good. The pragmatic strategy I am describing here differs in supposing that "external" problems—including shared social problems recognized across traditions and cultures—can drive internal arguments. MacIntyre agrees that the conceptual resources of a tradition take their meaning from the contingent social practices of moral communities, but he thinks that traditions differ so much that their conceptual resources must be understood exclusively within the terms of the internal argument of a tradition.[53] Pragmatic borrowing and planetary problems pose threats to this view of tradition. But if the internal arguments of moral traditions develop at least in part from ongoing attempts to make traditions capable of meeting shared political challenges (as Stout protests to MacIntyre), then pluralist borrowing for wider social reform purposes does not necessarily fragment a tradition.[54] On the contrary, bricolage may create repertoires of action that allow a community to assimilate responses to social problems within their ongoing argument over the good. Because Christian civil rights projects drew on multiple moral inheritances they were able to use responses to white racism to sustain the possibility of loving enemies and keeping faith with God's justice. The tactics of overcoming racism were, for them, the tactics of faith.

A strategy of Christian ethics that expects responses to social problems to renegotiate the meaning of traditions accrues the sort of participatory and activist dimensions described in Cornel West's "prophetic pragmatism." West wants skilled cultural actors to help communities cultivate an "emancipatory social experimentalism" that functions as a "quest for wisdom that puts forth new interpretations of the world based on past traditions."[55] For West, "organic intellectuals" help communities find new capacities in their moral inheritances, inventing possibilities for cultural reforms that in turn enable communities to take responsibility for society's deepest and most difficult problems. King is exemplar for West as well; he is "the most significant and successful organic intellectual in American history."[56]

In a theological version of a pragmatic strategy, King was successful not merely because he borrowed resources from cultural inheritances in a politically useful way, but because he preached that Christian communities needed the tactics supported by that borrowing in order to remain faithful to the way of Jesus. Indeed, King's struggle for faith drove the tactical engagement needed to borrow well in the first place. King's pragmatism is theocentric in a way that West's pragmatism does not seem to fully appreciate. "What sets him apart from exemplary organic intellectuals of the past such as W. E. B. DuBois or Frederick Douglas," writes Luther Ivory, is his "God-centeredness." The problem of American racism compelled the movement's moral work, which King sought to understand as always also a response to God.[57] King's style of taking and stitching multiple inheritances presented tactical responses to the problem at hand as concrete ways to participate in God's redemptive responses to evil. His interpretation of God's purposes could shift through tactical experience. For example, King's early views on love and power were shifted by the student sit-in movement. Persons putting their bodies on the line in a drama of confrontation with social evil was compelling to King because it seemed to have the shape of Christ's way of acting. In the unexpected use of that drama, King learned from movement actors new tactical approaches for opening possibilities of love in the midst of overwhelming power.[58] By adapting love to meet the shifting powers of racism, they sustained love's possibility for moral agents. Learning what love could do, they learned more deeply what it means.

King's theological commitments took shape through social confrontations. He "combined revolutionary consciousness with a radical pragmatism," writes Ivory.[59] His was not the sort of instrumentalist realism that constrains ethical possibility to the perceived limitations of power structures. King's theocentric pragmatism sought concrete opportunities for transforming racist and impoverishing social relations, in the faith that their attempts answered a God whose action always exceeds and transforms the situation. Christian love is not "applied" to social wounds; it arises from wounds as participation in God's way of incorporating the wounds into God's body. Participating in movements that meet the needs of the moment can be, in faith, participation in God's action for the world.

Understanding King's social ethics in that way still requires an account of how Christian action is a cultural practice and of how Christian belief matters for changing cultural practices. My point in this section was to outline a basic strategy of Christian social ethics that begins from problems and attends to how reform projects use their traditions to create faithful responses. In order to claim that this strategy is better for addressing unprecedented problems like climate change, I need to defend the view of culture it assumes and explain the role of theological invention within it. So the next section revisits "Christ and culture" with a view to the difference it makes for the basic strategies of Christian ethics.

CHRIST AND CULTURE

The shorthand of "Christ and culture" to identify cultural strategies of Christianity comes from H. Richard Niebuhr. Even while readers questioned the accuracy of Niebuhr's five types, the book influenced generations of Christian ethics by making models of cultural engagement central to interpreting Christian social practice.[60] The debates over those models of engagement, however, sometimes fail to consider what is a culture. The most important assumption in Niebuhr's book is not his preference for one type (Christ transforming culture), but the idea of culture underlying all five types. In this section I pay heed to a series of theologians who are concerned that (North American) Christian social practices have been tactically misoriented, because they chronically misconceive how cultures work. They point to social theorists who displace thinking of culture as a coherent worldview in favor of thinking of culture in terms of strategies of action. Those views of culture offer additional reasons to choose a pragmatic strategy of Christian ethics, especially when facing unprecedented problems.

Different theories of culture, Kathryn Tanner argues, make for different styles of theological practice. Tanner observes that as Niebuhr extended Troeltsch's ideal religious types, he assimilated the Weberian understanding of culture that Troeltsch assumed. So for Niebuhr "culture in all its forms and varieties is concerned with the temporal and material realization of values." Superimposed on nature, "the world of culture is a world of values," measured by their benefit to humanity and conserved through social organization. Culture is about realizing ethical values, and the task of Christian ethics lies in measuring prevailing cultural values against Christian ones. With a better view of culture, argues Tanner, the role of theological interpretation shifts—and with it the task of Christian ethics.[61]

Some post-liberal theologies turn to ideas of culture that allow them to interpret Christian practices as linguistic performances, the meaning of which lie in the particular interpretive world (or "language") that they make. This view helpfully reconceptualizes the "Christ and culture" thematic by beginning to render those two terms more fluid to what participants are doing. The linguistic pragmatism of George Lindbeck and Stanley Hauerwas refers the meaning of theological ideas to their "grammatical" function within the language (Lindbeck) or narrative (Hauerwas) of Christian churches.[62] So the meaning of Christ lies in the contingent discursive practices of ecclesial communities attempting to "speak Christian" or to tell the Christian story. That view of culture seems idealized, however; it seems insulated from the flux and border-crossing of its participants. Both views borrow from the anthropologist Clifford Geertz, who argues for seeing religions as cultures, and who thinks of culture as a coherent worldview which makes intelligible the social practices within its boundary.[63] With a view of culture as a comprehensive scheme of interpretation that lends intelligibility to Christian practice, theology inevitably orients itself toward identifying and strengthening the boundaries. If the boundary of a cultural system defines the interpretive scheme that lends certain practices of life their distinctiveness and intelligibility, the theologians must protect that boundary from outside incursions. That helps explain why Milbank and Hauerwas want to defeat the question of "Christian ethics and social problems": responding to the problems of an alien culture would introduce exotic solvents into the linguistic system that maintains Christian identity. Understanding culture as a worldview and Christianity as a culture orients theological ethics toward defending a Christian worldview.[64]

Tanner argues that theologians have reasons not to accept that view of culture, and here she is joined by sociologists and philosophers. The sociologist James Hunter criticizes prevalent models of culture in Christian thought. "The dominant ways of thinking about culture and cultural change," he writes, "are based on both specious social science and problematic theology." Across the ideological spectrum, Christian social thinkers imagine culture as a worldview and so conceptualize the task of social reform in terms of transforming moral consciousness. Focusing on ideal worldviews, thinks

Hunter, "ignores the way culture is generated," which happens within the institutions, community structures, and networks of power that use culture as a resource to organize the daily lives of moral agents.[65]

James K. A. Smith calls for a moratorium on worldviews. Smith wants Christian cultural engagement to stop overestimating the influence of cognitive moral perspectives and instead pay closer attention to how social practices form persons into habits of desire. Theologians should think of social practices (from shopping to warfare) as cultural liturgies, says Smith; they function as a "pedagogy of desire," shaping agents into dispositions to a practical inhabitation of the world. Because agents do not necessarily recognize and intend the interpretive frameworks that are reproduced by the social practices in which they participate, focusing reform on those ideas misses how moral formation happens and how cultures work. It misses the embodied practices that generate worldviews and that carry the culture that shapes us.[66]

The dissenting ideas of culture at work here come more clearly into view with Pierre Bourdieu's sociology (to whom Tanner, Hunter, and Smith each refer).[67] For Bourdieu, the organizing center of culture is a *habitus*, a set of practical, interpretive relations to the world: "durable, transposable dispositions, structured structures predisposed to function as structuring structures . . . which generate and organize practices . . . without presupposing a conscious aiming at ends."[68] In other words, agents interpret their world through practical actions, which in turn produce the interpretive structures that make the practices possible. A *habitus* shapes an embodied, practical sense of a world. Like the sense of a game, it enables agents to function, anticipate, and innovate in ways that sustain the meaning of the game. Agents therefore participate in social practices that are already structured toward the end of reproducing the world in which those practices have their sense.

Except in the odd cultural field of academics, agents do not usually interpret their world by theorizing with ideas and values, but by participating in the practices through which a culture reproduces an interpretive scheme. The worldviews that seem to explain the purposes of action, maintains Bourdieu, come after the fact, as the product of intellectual inquiry. Moral agency happens at a different moment, within the creativity that sustains a pattern of acting. The *habitus* is an "art of inventing," which makes agents capable of producing responses to situations—an "infinite number," says Bourdieu, whose diversity is limited only by the extent to which structures can make them intelligible as recognizable responses to a real situation. The "unpredictable confrontation between the habitus and an event . . . can exercise a pertinent incitement on the *habitus* only if the latter snatches it from the contingency of the accidental and constitutes it as a problem by applying to it the very principles of a solution."[69] A functioning culture makes problems for its participants.

Bourdieu's view of culture presents a difficulty for any sustainability ethic because action seems limited by what a culture can recognize as a problem, which is only those situations for which the *habitus* already has the principles of a solution.[70] A functional culture makes only problems that its participants can solve. What about unprecedented problems that threaten the continuation of a cultural pattern of life? As we saw in the case of climate denialism in chapter 1, the *habitus* produces "avoidance strategies" in order to suppress recognition of threats that its range of creativity cannot meet.[71] In order to think that it can face unprecedented problems, Christian ethics needs an understanding of culture more open to change.

Charles Taylor helps open the possibility of change. When Smith calls for a moratorium on worldviews he proposes in its place the "social imaginary" of Taylor. An imaginary refers beyond intellectual schemes to the implicit meanings in lived experience that carry a common understanding, making possible shared practices. Similar to Bourdieu, Taylor thinks of a social imaginary as embedded within the social practices which it makes possible.[72] However, Taylor thinks that the various arts by which people use their "cultural repertory" can lead to epochal shifts in the social imaginary and even the emergence of a new understanding of self. Taylor's *A Secular Age* narrates a historical transition in European civilization from a permeable, social self to a "buffered self" with a disciplined interiority. Although driven by Christianity's reform spirit, the immanent humanism it makes possible eventually becomes the new common sense imaginary. Taylor thus provides a view of culture in which the normative creativity of reform efforts can create new cultural options, but does so within a sobering historical account of ironic (and maybe tragic) outcomes. Theological inventions of new cultural capacities led to ideas and practices that shifted the background imaginary of European societies toward a buffered, anthropocentric culture that eventually made faith in a world-transforming God less intelligible. Attempting to restore that faith through a clash of ideas will not work because a culture's common sense is (as Smith sees) carried and reproduced in everyday trips to the mall.

Taylor's theory of culture keeps attention on the everyday practices that shape agents into a sense of the world, while his history of modern European culture forces Christian ethics to reckon with a more intense challenge than mere pluralism. For after the epochal shift to an immanent frame, Christian social ethics must decide how its reform practices matter within cultures whose social imaginaries may not recognize those practices as intelligible options. Christian responses to social problems may not even count as one cultural option among others if their distinguishing characteristics (e.g., supposing a transcendent God confronts humanity in climate change) cannot appear as an option at all. If that is the case, why should Christian ethics respond to social problems at all?

To suppose that the sustainability problems of a secular age matter for Christian ethics, we need (1) an account of culture in which theological creativity can make a difference for social reform even when Christian practices no longer determine the social imaginary of a culture. In order to make that a respectable project for Christian ethics, we also need (2) a theology in which inventing responses to sustainability problems counts as a central practice of faith.

First, the account of culture. Sociologist Ann Swidler agrees with accounts like those of Bourdieu and Taylor which displace the explanatory role of values, worldviews, and other ideal symbols. "The significance of specific cultural symbols," writes Swidler, "can be understood only in relation to the strategies of action they sustain."[73] In the United States, she observes, ideas of culture and ethics have been shaped by two main views: the view of Geertz that a unified worldview shapes action, and a view derived from Weber that cultural values set the goals for action. Neither view stands up to empirical sociological research, claims Swidler. "Culture in fact drives contemporary social change," she says, agreeing with Geertz and Weber, "but not in the way conventional sociological models suggest." Culture shapes social action "by furnishing a repertoire of capacities for action that can be mobilized to achieve new objectives." Swidler's research into how Americans talk about love and relationships shows that "cultural meanings operate less as logical structures that integrate ends and means, and more as tools and resources that cultivate skills and capacities that people integrate into larger, more stable 'strategies of action.'"[74]

By supposing that new ways of organizing action are developed as agents redeploy the resources of their "cultural toolkits" to meet new challenges, Swidler puts social practices at the center of cultural interpretation in a way that allows a greater range of social change than Bourdieu anticipates. Through "the reappropriation of larger, culturally organized capacities for action" agents received patterns of acting in different ways to invent new capacities for action.[75] Those new patterns of action in turn allow agents to develop conceptual capacities for recognizing new problems which they could address by reappropriating their cultural inheritances anew, thus anticipating further possibilities for cultural change.

Worldviews and the task of changing values still have their place in this account. A culture's repertoire of action always admits a diversity of strategies, practices of cosmological criticism among them. In "unsettled" times especially, says Swidler, agents may try ideological constructions that explicitly propose new ideas, worldviews, and values as ways of arguing for new strategies of action that seem to better meet contextual problems. A pragmatic view of culture therefore retains a role for rethinking basic metaphors and narratives, especially in the face of unsettling social challenges. (Chapters 4 and 5 show how appeals to ecological cosmologies play exactly that kind of role.) Such ideological reconstruction is an important tool for solving problems.[76] For Swidler, culture is a "'tool kit' of symbols, stories, rituals, and world-views which people may use in varying configurations to solve different kinds of problems."[77] The meaning of culture is made in the ways that agents use its components to solve problems.

Here we have an account of culture that explains how agents might create new capacities of moral agency as they face new problems. In this account of culture, Christian ethics (or any reform-oriented moral project) does not need to first establish its worldview in the hearts and minds of those whose world it would change. If cultures change in something like the way Swidler suggests, then theological communities should instead focus on using cultural resources in odd and innovative ways. They do not have to approve or reconstruct the cultural symbols in order to use them to open new possibilities for faithful action. (A group does not have to approve of mall shopping in order to use the practice in unexpected, ironic ways.) We could think of Christianity, then, not as its own kind of culture, but as a characteristic style of using culture in order to open unexpected patterns of action.

Second, the theology of cultural invention. Tanner supplies *theological* reasons to think of Christian action as a style of cultural use. "Christian practices are always the practices of others made odd." The Christian difference from culture is not a boundary that falls along internal narratives or language games, but a boundary made by participating in culture in odd ways. All the interesting theological production happens not safely inside some boundary, as if Christianity were a territory, but in an ironic reproduction of culture that happens at the boundary it makes. Its style is characterized not by a shared ultimate symbol, but by a shared ultimate strategy: to refer all things to God, and thereby constantly reopen a space for responsiveness to God. In this view, Christian community forms by tactical uses of culture rather than as an alternative culture altogether. "Because God is the God of the whole world, and not just of our religious lives," Christian faith attempts to bring a double-voicedness to all the relations in which its members live.

Christian social existence is not "alien" inasmuch as it is ironic. "Prophetic objections to the wider society are maintained, not by isolation, but by the indefinitely extended effort to alter . . . whatever one comes across through sustained engagement with it."[78]

Christian efforts to open spaces for discipleship within a modernist social imaginary should therefore style themselves not so much as counter-cultural but as ironic: deftly combining use of theological traditions with uses of a humanist culture in order to open possibilities for responsiveness to the God who always exceeds any such effort. Theologians need "artisan-like inventiveness" and "tactical cleverness" in order to keep solving an inexhaustible problem: how to reflect in word and deed human responsibility before God.[79] Tanner's argument suggests that Christian styles of cultural action have a special impetus for constant creativity, for their fundamental problem—how to respond to a God beyond all creaturely goods—can neither be solved nor avoided. Christian cultural production happens in the gap between a saving, transcendent God and the finite possibilities for creaturely action. That gap makes Christian practice constantly self-critical, recognizing the inexhaustibility of its project, and therefore critically open to the possibilities it might learn and make from the surrounding culture.[80]

Theological strategies of culture may then allow for more inventiveness than either Bourdieu or Swidler anticipate. Tanner's sense of bricolage here differs from Stout's, in that Tanner sees the creativity of a figure like King sourced from a gap between a transcendent God and finite creatures. Whereas Stout imagines the bricoleur stitching together cultural resources to meet "the needs of the moment," the verticality in Tanner's version of bricolage implies the capacity to reinterpret social needs, reconstructing social problems in order to confront a theological problem: how to faithfully answer God. On the other hand, however, Stout highlights the role of contextual needs in driving moral creativity in a way that Tanner's metaphor of style can suppress. Theological inventiveness may sometimes simply effervesce, as Tanner's account implies, bubbling up toward God from various cultural scenes. But the moral inventiveness at the center of Christian social ethics has definite occasions: it arises from the scene of a wound. In King we see moral creativity supporting tactical responses to definite problems (Stout's sense of bricolage), undertaken as ways to keep responding to God (Tanner's sense). For King, the theological gap that elicits the creativity of faith opens in the moral gap between a particular problem and possibilities for addressing it. Concrete problems mediate the problem of faith when their demand is received as a demand from God. Responding to "unprecedented" and "wicked" problems thus becomes part of responding to the unavoidable and overwhelming problem of faith: answering God.

With the account of culture from Swidler and of theological creativity from Tanner, a pragmatic strategy of Christian ethics can expect practical innovation in the gap between social problems and competencies of action. Moral incompetence before climate change does not then defeat the possibility of Christian ethics but should rather incite the initial responses that begin its inquiry. It is not the task of Christian ethics, in this strategy, to close the distance between the apparent demands of climate change and current moral competencies by proposing ideal values which could serve as the basis for better practices. The task of Christian ethics is rather to help the tension of that moral gap drive reform projects that are culturally and theologically productive. The social ethicist's task, in the account I am developing here, is shaped by strategic participation in the reform efforts of communities using their traditions to respond to demands.[81] King exemplifies pursuit of that task, showing the theological ethicist as a uniquely trained participant in movements that draw on cultural repertoires as they attempt to invent responses to problems that seem to demand faithful answer.

I have now offered reasons from social theory and from theology for Christian ethics to adopt a pragmatic strategy, at least for confronting problems like climate change that need moral innovation. Christian ethics should work from problems rather than worldviews because problems mediate theologically charged demands, thus driving the inventiveness of communities seeking to open practices of faith through their responses. Christian ethics should work with the movements using religious traditions and other cultural inheritances to generate possibilities of practical faith because the creativity of these movements fits with compelling accounts of how cultural change happens.

One final point remains in this section. Sometimes debates of "Christ and culture" make it seem that "Christ" is the possession of the church and "culture" the province of corrupting temptations. A pragmatic strategy of Christian ethics changes those debates by implying that the relevant moral community here is characterized not by its proprietary Christian language but by its capacity to invent concrete possibilities of faithful practice. Luke Bretherton's description of Christian political practice helps illustrate the point. Bretherton wants Christian ethics to orient itself toward developing responses to God from existing relationships and practices. He takes Christian inhabitation in structures of culture—including market and state—not as an obstacle to overcome but as the condition for responding to God. The "missiological orientation of the church" means that it cannot be content to merely resist the world or to await the world's conversion to the beliefs by which the world could become church. Rather, it "entails combining active investment in Babylon's wellbeing with faithful particularity," such that the church "acts in expectation of [Babylon's] transfiguration."[82] The way Christian communities learn how grace overcomes the world is by constructive investment in its well-being.

Constructive investment in the well-being of the world sounds to some theologians like compromise and complicity. However, it orients Christian ethics to the embodied practices in which morality is lived and renegotiated, and thereby performs a language of witness intelligible to other moral worlds. Christian hopes for moral transformation and social salvation dwell in the concrete. If ethics hopes to reeducate desire and stimulate social change, argues Anna Peterson, it must work with everyday practices, cultivating and opening them as "moments of grace" in which transformation happens.[83] Moreover, Christian responses to social problems, produced in self-conscious relation to other cultural productions, become an important missiological activity in pluralist cultures. Graham Ward explains how projects for social faithfulness form a key part of Christian witness. "What characterizes Christian social practices in the world, Christian poiesis, is a governing soteriology that pursues social transformation by means of opening up new utopian possibilities in the prevailing cultural Zeitgeist."[84] By inventing responses to climate change that make faithful response possible, Christian projects may open cultural space for other kinds of response. The ironic, double-voiced uses of culture become cultural production that other groups may use, for their own purposes and with their own ironies, but hopefully in ways that make them more competent to a problem all cultures face.

Christianity offers itself to the wider culture, then, through its unique way of trying to give answer to God for shared problems. In pluralist societies, Christian communities perform the claims of their own (particular and marginal) standpoint through projects which enact cultural opportunities made by Christian faith. Ward calls this view an "operative pragmatism" since the content of Christian claims hangs on these provisional, contextual practices. Christian performance can bring about social change insofar as other standpoint communities find the performances compelling; "cultural transformation takes place on the basis of these operational pragmatics that are brought into play with any intentional project." In Ward's view, Christian ethics can understand the inventions of Christian social projects as marginal cultural products that might, insofar as they are compelling responses to shared demands, interact with the wider social imaginary in which they participate. That marginal role may be especially important in an era anxious for sustainability, in societies looking for possible futures. As Christian social practices attempt to enact the body of Christ, says Ward, they "practice the future like practicing a foreign tongue."[85]

In this section I have argued for an account of culture and of the role of theological production within it that allows Christian ethics to interpret social problems as occasions for theological and moral invention. Christian ethics should work with creative projects as sites of that invention, on the view that they can keep generating more adequate and more faithful possibilities, and based on the assumption that, insofar as they demonstrate novel capacities of responses, they may become compelling to other moral communities. In order to explain where to find such projects, I now need to clarify the role of Christian communities in this strategy.

CHURCH PRACTICE

Appeals to the practices of Christian communities occupy the center of some important accounts of Christian ethics—most visibly in the work of Stanley Hauerwas. We have seen that Hauerwas organizes ethics around the performance of church, and that he rejects methods that would seem to deprioritize formation of Christian character for the sake of social responsibility. Critics like Jeffrey Stout have objected that such appeals to church suppress attention to social problems and conceal the participation of Christians in shared civic arrangements. By arguing for Christian ethics to work on social problems through engaging the practices of Christian reform efforts, I have been developing a position that borrows from pragmatist ideas of both. My appeal to Christian reform projects follows a post-liberal sense that the meaning of moral concepts lies implicit in the practices which use them, and I have argued that competent uses are characterized by efforts to respond to the world's wounds. I let the demands of social problems test the fittingness of Christian practice, yet I also insist that those practices reinterpret the problems they address and reframe the demands they pose. I will now explain that position further by engaging the debate between Hauerwas and Stout, and illustrate it by arguing that it makes the best sense of Martin Luther King and of Dietrich Bonhoeffer.

A pragmatic strategy of Christian social ethics must answer the worry of Hauerwas that it identifies the church with some need for a social reform project. Since the social gospel movement, theologians have been rightly wary of enthusiastic reform programs that would identify the mission of Christ with social meliorism. H. R. Niebuhr worried about those sorts of pragmatisms, calling them "banal, Pelagian theurgisms in which men were concerned with the symptoms of sin, not its roots." He could be searing with regard to projects "which expected to change prodigal mankind by improving the quality of the husks served in the pigsty."[86] A practical sensibility should not lead churches to identify their gospel of transformation with some project of modest improvement—or worse, with a mere principle of continuation in "sustainability."

Hauerwas and Yoder think that Niebuhr nonetheless remains too pragmatic himself, and they blame the loss of church in Christian ethics on a concern for responsibility. Insofar as it organizes around responsibility for social problems, claims Yoder, the field of Christian ethics starts by assuming the irrelevance of Jesus. Yoder opens his *Politics of Jesus* in sarcastic protest of the notion that social ethics should "measure what is 'fitting' and what is 'adequate;' what is 'relevant' and 'effective;' . . . 'realistic' and 'responsible.'" Those slogans (which come from the two Niebuhr brothers) amount to a situational ethic, he thinks, guided only by the day's "common sense" and secular sciences of reality.[87] Hauerwas and Yoder force a pragmatic strategy of Christian ethics to prove how bearing responsibility for the world's problems is a way of participating in the reality of Christ experienced in the church. In the last section I explained how responses to social problems could be understood as participations in Christ, but where are the communities in which that actually happens?

Church happens in two ways in my account. Let me begin to explain by answering another sort of worry about pragmatism in Christian ethics. In a powerful ecumenical essay interpreting the past century of social ethics "under the sign of the cross," David Hollenbach worries that the ironic pluralism of pragmatist thought can suppress responses to human suffering. With Richard Rorty in mind, Hollenbach laments that, in responses to social wounds, pragmatists teach that "'simply coping' is the best we can aspire to," such that "what we may hope for becomes 'survival—for the time being.'" Christian ethics refuses mere survival (and mere sustainability) by seeking a "reality behind the conflicts and brokenness of the world that may be a source of reconciliation."[88] How can Christian ethics name that source, that reality beyond realities, in a pluralist world? Hollenbach argues that the cross reveals God's participation in all human suffering and God's solidarity in all struggles against dehumanizing violence. The particularist Christian symbol of the cross thus supports all social practices that develop solidarity with human suffering. Wherever a moral community develops its ethos by bearing suffering as part of a strategy of confronting social brokenness, Hollenbach's view implies, Christian ethics should interpret it as practically participating in the reconciling reality of Jesus Christ.[89]

Hollenbach's response to Rorty's school of pragmatism supplies what a theological pragmatism needs: the suggestion that the reality of church may be experienced in responses to social wounds. Responsibility may—sometimes, under cruciform conditions—be a form of participating in Christ. Hollenbach does not venture the further implication: that "church" can take place beyond the bounds of normal ecclesial structures and Christian identities. But with the view of moral culture I describe in this chapter, Christian ethics should anticipate unauthorized cultural productions that "do the cross" better than the outreaches of official churches or self-identifying Christians. That is precisely how King interpreted the cruciform love of movement protestors: often ventured without sanction of the official churches and sometimes by non-Christians, they did Christ better than the institutions and people claiming his name. If that holds, then the politics of Jesus are not the sole possession of communities devoted to confessing Jesus. Others may better see what the Christian repertory can do in some context, and may improvise on its pattern of acting in a way that is so compelling that it becomes an icon of faithfulness. Christian action, that is to say, may show up beyond Christian churches and within projects that do not identify themselves as Christian. That should not surprise: it does not seem uncharacteristic of the mission of God to move beyond its institutional sponsors.

The moral community of Christian social ethics may appear, then, wherever communities of shared practice (even if not shared identity) create ways of bearing responsibility for the world that—eventually and upon theological reflection—Christian churches adopt into their repertory of faith. That view keeps Christian ethics accountable to concrete ecclesial practices while accounting for the boring, pitiable character of most churches. Christian social ethics remains an activity of and for the contingent practices of the church (as Hauerwas wants), but those practices might appear outside the institutions that go by the name. An important task of Christian ethics, therefore, involves interpreting where church happens, in order to find the sites where communities of shared practice are inventing ways to respond to the wounds of the world. Creative problem-focused communities of responsibility often develop beyond the boundaries of visible churches, which they regularly criticize and cajole. Reform projects may reject conventional churches in frustration at their inert complacency, may confess on behalf of them, or may form in indifference to religion in general. The confessional identity of their members, I contend, is not the most interesting or important thing about them.

Christian ethics therefore faces some ecclesiological dissonance: the contingent social practices that make the meaning of the church can (and often do) occur outside churches. How to make sense of that paradox? Hauerwas and Stout agree that the meaning of ethical ideas depends on contingent social practices. They disagree on where those practices happen, on what sort of community can function as "church." Stout and Hauerwas can both follow a linguistically pragmatist claim that in Selma in 1965, "agape" meant what the political tactics of a civil rights movement made it mean. The question is whether Christian ethics should recognize that meaning as an authoritative instance of Christian love. Stout would want the field to do so and thus show how Christian traditions can make useful contributions to democratic liberalism by deploying their inheritances to meet shared social needs. For Hauerwas it depends on whether the Selma movement community counts as a church, and it is not clear from his descriptions of church how a Christian story-telling community in Selma in 1965 could have made civic desegregation part of its mission, or recognized the civil action of other groups as participation in the mission of Jesus. It is not clear, that is, how segregation outside the church could appear as a problem nor how tactics to confront it could be undertaken as proper theological exercises.

When Hauerwas insists that "the first social ethical task of the church is to be the church," he means more than that Christian social ethics depends on the contingent discursive practices of communities using the repertory of faith. He also has a substantive account of the practices that make a church.[90] "Being the church," for Hauerwas, primarily means narrating its own existence. Protecting the conditions of telling and understanding its own story, he thinks, requires refusing responsibility for the world's problems. Christian ethics should respond to political debates over war or health care allocation by turning them into occasions for the church to retell its story, and so establish anew the discursive boundary of church from world.

Stout impugns Hauerwas not for his Christian particularism, but for the way he lets Christians think that they inhabit a different cultural world with different problems. Stout worries that Hauerwas combines MacIntyre's internalist sense of tradition with an Anabaptist critique of "the world" adapted from Yoder. In combination, those two elements alienate Christian storytelling from social responsibility. It is not his sources that Stout dislikes, but what the bricoleur has made from them. Church appears as the performance of anti-civic apathy for the sake of maintaining Christian identity. When Hauerwas's concern for the distinctiveness of the Christian lexicon leads him to warn against "alien" discourses of justice and rights, Stout thinks that the anti-civic performance begins to deprive Christians of concepts the church once thought important for enacting the faith (as recently as Selma 1965). The consequence is not rigorous performance, but complacent irresponsibility: "Many of Hauerwas's readers probably liked being told that they should care more about being the church than about doing justice to the underclass. At some level, they knew perfectly well how much it would cost them to do justice. So they hardly minded hearing . . . that following Jesus involves little more than hating the liberal secularists who supposedly run the country, pitying poor people from a distance, and donating a portion of one's income to the church."[91] Stout is saying that Hauerwas's rendition of ecclesial performance appears neither civic nor Christian.

Now Hauerwas would object that he dislikes appeals to "social justice" because he thinks that slogan has required *too little* of privileged Christians. "Church" for Hauerwas names an arduous school in the virtues of love and justice.[92] Yet he opens the door to criticism of his church as cheap grace by refusing to let it be shaped by the problems of the social systems in which it participates. Because response to social wounds is not an important exercise in that school, Hauerwas's church begins to appear comfortably abstract. Because concrete responsiveness to social context does not matter for the church's performance of itself, Hauerwas's church seems not just alien but disembodied. It is difficult to say where one could join one of these churches. While regularly critical of most of the visible options he sees, Hauerwas seems uninterested in offering directions to any particular body. The idea of church seems important to him primarily for its service in identifying the boundary of Christianity and thus for organizing the work of Christian ethics. The actual existence of any particular church goes without observation.

The absence of concrete instances of church becomes especially evident where appeals to it are strongest. In Milbank the church is "the difference from all other cultural systems," a strangely wonderful culture that overturns the world's corrupt loves by true charity and counters its distorted economies with true gift.[93] Where might one join? No empirical, joinable communities, it turns out, actually embody that life. Once upon a time such communities may have existed as a real society, but the church has since been dissolved by modernist (nominalist! Scotist!) nihilism. So in the same moment that the world is reinterpreted by the light of the church, it is also told that, sadly, membership is not quite a possibility. With the church in eclipse, "the theologian feels almost that the entire ecclesial task falls on his own head."[94] How good for academic theology: one cannot really join church, but theologians can keep using it to fund their social criticism. Thus the late-modern solution to Christian social ethics: theologians interpret society by the practices of churches which exist only in their own rhetoric. Christians can go to church virtually, by reading the theologians who invoke the virtues of a lost colony.

It is not only outsiders like Stout who find such views the nadir of insulated irresponsibility. So does any Christian community that interprets the church as a concrete, a response to the world's suffering as embodied as is the cross. A responsibility ethic may be more ecclesial, I am arguing,

than some confessionalist accounts that take themselves to be zealous for
the priority of church. If church takes form by taking responsibility for the
world's problems, as a way of answering God, then confronting social problems functions as a site of revelation. In *The Responsible Self*, Niebuhr allows
that suggestion with the formula: "God is acting in all actions upon you.
So respond to all actions upon you as to respond to his action."[95] That view
of responsibility implies that the contextual experience of social problems
mediates the demanding action of God, and so become sites of response to
God. Of course reckless human powers have made these problems; just so,
God summons a response within the context and relations driving the crisis.
That is how the church "overcomes the world": by learning to bear responsibility for problems whose demand comes from the God who, in body, bears
responsibility for what is going on in the world.

When Niebuhr seeks vocabulary for what fitting responses mean for the
church, his language becomes, in spite of himself, theurgical and christo-
centric—and strikingly less Protestant in image. Summoned into existence
by its responsibility before God, the church is "that part of human society,
and that element in each particular society, which moves toward God." That
association becomes a church by moving toward God in a corporate act of
bearing responsibility, "as the priest acting for all." Social responsibility is
not an expression or outreach of the church, then; it is its participation in
Christ. In responsibility it offers "a demonstration of love of God and neighbor" in which "the deed of Christ is reduplicated."[96] As Niebuhr's language
bends toward theurgy, it recalls patristic images of the church as a microcosmic liturgical laboratory, where is made the reality of Christ for the world.
Liturgy, the central Sunday act of churches, includes inventing ways to bear
the world's wounds before God.

A view like that seems to explain the notion of church in King's work.
One could actually join what King did not hesitate to call a "colony of
heaven," for it appeared in the streets of Birmingham, bearing wounds and
so proving the possibility of agape.[97] For King, the reality of Christ was no
rhetorical invocation of lost society's difference from a racist world; it was
instead a summons to concrete practices of self-sacrificial love for enemy
and neighbor. If Christian social ethics depends on the church, the church
could be found, militantly responsible, marching in the streets, bearing
blows, suffering imprisonment, enacting justice, offering redemption. Not
all participants in this church were Christian, noted King, who thus faced
the paradox that the reality of church may be practiced by those who are
not members of churches. The reality of Christ was made by the suffering
of many who were not Christian, were not even religious, in communities
that did not always understand themselves as church but were willing to

undergo the discipline of nonviolent love. As King pastored this "church," he found himself wondering over the many institutions that called themselves church but would not join the embodied reality of Christ. It tempts one toward locating the real church in some theological imagination, he reported; "maybe I must turn my faith to the inner spiritual church, the church within the church, as the true ecclesia and the hope of the world." He was saved from that temptation, he writes, by Christians who recognized the reality of the gospel in the movement, who saw the movement as the living reality of the church in that moment, and gave themselves to it.[98]

Dietrich Bonhoeffer faced that paradox even more intensely. The theologian who began his career celebrating the church as the concrete social existence of God's reality for the world came to the end of it witnessing the collapse of even the "confessing" churches and working instead for a political resistance group. Like King, Bonhoeffer came to understand his political participation as still a way of participating in God's reality. Late in life he wrote: "In Christ we are invited to participate in the reality of God and the reality of the world at the same time, the one not without the other." The invitation comes to us, Bonhoeffer sees, without offering moral rules of participation, but only a call to interpretive discernment: "The Christian ethic asks, then, how this reality of God and of the world that is given in Christ becomes real in our world."[99] Like King, Bonhoeffer discovered that the reality of Christ may become real within the actions of those not belonging to churches. At the same time, like Niebuhr, his ecclesial ethic takes on theurgic tropes as he searches for language of Christ's body becoming concretely real within a wounded world: "the reality of God demonstrates itself only as it places me completely in the reality of the world." In times when the official churches betray the reality of Christ, "the gospel will instead demonstrate itself in the few remaining figures who are just, truthful, and humane."[100] Bonhoeffer knows the church not as an ontic foundation but as a social operation: the reality of Christ makes itself known through the actions of those risking themselves in order to bear responsibility for the wounds of their world.

So does his "religionless Christianity" reduce the church into noncreedal humanitarian programs? Bonhoeffer explicitly excludes any "myopic pragmatism" that would reduce responsibility to social utility; what matters is whether a particular project shapes action in accordance with the reality of creation.[101] The final meaning of created reality must be interpreted theologically, but Bonhoeffer rules out deciding which actions are in accordance with reality on the basis of who performs them (whether they are Christian or not). Responsibility for the world as it actually exists in Christ may be conducted by those with no belief or interest in Christ.

King and Bonhoeffer, I would argue, leave us with two senses of "church" for Christian ethics: those communities that gather in word and sacrament to tell the story of Jesus, and those communities that make the reality of Jesus by bearing responsibility for the world's suffering. The former maintain the interpretive lexicon for recognizing the latter. Confessing churches cultivate the narrative which tells the shape of Christ's becoming evident in the world, which may happen elsewhere. Charles Marsh calls that persistent "elsewhere" the "beloved community," which King sought wherever it might appear. "The church establishes the hidden meaning of beloved community," writes Marsh, "even as beloved community makes visible that meaning in ways the church often may not." When churches fail to hear the summons of God in the world around them, they can be grateful that the Spirit brings forth responses from elsewhere. If this elsewhere is alienated from the church, that is no reason to despise it. "The church should not be envious of her children," says Marsh, writing with Bonhoeffer's meditation on good people, "but should listen to them and should learn lessons as they catch a glimpse of a better future under a different banner than Christ . . . Christians should receive with gratitude the opportunity to participate in a common human struggle for a just world." For that opportunity, that struggle, is the gift of Christ's body, and thus the real life of the church.[102]

The confessionalist theologians have something right when they insist that the language of Christianity depends on the practices of the church. They are wrong only in supposing that church happens only among those who tell the story. The reality of the church may appear wherever the reality of Christ demonstrates itself among those responding to the world's realities. Social problems may legitimately determine the tasks of Christian social ethics, without reducing the field to religious support for social programs or conflating the church with a social justice movement. Because the reality of Christ always exceeds any practice, it exceeds the performance of any project. One important task of Christian ethics is to continually insist on that excess. For that, Christian ethics needs the narratives of confessing church communities. Often those "story-formed" communities tell the story insipidly and poorly, especially when they become obsessed with the preciousness of their own identities. But their story anticipates embodied performances which enflesh the narrative, cultural improvisations which bring the reconciling reality of God to life. A second task of Christian ethics is to interpret where that community is happening. In a pragmatic strategy, ethicists cannot know in advance by devising tests of belief, worldview, or narration; the way of Christ opens itself by participating in the reality of the world.

CONCLUSION

This chapter has described two basic strategies of Christian social ethics formed by different methods of confronting social problems. It has developed a pragmatic strategy by presenting reasons from theology and social theory to prefer its view of culture and its account of the relation between Christian practice and cultural change. Most importantly for a book on sustainability problems, a pragmatic strategy explains how unprecedented problems can drive moral adaptation. To allay common suspicions of pragmatism, I have argued that moral adaptation functions theologically as a practice for sustaining faith. Christian ethics can then work with incompetent responses to sustainability problems on the supposition that they offer both a site of moral production and an important way that Christian communities sustain their faith.

By focusing on the tensions between theological production and the demands of a problem, Christian ethics need not arrive on the scene of social problems with an already complete theory. Ethics might rather begin in recognition of incompleteness—of something that compels a response not yet fully given. That production may not necessarily happen through self-critical reconsideration of a community's worldview or its beliefs about reality. In fact, the least interesting part of a community's response is often what its authorized spokespersons say their beliefs mean for a problem. A pragmatic strategy supposes instead that Christian ethics should interpret difficult social problems in relation to communities already creating live strategies of response. Rather than proposing an arrangement of symbols, metaphors, and beliefs that could lead to new kinds of action, a pragmatic strategy supposes that the most important interpretive resources lie in the tactics communities use to make their traditions confront new problems. Ethicists can help realize the potential of those tactics by cultivating and criticizing a community's initial responses, working to make their trajectory more competent to the problems they face and more faithful to the traditions they use.

In the next two chapters I consider the role for particularist religious projects in global ethics and in the sciences of sustainability. Chapter 3 explains how a particularist and pragmatic ethic can contribute to the pluralist arena of global ethics. Chapter 4 explains how religious creativity makes a difference for science-based sustainability decisions. In both chapters cosmology makes a return, as I show how a pragmatic strategy sometimes needs the scope of reimagination that working with worldviews affords. Then chapter 5 returns to a concrete problem by tracing how responses to toxins have begun to adapt ideas of justice. Appeal to worldviews, I show there, plays an important role in expanding the competency of justice. The point of this chapter, then, has not been to condemn all talk of worldviews and attempt to install in its place the lexicon of problems and practices. Its point has been that Christian ethics should interpret efforts to create practical responses to overwhelming sustainability problems as struggles to keep faith with God's way of keeping faith with creation.

NOTES

1. Paul Ramsey, *Basic Christian Ethics* (New York: Scribner, 1950; Louisville, KY: Westminster John Knox Press, 1993), xxxii.

2. Traci West, *Disruptive Christian Ethics: When Racism and Women's Lives Matter* (Louisville, KY: Westminster John Knox Press, 2006).

3. Another reason for suspicion is the hostility of some pragmatic theorists toward religious belief, and especially toward theological modes of moral reasoning. Attempting to interpret those debates would distract the focus of this chapter, so I address this suspicion implicitly: by showing how processes of moral invention, which both pragmatists and theologians have distinct reasons to value, are sometimes driven by beliefs beyond those permitted by strictly materialist epistemologies.

4. Gary Dorrien, *Economy, Difference, Empire: Social Ethics for Social Justice* (New York: Columbia University Press, 2010), chap. 1; Paul T. Phillips, *A Kingdom on Earth: Anglo-American Social Christianity, 1880–1940* (University Park, PA: Pennsylvania State University Press, 1996).

5. Ernst Troeltsch, *The Social Teaching of the Christian Churches*, Olive Wyon, trans. 2 vols. (Louisville, KY: Westminster John Knox Press, 1992).

6. Troeltsch, *Social Teaching*, 2:1010–12.

7. Stanley Hauerwas, John Berkman, and Michael C. Cartwright, *The Hauerwas Reader* (Durham, NC: Duke University Press, 2001), 374.

8. John Milbank, *Theology and Social Theory: Beyond Secular Reason* (Oxford: Blackwell, 1993), 380–81.

9. Stanley Hauerwas and Samuel Wells, eds., *The Blackwell Companion to Christian Ethics* (Oxford: Blackwell, 2006), chaps. 3–4.

10. Jon Sobrino, *No Salvation Outside the Poor* (Maryknoll, NY: Orbis, 2008).

11. Ernst Troeltsch, *The Absoluteness of Christianity and the History of Religions* (Louisville, KY: Westminster John Knox Press, 2006), 193.

12. Gary Dorrien, *Social Ethics in the Making: Interpreting an American Tradition* (Oxford: Wiley-Blackwell, 2009), 61–84.

13. H. Richard Niebuhr, *The Kingdom of God in America* (Middletown, CT: Wesleyan University Press 1988), 193.

14. Niebuhr, *Kingdom of God*, 67.

15. Niebuhr, *Kingdom of God*, xxiii, 69.

16. H. Richard Niebuhr, *The Responsible Self: An Essay in Christian Moral Philosophy* (New York: Harper and Row, 1963; Louisville, KY: Wesminster John Knox Press, 1999).

17. On his legacies see William Werpehowski, *American Protestant Ethics and the Legacy of H. Richard Niebuhr* (Washington, DC: Georgetown University Press, 2002).

18. "Strategy" is a different category from those in methodological debates over universalism versus particularism and principlism versus casuistry. It aims to bring into view distinct styles of theological creativity and consider how they each make practical cultural proposals. The terms "strategy" and "tactics" appear in this chapter without intending the precise uses to which they are put in Michel de Certeau, *The Practice of Everyday Life*, Steven Rendall, trans. (Berkeley: University of California Press, 1984).

19. Niebuhr, *The Responsible Self*, 42–46, 107.

20. This is how James Gustafson takes the legacy of Niebuhr; see his introduction to Niebuhr, *The Responsible Self*, 13–18.

21. William Schweiker, *Responsibility and Christian Ethics* (Cambridge: Cambridge University Press, 1995), 5; William Schweiker, *Theological Ethics and Global Dynamics: In the Time of Many Worlds* (Malden, MA: Blackwell, 2004), 5.

22. Schweiker, *Theological Ethics and Global Dynamics,* 15.

23. Schweiker, *Responsibility and Christian Ethics*, 24–27.

24. Schweiker, *Theological Ethics and Global Dynamics,* 11.

25. David E. Klemm and William Schweiker, *Religion and the Human Future: An Essay on Theological Humanism* (Malden, MA: Blackwell, 2008), 12–15, 31–37.

26. Schweiker, *Responsibility and Christian Ethics,* 49–50, 207–16.

27. Klemm and Schweiker, *Religion and the Human Future*, chap. 3.

28. John P. Reeder, "What Is a Religious Ethic?" *Journal of Religious Ethics* 25, no. 3 (1997): 157–81.

29. Douglas F. Ottati, "How Can Theological Ethics Be Christian?" *Journal of the Society of Christian Ethics* 31, no. 2 (2011): 6, 5.

30. Gibson Winter, *Liberating Creation: Foundations of Christian Social Ethics* (New York: Crossroad, 1981).

31. Sallie McFague, *A New Climate for Theology: God, the World, and Global Warming* (Minneapolis: Fortress Press, 2008). Her metaphorical strategy is perhaps best described in Sallie McFague, *The Body of God* (Minneapolis: Fortress Press, 1993).

32. Emilie M. Townes, *Womanist Ethics and the Cultural Production of Evil* (New York: Palgrave Macmillan, 2006), 12, 19.

33. Another powerful exemplar of the cosmological strategy is Larry Rasmussen, *Earth Community, Earth Ethics* (Maryknoll, NY: Orbis, 1996).

34. James Gustafson, *Ethics from a Theocentric Perspective*, 2 vols. (Chicago: University of Chicago Press, 1981), 1:72.

35. Gustafson, *Ethics from a Theocentric Perspective*, 1:69–75.

36. Lynn White, "The Historical Roots of Our Ecologic Crisis," *Science* 155, no. 3767 (1967): 1205.

37. Willis Jenkins, "After Lynn White: Religious Ethics and Environmental Problems," *Journal of Religious Ethics* 37, no. 2 (2009).

38. Gustafson, *Ethics from a Theocentric Perspective,* 1:95.

39. Max L. Stackhouse, *Globalization and Grace: A Christian Public Theology for a Global Future,* vol. 4; *God and Globalization* (New York: Thoemmes Continuum, 2007), 31, 32.

40. Max L. Stackhouse, Peter L. Berger, Dennis P. McCann, and M. Douglas Meeks, *Christian Social Ethics in a Global Era* (Nashville: Abingdon Press, 1995), 11.

41. H. Richard Niebuhr, *The Responsibility of the Church for Society and Other Essays* (Louisville, KY: Westminster John Knox Press, 2008), 74–75.

42. For another pragmatist portrait of Niebuhr see, Victor Anderson, *Pragmatic Theology: Negotiating the Intersections of an American Philosophy of Religion and Public Theology* (Albany: SUNY Press, 1998).

43. For a view like this, see David L. Chappell, *Stone of Hope: Prophetic Religion and the Death of Jim Crow* (Chapel Hill: University of North Carolina Press, 2004).

44. West, *Disruptive Christian Ethics,* 9, 41.

45. On this similarity of liberationist and pragmatist approaches to ethics see Anna L. Peterson, *Everyday Ethics and Social Change: The Education of Desire* (New York: Columbia University Press, 2009), 127–37.

46. Mary McClintock Fulkerson, *Places of Redemption: Theology for a Worldly Church* (New York: Oxford University Press, 2007), 13.

47. Jeffrey Stout, *Ethics after Babel: The Languages of Morals and Their Discontents* (Princeton: Princeton University Press), 292.

48. Gustafson, *Ethics from a Theocentric Perspective,* 1:23–25. See also James Gustafson, *Can Ethics Be Christian?* (Chicago: University of Chicago Press, 1975).

49. John Howard Yoder, *For the Nations: Essays Evangelical and Public* (Grand Rapids, MI: Eerdmans, 1997), 76.

50. Stanley Hauerwas, *Truthfulness and Tragedy* (Notre Dame, IN: University of Notre Dame Press, 1989), 133.

51. Richard Sherlock, "Must Ethics Be Theological? A Critique of the New Pragmatists," *Journal of Religious Ethics* 37, no. 4 (2009).

52. Niebuhr, *Kingdom of God in America,* 12.

53. For his account of traditions see Alasdair MacIntyre, *Whose Justice? Which Rationality?* (Notre Dame, IN: University of Notre Dame Press, 1988). For his pessimism about intelligible moral deliberation in pluralist cultures see Alasdair MacIntyre, *After Virtue: A Study in Moral Theory* (Notre Dame, IN: University of Notre Dame Press, 1981).

54. Jeffrey Stout, *Democracy and Tradition* (Princeton, NJ: Princeton University Press, 2004), 135–39.

55. Cornel West, *The American Evasion of Philosophy: A Genealogy of Pragmatism* (Madison: University of Wisconsin Press, 1989), 214, 230.

56. Cornel West, *The Cornel West Reader* (New York: Civitas Books, 1999), 426.

57. Luther Ivory, *Toward a Theology of Radical Involvement: The Theological Legacy of Martin Luther King, Jr.* (Nashville: Abingdon, 1997), 111.

58. See Willis Jenkins, "Christian Social Ethics after Bonhoeffer and King," in *Bonhoeffer and King: Their Legacies for Christian Social Thought,* Willis Jenkins and Jennifer McBride, eds. (Minneapolis: Fortress Press, 2010), 243–57.

59. Ivory, *Toward a Theology of Radical Involvement*, 111.

60. H. Richard Niebuhr, *Christ and Culture* (New York: Harper and Brothers, 1951); D. M. Yeager, "H. Richard Niebuhr's *Christ and Culture*," in *The Oxford Handbook of Theological Ethics*, Gilbert Meilaender and William Werpehowski, eds. (Oxford: Oxford University Press, 2005).

61. Kathryn Tanner, *Theories of Culture: A New Agenda for Theology* (Minneapolis: Fortress Press, 1997), 36, 32.

62. George Lindbeck, *The Nature of Doctrine: Religion and Theology in a Postliberal Age* (Louisville, KY: Westminster John Knox Press, 1984).

63. Clifford Geertz, *The Interpretation of Cultures* (New York: Basic Books, 1973), chap. 4.

64. See Tanner, *Theories of Culture*, 97–106.

65. James Davison Hunter, *To Change the World: The Irony, Tragedy, and Possibility of Christianity in the Late Modern World* (New York: Oxford University Press, 2010), 5, 26.

66. James K. A. Smith, *Desiring the Kingdom: Worship, Worldview, and Cultural Formation* (Grand Rapids, MI: Baker Academic, 2009).

67. Tanner, *Theories of Culture* 192–93; Smith, *Desiring the Kingdom* 67; Hunter, *To Change the World,* 34, 36.

68. Pierre Bourdieu, *The Logic of Practice* (Stanford, CA: Stanford University Press, 1990), 53.

69. Bourdieu, *Logic of Practice*, 55.

70. See Scott Lash, "Pierre Bourdieu: Cultural Economy and Social Change," in *Bourdieu: Critical Perspectives*, Craig Calhoun, Edward LiPuma, and Moishe Postone, eds. (Chicago: University of Chicago Press, 1993).

71. Bourdieu, *Logic of Practice*, 61.

72. Charles Taylor, *A Secular Age* (Cambridge, MA: Belknap Press of Harvard University Press, 2007), 171–76.

73. Ann Swidler, "Culture in Action: Symbols and Strategies," *American Sociological Review* 51, no. 2 (1986): 283.

74. Ann Swidler, *Talk of Love: How Culture Matters* (Chicago: University of Chicago Press, 2001), 80–82, 187. On the relation of "strategies of action" to Bourdieu's *habitus* see *Talk of Love*, 247n11.

75. Swidler, "Culture in Action," 283.

76. Swidler, *Talk of Love,* 89–107.

77. Swidler, "Culture in Action," 273.

78. Tanner, *Theories of Culture,* 113, 103, 152.

79. Tanner, *Theories of Culture*, 166, 80–87.

80. See Kathryn Tanner, *The Politics of God: Christian Theologies and Social Justice* (Minneapolis: Fortress Press, 1992), chaps 1–2.

81. There are similarities in my account with what Michael Walzer describes as the "path of interpretation" for social critics; Michael Walzer, *Interpretation and Social Criticism* (Cambridge, MA: Harvard University Press, 1987).

82. Luke Bretherton, *Christianity and Contemporary Politics: The Conditions of Faithful Witness* (Oxford: Wiley-Blackwell, 2010), 191.

83. Peterson, *Everyday Ethics and Social Change*, 3–5.

84. Graham Ward, *Cultural Transformation and Religious Practice* (Cambridge: Cambridge University Press, 2005), 168.

85. Ward, *Cultural Transformation and Religious Practice*, 95, 170.

86. Niebuhr, *Christ and Culture*, 220.

87. John Howard Yoder, *The Politics of Jesus*, 2nd ed. (Grand Rapids, MI: Eerdmans, 1972; 1994), 8.

88. David Hollenbach, *The Global Face of Public Faith: Politics, Human Rights, and Christian Ethics* (Washington, DC: Georgetown University Press, 2003), 61, 62.

89. See also Ignacio Ellacuria, "The Crucified People" in *Mysterium Liberationis: Fundamental Concepts of Liberation Theology*, Jon Sobrino and Ignacio Ellacuria, eds. (Maryknoll, NY: Orbis, 1993): 580–603.

90. Hauerwas, *Hauerwas Reader*, 374.

91. Stout, *Democracy and Tradition*, 158.

92. Hauerwas, *Hauerwas Reader*, 380.

93. Milbank, *Theology and Social Theory*, 387–88.

94. John Milbank, *The Word Made Strange: Theology, Language, Culture* (Malden, MA: Blackwell, 1997), 1.

95. Niebuhr, *The Responsible Self*, 126.

96. Niebuhr, *Responsibility of the Church for Society*, 74–75.

97. Martin Luther King Jr., "Letter from Birmingham City Jail," in *Testament of Hope: The Essential Writings and Speeches*, James M. Washington, ed. (New York: Harper-Collins, 1986), 300.

98. King, "Letter from Birmingham City Jail."

99. Dietrich Bonhoeffer, *Dietrich Bonhoeffer Works*, vol. 6, *Ethics*, Reinhard Krauss, Charles West, and Douglass Stott, trans. (Minneapolis: Fortress Press, 2005), 55.

100. Bonhoeffer, *Ethics*, 55, 347. I translate "erweisen sich" in the first quotation with "demonstrate itself" (the translators use "is disclosed") to highlight the same verb appearing in the second quotation (where the translators do use "demonstrate itself" for "erweisen sich").

101. Bonhoeffer, *Ethics*, 260.

102. Charles Marsh, *The Beloved Community: How Faith Shapes Social Justice from the Civil Rights Movement to Today* (New York: Basic Books, 2005), 207–10.

CHAPTER THREE

Global Ethics:
Moral Pluralism and Planetary Problems

✦

A lawyer asked Jesus: "Who is my neighbor?" Jesus replied: "A man was traveling the road from Jerusalem to Jericho and was assaulted by thieves, who beat him and left him half-dead. A priest later came down that road, but when he saw him, passed by on the other side. . . . Later a Samaritan traveling the road saw the injured man, went to him, cared for his wounds and took him to an inn. . . . Which of these was a neighbor?"

Luke 10:29–37

Planetary problems call for a global ethic. Confronting a problem like climate change requires responsibilities shared across borders and traditions. Various moral provincialisms stand in the way of a cooperative ethic scaled to use of the atmosphere; many people bound their concern to their own nation, religion, class, generation, and species. Humanity needs to develop a moral membership that encompasses the scale of the problems it faces. A pragmatic approach to ethics of the sort I have been developing would seem to frustrate that task. Working from particular moral communities seems to forego principles that are authoritative across traditions and cultures. Working from religious communities in fact seems to intensify conflict among traditions and cultures. Working from contextual reform projects seems distant from the planet-wide scale of problems like climate change. This chapter explores the possibility of a pluralist global ethic, developed from the ground up, by investigating the role of religious reform projects in generating norms and practices that cross boundaries.

Global ethics negotiates the tension of multiple moral worlds inhabiting one shared planet. The same globalizing powers that force humanity to recognize that it shares one planet also bring its multiple moral worlds into deeper conflict.[1] How might moral agents formed within many worlds learn to cooperatively inhabit one planet? This chapter describes several notions of what a global ethic must accomplish and argues for a conception focused on shared problems and arising from boundary-crossing social practices. The chapter then introduces sustainability as a bridge-building concept that helps to organize pluralist debate over the priorities of collaborative projects. The idea of sustainability, I argue, probably cannot function as a universal norm or shared worldview, but it can facilitate pluralist deliberation over responses to planetary problems. It gains normative traction on problems like climate change only insofar as it informs reflection on practices of cooperation across moral worlds. The most important tasks for a global sustainability ethic lie in summoning agents into projects that cross alienating boundaries and in cultivating the shared commitments that can emerge.

GLOBAL ETHICS AND MORAL COSMOPOLITANISM

Consider the "survival strategy" of the indigenous peoples' climate justice movement that I described in chapter 1. The project defends indigenous cultural identity by making rights claims in order to force international response to climate change, arguing that failing to act amounts to genocide. Responding to the peril climate change poses to a sacred membership, the project also makes rights claims on behalf of Mother Earth.[2] In other words, the project attempts to protect conditions for the diversity of multiple moral worlds (diverse indigenous peoples) by deploying universalist discourse (human rights) and appealing to a unique cultural identity (indigeneity). On this basis, they make to the whole world a novel proposal carrying a cosmological vision (Mother Earth rights). Does that project cultivate or frustrate work toward a global ethic?

It depends on what a global ethics is and does. Various conceptions of global ethics depend on various notions of the term "global." It can refer to (1) the planetary scale of problems that ethics must address, (2) the globalizing social and ecological relations generating those problems, (3) the cross-border networks of agents pursuing projects to address shared problems, (4) worldwide consensus on basic values, or (5) universal moral foundations that support or oblige a worldwide consensus. In this chapter I defend uses of "global" in the first three senses while distancing the task of global ethics from positions (4) and (5). A global ethic is not necessarily the same thing as a world ethic or a universal ethic. It is not a worldview shared by or impingent upon every person on the planet. A global ethic is, in my view, an ethic that addresses problems with a planetary scale in a way helpful to the cross-border practices attempting to develop shared responsibilities for globalizing social and ecological relations.

Planetary problems (1) refer to problems arising from the cumulative, collective power of humans embedded in planet-wide networks. Climate change emerges from globalizing social and economic structures that organize how persons participate in earth's energy economy. Human poverty has become a planetary problem because persons are now impoverished through globally shared economic relations. Planetary problems thus have a distinctive structure: they emerge from the interaction of billions of persons and institutions pursuing various projects from different social positions and in different cultural worlds. Those interactions sometimes produce unwanted outcomes, and whether those outcomes are nonintentional or foreseen and accepted by powerful interests (or both), the entire network of agents bears responsibility for them. Planetary problems imply cosmopolitan responsibilities.

Globalizing social and ecological relations (2) therefore become an object of interpretation for ethics. Structural problems of global justice, says Iris Marion Young, are best understood in terms of participation: unjust or undesirable outcomes are made by the cumulative action of many persons pursuing (for the most part) socially acceptable interests. Less important than the motives, values, or goals of discrete agents are the systems that shape interactions among these agents. "Responsibility derives from belonging together with others in a system of interdependent processes."[3] The primary focus of change for global ethics is not then the consciousness of immoral individuals, nor is it bad behavior by nations and corporations; it lies beyond agents in the perversely functioning structures that organize their interactions.

Shifting the focus of ethics to structures of mutual belonging does not diminish the violence and injustice involved in climate change and impoverishment. Nor does it absolve individual agents of responsibility, nor exculpate the powerful of vicious indifference. Even if we did not make the systems that organize our relations to each other, and despite whether we despise their outcomes, we are at least, as Mary Hobgood writes, "accountable to others for the unearned advantages these systems routinely give us, as well as for how we contribute (often unwittingly) to [their] reproduction."[4] Participation in globalizing structures of relation imposes responsibility for how those structures function. Relative advantage within them increases personal responsibility for them. That includes responsibility for what Rob Nixon calls "slow violence"—the violence against persons and earth that is often invisible because it is attritional, incremental, and dispersed.[5] Climate change and impoverishment are problems produced by

structures of relation that conceal the violence they do. Continued conceal-
ment and collective irresponsibility is supported by the ignorance of participants, by indifference to the evils we participate in making, by laziness in
the face of practical difficulties, and by fear of acknowledging shared relations with strangers. Planetary problems are not directly caused by those
vices, but responding to them requires practical imagination to address the
structures of relation that do. Responsibilities for climate change and for
impoverishment need a strategy that recognizes shared material relations,
illustrates the violence they make, and creates cooperative projects to use
them in ways that reshape their outcome.

The cross-border networks of agents responding to problems (3) thus
form an indispensable source of global ethics. Hope that humans can address planetary problems across cultural differences and political alienations
depends on the persons and projects transforming perversely functioning
structures of relation. That hope depends on agents "*sans frontières*" who
specialize in moving across boundaries to create collaborative responses to
shared problems. In a shared planet of unevenly shared power and profound
moral differences, cultivating friendship across boundaries seems more important that trying to establish a shared faith, foundation, or worldview.
The project of globalizing justice and the effort to catch up with globalizing powers and relations begins by cultivating concrete possibilities of
civic friendship within those relations.[6] This differs from the conventional
approach in global ethics of first searching for universalizing principles in
moral traditions in hopes of isolating common ground for a shared theory of
justice.[7] Instead it convenes pluralist inquiry within the occasion of shared
problems produced by shared relations. Yet it still relies on cosmopolitan
virtues: global ethics needs agents capable of working beyond borders and
across boundaries to cultivate shared responsibilities for shared problems.

Those first three dimensions of global ethics describe a field of practical cooperation that generates enough transformative promise to resist a
skeptical yield to power. They make global ethics morally realist about the
planetary relations from which it starts, without yielding to *realpolitik* about
the impossibility of ethics before globalizing powers. Sometimes globalization is treated as an inexorable process impervious to political direction or
humane transformation. Against pseudo-realisms of market laws, technological inevitability, or civilizational clash, global ethics cultivates practices
that let humans still hope that their planetary powers have not yet defeated
their moral capacities. Doing global ethics from projects that transform
shared participation in perversely functioning systems into shared responsibility refuses to allow contingent arrangements of power to appear natural.
Globalizing market relations do not inevitably produce the impoverishing

outcomes that they do now, which a multitude of relationship-transforming economic projects continuously demonstrate.

A global ethic does not necessarily require a worldwide consensus (4) or universal foundation (5). If every human did share one moral world that would of course provide strong ground for confronting shared problems, which is why so many ethicists work on articulating universal values, obligations impingent on all moral agents, or a shared planetary story. Without a universal foundation for common moral citizenship or "a set of universal values applicable to all human beings," worry these theorists, "global problems could not then be tackled on any concerted basis."[8] It seems an intuitive assumption that confronting planetary problems requires a universal morality, but the cosmopolitan vision for a shared moral world can look past the actual diversity of humanity. Practical cooperation is delayed in wistful description of the shared moral world that would make it possible. If the first task for global ethics is to describe universal foundations and establish their acceptance within all our moral worlds, then it will likely never leave a metaethical prologue for practical problems. Global ethics, I argue, should rather let our moral worlds remain plural and seek those border-crossing projects and bridge-building discourses that support cooperative action on shared problems. A global ethic needs to generate just enough shared commitment to cooperate across difference, and should focus on cultivating provisional norms for that cooperation.

Because the modest ambitions of that conception may seem surprising given the scope and urgency of planetary problems, let me defend this approach to global ethics in relation to humanity's most successful cosmopolitan project: universal human rights. It was not until the twentieth century that crises in worldwide relations allowed ancient cosmopolitan longings to seek expression in an effective global ethic.[9] While the Greek schools of stoicism and cynicism produced citizen of the world ideals, and the emergence of world religious traditions was probably facilitated by their universalizing codes of conduct, neither of those kinds of cosmopolitanism supposed that they offered a practical ethic for a global society. They rather produced cosmopolitan ideas in order to criticize moral parochialisms.[10] Global social relations with planetary problems did not exist until the twentieth century, when two world wars put on terrible display the perils of a world of shared power without shared moral commitments.

Among the responses is the most successful cosmopolitan project humanity has yet created. The Universal Declaration of Human Rights (UDHR) was adopted in 1948 by the United Nations and ratified by nearly every nation, in "recognition of the inherent dignity and of the equal and inalienable rights of all members of the human family." Presenting itself as a "common standard of achievement for all peoples and all nations," the Declaration makes human rights an authoritative measure in every moral world. Securing "universal and effective recognition" of human rights became a global moral project, undertaken by ongoing civil and political efforts in every nation and culture.[11] Its universal scope, along with its success in continuing to build practical consensus, has made the UDHR seem an initial "stepping stone" toward a globally shared moral world.[12]

In one view, the UDHR represents a moment of advance toward a universal morality. Peter Singer makes this kind of case for global ethics. Singer in fact helped create the field of global ethics with an early article on the moral obligations of affluent persons to distant starving persons. Distance, Singer argued there, is no longer a morally relevant category on a planet linked by shared economies and immediate communication.[13] Singer now extends the case against the moral relevance of distance in his *One World*, arguing that ethics must enlarge humanity's sense of moral community to fit the actual community in which it lives. We already live in "one economy" and "one climate," so we need one ethic—one moral world.[14]

What is the relation of that prospective one world to the many moral worlds that humanity currently inhabits? Extending cosmopolitan critiques of parochialism, Singer ridicules the hypocritical moralities of provincial memberships. US citizens benefit from international economic relationships yet regularly ignore needs beyond their national borders. And it is not because we respond so robustly to the needs of compatriots; supposed obligations to one's community and family function as excuses for lavishing consumer goods on near relations (especially oneself) while failing to help those in desperate need. Singer's argument against the moral significance of proximity is compelling to anyone scandalized by indifference to avoidable suffering. While Christian ethicists usually reject Singer's utilitarian framework, they often appreciate his argument that national, cultural, and relational borders produce unwarranted indifference to those beyond them and permit hypocritical selfishness.

Yet dismantling borders begins to make difficulties for Singer's agents and for universalist cosmopolitanism in general. Proximity and membership seem important for the formation of moral agents who *can* respond to the suffering of others. Cosmopolitan citizenship seems at once too thin and too encompassing: the global citizen can seem a disembodied calculator attempting to cipher a response to a planet of claims. To counter this "vertigo of political responsibility," says Young, ethics should articulate obligations of global justice within the particular relations that generate injustice.[15] Global justice does not require indifference to one's location; on the contrary, it should take shape within the global social relations that already connect agents. I agree with David Hollenbach that responsibility for global common goods must protect the relationships that make moral agents. Persons become moral agents through embodiment in particular places and participation in specific communities. Empathy is learned through family and friendships; practical reasoning is developed in schools, careers, and vocations; moral imagination is cultivated through cultural practices. An entirely generic universalist cosmopolitanism would undermine the particular relationships and local memberships that make moral agency possible.[16]

Privileging proximity may also be important for preserving the humanity of persons in need. Eric Gregory observes that one reason Christian ethics has taught an "order of love" is to preserve the importance of particular relationships with concrete persons. Gregory agrees with Singer that naturalized notions of moral order have become excuses for indifference and selfishness, so he reminds readers that in Christian thought proximity is a feature of contingency and embodiment. We have greater obligations to those near to us, not because of some particular status they have (identity, membership), but because we have happened into relationship with them. That seems the point of the Good Samaritan story; what matters for neighbor-love is not shared membership but near need. Proximity includes family members as well as the hungry stranger with whom our paths cross, the refugee requesting asylum with us, and even the enemy to whom we might show mercy.[17] Christian cosmopolitanism, agrees Luke Bretherton, is not generic piety toward humanity, but concern for the particular neighbors with whom we find ourselves in relationship.[18]

Precisely in order to preserve universal regard for every person, therefore, global ethics should resist some forms of universalism, because it needs to retain the sort of particular relations that cultivate agents who can respond well to the needs of others. Global ethics should then endorse the universality of the UDHR as a set of practices that are so apt for responding to vulnerabilities that they have become normative for confronting the globalization of modern political relations. Global ethics should resist interpretations of the UDHR as a foundation for establishing one moral world. Singer is right that shared global relations generate border-crossing obligations, but his universalism seems unhelpful when it suggests that globalization exhausts continued roles for proximity in realizing obligations of justice. Globalization creates moral proximity through the *particular* global social relations in which agents are embodied. As the indigenous climate justice movement shows, human rights may be deployed to protect the multiplicity of moral worlds from a universalizing dominant culture. The movement uses a universalist device to *resist* attempts to civilize indigenous peoples into one moral world.

For Christian ethics that sort of proximity still seems too passive. In Gregory's and Bretherton's accounts, proximity *happens* to agents: we find ourselves in families and nations, and sometimes, like the Good Samaritan, we come across needy outsiders. Within global structures of mutual relation, that passive proximity generates rigorous obligations; indeed, concern for those to whom we are connected through the structures of relation driving planetary problems generates obligations beyond what many privileged persons are willing to recognize.

However, Christian practices not only respond to contingent proximity; they should also seek to create it. There is a border-crossing impulse to Christian neighbor-love: it does not stop at recognizing nearby others as neighbors, but seeks to become a neighbor to others across alienating distances. Responding to injustice and need happens not only by Good Samaritan happenstance, but by going into streets to find the poor and along distant roads to invite strangers to a shared feast (see Luke 14:15–24). Love seeks proximity with those who might otherwise remain far apart by moving across boundaries to make relationship. Leonardo Boff writes that Christians should not ask themselves who is their neighbor, but rather how they can cross social and ethnic boundaries to share in God's mission.[19] Neighbor-making love creates conditions for expanded claims of justice because, as love moves across boundaries, it expands the arena of justice by creating new relationships.

I do not mean to imply that the human rights project needs a missiological account of *agape*. It does, however, rely on a kind of moral border crossing. I have so far argued that global ethics should understand cosmopolitan obligations as embodied practices undertaken within and for particular social relations, rather than as expressions of a universal value system. Responding to problems of injustice or dysfunction in those relations without a universal foundation does require normative practices that judge and change contexts of agency. A global ethic content to work with agents embodied within many moral worlds therefore needs some account of how cross-world, cross-border projects can make shared global relations more just or more sustainable, while at the same time generating practical concepts of "justice" or "sustainability."

The human rights project succeeds not because all humanity now shares a foundational value system. It succeeds because using rights to confront the human jeopardies serially produced within modern political structures helps to generate a cross-cultural sense of human dignity. Human rights claims, whether by legal process or informal appeal, draw attention to politically produced threats by creating a field of social interactions organized around the dignity of an individual rights holder. The universal authority of human rights rests not in a shared ontology but in the continued performance of social practices that keep producing a (provisional and contested) vision of human dignity. "When human rights claims bring legal and political practice into line with their demands," Jack Donnelly argues, "they create the type of person posited in that moral vision." That does not mean that rights are arbitrary moral inventions. It rather supposes that human rights are shared social practices that interpret what persons share across moral worlds. The interpretive and constructive function of human rights explains what Donnelly calls their "possession paradox:" rights claims are made precisely when the moral reality they protect has been made insecure. Persons claim rights when threatened with the loss of some aspect of human dignity constituent of being a person. Claiming a right sets in motion an agreed upon set of normative practices that argue over the shared human nature in which they are grounded. "Human rights shape political society, so as to shape human beings, so as to realize the possibilities of human nature, which provided the basis for the rights in the first place."[20] As agents make rights claims within and across nations and traditions, a minimally shared moral anthropology begins to take shape within the many moral worlds humans already inhabit.[21]

Global ethics does not then need to first establish an ontological foundation for rights. It is more important to support the practice of rights claims, because they generate the (contingent, shifting, controversial, limited) vision of human dignity that they protect. The universal human rights project might best be understood as an evolving, adaptive set of responses to changing social conditions, driven by a more or less shared sense of the most grave and most remediable threats to being human.[22] Through the constant exercise and deployment of human rights claims to illustrate those threats, the project drives moral learning across traditions and contexts. Human rights have become universal across moral worlds to the extent that agents working with and across boundaries have adopted rights-shaped practices to interpret and confront shared problems.[23]

When agents deploy rights claims in odd or innovative ways, as the indigenous people's climate justice movement does, they therefore make a proposal to alter or expand the underlying account of human dignity. The indigenous climate justice project uses the universal lexicon of rights in order to insist that they do not share the kind of personhood native to industrial cultures, and to illustrate how their unique moral anthropology is under threat. The project uses rights concepts to argue that participation in an ecological membership (possessed of its own rights) should be seen as constitutive of human dignity. To the extent that their use of rights is adopted by agents within other moral worlds, they will have significantly changed the meaning of personhood carried by rights practices.[24]

A crucial task for global ethics therefore involves discerning which tools from what projects best interpret particular problems. Is poverty best confronted with human rights, or is it better interpreted within the practices of the human development project? Does it make sense to address climate change in terms of the rights of indigenous peoples, or is it better interpreted in terms of ecological conservation? Global ethics should take up those questions and those several projects without attempting to integrate them all into a comprehensive worldview. That would undermine the diversity of moral words and the mutual accountability they have wrought through these several projects.

My point in this section has been that the need for a global ethics to respond to planetary problems does not require establishment of universal foundations. I have made that case in relation to the most successful universal moral project—human rights—by arguing that attempts to find foundations may undermine the practices through which responsible agency is cultivated. An ethic of planetary problem solving needs practices of world-crossing cooperation, but working toward common goods does not depend on a universal and integrated vision of the good. Global ethics can be content with the "pluralistic ensemble of goods" generated by the global moral projects responding to shared problems.[25] Pluralist cooperation among agents from many moral worlds, I argue, affords a more resilient, more adaptable strategy of cooperating than does seeking one world of a shared vision.

PLANETARY DECLARATIONS

Two recent documents represent alternative visions for what a global ethic can accomplish and how to produce it. In the 1990s *The Declaration Toward a Global Ethic* and *The Earth Charter* separately sought to articulate a worldwide moral vision competent to planetary problems. The two documents represent different sensibilities: the Declaration names an already shared moral minimum while the Charter proposes an expansion of cosmopolitan regard beyond the human family to the entire community of life. So the Declaration and the Charter exhibit contrary impulses in global ethics: overcoming pluralist conflict by discovering worldwide consensus in the former, as opposed to expanding moral consciousness to meet new threats in the latter. They also respond to different fears: the Declaration worries about conflict among humanity's many moralities, while the Charter worries that humanity lacks a morality that encompasses the full membership of earth. Their respective ways of producing a global ethic therefore encounter distinctive difficulties, which I explain here in order to bring the challenge of global ethics and the role of religious projects into clearer focus.

The Declaration was adopted in 1993 by the Parliament of the World's Religions, which had commissioned Hans Küng to draft it, in consultation with religious scholars and representatives. Küng had already proposed that human survival depended on developing a "world ethic" through a dialogue among the religions.[26] The Parliament hosted that dialogue in order to affirm a consensus among its traditions that could ground new responsibilities.[27] The tension between ancient resources and new needs appears in the opening paragraphs. "Our world is experiencing a fundamental crisis," the Declaration opens, rooted in "the lack of a grand vision, the tangle of unresolved problems. . . . Too many old answers to new problems." Yet some old answers apparently have transformative potential: "An ethic already exists within the religious teachings of the world which can counter the global distress."[28]

It seems an odd stance: world society falters amidst divisive and archaic moralities, yet hope lies in the world's many religions. That stance is necessitated by the Parliament's conception of what a global ethic must do: "by a global ethic we mean a fundamental consensus on binding values, irrevocable standards, and personal attitudes." The Parliament wants to find already recognized universal ground in order to show humanity that we live in one moral world and should live by its code. The Declaration discovers that shared world in an overarching principle: "what you do not wish done to yourself, do not do to others."[29] The Declaration thus offers the world an authoritative paraphrase of an overlapping morality found in all religious traditions, yet recognizable by nonreligious persons, presented in the form of a consensus document used to condemn humanity's present divisions and call the world to transformed unity. When critics have not found those several tensions too many, they have complained that the result is too vague to matter to any particular problem. The world might agree to a golden rule principle while continuing to disagree, in nearly all the ways it already does, over shared responsibilities for climate change. A minimal paraphrase chronically underdetermines practical obligations.

More importantly, the traditions supporting that moral consensus may be incompetent to a problem like climate change. An ethic of fair reciprocity among persons may lie at the heart of many moral traditions but it excludes the rest of earth's membership. The anthropocentrism of the Declaration is not unique; much work in global ethics attempts to address planetary problems as if the only problem were finding agreement among humans—leaving unchallenged the prerogative of human power over the rest of life. Schweiker thus argues that "it is not enough to isolate common standards, values, and attitudes . . . if we leave in place a construal of the world that foils moral aspirations."[30] At least, a global ethic of sustainability must not be constrained to the anthropocentric assumptions of inherited moral worlds. The moral imagination required for meeting planetary problems must "enlist all the powers of the human mind and heart," say Kathleen Dean Moore and Michael Nelson in their introduction to an anthology of voices for a planetary ethic. It requires imagination to see ourselves in the eyes of our progeny, senses to listen to earth's full membership, the humility to overcome our own selfishness, and the will to refuse to let the powerful destroy what we love.[31] A global ethic must do better than confirm our inherited moralities; it must transform us.

The Earth Charter takes up that challenge by recontextualizing values and symbols from many traditions within a shared planetary membership. "We are one human family *and* one Earth community with a common destiny," the Charter opens. Developed in the years following the 1992 Earth Summit, the Charter sought to articulate an ethic for a "sustainable global society" amid growing recognition of shared planetary problems.[32] It seeks to expand inherited universal values (like human rights) into a shared planetary vision. Its lead drafter, Steven Rockefeller, therefore presents the Charter as both a culmination of the cosmopolitan declarations beginning with the UDHR and a significant expansion from what global ethics had previously included.[33] Unlike the Declaration, the Charter's vision does not constrain itself to moral values already shared; it rather articulates a transforming vision of a shared earth. "Fundamental changes are needed in our values, institutions and ways of living," without which we "risk the destruction of ourselves and the diversity of life." In the face of planetary problems, the world needs a new moral vision "to provide an ethical foundation for the emerging world community."[34] Unlike the Declaration's underdetermining principle, the Charter elaborates specifying norms in a cumulative account of an ethos appropriate for participating in earth's membership.

By presenting itself as a summons to *make* its commitments into a widely shared vision, the Charter attempts to expand cosmopolitanism beyond the human world through a process of cultural engagement.[35] Its universality is stronger than that of the Declaration, observes Nigel Dower, because "it is not a minimal core, but a tool for challenge." The Charter is both a declaration and a cultural manifesto. How one receives it depends on how one conceives the task of global ethics. Dower predicts that pluralists and pragmatists will raise objections about an attempt to generate a "21st century mythos or grand narrative" with universalist purchase. Even though the Charter works with values found in many traditions and is supportable by many moral worlds, its challenge to inherited moralities, combined with its ability to function as a worldview on its own, leads some to "a pragmatic rejection of cultural imperialism."[36] Such skepticism has less to do with any specific content in the Charter than with how it would function as a global ethic.

Sometimes its advocates describe the Charter functioning as the religious ethic of a world membership. When theologian Dieter Hessel writes that the Charter's principles "not only present a moral ecology of crucial values . . . they also provide an ethical standard," then others are right to worry that he understands the Charter's vision as an authoritative measure of all traditions.[37] Others hold the still stronger view that the Charter gives expression to a new form of spiritual consciousness. Rockefeller presents the Charter as "part of the quest for a spirituality and ethics adequate to the challenge of building a planetary civilization. . . . The objective is to give the emerging global consciousness the spiritual depth—the soul—needed to build a just and peaceful world community." Presented that way, the Charter can seem to propose a new religious tradition—and one with globalizing ambition. Rockefeller wants to deny that the Charter represents an incipient new religion, but he has said that it "produces its own unique form of religious consciousness" and that it calls inherited religions "to adopt a planetary consciousness."[38] Bron Taylor takes that line of thought to its conclusion, interpreting the Charter as one manifestation of an emerging "terrapolitan earth religion" that represents the likely evolutionary future of religion.[39] Whether or not the future of religion, Rockefeller and Taylor agree that a global ethic of sustainability requires the sort of worldview expressed by the Charter.

Mary Evelyn Tucker presents the religious task of the Charter more adroitly, explaining that it shows how the world's religions offer mythic resources for an ecological era of civilization and that the Charter offers back to religious traditions a concrete challenge of creating cultural change.[40] In this view, the Charter orients religions toward the guiding role they should play in developing the planetary consciousness that a global sustainability ethic needs. It does that by articulating the ethos of a common cosmology and shared membership, the values of which might be realized even within communities that do not understand themselves by a common creation story.[41] Tucker's explanation opens cultural space for the Charter to function differently than Taylor and Rockefeller think that a global ethic must. Perhaps values and commitments in the Charter might be deployed by communities working to confront planetary problems even when they do not start from a planetary consciousness.

Interpreting the Charter illustrates a central difficulty for any global sustainability ethic: to meaningfully address planetary problems it must simultaneously transform inherited moralities and demonstrate common ground. In a universalist view of the Charter's role in global ethics, it is hard to avoid the impression that it seeks to be the founding document of a new religious ethic. If Schweiker is correct that global ethics needs myth to re-narrate the world, and ethics supposes that the Charter presents a new eco-logical consciousness, then confronting planetary problems begins from the struggle to establish a moral world at once new and universal. That implies a very strong burden of cultural transformation as prologue to any practi-cal sustainability norms. However, global ethics does not necessarily need to work down from a declared vision into practical responsibilities. Shared practical responses to planetary problems might generate shared concepts for a global ethic from below.

GLOBAL ETHICS FROM BELOW: THE CREOLE OF COOPERATION

Informed by liberation theologies and postcolonial analyses, some ethicists working for ecological responsibilities of the very sort envisioned by *The Earth Charter* nonetheless resist efforts to declare a universal vision. They question how a global ethic so conceived would function in conditions of North Atlantic domination. An ethic with ambition to transform lived mo-ralities across the world in the light of its novel vision could easily become globalizing cultural imperialism. Their dissent is not merely localist and conservative, however, for they often support projects in which cosmo-politan commitments and transforming spiritualities emerge. The differ-ence lies in supposing that a global ethic should be cultivated "from below," through pluralist collaborations to address particular problems. I explain this alternative path to a global ethic by first observing critical reception of the Declaration and the Charter by Christian ethicists, then explain how shared moral norms can emerge from reflection on cross-border practices, and then interpret the idea of sustainability as that sort of norm.

Focusing the task of ethics on declarative documents distracts atten-tion from the global social movements in which shared concepts and com-mitments are forged. Martin Robra argues that the Declaration obscures the process by which a global ethos actually develops. Such texts offer "a tool for the process of interaction, networking and developing a shared lan-guage," but they obscure that use when they present themselves as finished and authorized products.[42] For a similar reason Konrad Raiser of the World Council of Churches (WCC) counseled delay in presenting the Charter to the UN because he thought it needed more time to "test out the evocative potential in different religious and cultural contexts." Its language will become valid, he argued, to the extent that it is successfully adopted within multiple and diverse contexts.[43] Like any language, a global ethic must express values and concepts already in use or implicit within shared practices. To the extent that it does, a declaration may be used to further cultivate those practices.

A global ethic depends on agents who cross the borders of moral worlds to work on shared problems, who then find that reflection on shared practices needs shared concepts, and who then begin to collaborate in generating those norms. Collaborative projects may generate normative concepts by borrowing concepts from various traditions and putting them to new social uses. For example, the indigenous climate justice movement borrows from human rights discourse and from traditional cosmovisions in order to invent concepts that support a project of cooperative confrontation across much cultural diversity. Their project does not want to overcome that diversity; in fact, it works to protect the conditions for multiple cultural ways of life on a planet being reshaped by climate change. They adapt rights and cosmovisions to organize confrontation with climate change, but they do not want the universalism of their appeal to imply that they all share the same moral world. That example illustrates how global social movements can exhibit impulses both for and against a universal ethic. On the one hand, movements use universalizing concepts to cultivate commitments across borders in the face of a shared problem. On the other hand, they resist globalizing power by resisting dominant global discourses for framing climate responsibilities. Developing shared responses to planetary problems may include resistance to "civilization" into one moral world. Planetarity does not mean globalism, as Gayatri Spivak would say.[44]

The Charter tries to absorb both cosmopolitan and postcolonial impulses, but Robra thinks that it does so by relegating the (mostly southern) voices of postcolonial pluralism to the subprinciples, while (typically northern) voices for a universal ethic dominate the main principles. Robra recounts that decades of WCC initiatives to link sustainability and social justice generated similar resistance from global South churches to universalizing moral synthesis. Eventually the WCC settled on affirming "an anti-systemic covenant between different global movements rooted in biblical affirmation." Thus, it created space for common action by recognizing theologically and ideologically particularist social movements as "the major actors for an emerging global ethos legitimized by the aspirations of the people and their struggles."[45]

At stake here is whose agency shapes a global ethic, and where ethicists look for sources of moral transformation. Postcolonial and pragmatist critics

agree on organizing the task of global ethics from the projects and movements that attempt to work across moral worlds to address planetary problems. Assuming pluralism does not concede hapless relativism or intractable
parochialism. It assumes that agents are embodied in particular contexts and
shaped differently by their respective moral worlds. Emilie Townes argues
that interpreting structural evils may in fact require the countermemory and
subversive imagination of those who resist cultural homogenization. Ethics
needs multiple moral worlds in order to develop meaningful norms of cooperation. "The universal, then, is created in the creolization of discourses,
not in the austere terrain of monochromatic abstract conceptualizations."[46]
Global ethics need not establish conditions of possibility for abstract agents
to occupy the same ground. Global ethics needs creoles of cooperation, and
those arise from agents working specific problems, within structures of relation that connect them to other moral worlds and from projects created by
people trying to make those relations better.

Developing global ethics from below, I am arguing, stands a better
chance of making pluralism productive rather than defeating. Resolving
conflicts among multiple moral views seems more likely to succeed within
specific contexts of cooperation than in conceptual foundations. If we really care about resolving practical problems rather than metaethical ones,
argues Jeffrey Stout, we should "proceed on an ad hoc basis, keeping the
scope of comparison as narrow as possible."[47] We need just enough moral
language in common to treat particular problems, and we can create those
languages piecemeal. Human rights, says Stout, represent one successful
moral creole, borrowed from many sources and developed through use by
many speakers.[48] Disagreements over its foundations do not imperil the vocabulary so long as speakers keep using it in mutually intelligible ways. In
fact, its internal pluralism—its lack of sure cultural foundation—may be a
reason it is so widely adopted.

In addition to liberationists and pragmatists, this sort of argument also
appears among religious ethicists concerned for the embodiment of moral
agency. Elizabeth Gerle criticizes the Declaration because it appeals to religion as an abstract authority for a universal norm, rather than the living
reality of projects and networks. Reflecting on work in the WCC, Gerle observes that consensus builds in the context of concrete commitments.[49] Jean
Porter likewise criticizes the Declaration for its assumption that a pluralist
world needs a universal consensus guaranteed by religion in order to face
its problems. Global ethics does not begin in a choice between universalism
or relativism, she writes; it "begins by looking for specific points of agreement and working toward a consensus, perhaps only limited and provisional
but still workable on that basis." She points to Catholic scholars working on

human rights without appealing to a universal account of human nature. Provisional agreement on certain rights protections may be all we can hope for among moral traditions. But it also may be all that is needed: "it is not clear that we do need a global ethic, with or without religious foundations to resolve moral conflicts across national boundaries. It may be enough to bring an attitude of openness and a willingness to look for a basis of ad hoc agreement to situations of potential conflict."[50]

Other Catholic social ethicists counter Porter's pessimism toward the prospects of a global ethic by emphasizing the constructive potential of an ad hoc approach. Lisa Cahill and David Hollenbach argue that practical agreements wrought across moral worlds create shared commitments to particular goods. Cahill argues that we should think of global ethics "as an intercultural process serving the common good through experience-based consensus about the truth of moral relationships." Truth is learned through relationships of solidarity with others committed to confronting shared problems. Practical reasoning through concrete problems can lead to shared understandings of reality. "Moral truths, both particular and general, are re-alized inductively, experientially, interactively, and in the midst of concrete human problems and projects."[51] Shared moral resources for confronting shared planetary problems can grow from the ground up.

Consider as evidence the fact that at least four major "state of the world" reports are published annually. Each describes some planetary problem from within a shared project of addressing it. Human Rights Watch tracks violations of human dignity; World Watch documents environmental de-struction and ecological change; the World Bank and the UN Development Program issue competing accounts of impoverishment and economic devel-opment. Each is issued in expectation that agents from many moral worlds will find their appeals reasonable, their descriptions compelling, and their recommendations worthy of support. The reports do not offer foundational accounts of the good and the right by which to make sense of their projects. Yet each cultivates minimal norms of description and responsibility that arise from pluralist reflection on a shared problem, and each offers those norms and their assumptions to revision in light of experience.

Critical to the development of the guiding concepts within those proj-ects are the social practices that produce them and thereby create arenas for shared practical reasoning across moral worlds. The concepts and norms of global ethics arise from practices that move across significant human bound-aries in order to create solidarity in bearing one another's problems. Cahill thus appeals for "boundary-crossing creativity" and solidarity with those suf-fering the world's problems most acutely. "The possibility of global ethics, then, should not be pondered in the realm of abstract or deductive reason alone, but through engagement with practical, political affairs."[52] Again, ethics happens by participation.

For Christian ethics, that engagement takes a christoform pattern: it moves across boundaries to the far and forgotten places of alienation to seek God's solidarity with those suffering powers of evil, violence, and exclusion. Hollenbach thus argues that the particularist symbol of the cross should function to make Christian ethicists support all practices of solidarity with suffering, no matter the moral worlds that generate them.[53] In the last chapter I showed how Dietrich Bonhoeffer and Martin Luther King interpreted practices of bearing responsibility for the world as forms of participation in the reality of Christ. A Christian global ethic should not appear then as a globalized ethos of Christian identity, or as religious authority for universal values. If some moral good is found through embodied work across borders of alienation to bear responsibility for the world, then the important theological tasks lie in summoning Christians and others to participate in those practices, and in helping them to make sense of the experience.

The chief difficulty for global ethics on this account lies not in meta-ethics but in the plain fearfulness and reluctance of persons to move beyond the boundaries that secure their own identities. Creating the sort of cross-border projects that cultivate shared commitments is the most difficult and most important task for global ethics. Willingness to enter into those relationships requires a certain cosmopolitan acknowledgement that we already participate in relationships that extend beyond national, cultural, and religious borders. (Stephen Gardiner suggests that one reason US citizens may be reluctant to face climate change is that doing so would acknowledge their involvement in global social relations.)[54] So a pragmatic approach, working from below, does need a planetary perspective. Crossing borders to work with strangers is not a supererogatory option. It is an obligatory response to our participation in globalizing networks of power that exceed the reach of our moral and political memberships. It needs ethicists who themselves cross boundaries of identity, discipline, and tradition to participate in working on problems. Developing a creole of cooperation among multiple worlds relies on inhabitants of those worlds attempting to make the best they can of one another's efforts to respond to the problems of a planetary membership.

The neighbor-making love of Christian ethics adds a further cosmopolitan disposition. A creole of cooperation is more likely to emerge if inhabitants of different moral worlds listen to one another as neighbors. Christian faith generates strong reasons for members of its moral world to hold a cosmopolitan disposition because it refuses to let national, cultural, or other human borders determine who may count as a neighbor. (It should so refuse, anyway; in actuality borders continue to overdetermine work in Christian ethics, which Daisy Machado has shown in a disruptive reflection on the theological function of the US border.)[55] Even confessional borders cannot exclude. With the theological account of global ethics from below developed by Cahill and Hollenbach, and the theological pragmatism I defend in chapter 2, even the religious border that differentiates a Christian world from others cannot function to secure Christian identity. It must serve the purpose of seeking how God moves across all borders to reconcile creatures—as the religious border does in the parable of the Samaritan. The particular belief that all goods unite in Christ, the one who crossed the border to make God neighbor with the alienated, frees Christian practice to participate in pluralist projects seeking common goods from many grounds, without worrying over their Christian status. It suggests that Christian faith embodies itself (becomes particular) by moving across the borders of Christian identity.

COMMON GOODS AND MIDDLE AXIOMS

What if the differences among moral worlds run so deeply that cooperation appears impossible? Does doing global ethics from below give up on universal norms? What if the shared ground made by cross-border projects remains narrowly anthropocentric? The wager of this method of global ethics is that sufficient norms can eventually be learned by participating in projects that respond to shared problems. Long reflection across cultures on that participation may even lead toward consensus norms with the force of universality (like human rights). Where those shared concepts seem inadequate, projects may attempt to illuminate further imperiled goods with transforming proposals (like Mother Earth rights), thus putting pressure on the practical consensus hosted by a norm. The point is that prior agreement on universal norms or a vision of the good is not required for the sort of cooperative practices that build provisional commitments to particular shared goods.

Christian ethics can have confidence in starting from below when it has an account of the common good which holds that all of creation's goods cohere in the God who transcends creation. Theological ideas of the common good affirm the possibility that social learning about particular goods can happen without shared beliefs about their coherence in God. Theological confidence in the transcendent good supports an ethic of the common good in which persons from quite different moral worlds can reason together about the conditions by which their lives are sustained, even if they have no shared language about how those particular goods fulfill some account of the ultimate good. Theological affirmation thus warrants a pluralist moral epistemology toward provisional common goods, but the point is not that one must hold that theological warrant. Other traditions may affirm similar possibilities of pluralist moral learning with other ideas. In any case, agents do not need to endorse any belief about its possibility in order to learn. So a Christian ethic of the common good should focus on the practices of cooperative moral learning before it tries to establish the beliefs that make it possible.

Talk of the common good often appears when Catholic social ethicists engage political economy and human development. The common good offers a middle ground theological vocabulary, rooted in creation's ultimate end in God while compatible with many views of human flourishing and social justice. The Vatican II document *Gaudium et spes* defines the common good as "the sum of those conditions of social life which allow social groups and their individual members relatively thorough and ready access to their own fulfillment."[56] Yet the common good does not just give a Christian name to universalist cosmopolitanism, as Hollenbach explains, because it insists on "the moral significance of local and particular relationships."[57] The various goods constituitive of the common good are learned through participation in moral relationships, especially within communities responding to human suffering. Hollenbach thus affirms a pluralist way to moral truth through a particularist confession: we learn moral truth through cruciform relationships of justice and solidarity. Again, the fundamental choice in global ethics is not for or against universality, nor for or against Christianity, but whether to be within or without solidarity.[58] The fundamental moral decision is whether or not we will be neighbors.

The provisionality of the common good to a transcendent ultimate good prevents those middle axioms from becoming absolute norms. Theologies of the common good prevent social projects from supposing that they can finally achieve the good. Neither economic growth, nor human development, nor human rights, nor ecological sustainability—the chief norms of each of those four state of the world reports—stands as an ultimate good. By relativizing the claims of lesser solidarities even as it holds that their various goods do cohere, a theological account frees agents to build solidarities in confidence that, as Hollenbach puts it, "the common good that can be achieved in history is a pluralistic ensemble of goods."[59] Faith in the ultimate end of all moral worlds opens up a space of inductive practical reason between the particular and the universal. The space of the common good accommodates multiple moral projects seeking the goods of humanity and of creation, provisionally dampens conflicts among them, and invites reflection on their discoveries and challenges.[60]

As those practices generate shared commitments—as human rights practices generate a shared commitment to human dignity, for example— theologians can try to explain to others why they think Christian beliefs best interpret those commitments within a more comprehensive account of the good. Of course, the pluralist exchanges may also revise Christian understandings. For example, participating in responses to biodiversity loss should lead Christian communities to better integrate appreciation for ecological commons.[61] Cahill and Hollenbach both seem ecologically insufficient in their account of the common good, but their practical epistemology of the good implies that their understandings would expand as problem-solving, solidaristic relationships discover broader dimensions of moral truth. Theological communities learn the common good through participation in social projects that cross borders of culture, faith, discipline, and power in order to defend some good.

The idea of the common good thus facilitates practical solidarity in a pluralist world. Highlighting its uses in social encyclicals over a century, Dennis McCann argues that the common good "is best understood, not in essentialist terms as a logical explication of what is already implicit in the concept, but in pragmatic terms." It supports and unfolds from projects that can cultivate understanding of shared goods. That functional account invites the search for many subsidiary middle axioms.[62] "Social justice" and "human dignity" are important middle axioms with global currency; in the next section I explain "sustainability" as another.

Middle axioms arise from cross-border projects. Feminist and liberationist movements situated in "global theological flows," argues Robert Schreiter, have been especially important sites for the production of middle axioms. Schreiter picks up the concept from Charles Villa-Vicencio, who himself retrieved it from mid-twentieth century Anglican ethicist J. H. Oldham in order to explore how churches in South Africa could contribute to the country's reconstruction. "Truth and reconciliation," as a political practice for addressing legacies of violent oppression, has become a transnational middle axiom because of the South African experience. While open to theological elaboration, "truth and reconciliation" is not a Christian command or particularist ideal; it is a set of pluralist political practices whose test lies in whether, over the long run, it helps overcome enmity. In Schreiter's definition, middle axioms are "evolving principles reshaped by the continuing encounter with an evolving society and tempered by the eschatological proviso that all social proposals work under."[63] Middle axioms are different than "applied theology," then. They represent an inductive, contextual method for churches to understand and interpret their context in ways that facilitate ongoing social encounter.[64]

Middle axioms have been criticized from multiple quarters. The objections raise difficulties for an inductive way to common goods and specifically for sustainability discourse. Liberationists object that mediating concepts imply modest incrementalism and concession to the ideology of contemporary powers. Their political contingency underscores their weakness: if "truth and reconciliation" is merely a bridge-building concept warranted by its contextual usefulness, then speaking "truth" to power seems less revolutionary, and "reconciliation" might just name capitulation. When appeal to middle axioms attempts conceptual mediation of deep divisions, Timothy Gorringe warns against "pouring the oil of middle axioms on the troubled waters of social conflict."[65] Notice how the idea of "sustainable development" has been used to evade rather than confront important conflicts between economic growth and ecological protection. Better to meet those conflicts directly than try to soften them. Middle axioms can support a policy-oriented managerialism that insulates economic powers and cultural practices from theological critique.[66]

Those criticisms express the worry that middle axioms undercut the transformative power of theological ethics. Some of the worry may derive from a model of theological ethics focused on the ideals and authority of a Christian worldview—on ethics "from above." If, on the other hand, Christian ethics supposes that middle axioms arise from what are already missional practices, then they may look less compromising. William Danaher argues that middle axioms derive from a "missional ecclesiology," in which churches seek ways of "creatively practicing the politics of the kingdom" in a pluralist world. Danaher's example is the Millennium Development Goals. To confessionalist Christian ethicists chary of human development goals undetermined by a theological narrative, Danaher replies that the church should expect *ad hoc* points of social transformation to emerge from Christian mission practices. As long as God's mission of transformation is the focus, and not boundaries of religious identity, then Christian communities can look for ways to join in that mission wherever they find it.[67] Just because middle axioms are limited and provisional does not mean that they are inimical to faith. We should think of middle axioms, writes Cahill, as "interactive points of interdisciplinary collaboration when social needs and Christian values reach a working arrangement."[68]

Theological communities need not be uncritical of that working arrangement. On the contrary, by understanding its support of middle axioms to emerge from border-crossing practices that seek common goods, and interpreting those practices as ways that Christians seek the mission of God, Christian ethics has theological ground to continually test and criticize concepts of shared goods. The Millennium Development Goals may have too limited a notion of human personhood or represent an inchoate set of social goals. But surely they name a number of specific goods also implicit in Christian mission practices. It should be no scandal to Christian particularity that responses to poverty and illness lead persons from other traditions to similar moral conclusions. A theological ethic of the common good expects that convergence, and by explaining how Christian mission practices interpret the goods named by human development projects within a wider account of the good, they drive continual reflection on the provisional goals of global commitments. The Christian ethicist's worry with the Millennium Development Goals should not be that they are insufficiently Christian but that they are insufficiently funded and half-heartedly pursued.

Objections that middle axioms remain too moderate and accommodationist state important cautions for any pragmatic approach to global ethics. The moral creole of such projects is likely to be minimalist and functional, creating only as much shared commitment as needed to deliberate together over problems. Projects may not yield a language at all, but—like the Millennium Development Goals—a mere list of commitments. The relevant moral minimum here is, as Michael Walzer argues, not the discovery that everyone is committed to the same values, but that, like a protest march, all the participants have joined in a response to a crisis. A minimal morality facilitates a pluralist encounter for interpreting the crisis.[69] We need those commitments in order to have shared ground for questioning impoverishing structures or dehumanizing powers. We need to have some shared concepts in order to question whether the march is moving in the right direction. Middle axioms offer provisional norms and intercultural space for hosting debate about those norms, the problems they confront, and the shared practices from which they arise. In the next section I explain how "sustainability" functions that way.

THE IDEA OF SUSTAINABILITY

I have argued that thin but universalizing norms can emerge from pluralist projects to confront shared problems. Their purpose is to facilitate learning and reflection on cross-border projects as a kind of moral creole. One task of global ethics, in my account, is to criticize those norms so that they function more helpfully and more adequately within the projects they support. Ethicists might wish that a project used different norms, metaphors, or ideas, but they should begin from the moral creole that participants in the project already use. After they understand the range of argument a moral creole permits, and how it supports pluralist learning about a problem and the goods it imperils, then ethicists might argue for a different norm.

Beginning from speculation about the best possible norm for some problem fails to start from a creole already spoken.

This section examines sustainability as a norm that helps to organize pluralist response to planetary problems. Sustainability has gained currency across the sciences and humanities as an idea around which to organize research programs on planetary problems (more on this in the next chapter); it names stated objectives in many kinds of institutions, including those of the international community; it is used in many cultural contexts and has become ubiquitous in some. Whatever the drawbacks of this word, observes theologian Rachel Muers, sustainability is "on the way to becoming a basic ethical term, a term used to refer to a complex and contested understanding of the good."[70] It has become an intercultural, interdisciplinary site for debating human responsibilities for globalizing social relations in times of ecological change, economic uncertainty, and environmental destruction. Muers observes that theologians sometimes make the mistake of simply adding religious force to the importance of the concept—as if sustainability were a universal ideal in need of religious support. That point is crucial for global ethics: sustainability is not a principle to apply, nor a value to either favor or disfavor, but a pluralist site of cultural renegotiation in which societies interpret basic ideas of justice and the good by reckoning with the problems created by emergent human powers. The point of this section, let me be clear, is not to endorse sustainability or imply its priority over other norms; it is to critically examine how a candidate concept for global ethics functions to support practical pluralist deliberation.

Definitions

The idea of sustainability carries paradoxical dimensions. On the one hand, it is a bare norm of prudence: do not undermine survival. On the other hand, in the context of anthropogenic change of basic systems, that minimal norm forces reflection on the goals of economy, the value of nonhuman life, the role of humanity within earth, and what we hope for the future. In the debate over what societies should sustain and why, we are forced to reflect on what sustains humanity and why. Precisely because the basic norm of sustainability is so minimal, the fact of its jeopardy involves debates over comprehensive beliefs and values.

Philosopher Andrew Dobson describes three approaches to the variety of ideas of sustainability: definitional, discursive, and typological.[71] I employ each approach to clarify uses of the term. Definitional approaches propose and defend a summary articulation of sustainability. In its literal rudiments, sustainability means a capacity to maintain some entity, outcome, or process over time.[72] The term was first employed by resource managers to refer to maintaining yield over time; hence, agriculture, forest management, and financial investments are sustainable if the costs and extractions of the activity do not exhaust the resources on which it depends. In recent decades the term has been used to assess threats posed by human action to basic ecological and social systems on which humanity depends. The basic intuition remains: that some activity runs the risk of exhausting resources or conditions on which it depends.

Beyond that definitions vary widely. Larry Rasmussen begins his essay in *Ethics for a Small Planet* with the statement that "'sustainability' is the capacity of natural and industrial systems to survive and thrive together indefinitely."[73] A religious ethicist might prefer Robert Nelson's formulation: "To ask whether a society is sustainable is to ask whether its people are living according to God's commands."[74] Or she might prefer the definition from *Caring for the Earth*: "improving the quality of human life while living within the carrying capacity of supporting ecosystems."[75] Those all seem different from Robert Solow's classic definition: "the obligation to leave the future the capacity to be as well off as we are."[76]

Behind each definition, of course, is a different project. Rasmussen is preparing to criticize development ideas in a social justice account of population and consumption, while *Caring for the Earth* wants to harmonize with development discourse, in order to make a case for conserving ecological capacities. Nelson uses sustainability to question the ideology of economic growth, while Solow's definition assumes economic growth as the basic logic of human welfare. One could go on proliferating definitions, and critics often do when they want to criticize the incoherence of sustainability discourse. However, if sustainability represents not a general norm but a site of learning and reflection about the integration of human and ecological systems, then ethics does not need an authoritative definition to resolve debate. It just needs to make the debates more searching and useful.

Historical Emergence

A discursive approach tracks the historical emergence of sustainability concepts. One of the earliest uses of the term "sustainability" to address human environmental impact appears in a 1969 International Union for Conservation of Nature (IUCN) document describing as its mandate as "the perpetuation and enhancement of the living world . . . so as to achieve the highest sustainable quality of life."[77] The publication that may have done the most to provoke public thinking of earth systems, the 1972 *Limits to Growth* issued by the Club of Rome, argued that human economies had reached the planet's biophysical limits and called for scaling back economic activity.[78] Although the term "sustainability" nowhere appears in it, the report's account of conflict between ecological limits and human growth was influential for subsequent uses. That same year the Stockholm Declaration, issued by the conference which established the UN Environment Programme, argued that "the capacity of the earth to produce vital renewable resources must be maintained."[79] Two years later, in 1974, the Cocoyoc Declaration, adopted by the participants in a small UN symposium, used sustainability for the first time as a concept for uniting conservation and social development.[80] The major public debut of sustainability as a practical norm for confronting planetary problems appeared in a 1980 conservation strategy document from the IUCN, which connected ecological integrity and social poverty in its call for a program to protect the conditions of flourishing for all.[81]

Theological debates attended the public emergence of the sustainability idea, helped bring it to international prominence, and then raised critical concerns about continuing to use it. As early as 1974 the WCC was discussing the idea of sustainability, and by 1975 had initiated a major program on a "Just, Participatory, and Sustainable Society."[82] One of the first uses of sustainability to integrate commitments to ecological protection with justice for the poor thus appeared in a church gathering.[83] The 1975 WCC assembly used the concept to connect its support for pro-poor liberation theologies with emerging international concerns about environmental problems. Theological uses helped transform sustainability from a resource management concept into an integrative idea of social ethics.[84] But by the time the IUCN had picked up that use, WCC gatherings were already doubting whether the term could bear the multiple projects it had accreted.

The idea of sustainability came to worldwide prominence in 1987 through the World Commission on Environment and Development publication *Our Common Future*, which addressed tensions between economic growth and environmental degradation by using the hybrid concept, "sustainable development." In its famous definition, "sustainable development is development that meets the needs of the present without compromising the ability of future generations to meet their own needs."[85] Although it did notoriously little to specify what needs those are, *Our Common Future* was important for focusing on intergenerational obligation and for making "sustainable development" a principle of political economy that could integrate environmental, economic, and social commitments.[86] The absorptive capacity of the idea of sustainability helped create political support for an international conference addressing environmental issues, thus opening the way for the 1992 "Earth Summit" in Rio de Janeiro. A decade later, when the UN held the World Summit on Sustainable Development in Johannesburg, "sustainability" had accreted not only "economic development" but nearly every other social goal produced by the previous decade of world summits. Sustainability had become a watchword for the interconnection of everything good—and ideological cover for some things bad.[87]

Precisely because of that ideological accretion, the WCC turned away from the idea of sustainability as an integrating norm. Already, by 1983 the WCC program on the "sustainable society" had been replaced with the "integrity of creation," in a new program unit on "Justice, Peace, and the Integrity of Creation," which has endured since. WCC participants worried that the idea of sustainability would compromise projects for the liberation of the poor and for the protection of ecological integrity. The titles of the new program unit disaggregated the basic commitments: social justice and the integrity of creation. By the time of the 2002 Summit, the WCC joined other religious communities in trying to disentangle social justice priorities from the market globalization ideology shaping "sustainable development." The discourse of sustainability, they thought, was beginning to sustain the wrong sort of world. Thus the ecclesial institution that helped launch the public career of sustainability soon discovered missional reasons to criticize its success.[88]

Types of Sustainability

Discriminating types of sustainability helps clarify what is at stake. Types are sometimes categorized as weak or strong, brown or green, or they are plotted along a range from technocentric to ecocentric or humanist to preservationist. The key differentiating point among the varieties is their object: what should be sustained? Types of sustainability often divide by assumptions they use to answer that question. One of the most important assumptions concerns the multiplicity of goods at stake. Can multiple social goals be measured by a common standard, or are they irreducibly diverse? From a perspective holding the fungibility of moral values, societies aim to preserve one key value, usually measured in terms of human welfare. A pluralist perspective holds that societies must aim to preserve multiple values which may be both incommensurable and competing. These might include human welfare, preservation of other species for their own sake, ecosystem integrity, political goods such as democracy or human rights, and cultural goods such as traditional ways of life. Value pluralists usually insist that those goods are not substitutable for one another, such that loss of one might be perfectly compensated by the gain or protection of another.

The difference between "strong" and "weak" versions of sustainability turns on those points of fungibility. "Strong sustainability" requires preservation of multiple goods, and insists that they cannot be substituted for one another in some common measure. Generally, strong sustainability requires protection of ecological goods, such as particular species or the functioning

of particular ecosystems, and assumes that those goods may conflict with
some goods of human welfare. It may also include nonsubstitutable protection of social or political goods. "Weak sustainability" incorporates all the
goods at stake within an expansive account of welfare. It usually includes
"natural capital" and "social capital" when calculating welfare decisions, and
seeks a common measure to allow one metric of decision making.[89]

Those types of sustainability involve background pictures of the relation
between human and ecological systems. If an ethicist thinks that ecological
systems pose hard limits to the human economy, she may endorse a nonsubstitutable view in order to emphasize biophysical limits on human agency.
If, on the other hand, an ethicist thinks that economic development creates
resources as it uses others, then she is more likely to endorse a substitutable view, in the view that human creativity overcomes limits and reduces
scarcity. Unfortunately those background pictures often correspond to disciplinary location; economists tend to adopt the latter and ecological scientists the former. That forces citizen observers to decide among competing
background pictures of the world.

Different disciplinary frameworks thus tend to give rise to competing
models of sustainability, each with an assumed priority for some good. *Economic models* illuminate dimensions of human welfare at risk of irrational use
of resources. Here sustainability poses an investment problem, in which societies must use returns from the use of natural resources in order to create
new opportunities of equal or greater value. When observers find features
of the model odd—such as valuing the existence of a species or discounting costs to the future into vanishing significance—they turn to the models of other disciplines.[90] *Ecological models* illuminate risks posed by human
powers to biological functions and ecological systems. They may focus on
ecological goods for the sake of human dependence on them or for their
own intrinsic value; but however warranted, the model interprets conflict
between human economies and ecological systems. *Political models* propose
to sustain social systems that realize human dignity or protect fundamental
values (such as democracy or human rights). They interpret sustainability
problems as the jeopardy of certain political goods and the consequence of
political conflict.[91]

Pluralist Bridge Concept

The idea of sustainability thus involves multiple moral commitments and
conflicting models of reality. Some critics worry that it bears too many
agendas with too little clarity to be of any practical use.[92] In line with
worries that emerged in WCC processes, religious ethicist Clare Palmer

worries that its malleability makes the idea of sustainability not just incoherent but supine to the powers that occasion its need. Conceptual ambiguity, she argues, undercuts resistance to social injustice and permits totalizing use of the planet by human power.[93] Philosopher Aidan Davison intensifies the complicity by arguing that sustainability discourse shores up faith in human progress and particularly in a human ability to save ourselves. Debating models and meanings of sustainability distracts attention from its quasi-religious function as a paradoxical salvation story that supports the extension of human power over the earth in order to rescue the earth from human powers.[94] By accreting and absorbing matters of a religious depth, the idea of sustainability may thus work to subjugate religion and ethics to imperatives of power.

Sustainability discourse can certainly function as a secular salvation idea. When it does it threatens ethical reasoning in both religious and nonreligious modes. Considered as a "secularized eternity," a salvation concept for humans who imagine the survival of their own power as the most significant thing in the cosmos, the idea of sustainability begins to corrode rather than cultivate moral capacities.[95] Even where the idea does not offer moral cover for exploitative powers, Christian ethics has no interest in supporting a poor substitute for the hope of Christ or a weak analogue of rescue from sin. And any ethic must be wary of how the idea of sustainability can absorb and suppress questions about the ultimate good and the human purpose in earth.

However, as a site of open cultural contest about the goods of life, conducted in new appreciation of human embeddedness in systems of life, sustainability may offer an idea that ethics can use to think through planetary problems. In this view the unresolved plurality of sustainability is a strength. "The power of the concept of sustainability," writes John Robinson, "lies precisely in the degree to which it brings to the surface these contradictions and provides a kind of discursive playing field in which they can be debated." The open idea of sustainability invites interdisciplinary, multicultural reflection on engaged experiments in learning from specific problems. It is not really a definition, argues Robinson; it is a political act.[96] Brian Barry turns that discursive way of understanding sustainability into a substantive norm by appealing to the requisite conditions of the debate. If sustainability stands for important cultural contests over fundamental goods, and choosing one's own good is a basic point of justice, then environmental and social conditions for the debate must be maintained. Destroying biodiversity impoverishes conditions for arguing over whether and how it is a sustaining good. If "the core concept of sustainability is . . . that there is some X whose value should be maintained," Barry argues that value includes the practice of arguing over whether and how some "X" sustains us.[97] Barry thus makes access to a meaningful argument over sustainability a summary of what it practically entails.

Global ethics does not need a universal ideal of sustainability in order to have the beginnings of a normative ethic. The irreducible plurality raises important arguments in the context of real problems, which helps societies understand the ecological and social conditions required for sustaining good arguments. We cannot conduct a good argument over the importance of biodiversity after it is lost. As a middle axiom, a provisional concept for organizing argument, the idea of sustainability can help open transdisciplinary, cross-cultural dialogue about confronting planetary problems. But those debates cannot be held abstractly; they need pluralist social practices of response to those problems, from which they can learn.

Religious and philosophical ethics may play an important role in that debate by articulating the ethical dimensions it involves and holding open its search for adaptive norms. Mary Midgley argues that philosophy can criticize the "anthropolatry" of sustainability discourse that lets societies avoid the deep questions raised by the kinds of problems their power is creating. Part of the point of philosophy, she thinks, is to suspend the assumptions that let societies evade important questions—such as what attitude creatures with such power over earth ought to take toward a cosmos in which we have such a small part.[98] Much theological engagement with uses of the idea of sustainability does something similar by questioning the ultimate value of assumed social imperatives (e.g., development, growth, or even human survival). By situating the relation of human and ecological systems within a broader economy of God, theological ideas can raise metaethical questions about background assumptions of how we think we are sustained. The point is not that Christian ethics has authority to decide among types and models of sustainability, but that a theological ethic can surface the background assumptions and deep moral questions at stake in the conceptual variety. It may be theology, ironically, that can keep sustainability from functioning as an empty salvation concept by opening it to the deep moral questions it involves. Religious modes of ethics may then help sustain the social learning required for a pragmatic strategy of sustainability ethics.

This section has shown that sustainability is not itself an ethic that can be applied. It is an open norm used by various disciplines and projects to interpret the problems produced by globalizing social and economic relations. As a shared conceptual space for various modes of criticizing a cultural gap between the problems humanity faces and its present capacities to take responsibility for them, sustainability works as a bridging concept. It creates connections across cultures and social goals, and offers a new epistemic link between scientific research, cultural reflection, and social change.[99] The important question here is not what sustainability means, but whether the practices of response from which it emerges can elicit adaptive transformations in cultural action sufficient to protect the goods at jeopardy of human powers.

CONCLUSION

This chapter has argued for developing global ethics from the cross-border practices of agents collaborating to respond to planetary problems. Its most important products are not documents and declarations, but the moral creoles and middle axioms generated from pluralist reflection on shared problems. Christian ethics should speak those creoles in order to support pluralist reflection on projects attempting to take responsibility for the structures and powers that imperil shared goods. In a theological account of the common good, pluralist practices of response to planetary problems form sites of dialogue across multiple moral worlds for learning about the goods that sustain us. Agents from different moral traditions may not find a common moral foundation by working together. In fact, neocolonial dynamics of power should make ethicists wary of trying to discover or make one moral world. Collaboration across boundaries of difference and alienation can, however, foster forms of practical friendship that support pluralist responsibilities for shared habitat. The most difficult and most important moral task for global ethics lies not in metaethics but in overcoming the everyday fear, alienation, and indifference that prevents persons from cultivating relationships across borders. In other words, loving neighbors remains the most important moral task. Global ethics begins by seeking out practical friendship with those from whom we are separated in world and yet united in planetary peril. The exigency of shared problems simply makes doing so a condition of survival as well as a practice of love.

This chapter introduced the idea of sustainability as the sort of norm (open, contested, multivalent) that might emerge from cross-border cooperation. For global ethics, sustainability functions among multiple moral worlds and competing disciplines as a middle axiom for interpreting the common goods at stake in the problems we face. I suggested that religious ethics may have a role to play in keeping the idea of sustainability open to the basic questions raised by planetary problems, and in addressing worries that an ethic of sustainability cannot generate the deep cultural changes needed to confront those problems.

My approach to global ethics moves from the scales in which agents are formed (communities, traditions, relationships, projects) toward the scale at which problems form (structures, systems). By arguing that the meaning of sustainability lies in the projects it supports, and by focusing on the way that Christian theological traditions support pluralist moral creoles, I have presented an approach to global ethics that works toward practical responsibilities for planetary problems without a universal worldview or shared foundation. Projects of responsibility, and the provisional norms they generate, can scale up to meet planetary problems by gaining support from multiple moral worlds. I turn to develop those suggestions in the next two chapters, showing in chapter 4 the role for religious creativity in the adaptive learning model of sustainability science and then, in chapter 5, the way that community-based environmental justice movements are expanding the meaning of justice.

NOTES

1. I borrow the trope "many moral worlds" from William Schweiker, *Theological Ethics and Global Dynamics: In the Time of Many Worlds* (Malden, MA: Blackwell, 2004).

2. See the "Indigenous Peoples' Declaration," World Peoples' Conference on Climate Change and the Rights of Mother Earth, Cochabamba, Bolivia, April 21, 2010, and further commentary in chapter 5.

3. Iris Marion Young, *Responsibility for Justice* (New York: Oxford University Press, 2011), 105.

4. Mary Elizabeth Hobgood, *Dismantling Privilege: An Ethics of Accountability* (Cleveland: Pilgrim Press, 2000), ix.

5. Rob Nixon, *Slow Violence and the Environmentalism of the Poor* (Cambridge, MA: Harvard University Press, 2011).

6. See Richard W. Miller, *Globalizing Justice: The Ethics of Poverty and Power* (New York: Oxford University Press, 2010).

7. For projects organized on this convention, see William Sullivan and Will Kymlicka, eds., *The Globalization of Ethics: Religious and Secular Perspectives* (New York: Cambridge University Press, 2007); Gene H. Outka and John P. Reeder, eds., *Prospects for a Common Morality* (Princeton, NJ: Princeton University Press, 1993).

8. Nigel Dower, *World Ethics: The New Agenda*, 2nd ed. (Edinburgh: Edinburgh University Press, 2007), 2; Robin Attfield, "The Shape of a Global Ethic," *Philosophy and Social Criticism* 32, no. 1 (2006): 5–7.

9. On the distinction of "moral cosmopolitanism" from political and other varieties, see Charles Beitz, "Cosmopolitanism and Global Justice," in *Current Debates in Global Justice*, Gillian Brock and Darrel Moellendorf, eds. (Dordrecht, Netherlands: Springer, 2005).

10. Kwame Anthony Appiah, *Cosmopolitanism: Ethics in a World of Strangers* (New York: W. W. Norton, 2006).

11. Universal Declaration of Human Rights, G. A. Res. 217 (III) A, UN Doc. A/RES/217(III) (Dec. 10, 1948), Preamble.

12. Marcus Braybrooke, ed. *Stepping Stones to a Global Ethic* (London: SCM Press, 1992).

13. Peter Singer, "Famine, Affluence, and Morality," *Philosophy and Public Affairs* 1, no. 3 (1972). On the legacy of that essay, see the discussion in Deen K. Chatterjee, ed., *The Ethics of Assistance: Morality and the Distant Needy* (Cambridge: Cambridge University Press, 2004).

14. Peter Singer, *One World: The Ethics of Globalization* (New Haven, CT: Yale University Press, 2002).

15. Young, *Responsibility for Justice,* 124.

16. David Hollenbach, *The Common Good and Christian Ethics* (Cambridge: Cambridge University Press, 2002), 221.

17. Eric Gregory, "Agape and Special Relations in a Global Economy: Theological Sources," in *Global Neighbors: Christian Faith and Moral Obligation in Today's Economy*, Douglas Hicks and Mark Valeri, eds. (Grand Rapids, MI: Eerdmans, 2008).

18. Luke Bretherton, *Christianity and Contemporary Politics: The Conditions and Possibilities of Faithful Witness* (Malden, MA: Wiley-Blackwell, 2010), chap. 3.

19. Leonardo Boff, *When Theology Listens to the Poor* (San Francisco: Harper and Row, 1988), 8–9.

20. Jack Donnelly, *Universal Human Rights in Theory and Practice*, 2nd ed. (Ithaca, NY: Cornell University Press, 2003), 14–16.

21. "Contrary to what many people think, world convergence will not come through a loss or denial of traditions all around, but rather by creative reimmersions of different groups, each in their own spiritual heritage, traveling different routes to the same goal." Charles Taylor, "Conditions of an Unforced Consensus on Human Rights," in *Global Ethics: Seminal Essays*, Thomas Pogge and Keith Horton, eds. (St. Paul, MN: Paragon House, 2008), 427.

22. Henry Shue focuses on "predictable remediable threats" of deprivation of what seems basic to human dignity; Henry Shue, *Basic Human Rights: Subsistence, Affluence, and U.S. Foreign Policy,* 2nd ed. (Princeton, NJ: Princeton University Press, 1996), 33.

23. See Ann-Belinda Preis, "Human Rights as Cultural Practice: An Anthropological Critique," *Human Rights Quarterly* 18, no. 2 (1996): 286–315.

24. See Willis Jenkins, "Religion and Environmental Rights," in *Religion and Human Rights: An Introduction*, John Witte and M. Christian Green, eds. (New York: Oxford University Press, 2011): 330–45.

25. Hollenbach, *The Common Good and Christian Ethics,* 242.

26. Hans Küng, *Global Responsibility: In Search of a New World Ethic* (New York: Crossroad, 1991).

27. For more on the process, including the contributing role of Leonard Swidler's separate initiative for a global ethic, see Hans Küng and Karl-Josef Kuschel, *A Global Ethic: The Declaration of the Parliament of the World's Religions*, special ed. (New York:

Continuum, 1993), 43–53; Leonard Swidler, "Toward a Universal Declaration of a Global Ethic," *Journal of Ecumenical Studies* 42, no. 3 (2007). Sallie King objects that the process was neither dialogical nor representative; see Sallie King, "A Global Ethic in Light of Comparative Religious Ethics," in *Explorations in Global Ethics*, Sumner Twiss and Bruce Grelle, eds. (Boulder, CO: Westview Press, 2000): 118–40.

28. Parliament of the World's Religions, *Declaration toward a Global Ethic* (Chicago, September 1993), preface and section 1. www.parliamentofreligions.org.

29. Ibid., sections 2, 3.

30. William Schweiker, "Whither Global Ethics? Moral Consciousness and Global Cultural Flows," *Journal of Ecumenical Studies* 42, no. 3 (2007): 15.

31. Kathleen Dean Moore and Michael P. Nelson, *Moral Ground: Ethical Action for a Planet in Peril* (San Antonio, TX: Trinity University Press, 2010), xxiii.

32. The Earth Charter, Preamble (emphasis mine).

33. Rockefeller, "Earth Charter," in *The Spirit of Sustainability*, Willis Jenkins, ed. (Great Barrington: Berkshire Publishing, 2010), 115–18; Steven Rockefeller, "Ecological and Social Responsibility: The Making of the Earth Charter," in *Responsibility*, Barbara Darling-Smith, ed. (Lanham, MD: Rowman and Littlefield, 2007).

34. The Earth Charter, Preamble.

35. See Peter Corcoran et al., eds., *The Earth Charter in Action: Toward a Sustainable World* (Amsterdam: KIT Publishers, 2005).

36. Nigel Dower, "The Earth Charter and Global Ethics," *Worldviews: Environment Culture Religion* 8, no. 1 (2004): 19, 25–26. For a pragmatist view of the Earth Charter, see Bryan Norton, "Biodiversity and Environmental Values: In Search of a Universal Earth Ethic," *Biodiversity and Conservation* 9 (2000).

37. Dieter T. Hessel, "Integrated Earth Charter Ethics," *Worldviews: Environment Culture Religion* 8, no. 1 (2004), quoted at 48. See also Gordon D. Kaufman, "The Theological Structure of the Christian Faith and the Feasibility of a Global Ecological Ethic," *Zygon: Journal of Religion and Science* 38, no. 1 (2003).

38. Steven Rockefeller, "Global Interdependence, the Earth Charter, and Christian Faith," in *Earth Habitat: Eco-Injustice and the Church's Response*, Dieter T. Hessel and Larry Rasmussen, eds. (Minneapolis, MN: Fortress, 2001), 103. The phrase "produces its own unique form of religious consciousness" was offered during public remarks at *Journey of the Universe Conference*, Sept. 26, 2011, Yale University.

39. Bron Taylor, *Dark Green Religion: Nature Spirituality and the Planetary Future* (Berkeley: University of California Press, 2009), chap. 9.

40. Mary Evelyn Tucker, *Worldly Wonder: Religions Enter Their Ecological Phase* (Chicago: Open Court, 2003).

41. Brian Swimme and Mary Evelyn Tucker, *Journey of the Universe* (New Haven, CT: Yale University Press, 2011).

42. Martin Robra, "Affirming the Role of Global Movements for Global Ethics," *The Ecumenical Review* 52, no. 4 (2000): 476.

43. Quoted in Robra, "Affirming the Role of Global Movements for Global Ethics," 476. See also Conrad Raiser, "Global Order and Global Ethic," *Concilium*, no. 4 (2001): 19–25.

44. Gayatri Spivak, *Death of a Discipline* (New York: Columbia University Press, 2005), chap. 3.

45. Robra, "Affirming the Role of Global Movements for Global Ethics," 475–76.

46. Emilie Townes, *Womanist Ethics and the Cultural Production of Evil* (New York: Palgrave Macmillan, 2006), 23.

47. Jeffrey Stout, "On Having a Morality in Common," in *Prospects for a Common Morality*, Gene Outka and John Reeder, eds. (Princeton, NJ: Princeton University Press, 1993), 219.

48. Jeffrey Stout, *Ethics after Babel: The Languages of Morals and Their Discontents* (Boston: Beacon Press, 1988), 80–81.

49. Elizabeth Gerle, *In Search of a Global Ethics* (Lund, Sweden: Lund University Press, 1995).

50. Jean Porter, "The Search for a Global Ethic," *Theological Studies* 62, no. 1 (2001): 118.

51. Lisa Cahill, "Toward Global Ethics," *Theological Studies* 63 (2002): 329, 334.

52. Cahill "Toward Global Ethics," 330, 335. See also Lisa Cahill, "Globalization and the Common Good," in *Globalization and Catholic Social Thought*, John Coleman and William Ryan, eds. (Maryknoll, NY: Orbis 2005).

53. David Hollenbach, *The Global Face of Public Faith: Politics, Human Rights, and Christian Ethics* (Washington, DC: Georgetown University Press, 2003), 64–67.

54. Stephen Gardiner, "A Perfect Moral Storm: Climate Change, Intergenerational Ethics, and the Problem of Corruption," *Environmental Values* 15, no. 3 (2006).

55. Daisy Machado, "The Unnamed Woman: Justice, Feminists, and the Undocumented Woman," in *A Reader in Latina Feminist Theology: Religion and Justice,* Maria Pilar Aquino, Daisy Machado, and Jeannette Rodriguez, eds. (Austin: University of Texas Press, 2002): 161–76.

56. *Gaudium et spes,* par. 26.

57. Hollenbach, *Common Good and Christian Ethics*, 221.

58. Hollenbach, *The Global Face of Public Faith: Politics, Human Rights, and Christian Ethics*, 54–69.

59. Hollenbach, *Common Good and Christian Ethics*, 242–43.

60. See Max Stackhouse, "The Common Good, Our Common Goods, and the Uncommon Good in a Globalizing Era," in *In Search of the Common Good*, Dennis McCann and Patrick Miller, eds. (New York: T. and T. Clark, 2005).

61. See John Hart, *Sacramental Commons: Christian Ecological Ethics* (Lanham, MD: Rowman and Littlefield, 2006).

62. Dennis McCann, "The Common Good in Catholic Social Teaching: A Case Study in Modernization," in *In Search of the Common Good*, Dennis McCann and Patrick Miller, eds. (New York: T. and T. Clark, 2005), 126, 143.

63. Robert Schreiter, *The New Catholicity: Theology between the Global and the Local* (Maryknoll, NY: Orbis, 1997), 111.

64. Dennis McCann, "A Second Look at Middle Axioms," *Annual of the Society of Christian Ethics* (1981): 73–96.

65. T. J. Gorringe, *A Theology of the Built Environment* (Cambridge: Cambridge University Press, 2002), 2.

66. Michael Northcott, "The Market, the Multitude, and Metaphysics: Ronald Preston's Middle Way and the Theological Critique of Economic Reason," *Studies in Christian Ethics* 17, no. 2 (2004), 104–17.

67. William Danaher, "Healing Broken Bodies: The Missional Ecclesiology behind J. H. Oldham's Middle Axioms," *Anglican Theological Review* 92, no. 2 (2010).

68. Cahill, "Globalization and the Common Good," 53–54.

69. Michael Walzer, *Thick and Thin: Moral Argument at Home and Abroad* (Notre Dame, IN: University of Notre Dame Press, 2006), 17–18.

70. Rachel Muers, *Living for the Future: Theological Ethics for Coming Generations* (New York: T. and T. Clark, 2008).

71. Andrew Dobson, "Environment Sustainabilities: An Analysis and a Typology," *Environmental Politics* 5, no. 3 (1996); Andrew Dobson, *Justice and the Environment: Conceptions of Environmental Sustainability and Dimensions of Social Justice* (Oxford: Oxford University Press, 1998).

72. This section draws from Willis Jenkins, "Sustainability Theory," in *The Spirit of Sustainability,* Willis Jenkins, ed. (Great Barrington, MA: Berkshire Publishing, 2010): 380–84; Willis Jenkins, "Sustainability," in *Grounding Religion: A Field Guide to the Study of Religion and Ecology*, Whitney Bauman et al., eds. (New York: Routledge, 2011): 96–112.

73. Daniel Maguire and Larry L. Rasmussen, *Ethics for a Small Planet: New Horizons on Population, Consumption, and Ecology* (Albany: SUNY Press, 1998), 67.

74. Robert H. Nelson, "Sustainability, Efficiency, and God: Economic Values and the Sustainability Debate," *Annual Review of Ecology and Systematics* 26 (1995): 54.

75. IUCN, UNEP, and WWF, "Caring for the Earth: A Strategy for Sustainable Living," (Gland, Switzerland: 1991).

76. Robert Solow, "Sustainability: An Economist's Perspective," in *Economics of the Environment: Selected Readings*, Robert Dorfman and Nancy Dorfman, eds. (New York: W. W. Norton, 1993).

77. Quoted in W. M. Adams, "The Future of Sustainability: Re-Thinking Environment and Development in the Twenty-First Century" (paper presented at the IUCN Renowned Thinkers Meeting, 2006).

78. Donella H. Meadows, *The Limits to Growth: A Report for the Club of Rome's Project on the Predicament of Mankind* (New York: Universe Books, 1972).

79. Report of the UN Conference on the Human Environment (Stockholm 1972), Principles 2 and 3.

80. The Cocoyoc Declaration (Cocoyoc Mexico, Oct. 12, 1974), UN/Doc. A/C.2/292.

81. IUCN, UNEP, and WWF, "World Conservation Strategy" (Gland, Switzerland: 1980), chap. 1. See Sharachchandram Lele, "Sustainable Development: A Critical Review," *World Development* 19, no. 6 (1991).

82. See David Hallman, "Climate Change and Ecumenical Work on Sustainable Community," in *Earth Habitat: Eco-Injustice and the Church's Response*, Dieter T. Hessel and Larry L. Rasmussen, eds. (Minneapolis, MN: Fortress Press, 2001).

83. The first use of sustainability to unite conservationists and economic development advocates may have been in the Cocoyoc Declaration (Mexico, 1974).

84. Peter W. Bakken et al., *Ecology, Justice, and Christian Faith: A Critical Guide to the Literature* (Westport, CT: Greenwood Press, 1995), 9ff.

85. World Commission on Environment and Development, *Our Common Future* (New York: Oxford University Press, 1987), 43.

86. See Chris Sneddon et al., "Sustainable Development in a Post-Brundtland World," *Ecological Economics* 57, no. 2 (2006).

87. D. G. Victor, "Recovering Sustainable Development," *Foreign Affairs* 85, no. 1 (2006).

88. See Larry Rasmussen, "Christianity and Sustainable Communities," in *The Encyclopedia of Religion and Nature*, Bron Taylor, ed. (New York: Thoemmes Continuum, 2005).

89. See Alan Holland, "Sustainability," in *A Companion to Environmental Philosophy*, Dale Jamieson, ed. (Oxford: Blackwell, 2003); Micheal Jacobs, "Sustainable Development as a Contested Concept," in *Fairness and Futurity*, Andrew Dobson, ed. (Oxford: Oxford University Press, 1999); Andrew Dobson, *Justice and the Environment: Conceptions of Environmental Sustainability and Theories of Distributive Justice* (Oxford: Oxford University Press, 1998), chap. 2; Herman E. Daly, "Toward Some Operational Principles of Sustainable Development," *Ecological Economics* 2, no. 1 (1990); Robert Costanza and Herman E. Daly, "Natural Capital and Sustainable Development," *Conservation Biology* 6, no. 1 (1992).

90. See Herman E. Daly, "Toward Some Operational Principles of Sustainable Development," *Ecological Economics* 2, no. 1 (1990).

91. Joan Martinez-Alier, "Ecological Distribution Conflicts and Indicators of Sustainability," *International Journal of Political Economy* 34, no. 1 (2004). Amartya Kumar Sen, *Development as Freedom* (New York: Knopf, 1999). See Sneddon et al., "Sustainable Development in a Post-Brundtland World."

92. Bob Pepperman Taylor, "Comments on Sustainability," in *The Moral Austerity of Environmental Decision Making: Sustainability, Democracy, and Normative Argument in Policy and Law*, John Robert Gillroy and Joe Bowersox, eds. (Durham, NC: Duke University Press, 2002); Julianne Lutz Newton and Eric Freyfogle, "Sustainability: A Dissent," *Conservation Biology* 19, no. 1 (2005); John Robert Gillroy, "Sustainability: Restricting the Policy Debate," in *The Moral Austerity of Environmental Decision Making: Sustainability, Democracy, and Normative Argument in Policy and Law*, John Robert Gillroy and Joe Bowersox, eds. (Durham, NC: Duke University Press, 2002).

93. Clare Palmer, "Some Problems with Sustainability," *Studies in Christian Ethics* 7, no. 1 (1994).

94. Aidan Davison, "Ruling the Future? Heretical Reflections on Technology and Other Secular Religions of Sustainability," *Worldviews: Global Religions, Culture, and*

Ecology 12, no. 2–3 (2008). Aidan Davison, *Technology and the Contested Meanings of Sustainability* (Albany: SUNY Press, 2001), 32–38.

95. Joachim Radkau, *Nature and Power: A Global History of the Environment*, Thomas Dunlap, trans. (Washington, DC: Cambridge University Press, 2008), 148.

96. John Robinson, "Squaring the Circle? Some Thoughts on the Idea of Sustainable Development," *Ecological Economics* 48 (2004): 382.

97. Brian Barry, "Sustainability and Intergenerational Justice," in *Environmental Ethics: An Anthology* (Malden, MA: Blackwell, 2003), 492, 493.

98. Mary Midgley, *Utopias, Dolphins and Computers: Problems of Philosophical Plumbing* (New York: Routledge, 2000), 129. See also Mary Midgley, "Sustainability and Moral Pluralism," *Ethics and the Environment* 1, no. 1 (1996).

99. Sneddon et al., "Sustainable Development in a Post-Brundtland World"; R. Paehlke, "Sustainability as a Bridging Concept," *Conservation Biology* 19, no. 1 (2005).

CHAPTER FOUR

Sustainability Science and the Ethics of Wicked Problems

✦

Learn to do good, seek justice. . . . Come now, let us argue it out, says the Lord. . . .

Isaiah 1:17–8

Truth grows up from earth and righteousness peers down from heaven.

Psalm 85:11

Over the last three chapters I have offered reasons to resist the cosmological temptation to do ethics from religious worldviews in order to develop a pluralist, problem-based approach. In this chapter I argue the other side: that, in order to face the most complex problems, a pragmatic strategy needs the cosmological facility often found in religious thought.[1] Here I contend with environmental pragmatists who disdain calls for changing worldviews and ignore religious communities in their attempt to build consensus on science-based policy solutions. Their sort of pragmatism, I argue, seems poorly equipped to meet the most difficult problems because it seems captive to ethical incompetency and social injustice. Problems that exceed a culture's ethical competencies threaten the sciences that research them because societies cannot interpret environmental feedback into revised patterns of action. A science-based, problem-focused ethic of sustainability needs the process of managing problems to drive cultural transformation. It needs communities that can rethink inherited ways of life and invent new cultural possibilities.

Consider the problem of managing the Chesapeake Bay. Agriculture and development throughout its watershed have driven ecological changes, including eutrophication and biodiversity loss, manifest most visibly in the collapse of commercial oyster stocks, loss of habitat for native species, and invasion of nonnative species. How can the diverse and factious political community that inhabits this watershed recognize common goods and forge shared responsibilities? What role should science play in setting objectives? Complicating those questions is the reflexivity of human and environmental systems. As oyster stocks collapse, coastal housing development becomes more important, driving further ecological change and changing social goals. How can a changing watershed community deliberate over the future of a changing bay?

In the last chapter I presented sustainability as a concept for negotiating moral pluralism. However, a pragmatic sustainability ethic must overcome the limitations of working within dysfunctional and unjust moral cultures. Without attention to structures of power and the way those structures are supported by popular ethical ideas, accommodating moral pluralism can amount to accommodating social domination. What if the community attempting to manage a watershed is racist and greedy? What if a culture is too anthropocentric and ignorant to rightly understand its problems? A pragmatic strategy would be complicit with social injustice and ecological catastrophe if it were constrained to work with the moral mainstream of corrupt cultures. In those cases, a science-based ethic of sustainability needs facilities of cultural transformation. When religious projects operate as culture-transforming practices, they open imaginative possibilities from cultural inheritances that become important to a broad problem-solving ethic. In this chapter I argue that a science-based pragmatic ethic needs religious imaginations and cosmological questions to make pluralist societies more capable of taking responsibility for their powers.

I do not argue here that science needs a religious foundation or must be guided by transcendent values. I claim that the sciences of sustainability need to incorporate the capacities of cultural transformation that religious communities sometimes cultivate. That implicates the sciences in tasks of cultural engagement that they usually prefer to leave to other disciplines. Yet the sciences of sustainability depend on learning from problems as societies manage them, and so depend on societies learning to manage well. Religious reform projects can (sometimes) demonstrate how to make moral sense of humanity's changing participation in earth systems. Used adroitly, worldviews and narrative interpretations of the changing human context can facilitate adaptive social learning by helping public debates over sustainability host the deeper questions at stake. When that happens, religious ethics finds itself in a newly productive relation with the environmental sciences.

At stake in this chapter is the role of culture in the science of sustainability, and with it, the relation of the natural sciences to the moral humanities. This chapter sketches a way for environmental sciences, interdisciplinary ethics, and the religious humanities to work together to create capacities of adaptive learning. After explaining the ethical entanglement of sustainability science, it addresses tensions between science-based management and cultural transformation. Is sustainability about managing problems or transforming cultures? I attempt to have it both ways by showing how to connect problem-solving and cultural change such that societies learn new ways of life from the process of confronting their most difficult problems. I explore several cases where religious communities have helped make that connection, illustrating why an inclusive justice and expansive cosmological imagination are necessary conditions for learning an ethic of sustainability.

ETHICAL SCIENCES

Ecology is sometimes treated as a moral worldview as well as a natural science. Environmentalists often invoke ecology as a normative view of nature, characterized by a holistic order against which much human action appears disruptive. In popular culture as well as the environmental humanities, and especially in religious ethics, "ecology" first names a worldview shaped by appreciation and care for the complex relations supporting natural states such as stability, balance, or beauty. Secondarily, it is a natural science that researches the principles of nature's economy and the problems of human interference, thus providing information needed for properly "ecological" policies.[2] Invoking the dictum of Aldo Leopold, famous ecologist and moralist, buttresses that view: "A thing is right when it tends to preserve the integrity, stability, and beauty of the biotic community. It is wrong when it tends otherwise."[3] For many that functions as a little summa of the morality established by ecological science. An ethic of sustainability begins, in this view, by adopting "the ecological worldview" and following its natural laws.

However, establishing that worldview from the practice of ecological science proves elusive. Researchers find it difficult to establish structuring principles of biotic communities, let alone the evaluative concepts of stability, integrity, beauty, or balance. Flux and chaos seem just as present in ecological systems, which makes it difficult to predict change and impossible to establish normative states of nature. In fact, scientists debate whether ecology can ever produce predictive laws about how ecosystems function. Perhaps ecology is merely a discipline of case studies, distinguished by local descriptive investigations of particular biotic communities.[4] If so, then ecological science cannot supply an ecological worldview because it cannot provide a picture of natural order that could also function as a model of moral order. The science of ecology cannot supply moral foundations.[5]

Ecology is nonetheless ethical. Insofar as it is a science for researching and managing problems that matter to human survival and flourishing, it is a goal-directed and value-laden endeavor. Most ecological research is organized in response to urgent social problems related to changing environmental systems. Analogous to medicine, ecology is a science-based practice of understanding and managing problems of biotic health. Its facts arise within practices that presuppose evaluative commitments.[6] Ecology is an ethical science, then, not because it supplies a worldview but because it is a practice for confronting problems that matter to basic human interests. Resolving those problems depends on science producing knowledge that matters, both for pursuing those interests and also for critically evaluating them. As in medicine, that depends on ecological managers working from evidence grounded in good research—rather than "ecological" intuitions about what makes for biotic health.[7]

I have just observed, however, that ecology lacks an account of normative states of nature and cannot supply predictive laws. How then can it manage environmental systems in better or worse ways? Responsibility for problems requires some predictive capacity of how communities and systems will change under different management policies, as well as some evaluative criteria for sorting desirable and undesirable changes. For ecological science to help the Chesapeake watershed decide whether to cull invasive mute swans, for example, it must be capable of explaining how a management action would affect the ecological community and why the outcome would be a good one. Ecologist Oswald Schmitz helps establish predictive capacity in a science without laws. If ecologists consider systems as open theaters in which evolutionary acts play out, then they can identify "the ground rules for the improvisation" of organisms and species, and so explain emergent properties of a system even without predictive laws.[8] Then, like physicians, ecologists can make sufficient predictions to diagnose environmental ailments and prescribe means to restore health.[9] Environmental scientists may even, like physicians, take themselves to have duties of public advocacy, promoting health as an important goal in the public mind and commending its component behaviors.[10]

Evaluative criteria inherent within the practice of ecological science are more difficult to find. Unlike medicine, the goals of ecological management involve a wider scope of controversy. The meaning of health varies across human bodies much less than across biotic communities, so controversies over the goals and values of medical practice are more contained. What does

"health" mean for an ecosystem? Does it refer to ecosystem services ame-
nable to human welfare? Does it include qualities of biodiversity for their
own sake? Does it protect interests of nonhuman species or consider the
future of evolutionary systems? The basic goals that constitute the organizing problems for this science may range from simple human survival to protection of biodiversity to preservation of species and landscapes.[11] Without
inherent criteria, ecological science needs to conduct research in a way that
helps broader society to critically evaluate the goals that shape what counts
as an ecological problem, and so, in turn, what the science must do.

The idea of sustainability hosts that evaluative deliberation by functioning as a proxy goal for interpreting and managing ecological problems.
"Sustainability science" has begun to emerge as a way of doing science in
response to the problems created by anthropogenic change, in collaboration
with multiple disciplinary approaches to interpreting human systems.[12] The
idea of sustainability here convenes an intersection of the natural sciences
and moral humanities to interpret new challenges. The sort of problems
that sustainability science attempts to understand do not permit separate
roles for the sciences and the humanities. Understanding a problem like
biodiversity loss in the Chesapeake needs fundamental scientific research as
well as critical reflection on the social patterns driving the problem and the
cultural interests constructing it. Sustainability science aims to draw on the
range of disciplines needed to support a science-based approach to making
societies more competent to understand and manage the problems of their
own power.[13]

Involving science in cultural reform creates uneasy tensions for an institution whose credibility depends on its methodological distance from values
and politics. But in conditions of pervasive human influence in ecological
systems those tensions are unavoidable. Research into the problems that
matter to this science cannot help but participate in cultural responses that
evaluate what a problem means, in turn shifting how an ecological system
functions, and then perhaps shifting how that culture understands itself.
Better, then, for sustainability science to explicitly and carefully work with
those tensions than attempt to conceal them.

On this score leading scientists have been ambivalent: they often affirm
the goal-driven character of sustainability science but seem unsure of how
to treat cultural uncertainty about those goals. Consider Jane Lubchenco's
call for a "new social contract for science," proposed while president of the
American Association of the Advancement of Science. The extent of human
power over the planet requires science "to address the most urgent needs of
society, in proportion to their importance," with a view to guiding human
action. As society's needs have changed with its extensive powers, it needs

a science that can investigate all dimensions of the "grand experiment with our planet"—including economic and political dimensions. Science, she says, must produce "knowledge to manage the planet" in ways that meet basic social needs.[14]

But how should science function in conditions of uncertainty over what needs are basic? To help societies understand and meet their most important problems, science needs to connect knowledge for managing with critical reflection on how and why we are managing. Doing "ecology for a crowded planet," says a cohort of leading environmental scientists, requires investigating how human agency shapes ecological systems, assessing which ecological services societies can afford to lose or technologically replace, and articulating the policy responses needed to meet criteria of sustainability.[15] Yet in the last chapter we saw competing models of sustainability and debate over its meaning. So how can the science of managing the planet incorporate that uncertainty in ways that cultivate better responsibility?

Sustainability science is what Silvio Funtowicz and Jerome Ravetz call a "post-normal science." It tries to solve problems that involve epistemic and ethical uncertainties. If the problems of sustainability science arise from planetary experiments in which human management is both inescapable and irreducibly controversial, then science must develop methods to conduct credible research in conditions in which the criteria for good management remain unknown and controversial. Managing the Chesapeake Bay represents this sort of problem: science must credibly investigate how humans are reshaping ecological systems in the midst of political controversy over how to interpret those changes and over what sustainability should mean. Funtowicz and Ravetz criticize Lubchenco for not admitting ethical uncertainty into her manifesto for sustainability science, as if the "values" character of this science was merely that it produces knowledge for (uncontroversial) social goals. Its task is rather more elusive: to produce knowledge that helps societies interpret and reassess the goals of its pursuit.[16]

Unlike "normal science," ethics cannot be bracketed into cultural moments before and after research. Moral learning is unavoidably part of the research of sustainability science. "The practice of research must of necessity become a form of social learning," write researchers reflecting on the management of European watersheds. If watersheds function both as ecological processes and political processes, then doing science for maintaining a sustainable biophysical system includes participation in a broad political process of deliberation over what that means.[17] Working on problems for which it is unclear what would count as an acceptable solution requires sustainability science to open cultural space in which societies can reflect on the goals organizing its research. The humanities thus become increasingly important to the practice of ecological research. Not only is culture an increasingly significant part of the phenomena science must interpret in order to understand environmental change; science is also engaged in adapting social behavior to its changing context. An important criterion for the credibility of research, then, is methodological inclusion of cultural and ethical criticism.[18]

The emergent ecological role of human power thus makes for uneasy intimacies among science and ethics. As ecological systems increasingly come under human management (accidental or purposeful), the conceit of separated knowledges of fact and value can no longer be maintained. Science can no longer play the role of supplying natural facts to policy processes that then interpret their normative meaning. Sustainability science operates after the exhaustion of nature as a positivist concept for insulating facts from values. For science that means unavoidable engagement with moral culture. For ethics that means the end of the "natural" as a useful evaluative category.

The stage thus seems set for religion and science to rediscover overlapping interests. After two centuries of mutual separation (the boundary skirmishes only affirming their mutual territories), the convention that religion and science represent separate, nonoverlapping magisteria cannot work where research problems come constructed in practices that carry interpretations of the meaning of life.[19] Medical science, where so many problems arise at the horizon of death and its meaning, already recognizes the need for integrated knowledges. That is one reason why biomedical ethics has hosted productive engagements of scientists, philosophers, and religionists. An analogous field is emerging for the sustainability sciences, in which problems take shape from responsibilities for social survival, for the existence of other species, and for the future of life's evolution.

The pervasive human power of the anthropocene exhausts nature as a neutral standard at the same moment that it makes ecology the scene of momentous moral decisions. Writing against the view that ecological science can on its own set the meaning of sustainability, biologist David Lodge and historian Christopher Hamlin observe that "it is not a matter then of doing things nature's way, but rather of deciding which of nature's ways or forms we want to establish, maintain, restore or change."[20] When scientists write that "humanity's dominance of Earth means that we cannot escape responsibility for managing the planet," as have Peter Vitousek and Jane Lubchenco, then religious ethicists like Larry Rasmussen are right to see "the ascendancy of ethics."[21] The sustainability sciences and the moral humanities rise together in significance, because taking responsibility for humanity's planetary experiment requires deciding on basic values and interpreting the meaning of humanity's role in earth. There is no way to research that experiment without participating in it, so no way for science to avoid responsibility for what humanity chooses to maintain, restore, and change. Geologist Paul Reitan therefore argues that sustainability science carries a mandate to transform cultural worldviews.[22] In that case scientific practice absorbs a cultural task that has often been considered (and avoided) as a basically religious enterprise.

Those are welcome conclusions for religious ethicists who enjoy new-found relevance to scientific research, but underscoring the moral and cultural dimensions of ecological research seems perilous to the integrity and authority of science. Research on climate change and biodiversity is already subject to hostile social reception and ideological misconstruals. Affirming its reliance on uncertain ethical ideas may make its findings seem arbitrary, thus making sustainability science even more liable to charges of ideological capture. Inviting the humanities (especially religious ethics) into the practice of science would seem to embed science in intractable culture wars.

Two counterpoints limit that liability. First, recognizing that science participates in moral culture does not reduce its findings to arbitrary notions. It presses science to include other disciplinary methods in constructing the problems it researches. Scientific method, including rigorous effort to bracket commitments and eliminate bias, remains regulative. Just because facts about reality are always produced through valued commitments does not mean that their reliability cannot be tested. It rather suggests employing more disciplinary methods to criticize and improve the reliability of scientific knowledge.[23] Indeed, by assuming some ethical uncertainty about its social mission, science-based management practice can insist on working from problem-driven evidence rather than general intuitions.

Second, science evaluates and reshapes moral culture. As it integrates methods of cultural criticism, sustainability science can research how social values, goals, and practices affect ecological systems. Explaining and predicting how systems function under different policy conditions tests the performance and feedback of various choices. The findings may not be definitive for which choice is better (the Chesapeake community may prefer coastal housing over oysters), but its findings force society to take responsibility for the ecological implications of its commitments. So science-based research contributes to the formation of a broad ethic of sustainability by making knowledge of how ecological systems function a reflection of how moral culture functions.[24] Sustainability science helps produce a culture of sustainability by depicting the ecological consequences of our ways of living.

Ecological restoration projects are a good example. Projects to restore a degraded ecosystem to a previous state or desired functionality require evidence-driven scientific management. Yet these projects include irreducibly evaluative decisions about their goals and criteria. Without an unchanging natural ideal, what benchmarks should be used assess successful restoration? Which species to introduce and which to extirpate? What priority for values of beauty, wildness, diversity, and ecological services? Ongoing research and management portrays the outcome of those decisions, perhaps leading to critical reassessment. The restoration process therefore produces knowledge both about the system and about the values guiding its management. When ecological restoration projects involve wide civic participation, the process may also generate new values and commitments. Involving citizens in removing invasive plants, counting species, or daylighting streambeds generates a "culture of nature."[25] So a science-based practice generates moral culture as citizens participate in sustaining the ecological communities in which they live. The experience may even drive cultural transformation. Scientist Robert Jordan argues that the public experiments of restoration ecology should be understood as "performative ontologies," functionally similar to religious rituals in which participants enact and narrate what is sacred in their world. Science should embrace this "sacralization of research," argues Jordan, and "make science an occasion for sacrament and the creation of higher values."[26] Religious ethicist Gretel Van Wieren has recently developed those suggestions, showing how a framework of science-based restoration as "public spiritual practice" can provide a forum for hosting and deliberating the many controversies over restoration projects.[27]

Restoration ecology thus exemplifies the general hope of sustainability science: that wide cultural involvement in problem-driven science can cultivate the ethic needed for societies to meet their challenges. If incorporated into the practice of managing problems, ethical uncertainty and moral pluralism need not paralyze society but can help drive adaptive learning. Here we come to a crucial question about how much cultural change the practice of sustainability science can expect to generate. Does adequate adaptive change require transforming cultural worldviews, or can a pluralist ethic of management generate satisfactory solutions to the problems at hand?

The pragmatic strategy of religious ethics that I have been developing would seem to prefer the latter, but here I argue (against other pragmatists) that a sustainability ethic needs capacities of cultural transformation opened by cosmological thinking. It does not need to begin from a particular religion or worldview, but in order to cultivate competency for complex problems it does need the capacities of cultural critique opened by reflection on fundamental narratives and ideas. The practices of managing problems and restoring ecosystems must be able to interpret and change perverse, dysfunctional, or unjust cultural practices. That requires capacities of critical reflection and cultural dissent. An adaptive ethic must include a dimension of what Martin Luther King called "maladjustment."[28] An experimental pragmatism, developed from science-based interaction with earth, needs the transformative capacity of a prophetic pragmatism.

ENVIRONMENTAL PRAGMATISM AND CULTURAL TRANSFORMATION

In chapter 2 I argued for a pragmatic strategy of theological ethics, responsive to concrete problems and adaptive within received traditions. In the field of environmental ethics a similar line of pragmatism has emerged, also objecting to cosmological modes of ethics, also oriented to specific problems and lived moral culture. Ethics need not start by revising beliefs about nature and humanity, these ethicists argue; it can start from problems arising in the scientific practices of managing for sustainability and seek broad cultural consensus. However, by focusing ethics on incremental policy improvements, a pragmatic approach seems to surrender criticism of power structures and bad ideologies, thereby weakening possibilities for deeper cultural changes that the most challenging problems may require. Critics therefore worry that a pragmatic ethic of sustainability becomes an ethos of accommodation that cannot challenge incompetent or perverse cultures. A pragmatic approach must then prove that possibilities for transformative social change reside in the experimental process of confronting problems. It needs to show possibilities for the sort of moral invention that religious reform projects can generate.

In spite of their calls to engage lived moral culture, however, environmental pragmatists serially overlook religious communities and faith-involved practices. The absence may be related to the association of religion with the cosmological style of ethics that pragmatists reject.[29] Religious communities tend to highlight beliefs about nature, God, and reality when explaining their commitments, and religious ethicists usually focus on revising beliefs and worldviews. But pragmatists think that "urgent calls for new environmental worldviews and radically revised ontological schemes" exacerbate metaethical paralysis in the ethics of sustainability. They "only lead ethicists' attention away from the resources already present within our shared moral and political traditions."[30] Cosmological preoccupations explain why "it is difficult to see what practical effect the field of environmental ethics has had on the formation of environmental policy."[31] Entanglement with religion may explain why. Bryan Norton argues that because environmental ethics took shape in the legacy of Lynn White's ecological critique of Christianity, even when ethicists were indifferent to the religious debates they followed White's assumption that environmental ethics must begin by reassessing beliefs about the human place in nature.[32]

So the pragmatist inattention to religious culture may represent something more principled than the reflexive disdain for religion sometimes found in the sciences. The pragmatists object to a method of ethics focused on beliefs and worldviews because they think it alienates moral reasoning from science-based problem solving. Since religious responses to environmental problems often adopt a cosmological form of response, they seem to represent just what the pragmatists think wrong with environmental ethics in general: they propound foundational ideals that do not motivate a broad public or help warrant realistic policy changes, and so stand irrelevant to the mandate of ecological research and management. Distant from lived moral culture and from concrete environmental problems, cosmological approaches do little to repair the rupture of science and culture; indeed they seem to tempt ecology to become "religious" in its mode of cultural engagement. Environmental pragmatists want the ethics of sustainability to focus less on changing worldviews and more on building science-based support for solutions to shared problems with the moral resources already held by citizens.

Environmental pragmatists thus introduce their ethic of contextual problem-solving by pressing the dilemma between deep cultural change and practical political engagement. They want ethics to become more practical in two ways: (1) by working with available moral resources, (2) for the sake of resolving specific policy problems. Andrew Light thus asks ethicists to "work within traditional moral psychologies and ethical theories that people already have" in order to create links between existing moralities and the cases that matter to agents working on environmental problems. Practical ethics entails working with the commitments that people already hold in order to generate "creative ways to persuade a variety of people" to adopt solutions to real problems.[33] Instead of developing a philosophy of nature, ethics should help communities resolve their problems. If we begin with environmental policy dilemmas, say Ben Minteer and Robert Manning, we can appeal, "in experimental fashion, to the tools of ethical theory in achieving a resolution."[34] In this "toolkit" view, ethics puts cultural values to work for "the practical dilemmas of forming a moral consensus around environmental issues."[35] A public need not share beliefs in order to initiate practical action. Norton's "convergence hypothesis" supposes that adherents of diverse environmental worldviews will, by participating in processes of managing specific issues, converge on similar policies.[36]

This approach to sustainability, however, seems limited by mainstream cultural values and overdetermined by the way problems arrive already framed within background social structures. What if a culture's moral inheritances can no longer be trusted? A culture might be so enthralled with economic growth, and so ideologically buffered from the relations with God or nature that could interrupt that thrall, that it no longer recognizes value beyond markets. What if policy dilemmas arrive into debate already distorted by powerful institutions resisting change? A pragmatist attempt to mediate conflict among poor alternatives would just perpetuate structural dysfunction. "Approaching environmental problems and conflicts with the open-minded, respectful, and practical disposition suggested by pragmatists," argues Robyn Eckersley, "can be positively foolhardy when there are more powerful forces arrayed around the negotiating table."[37] Pragmatism seems innocently malleable by whatever ideas and institutions hold social power.

Still worse, what if a culture's moral traditions constrain it from understanding its challenges because those very traditions lie at the root of the problems? A culture organized around the assumed good of human expansion, or by otherworldly visions, may need to question the narrative by which it is living. Eckersley thinks that the tradition of liberal humanism stands on an unjustified exclusion of nature from moral and political standing, the consequences of which show up in environmental destruction. Others point to instrumentalist metaphors of nature, religious immaterialism, or neoliberal economics. Addressing sustainability problems thus warrants reconsideration of inherited cultural worlds, but pragmatism tends "to take too much as given, to avoid any critical inquiry into 'the big picture' and to work with rather than against the grain of existing structures and discourses."[38] If our moral culture is dysfunctional, then ontological reflection and a new worldview would seem requisite, while contextual problem-solving would appear complicit with catastrophe.

Pragmatists employ three kinds of response to questions about cultural competence—two unconvincing and one more promising. First, they try to vindicate optimism in current moral culture. Minteer and Manning, for example, conduct a survey of values among Vermont's citizenry in order to show convergence on forest management policies. They can then appeal to John Dewey's "faith in the capacity of the intelligence of the common man to respond with common sense to the free play of facts and ideas" in order to suppose that pluralist moral culture will eventually yield decent environmental policies.[39] Those who do not share faith in common sense or the free play of facts, however, find that appeal unconvincing. Vermont's forested landscape may inspire confidence, but not Appalachia's mountain-top moonscapes or Mississippi's cancer alley. To what can ethics appeal when a public approves policies that lead to ecological collapse or social injustice?

Environmental justice projects often must challenge outcomes of the "free play of facts and ideas" within unjust societies. In order to protect themselves from toxic outcomes of mainstream common sense, these projects often appeal to foundational principles of justice and make ontological claims about the ecological dimensions of human personhood. That may be why the pragmatists generally overlook them, but as problem-driven forms of a local sustainability ethic, protesting dominant constructions of sustainability issues, they should be central to the pragmatists' account. Considering pragmatism and social power, I turn to environmental justice projects in the next chapter. My point here is that ignoring strange projects and minority moral communities makes a contextual ethic vulnerable to social injustice and oddly selective of the experience that counts. When a state is 96 percent white, as is Vermont, appealing to "intricate portraits of the region's complex and evolving moral geography," as do Minteer and Manning, could mean legitimating a landscape morality that excludes strangers and exports toxins.[40] Moral appeals to place are ambiguous. The structural racism in American landscapes of toxic risk warns of the potential for celebrations of local moral geography to drift toward "ecofascism."[41] When Norton roots sustainability ethics in a community's impulse to perpetuate "place-based values" as a "community performative act" of political identity and self-definition, what keeps sustainability from perpetuating exclusion and domination?[42]

Pragmatists sometimes meet the difficulty of unpalatable moral values with a second tack: narrowing the range of citizens that the pluralist experiment includes. Norton's convergence hypothesis stipulates that it is the values of "environmentalists" that will eventually converge on shared policy objectives.[43] Light refers to "the environmentally concerned" as the participants who matter.[44] When faced with objectionable moral agents, therefore, an ethicist can exclude them from the problem-solving community. Light does this in response to the specter of fascism while Norton excludes narrow-minded anthropocentrists. Holmes Rolston rightly objects that this tack vindicates a pragmatic strategy by selecting only approved participants in pluralist problem solving: those who are reasonable, just, and environmentally sensitive. Such narrowing does not avoid metaethics; it simply defers it to an undefended account of the criteria for admission. What counts as reasonable and environmentally sensitive, wryly observes Rolston, seems to rely on Rolston's own (ontological) theory of intrinsic value. Norton's notion of the problem-solving community assumes that some participants hold an ecocentric philosophy of the sort that Rolston constructs.[45] Pragmatism thus seems to rely on the political presence of theories produced by the ontological strategy it rejects. Even if that borrowing can be defended, how do narrowed communities of select problem-solvers exercise a reform influence on the rest of moral culture?

The pragmatists offer a third way of answering the criticism that their strategy cannot generate cultural reform: sometimes they suggest that the exercise of solving problems itself generates better relations of nature and culture. Support for this meliorist experimentalism also traces to Dewey, who held that a democratic people can democratically learn from interaction with its environment, simultaneously adapting itself and its environment.[46] Environmental pragmatists argue that sustainability problems are an occasion for adaptive learning from environments through adaptive management of them. Norton provides the most robust account of sustainability as meliorist experimentation by presenting adaptive ecological management as a process that generates both the understanding and the commitments needed to continue resolving problems: "the epistemology of adaptive management thus provides for gradual progress and improvement of both our belief system and our preferences and values, by using experience to triangulate between temporarily accepted beliefs and values."[47] Adaptive learning implies a provisionality and fallibilism in received cultural ideas, which can be revised through feedback from experience. As communities "progressively improve their natural and built environments," writes Minteer, "new knowledge and novel values can emerge from reflective and well-planned human activity."[48]

Managing problems, in other words, transforms culture. The pragmatists thus take an irenic stance toward moral pluralism, scientific ignorance, and political uncertainty, seeking to make each a source for cultural change. How much change can their approach generate? Is it enough to make science and culture capable of meeting our most difficult sustainability problems?

MANAGING CHANGE

Adaptive management usually refers to an integration of research and policy that allows researchers to investigate ecological systems in concert with management plans that influence how they work. In 1978 ecologist C. S. Holling proposed it as a method for researching the multiple uncertainties involved in natural resource management. Holling was concerned that management practices incapable of working with uncertainties were imperiling ecological systems by decreasing their resiliency.[49] By deploying several policy schemes at once over large scales, scientists could assess how ecological systems function under different conditions of human influence. Resource managers could then adapt policies to find the most effective ways of meeting social goals.[50]

Holling initially described a method for conducting research for a narrow set of research problems, but adaptive management has since been used as a model of social learning. In a book reflecting on the Columbia River watershed, Kai Lee presents adaptive management as a way to use an ecosystem as a policy laboratory for the whole civic community. At the broadest scale, the model supposes that economies and cultural patterns of inhabitation are environmental experiments. If science can create reliable ways to learn from those experiments, it helps make the search for sustainability into an experience-driven process of cultural reflection.[51] Holling affirms that extension of the adaptive management concept, agreeing that it might rescue the idea of sustainability by demonstrating how its ideological plurality and openness can support an integrative mode of science connected to a wide scene of social learning.[52]

Holling writes that adaptive management opens a view of nature and society at once more integrated and more dynamic than he originally suspected. Because ecological and social systems now seem more unpredictable and more reflexive than he imagined in the 1970s, Holling has come to argue for "policies and actions that not only satisfy social objectives but also achieve continually modified understanding of the evolving conditions."[53] Doing so may require dimensions of critical cultural analysis, including rethinking metaphors of nature and theorizing the relation of environmental and cultural change.[54] In other words, managing sustainability problems so as to learn from them may require philosophical and metaethical analyses of the sort that pragmatists seem to rule out. Is there a role for "cosmological" thinking in science-based experimental problem solving?

Norton thinks that adaptive management can generate new metaphors and ideas without resorting to cosmology or religion. Theories and value commitments arise from satisfactory responses to sustainability problems marked by descriptive and ethical uncertainty. Norton thus marries a post-normal view of sustainability science to the epistemology of American pragmatism. Facts and values arise together as a political community revises its understandings and its goals as it learns from policy responses to problems. Over time, the community discovers more adequate guidelines and descriptions and comes to adopt beliefs and commitments that prove themselves reliable for successful management. For Norton, the point is not to make ethical theory more ecological, but to make the practice of ecology into a form of ethics. The ethics of sustainability, he hopes, "may someday be seen as an important subfield of adaptive management science."[55]

Put that way, adaptive management seems to permit a typically American evasion of philosophy.[56] By offering a philosophy of management rather than an ecological ethic, Norton offers an experience-driven epistemology of social progress, rather than a moral philosophy by which to criticize society's values and practices. Norton can be optimistic about ameliorative

resolution of moral disagreement because he holds that as citizens with dif-
fering views participate in a broad process of managing sustainability problems, they adapt their views as they learn.[57] The upshot is characteristically
pragmatist: an ethic of sustainability should avoid ontological foundations
and adversarial social criticism in order to develop compelling experiments,
on the notion that moral pluralism will be constrained by the reality that is
cumulatively tested by experience.

Learning from the experience of environmental change requires minimal claims about reality or challenges to established interests. It merely
holds that humans shape ecological systems and that over time cultures
transmit better or worse ways of living within those systems. Ethics need
not threaten established powers or revise conventional worldviews; it need
only invite citizens into a reliable process for considering how a society
is shaping its environment.[58] If interests must be adjusted or worldviews
changed, the management process provides the process for doing so. As
a community faces problems that pose threats to perpetuating its way of
life into the future—tension between its moral ecology and its physical
ecology—it can clarify and change its moral culture. Adaptive management
thus serves as a reform-oriented progressivism, in which citizens use the
conceptual space of sustainability to respond to problems as "occasions for
reflection, deliberation, and compromise regarding how well the community is living up to its commitments."[59] Adaptive ecological management
functions for adaptive cultural change.

If so, adaptive management may supply a missing cultural function in
societies whose moral wisdom has come apart from its environmental experience. Fikret Berkes, Johan Colding, and Carl Folkes argue that adaptive
management might perform a cultural function in industrial societies akin
to that of traditional ecological knowledge: "a cumulative body of knowledge, practice, and belief, evolving by adaptive processes and handed down
through generations by cultural transmission." Fulfilling an analogous role
in industrialized societies, adaptive management works as a science-based
process for learning over time from ecological systems, and so "can be seen
as a rediscovery of traditional systems of knowledge."[60] Moral adaptation
happens not by expanding the realization of some ideal, but by learning
from experience and aligning beliefs and commitments accordingly. As with
biological evolution, ethical change may not represent "progress" toward
an ultimate goal but rather an adjustment to changed conditions at once
innovative and path dependent. If it succeeds in reproducing a cultural system over time, it proves adaptive. Leopold wrote that "nothing so important as an ethics is ever 'written' . . . it evolves in the minds of a thinking
community."[61] Here lies the rightful legacy of Leopold, argue Norton and

Minteer: not as a radical ecocentric philosopher but as a practical ecologist who demonstrated what a public can and should learn from its experience with its landscape.[62]

Some scientists object to this expansive use of adaptive management, contending that what was conceived as a method for normal scientific experimentation cannot be extended into a model of ethics. Doing so makes science bear too great a role in social change and may shortchange the importance of critical moral reason developed in other cultural arenas—like religion and philosophy. The concept has become so popular, say Gregory et al., that adaptive management is "too often used as a euphemism for environmental management plans that admit to the need for learning in the face of ecological uncertainty."[63] When undisciplined by experimental rigor, adaptive management seems to involve science in exactly what its method attempts to exclude: politics and morality. Schmitz agrees that involving political management in the learning process about environmental problems makes social values part of ecological research. He avers, however, that generating and justifying those values happens in a different cultural domain. Sustainability is the basic objective for adaptive management, Schmitz agrees, but establishing and justifying its meaning happens outside the scientific process. Society must "change its ethical perspective about nature," but that is not something scientists make happen. Managing for sustainability depends on "a realignment of ethical thinking in which market and natural economies are viewed as intertwined and interdependent."[64]

That is a cosmological point: a general ecological perspective seems necessary in order to initiate a science-based social learning process. Recognizing that humanity is in fact running planetary experiments for which it should take better responsibility requires accepting the basic point Leopold labored to establish: societies must recognize themselves as participants in ecological communities. Schmitz is arguing that the ability to learn from adaptive management depends on a prior moral vision. Lee ends his book on a similar note: management ideas are not enough for meeting social problems that "will redefine the place of our species in the natural order." To do so, thinks Lee, capitalist cultures need to rethink relations of prosperity, poverty, and ecology in order to develop "a vision of appropriate human endeavor on the planet we inhabit."[65] Norton's attempt to locate that revisioning process within adaptive management, thinks Lee, just contributes to muddied appropriations of adaptive management as a philosophical metaphor.[66] Successful science-based management depends on cultural reforms which science cannot itself produce.

Schmitz remembers that Leopold also wrote that "no important change in ethics was ever accomplished without an internal change in our intellectual emphasis, loyalties, affections, and convictions. The proof that conservation has not yet touched these foundations of conduct lies in the fact that philosophy and religion have not yet heard of it."[67] Now that philosophy and religion have heard of conservation, perhaps they should take the lead in changing convictions and altering the foundations of conduct? The capacity of society to learn from ecological management seems to depend on shifts in imagination and human understanding—the sort of thing in which philosophy and religion specialize.[68]

When pragmatism excludes cosmological modes of argument, it suppresses forms of cultural reform that it seems to need. Norton's theory of adaptive management seems incapable of seeing the way that political injustice or bad narratives determine environmental experience. If the problems that management tries to solve arise from a massive project of colonial exploitation or human domination over nature, then any learning from experience would support solutions that perpetuate that background ethos of power. To avoid that complicity, ethics may need the religious capacity to reconsider the basic story by which a culture lives.

Consider that from pragmatism we inherit William James's proposal for "war against nature" as a uniting cultural project.[69] "Ecological management" is a slightly gentler metaphor but it still rallies humanity around a project of controlling earth for human benefit. Religious historian Louis Dupré traces the beginning of pragmatist thought in modernist science (expressed in Bacon) and modernist Christianity (expressed in Puritanism), which conspired to create an idea of nature with no inherent ends, save those invested in it by human purpose. So began the socialization of nature into human projects, and with it the very idea that we know nature primarily as a "problem." Science and philosophy "changed into a practical, problem-solving activity accomplished for the purpose of forcing nature to respond," giving rise to "the characteristically modern belief in the unlimited human ability to conquer nature by rational methods with an unshakable confidence in a state of universal happiness that would follow from this conquest." The pragmatist view of humans as tinkering experimenters who learn a sustainability ethic by solving problems appears less benign when situated within that cultural history. Without an alternative narrative that integrates the purpose of human agency with the goods of earth, a problem-solving ethic seems certain to perpetuate disenchantment and domination. However worthy the diverse social goals of sustainability, notes Dupré, "without a common teleology that integrates humanity with nature, the mastery of nature becomes its own end."[70] At a planetary scale, a sustainability ethic modeled on adaptive management seems certain to become a technophilic form of "earth systems engineering," with every problem an opportunity to extend human power further.[71] In that case, as Aidan Davison argues, the discourse of sustainability functions "religiously" to support a domineering story of humans and nature.[72]

Precisely by avoiding religion, environmental pragmatism deprives itself of resources to prevent slipping into an uncritical piety. William French argues that theological modes have a critical advantage over pragmatic strategies because they can diagnose deep cultural pathologies and offer a counter narrative with a different paradigm of agency, integrated into a living sense of creation. French recommends Thomas Berry's new creation story as exemplar.[73] It is not only religionists who see the need for cosmology to shape ecological management. Many scientists have endorsed the Berry-inspired *Journey of the Universe*. They see it as the sort of integrative account of evolutionary history that can provide the participatory worldview needed for societies to begin learning from their sustainability problems.[74] Schmitz's account of ecological management closes by appealing for change in a basic perspective of reality. Lee thinks adaptive management needs an integrated account of humanity in earth's evolution. Berkes, Colding, and Folke observe the importance of a sacred ecology for the adaptive function of tradition in ecological knowledge.[75] Gunderson, Holling, and Light open the case studies in *Barriers and Bridges* with an epigraph from Teilhard de Chardin's *Hymn of the Universe*, suggesting that a problem-oriented sustainability ethic needs cultures that hear and sing a cosmic hymn.[76] In short, our leading ecological scientists think that worldviews must change in order for cultures to again learn deeply from science.

The process of adaptive management seems to need cultural change at a religious depth in order to get under way. Observing that the project of managing ecological systems anticipates a worldview different from the one of industrial power, religious ethicist Larry Rasmussen writes that "this sustainable adaptability ethic assumes, even centers, what many others do not, namely religious impulses as a substantive contribution."[77] Insofar as "the scientific worldview" refers to beliefs that drive cultural attempts to conquer nature, adaptive management invites reimagining humanity's role in earth. Perhaps the science anticipates a form of "sacred ecology" for the postindustrial world.

Now, the fact that mention of worldviews allows religionists to rush into the space of sustainability with a critique of science and a new account of reality, Norton would think, just goes to show why an ethic of sustainability must work from problems instead of cosmologies. Religion seems aggressively eager to displace the authority of science over the future of sustainability. However, Norton and other environmental pragmatists make it seem that any talk of worldviews and ontologies belongs to a metaphysically foundationalist strategy of ethics. But religious ideas, cosmologies, and alternative worldviews do not imply foundationalism. They may also function as important tools for solving problems. Creation stories and ontological paradigms can question assumed problem-frames, unjust social practices, and dysfunctional moral cultures. Maybe "managing nature" is a dysfunctional metaphor in a maladaptive imaginary, indifferent to social injustice and a shill for human power. "Why not," as Rolston wonders, "think of ourselves as authors who are writing the next chapters, or residents who are learning the logic of our home community?"[78] Questioning the basic metaphors that shape the production of ecological knowledge makes our science more accountable to our ideas of how humans participate in earth and what responsibilities we take ourselves to have.[79]

When a management frame obscures how humans participate in ecological destruction, conceals the concepts that construct problems, or surrenders criticism of environmental injustice, it makes problem-solving processes captive to dominant ideologies. Good management must be able to reflexively criticize assumptions and goals of its practice. The social learning on which sustainability science relies needs a way to host big questions about the goods of life and the purposes of humanity, and to do so in a way that does not paralyze responsibility. Religion and cosmology offer tools of cultural questioning that an adaptive management strategy seems to need.

WICKED PROBLEMS

I have argued that a generally pragmatic approach needs to incorporate religious modes of inquiry into the interpretation and management of sustainability problems. In order to treat the most difficult problems it also needs to involve religious communities—and not only because they are important political constituencies. Religious communities might in fact help vindicate the hope of environmental pragmatism. Working from specific problems with the moral values resident in a community (the pragmatist counsel) need not rule out transformative cultural reform (the cosmological promise), if communities can use their moral inheritances to invent adaptive responses to problems. For the problem of managing the Chesapeake Bay, which seems to overwhelm current competencies of responsibility, a pragmatic approach needs what cosmological and religious ethics can do: criticize social dysfunction and make transformative claims. It must show that ethics can transform what Leopold called the "foundations of conduct," while yet evolving from available values in critical experience of practical problems.

Consider first the problem of invasive mute swans in the Chesapeake. Managing invasive nonnative species usually involves both cultural and ecological uncertainty, and the resulting dilemmas have generated heated exchanges among philosophers and scientists. Philosopher Mark Sagoff claims that xenophobic metaphors illicitly drive research description (alien invaders!), which in turn drive aggressive control policies that do not make long-run evolutionary sense. Why should swans be prevented from living in the Chesapeake simply because they arrived recently? Biologist Daniel Simberloff retorts with bodies of evidence showing that invasives often increase extinctions of other species and degrade ecosystems, thus warranting strong disvalue.[80] Mute swans deplete underwater grass beds and drive away other birds, including endangered species. Simberloff seems to win the exchange but Sagoff's argument shows why policy debates over invasives can become polarized: describing the facts at hand always involves evaluative language, for which "nature" no longer offers an objective standard or an uncontroversial goal. The debates become animated when a management plan involves killing animals—especially when the public sees scientists shooting swans in the name of conservation. Why do native species warrant destruction of outsiders? Do holistic ecological goals cancel any moral claim that individual swans might make on human responsibility?[81] Taking responsibility for ecological change thus presses communities to decide what changes they should try to control and how to think about human power in relation to ecological communities and to individual organisms.

The moral implications of invasives management run broadly, but they may not require rethinking worldviews. An inclusive model of adaptive management focused on discrete cases of decision making offers promise for improving practical deliberations over invasives management. Philosopher Kristen Shrader-Frechette and biologist David Lodge argue that, by clearly discriminating descriptive and normative claims, scientists can at least help communities understand how invasives policy depends on incomplete scientific knowledge as well as independent cultural ideas. Patiently and carefully informing contextual deliberations can improve pluralist policy debates. With moral intuitions and scientific uncertainty acknowledged, a civic community can develop risk indicators responsive to accurate research and expressive of values that the community (over time) recognizes and accepts.[82] The case of the mute swans has helped the Chesapeake community consider its intuitions about anthropogenic change and nonnative species, to learn about the ecosystem function of grass beds, and to settle on nonlethal forms of swan management. So when its problems are carefully defined with the help of multiple disciplines, and the public is patiently engaged, management cases can drive a form of adaptive ecological learning.[83]

Seeing the promise of such case-based reasoning, some pragmatists propose that the ecological sciences develop a corollary field of practical ethics by organizing interdisciplinary deliberation around a set of standard cases—such as biomedical ethics does for medicine. Ben Minteer and James Collins propose "a new conceptual and analytical toolkit for ecologists and biodiversity managers that will help them deal with the moral questions raised by their work."[84] The received field of environmental ethics, they repeat, cannot do this because it is so preoccupied with changing world-views and arguing value theory. That does not help the professional training of ecologists and biologists who will face cases that involve deciding which species to save and which to remove, deciding whether and how to kill animals, and explaining those decisions to a divided civic community.[85] Just as we do not want physicians who merely follow professional codes while remaining obtuse to the human dimensions of each patient, we do not want ecologists incapable of responding to the moral complexity of particular cases.[86]

However, biomedical ethics is a troubling model for two reasons. First, its very success in becoming an independent field, institutionally oriented to the problems encountered in a discrete set of professional practices, has sometimes threatened its credibility. An applied ethics that focuses on re-solving the dilemmas created by contemporary health care practices cedes leverage to critique the context in which those dilemmas arise. For ex-ample, some end-of-life dilemmas seem produced by a war against death mindset of physicians and a scarcity of palliative care resources. Some inva-sive species dilemmas seem driven by xenophobic aggression and produced by land-use developments that escape critical attention. Overemphasis on cases, especially if deliberated among a narrow community of professionals, can blinker interpretive criticism of the problems it considers.

Biomedical ethics avoids blinkered captivity to professional cases be-cause its problems receive attention from diverse theoretical perspectives, creating lively interdisciplinary exchanges that keep moral inquiry open. Religious ethicists have been particularly active, inquiring into implicit nar-ratives of life and death, dominant metaphors of caregiving, and ideologies underwriting the unjust distribution of health care. Biomedical ethics suc-ceeds, it seems, precisely because it is not a management subfield but rather a formal intersection of disciplinary inquiries, shaped around practical re-sponses to specific problems and continually inviting modes of theoretical intelligence beyond the inductive reasoning of its own professionals.

Still more important is the second trouble: biomedical ethics and eco-logical ethics often face disanalogous problems. In biomedical ethics the problems are more contained because the range of objectives for practicing and researching health care limits the complexity at issue. Problems such as climate change are especially difficult to describe because they involve multiple units and scales of vulnerability; because they do not present themselves within a discrete set of professional practices; and because they involve a wider controversy of objectives. Moreover, environmental problems may pose basic threats to human societies in ways that biomedical problems generally do not.[87]

Some of the practical problems faced by the sustainability sciences are "wicked problems," characterized by such complexity that it seems hard to construct them as cases framed for scientific institutions and competencies.[88] Lee's description of the social complexity surrounding decisions about salmon and energy production in the Columbia River watershed seems so open to interpretive and normative variety that it is difficult even to find satisfactory concepts to describe the "problem." Climate change, we saw in chapter 1, involves a wider controversy of objectives, and poses basic threats to human societies in ways that invasives cases do not. With "no definitive formulation, no stopping rule, and no test for a solution," it escapes the competency of the sciences.[89] Making climate change into a practical case requires some evaluative decisions prior to any professional management activity. Yet as we saw in chapter 1, making those decisions requires the cultural imagination to overcome our ethical incompetencies.

Doing case-based reasoning from problems might work for managing the invasive swans, but not the entire Chesapeake Bay. Yet that is the scale at which most of the important sustainability questions matter. That raises doubt about whether an ethic modeled on adaptive management can deal with the most important and most challenging sustainability problems. While excellent for the discretely defined natural resource problems for which it was originally designed, say critics, adaptive management does not permit learning about problems with extensive spatial and temporal scales, high uncertainty, multiple social objectives, or unstable political support—exactly the features of our most important problems.[90] If pragmatism responds by narrowing the range of problems it considers, that makes a strategy developed for its practicality oddly impractical for society's most important challenges. Unless the success of a pragmatic strategy depends on excluding problems that it cannot handle, it must be able to turn wicked ecological threats into important cultural problems.

For wicked problems, which resist professional solutions because they outstrip a society's scientific and ethical competencies, a problem-based ethic needs communities that can invent new cultural competencies. To hold that wicked problems can be meaningfully managed, and so drive the adaptive learning on which a pragmatic ethic relies, it must explain how cultures can become capable of meeting new challenges. In chapter 2 I described an account of culture in which reform happens as agents redeploy their moral inheritances to create strategies of action for solving new problems. Rather than thinking of culture as a coherent scheme of interpretation, as a cosmology that orients action, I argued for views like that of sociologist Ann Swidler, who describes culture as a "'tool kit' of symbols, stories, rituals, and worldviews which people may use in varying configurations to solve different kinds of problems."[91] The meaning of those various tools inheres in the strategies of action they are used to sustain, and so culture changes as its participants use it to solve problems in new ways.

With that view of culture, pragmatists can anticipate cultural experimentation in gaps between the capacities of cultural action and new problems. In the face of wicked problems, their strategy in fact depends on culture-transforming creativity. Cultural transformation happens as communities of moral agents redeploy their cultural inheritances to create some strategy of action that makes them capable of meeting some problem. Not every strategy is successful or adaptive, of course. In chapter 1 I described several strategies deployed by Christian communities to address climate change, criticizing those with weak reflexive feedback from the problem itself. Cultures are susceptible to change by innovative reform projects, but those changes become adaptive only insofar as they are responsible to the problems arising in changing human-environmental systems.

The point here is that with a dynamic view of culture, pragmatists can suppose that complex ecological threats produce social experiments that seek to make a varied cultural inheritance capable of new things. To encourage that cultural experimentation, ecological managers should then go beyond merely inviting public participation toward actively facilitating new cultural inventiveness. For wicked problems, managers must do more than survey stakeholder values; they must ask stakeholders to change. For in the face of wicked problems, managers need citizens to make those values capable of sustaining new forms of cultural action. In other words, ecological managers must become skilled participants in moral culture, capable of recognizing and stimulating the inventive processes by which agents make culture capable of meeting new problems.[92]

The tasks of adaptive management again appear to involve deeper cultural conflict than pragmatists might want. For adaptive management to function as a general model for addressing wicked sustainability problems, it needs problems to begin to unsettle, challenge, and change basic behavioral patterns. It needs responsive and imaginative reform projects prepared to criticize the incompetency of their inherited repertory of action and to ideologically explain the advantage of their proposed alternative.

Reformers may propose a pattern of human behavior more appropriate to biodiversity loss by denouncing dominant values and metaphors of nature, naming and breaking with a cultural narrative of human dominion, or constructing a new "ecological worldview." If so, then a pragmatic ethic may sometimes *want* to see argument over ontologies and worldviews, because that argument signifies the creative cultural conflict that a problem-solving ethic needs. Cosmological debate represents intractable speculation only when not rooted in attempts to create new strategies of cultural action.

This model of moral culture thus opens the concept of adaptive management to a much wider, more pluralist, and more chaotic arena of cultural experimentation. For a problem like managing a watershed, the relevant management team extends beyond policy makers, ecological scientists, and "the environmental community," to all the actors using the watershed as both a living space and a space for cultural renewal. The most important participants here are not scientific experts but moral entrepreneurs—those who can create new capacities from cultural inheritances. Social critics and moral entrepreneurs often work with alternative worldviews, ontological value theories, and new ecological cosmologies in order to illustrate how sustainability problems pose important cultural problems. An ethic of adaptive management must see the uses of cosmology and work with those communities adept in moral invention.

RELIGIOUS REINHABITATION

Consider the case of Christian watermen families on Tangier Island, embroiled in conflict over a sustainable fisheries plan for the Chesapeake Bay. They initially resented the management proposal and used biblical themes of human dominion to support their resistance to what they saw as imposition of an environmentalist worldview. Policy conflict between Christian islanders and conservation scientists became overwritten as conflict between religion and science. Management conflict appeared stuck in intractable conflict between worldviews. When Susan Drake Emmerich, an evangelical Christian with anthropological and environmental education, came to the island, she saw potential for the conflict to be more productive.[93]

Participating in daily life on Tangier Island, Emmerich came to think that the religious inheritance which had thus far funded opposition to new management proposals could function differently without undermining its authority. Arriving in the island community with exposure to evangelical theologies of "missionary earthkeeping," Emmerich anticipated that the watermen could deploy biblical values to support an environmental management plan. Crucially observing that social change in this community was

driven by women and the church, Emmerich initiated reflective conversations among the women and then encouraged the local church to develop
its own biblically based ethic for managing the Chesapeake. Emmerich's initiative allowed the community to interpret fishery decline as a theological
problem open to interpretation by their own resources. Declining fisheries
now challenged their reading of scripture and their faith. Her recounting of
the response is dramatic: at a community church service, "fifty-eight watermen bowed down in tears and asked God to forgive them."[94] In Swidler's
terms, they deployed the practice of repentance to authorize a new pattern
of cultural action. Their stewardship metaphor offered ground for environmental, regulatory, and watermen groups to develop shared management
objectives.

The Tangier example illustrates more than an odd moral community finding its own peculiar vocabulary for participating in a management scheme.
It depicts a community discovering how to use its beliefs to learn from its
ecological context and change the pattern of action those beliefs support.
By interpreting scientific feedback about the state of the Chesapeake Bay
within their ethic of obedient stewardship, the watermen let science-based
ecological feedback mobilize and inform an internal logic of moral reform.
Biological data becomes an empirical marker of sin and faithfulness. The
wider public of the Chesapeake watershed need not share or understand
the community's beliefs in order to appreciate their demonstration of how a
management problem matters for the meaning of those beliefs. By turning a
fisheries problem into a theological problem, the watermen authorize other
moral communities with suspicions about "the environmental community"
or about environmental scientists to create similar forms of responsibility.
The very oddness of their cosmology proves that participating in science-
based practices of managing the Chesapeake is not a matter of having the
right worldview.

The watermen's stewardship metaphor may also begin to contest
the framing metaphor of responsibility. As ecological feedback about the
Chesapeake Bay shapes reflection on the adequacy of cultural response, the
watermen may eventually come to think that "management" represents a
pattern of action that prevents the wider watershed from adequately interpreting the problem or undertaking responsibility for it. In that case, they
could propose as a better interpretation of the problem their own model
of stewardship, with its notions of human sin, perverse political powers,
and accountability for creation. Mainstream moral culture need not adopt
the religious worldview to appreciate what its symbol of repentance accomplishes: an enactment of responsibility that connects personal integrity
with ecological health. Other moral communities in the watershed may find

compelling the watermen's personal self-examination and political critique, and may look for analogous ways to make their lived beliefs support actions accountable to ecological feedback from the bay. Or they may just use the theological interpretation of Chesapeake sustainability to pause in consideration of deeper moral questions possibly at stake and alternative metaphorical constructions of humanity's place in nature. The redeployment of tradition enacted by the religious watermen can thus illustrate to a wider moral culture unrealized possibilities of interpretation and action.

Effective management of the watershed thus requires managers who know how to help make cultural values do new things within the communities that hold them. That goes beyond the familiar claim that scientists should understand what citizens believe and communicate their facts more clearly in order to correct those beliefs. Adept participation in moral culture means that managers should open science-based management processes in expectation that participants can create new possibilities from their beliefs. To accomplish that, ecological managers need not contest the core values and beliefs of that community; they need to make communities take sustainability problems seriously. Like anthropologists, they should seek to understand how symbols, values, and worldviews function within lived moral worlds. Like activists, they should agitate those communities to make their toolkit support new responsibilities. Effective agitation requires a way of making the gap between social response and wicked problems pose a challenge to the core beliefs of a community—as watershed management was made into a theological problem by the community on Tangier.

This view suggests that a science-based pragmatism ought to be more engaged with religious communities, for two reasons. First, religious reform projects function as sites where received moral traditions are revised and authorized to sustain new patterns of action. Not just repositories of important cultural values, religions also represent dynamic processes of reinterpreting and reconsidering culture. Reform movements within religious traditions know how to make emergent social problems into important cultural problems. As they create authoritative changes, wider society may pick up strategies of action it finds approved and enacted by these reformers. Religious inventiveness may authorize other adaptive responses by showing how learning from ecological systems is also a form of learning moral responsibility. Religious communities make useful contributions to adaptive management processes, then, not primarily because they maintain certain values, but because they demonstrate capacities to make received values support adaptive strategies of action.

Yet pragmatists rarely recognize religious communities as part of moral culture. Religious communities and their values are absent in Norton and

Minteer, which raises doubts about the scope of their democratic inclusion and the reliability of their convergence notions.[95] No religious communities seem to reside in Lee's account of the Columbia River watershed. Light is unique among the pragmatists for mentioning religious communities, but when he does his hitherto creative notion of the ethical task appears flat: to articulate the values of "the environmental community" to some (apparently different) religious community.[96] The religious lacunae here represent more than a failure to recognize the motivating values of some segments of the population; ignoring religion misses a significant site of cultural creativity. In regard to problems that flummox the cultural capacities of even "the environmental community," religious communities may demonstrate capacities of cultural reform.

A second reason for pragmatists to engage religion: alternative metaphors and revisionary narratives sometimes prove crucial for remodeling a difficult problem. When religious projects use cosmology to think through practical problems, they open reflection on framing metaphors of agency or basic stances toward the universe. That can be a useful tool for working on some problems. Writing in response to the proposal of Minteer and Collins for a case-based ethics education for ecologists, the usually managerial Norton vindicates something like a cosmological proviso. When facing "messy problems, often involving conflicts among conflicting goods," says Norton, there are "varied complaints and varied explanations of what the problem is, often associated with varied value positions and perspectives." That is just when a pragmatist might want to reduce conflict to policy agreement. "But," surprises Norton, "it is in this messy dialogue about goals and aspirations that metaphors and similes allow the reconstruction of a problem." A process open to reframing a problem, he writes, "encourages 'social learning' at the deepest, metaphorical level—the kind of social learning that can 're-model' complex and wicked problems and improve communication by disentangling messes into addressable problems."[97]

Norton does not seem to have in mind metaphors like the Tangier watermen's Christ-centered discipleship, but his model suggests that their cosmological imagination offers an important tool. Cosmology can be especially important for working on wicked problems because it opens interdisciplinary self-reflection on how the broad cultural experiment is interpreted and modeled. The facility of religious communities for enacting integrative stories about humanity and their environment may be one that an expanded science of adaptive management needs in order to maintain critical openness. If Norton is right that adaptive learning from wicked problems may call for broad iterative reconceptions, then problem-solvers need tools to question the management metaphors that organize deliberation. A critical minority working with an alternative worldview may be important for making "management" the scene of ongoing interdisciplinary inquiry about how to best interpret the human experience of evolutionary and ecological participation.

For example, Sarah McFarland Taylor's study of "green sisters" shows a network of Catholic religious communities using cosmology as a tool for interpreting the appropriate register of religious and social response to sustainability problems. As they revitalize their forms of covenanted life, some of these communities use a "new universe story" in order to simultaneously "reinhabit" their Roman Catholic tradition as well as their ecological community. In Taylor's description, these communities use evolutionary cosmology as a framework for conceptualizing appropriate reform in care for their lands, their liturgies, and their witness. Living within an ecclesiastical institution that views them with suspicion and a society that views them as odd, the sisters can use the cosmology to create critical distance from the authoritative frames of the moral cultures in which they live. They do not, by Taylor's account, seem to adopt and apply the cosmology in the foundationalist way to which pragmatists object, but rather use it as an important imaginative instrument in what Minteer and Swidler would call their "toolkit." Taylor's metaphors of practical reason are, however, more horticultural: the sisters *graft* cosmological ideas into received traditions in order that their communities might *yield* and *sustain* new practices of life. Those metaphors fit with a model of reinhabiting earth rather than managing it, which makes a communicative proposal for remodeling how to think about sustainability problems.[98]

It is not only nuns who find cosmology useful. As we have seen, some of the scientists involved in expanding adaptive management into a sustainability science gesture toward cosmologies when trying to make sense of what must be so about the world for humans to simultaneously learn from it, take responsibility for it, acknowledge themselves threatened by it, and (sometimes) allow themselves to be awed by it. Management toolkits need not be threatened by radical beliefs and cosmological ideas, but should include them as heuristic tools available for making sense of an unprecedented research situation. In need of hypotheses with meliorist, adaptive consequences, researchers and policymakers facing a problem like climate change may then have reason to not only acknowledge but also seek out communities with reformist eco-social imaginations.

Those communities may sit at the odd margins of moral culture. Note that both the watermen and the green sisters come from minority communities; one from a culturally unique island and a threatened way of life, the other from a reformist network among a rare way of life. In the interest of

keeping open to critical interpretation of wicked problems, adaptive managers should know when to avoid the pragmatist counsel to "collapse" moral
pluralism into a weak anthropocentric policy consensus.[99] In the face of
the most complex, most uncertain, least understood problems, that tactic might delay the cultural conflict needed for deep adaptive learning. For
wicked problems, prematurely seeking policy consensus may stymie the
pluralist moral experimentation needed to invent new cultural capacities.
When facing sustainability problems that frustrate mainstream cultural
competencies, managers and ethicists might look away from the moral
mean and majority common sense in order to attend to peculiar imaginaries and marginal projects.

Minority moral strategies may, of course, themselves prove inadequate,
irrelevant, or perverse in regard to wicked problems. My argument merely
suggests that, despite pragmatist disdain and indifference, cosmological
arguments and marginal moral communities can sometimes make moral
culture function in new and better ways. Researching and responding to
wicked ecological problems depends on those problems becoming sites
that reconnect cultural imaginations with the environmental sciences and
that stimulate culture reform. Those reforms are sometimes supported by
constructing countercultural worldviews or new moral cosmologies. When
those cosmologies help a community reconnect its moral experience to
earth, they establish a vital condition for adaptive learning: they make problems in earth systems into problems of the moral life.

CULTURAL WATERSHEDS

Another religious project illustrates why justice is also a condition for adaptive learning. Not long after Kai Lee published his book on managing the
Columbia River watershed, the Catholic bishops of the area undertook a
three-year listening process with the region's communities and then issued
a pastoral letter: *The Columbia River Watershed: Caring for Creation and the Common Good* (*TCRW*). It is likely the first pastoral letter issued from the bishops
of a bioregion, rather than from a political or ecclesiastical jurisdiction.[100]
By setting their theological interpretation within the political ecology of the
watershed, the bishops aim to demonstrate how their particular beliefs make
a difference within a pluralist process of management. They have reason to
support and improve the problem-solving process because components of
a Catholic moral worldview are at stake. In order to maintain belief in creation's ordered common goods, *TCRW* needs to show that economic and
ecological goods can be sustained while remaining fundamentally committed to social justice. In order to maintain its moral anthropology, moreover,

it needs to hold that a way of managing the watershed for integrated goods can be learned by all persons, no matter their beliefs. The bishops thus have theological reasons to make the problem less wicked, including their belief that social justice names conditions for pluralist social learning to sustain the common good.

To prove the possibility, *TCRW* deploys key ideas from Catholic social thought in an unconventional way. It connects the idea of the common good, which as we saw in chapter 3 functions as a middle axiom for accommodating pluralism, to a diversely shared habitat such that diversity of agents, cultures, and creatures is a good in itself. It then suggests that people can learn the shape of creation's common good from this diverse social and ecological commons. "The watershed is the common home and habitat of God's creatures," which by its sustenance of life, "foster[s] the common good of all people who dwell here." Rightly approached, this shared habitat can teach humans not only middle axioms but higher goods because "the watershed, seen through eyes alive with faith, can be a revelation of God's presence."[101] For Catholic communities, that makes care of the shared commons a sacramental act, a creative medium by which humans can receive the presence of God.[102]

That sacramental ontology means something for non-Catholic citizens of the watershed as well, because it affirms that something of the truth is learned from managing well. The science-based process of adaptive management adapts finally not to arbitrary politics but to a deep integrity in earth and society. The right kinds of social and ecological responsibility, the letter implies, teach moral agents this integrity. Moreover, earth's integrity can be learned without holding particular theological beliefs about it. *TCRW* thus provides reason to think that communities can learn true harmonies of human and environmental systems through practices of responsibility for the watershed without holding a Catholic sacramental ontology.

For example, the bishops acknowledge that the indigenous peoples of the area already possessed such wisdom and apologize for the injustice of the church taking so long to recognize in their traditional ecological knowledge the integrity of creation that Catholic sacramental theology anticipates. For that they confess the church's complicity in a colonizing culture that alienated itself from the river and its people. Colonizing culture cut ties "with the Spirit, the earth and each other as well."[103] A people can learn the good from its habitat only insofar as its social conditions and cultural aptitudes allow it. While available to all persons, there are ethical conditions for learning the common good. Without openness to learning from creation and without inclusive justice, a science-based process of adaptive management does not learn what really sustains us. Colonizing cultures do not learn to adapt to earth without a sense of participation in an ecological membership and without a commitment to justice for all persons.

Catholic beliefs about human personhood offer an explanation of why those two conditions are necessary for adaptive learning. The possibility of humans coming to know an integrating good for creation is that humans are created in the image of God who creates and sustains the world. God "invites people to participate in divine creativity" by using the world justly and creatively, in care for its belovedness in God.[104] Protecting human dignity therefore entails preserving the social conditions for learning from one another as participants in the creation of God, and from creation itself. Economic livelihoods, human rights, and distributive justice are goods in themselves as well as epistemic conditions for learning how to sustain the goods of creation.

The anthropology underlying that claim conflicts with the anthropology implicit in environmental pragmatism. Whereas adaptive management conceives humans as instrumental experimenters, expanding human purposes through the world, the bishops present humans as participants in God's purposes for creation, and thus shaped by a story grander than their own. By showing how that claim makes a difference to the way decisions are made about the watershed, they implicitly question the views of humanity and nature implied in a management model. If adaptive management would teach us truths about ourselves and earth, and begin to transform us into those truths, its moral anthropology matters. Pragmatists might prefer to avoid such a metaphysical issue, but it matters for how adaptive management functions and what sort of moral agents it makes. (The next chapter shows what happens to human dignity without justice as a condition of ecological management.) They need not accept a Catholic account, but they must acknowledge the relevance of moral anthropology to concrete problems like managing the Columbia River watershed.

Adaptive management, in other words, must include reflection on how we should manage for own moral formation. In a 1980 essay on "the managerial ethos and the future of planet earth," Thomas Berry compared the inevitable fact of humanity's planetary management to the dysfunction of cultures shaped by engineering. Unless humanity would become engineers doomed to civilization failure, managers must manage for the transformation of humanity and culture. Through the wicked problems of an ecological era, thought Berry, earth is trying to teach humanity a new moral maturity.[105] That is the paradoxical task of sustainability: we must find ways to learn from creation how to be human on a human-dominated planet. "We are seeking patterns that connect us to a vaster destiny," say Tucker and Swimme, "a vital participation in Earth's unfolding." Participating in the creativity of the story tells us that "our own generativity becomes woven into the vibrant communities that comprise the vast symphony of the universe."[106]

That sort of cosmological account of humanity cannot answer how the Columbia River should be managed. While implied within any practical ethic of managing a watershed, creation stories and moral anthropologies underdetermine practical action. Especially in pluralist societies it is important to acknowledge that we cannot solve concrete problems by telling a new creation narrative. Even if one narrative were universally endorsed, its meaning would remain contingent on how agents use it to support strategies of practical action. Cosmologies do not work as foundations for a new era of civilization in the way Berry seemed to think; if they did, they would function awkwardly within pluralist politics and science-based processes of incremental cultural change.[107] As a critical tool for interpreting the context of our problems and making pluralist political processes reckon with implicit narratives, religious ideas like those of Berry and stories of the universe like that told by Tucker and Swimme can help drive creative cultural experiments. Especially when they make spiritual practices responsive to scientific research, as the Tangier community did, and offer ground for improving pluralist deliberation, as the *TCRW* did, religious projects can make fundamental questions drive social learning.

Ruling out cosmological or marginal approaches excludes critical tools for managing wicked problems. Adaptive responses must learn to admit comprehensive questions that question the competency of our moral culture without fearing that the questions will close down practical, science-based adaptation. When questions of cultural transformation are raised from within specific processes of confronting problems, they can stimulate the deliberative public on which such a process depends. Recognizing such questions need not shut down a practical, science-based process of learning sustainability. Ethicists may have a unique role to play here, not by rearranging cosmologies, but by helping pluralist processes reckon with comprehensive questions at stake in confronting difficult problems.

For the most complex problems, where human power appropriates and reshapes ecological systems, reflection on human purposes and on the sustaining goods of the world must be part of the cultural reflection involved in adaptive management. Revisiting the big questions is one way that humans learn from their embeddedness in ecological systems. If societies were to attempt to take responsibility for something like managing the Columbia River watershed *without* stepping back in reflection on the emergence of these powers in the watershed's evolutionary history, without considering the stories and metaphors that shape their sense of responsibility, without facing the questions about human purpose and earth's integrity that suspend belief in our powers—then their management would certainly fail. It would be doomed to uncritically repeating the cultural habits shaped by titanic human powers. That does not mean that we must agree on a common story in order to move forward; it only means that societies must recognize the depth of the questions to which our agency now inevitably gives answer in order to appreciate the gap between our predicaments and our capacities. Theological contribution can keep sustainability from functioning as an empty salvation concept by opening it to the deep moral questions it involves.

We cannot respond to the inexhaustibility of these questions or the multiplicity of stories by suppressing the questions and the stories. That would just permit the implicit narratives in our pursuit of wealth and power to stand as our civil religions. Humans already manage earth systems and must learn to do it together, as those uncertain of what is going on and ambivalent about our purposes on earth. Religious projects from many traditions can insist on this open moral anthropology: we seek sustainability as those creatures for whom the good of life stands as an open question and a defining search. We manage as creatures who live by questioning the good and so we must manage to at least sustain the conditions of good questioning. We manage as human creatures who know ourselves to desire more than a continuous supply of resources. Many religious traditions refuse to let humans think the meaning of our lives as individuals and as a species lies in our power or wealth. We desire to understand, to live in a meaningful story, to know and participate in what is really good. So we must manage as those who know we are not managers; we are more and other than managers, for we belong to earth and are open to graces not our own.

CONCLUSION

I have argued here for a kind of pragmatism committed to working on specific problems with moral culture as it finds it, yet not content to let communities flounder incompetently before complex threats. In the face of wicked problems, an ethics of sustainability needs to connect problem solving and cultural change, so that communities learn new ways of life from the process of facing their most difficult problems. This remains a pragmatic strategy because it remains disciplined to specific problems and seeks cultural reform through a science-based process of responding to them. It calls for further development of transdisciplinary collaboration among the sciences and humanities, and seeks better and broader engagement with lived culture. This sort of pragmatism holds a place for religious communities because they are significant participants in moral culture, and especially because they can function as sites of moral creativity, generating new cultural possibilities. It holds an important place for cosmological and philosophical approaches because it needs their critical and imaginative capacities to make problems drive deeper and more adaptive moral changes.

I observed that a shortcoming of pragmatic approaches is their weakness before powerful institutions and inherited patterns of domination. This approach must make a particular point, then, of attending to the experience of communities vulnerable to the ecological consequences of social power. In the next chapter I show how ecological experiments are reinterpreted by environmental justice movements contesting the mainstream framing of sustainability problems. What happens to a pragmatic approach when it starts from the problems and projects of disempowered communities?

NOTES

1. I am using "cosmological" not in reference to the astrophysical science but to the style of moral reasoning that I described in chapter 2.

2. An excellent history of ecology as science and ideology is Donald Worster, *Nature's Economy: A History of Ecological Ideas*, 2nd ed. (New York: Cambridge University Press, 1994). On the odd uses of ecology among religious thinkers, see Lisa Sideris, *Environmental Ethics, Ecological Theology, and Natural Selection* (New York: Columbia University Press, 2003).

3. Aldo Leopold, *A Sand County Almanac* (Oxford: Oxford University Press, 1949), 224.

4. J. H. Lawton, "Are There General Laws in Ecology?" *Oikos* 84 (1999). Daniel Simberloff, "Community Ecology: Is It Time to Move On?" *The American Naturalist* 163, no. 6 (2004): 787–99.

5. K. S. Shrader-Frechette and E. D. McCoy, *Method in Ecology: Strategies for Conservation* (New York: Cambridge University Press, 1993), chap. 1.

6. Hilary Putnam helps explain how the concepts of fact and value mutually presuppose one another, but this view of ecology does not depend on his theory of pragmatic realism, which understands physics in a similar way. My claim here is less sweeping, applying only to the environmental sciences that work on problems with obvious values and disvalues for societies. See Hilary Putnam, *Reason, Truth, and History* (New York: Cambridge University Press, 1981), chap. 6.

7. W. J. Sutherland et al., "The Need for Evidence-Based Conservation," *Trends in Ecology and Evolution* 19, no. 6 (2004).

8. Oswald Schmitz, *Resolving Ecosystem Complexity* (Princeton, NJ: Princeton University Press, 2010), 4–5.

9. Oswald Schmitz, "Restoration of Ailing Wetlands," *PloS Biology* 10, no.1 (2012): 1–3. Making similar points about the need for science-based policy within a medical model of conservation biology: M. E. Soulé et al., "Strongly Interacting Species: Conservation Policy, Management, and Ethics," *BioScience* 55, no. 2 (2005).

10. M. E. Soule, "What Is Conservation Biology?" *BioScience* 35, no. 11 (1985); D. Barry and M. Oelschlaeger, "A Science for Survival: Values and Conservation Biology," *Conservation Biology* 10, no. 3 (1996).

11. See Robert Costanza et al., eds., *Ecosystem Health: New Goals for Environmental Management* (Washington, DC: Island Press, 1992).

12. W. Clark and N. Dickson, "Sustainability Science: The Emerging Research Program," *Proceedings of the National Academy of Sciences* 100, no. 14 (2003); H. Komiyama and K. Takeuchi, "Sustainability Science: Building a New Discipline," *Sustainability Science* 1, no. 1 (2006); S. Levin and W. Clark, eds., "Toward a Science of Sustainability" (CID Working Paper 196, Center for International Development at Harvard University, May 2010).

13. R. Kates et al., "Sustainability Science," *Science* 292, no. 5517 (2001); Rafael Ziegler and Konrad Ott, "The Quality of Sustainable Science: A Philosophical Perspective," *Sustainability: Science, Practice, and Policy* 7, no. 1 (2011).

14. J. Lubchenco, "Entering the Century of the Environment: A New Social Contract for Science," *Science* 279, no. 5350 (1998): 495. See also J. Lubchenco et al., "The Sustainable Biosphere Initiative: An Ecological Research Agenda," *Ecology* 72, no. 2 (1991).

15. M. Palmer et al., "Ecology for a Crowded Planet," *Science* 304, no. 5675 (2004): 1251–52.

16. S. O. Funtowicz and J. R. Ravetz, "Science for the Post-Normal Age," *Futures* 25, no. 7 (1993).

17. Ray Ison et al., "Challenges to Science and Society in the Sustainable Management and Use of Water: Investigating the Role of Social Learning," *Environmental Science and Policy* 10, no. 6 (2007): 505. See also C. Blackmore et al., "Social Learning: An Alternative Policy Instrument for Managing in the Context of Europe's Water," *Environmental Science and Policy* 10, no. 6 (2007); K. Collins and R. Ison, "Jumping Off Arnstein's Ladder: Social Learning as a New Policy Paradigm for Climate Change Adaptation," *Environmental Policy and Governance* 19, no. 6 (2009).

18. Ziegler and Ott, "The Quality of Sustainable Science: A Philosophical Perspective"; R. Frodeman, "Redefining Ecological Ethics: Science, Policy, and Philosophy at Cape Horn," *Science and Engineering Ethics* 14, no. 4 (2008).

19. Stephen Jay Gould, "Nonoverlapping Magisteria," *Natural History* 106 (1997): 16–22.

20. Christopher Hamlin and David Lodge, "Beyond Lynn White: Religion, the Contexts of Ecology, and the Flux of Nature," in *Religion and the New Ecology*, Christopher Hamlin and David Lodge, eds. (Notre Dame, IN: University of Notre Dame Press, 2006), 7. For reflections on theology and science after the end of nature see David Albertson and Cabell King, eds., *Without Nature? A New Condition for Theology* (New York: Fordham University Press, 2010).

21. Peter M. Vitousek et al., "Human Domination of Earth's Ecosystems," *Science* 277, no. 5325 (1997): 499; Larry L. Rasmussen, "Ecology and Morality: The Challenge to and from Christian Ethics," in *Religion and the New Ecology*, David Lodge and

Christopher Hamlin, eds. (Notre Dame, IN: University of Notre Dame Press, 2006), 249.

22. Paul H. Reitan, "Sustainability Science and What's Needed beyond Science," *Sustainability: Science, Practice, and Policy* 1, no. 1 (2005).

23. See Donald Ludwig, Marc Mangel, and Brent Haddad, "Ecology, Conservation, and Public Policy," *Annual Review of Ecology and Systematics* 32 (2001).

24. For a review of theories of social learning in relation to sustainability ideas, see E. A. Parson and W. C. Clark, "Sustainable Development as Social Learning: Theoretical Perspectives and Practical Challenges for the Design of a Research Program," in *Barriers and Bridges to the Renewal of Ecosystems and Institutions*, Fikret Berkes et al., eds. (Cambridge: Cambridge University Press, 1995).

25. Andrew Light, "The Urban Blind Spot in Environmental Ethics," *Environmental Politics* 10, no. 1 (2001).

26. William Jordan, *The Sunflower Forest: Ecological Restoration and the New Communion with Nature* (Berkeley: University of California Press, 2003), 128.

27. Gretel Van Wieren, *Restored to Earth: Christianity, Environmental Ethics, and Ecological Restoration* (Washington, DC: Georgetown University Press, 2013).

28. Martin Luther King, Jr., "The Power of Nonviolence," in *A Testament of Hope: The Essential Writings and Speeches of Martin Luther King, Jr.*, James M. Washington, ed. (New York: Harper & Row, 1986): 15.

29. For more on religious studies and environmental pragmatism, see Lucas Johnston and Samuel Snyder, "Practically Natural: Religious Resources for Environmental Pragmatism," in *Inherited Land: The Changing Grounds of Religion and Ecology* (Eugene, OR: Wipf and Stock, 2011): 125–47.

30. Ben Minteer and Robert Manning, "Pragmatism in Environmental Ethics: Democracy, Pluralism, and the Management of Nature," in *Environmental Ethics: An Anthology*, Andrew Light and Holmes Rolston, eds. (Malden, MA: Blackwell, 2003), 319.

31. Andrew Light and Eric Katz, eds., *Environmental Pragmatism* (New York: Routledge, 1995), 1.

32. Bryan G. Norton, *Sustainability: A Philosophy of Adaptive Ecosystem Management* (Chicago: University of Chicago Press, 2005), 160–66. For more on White's legacy, see Willis Jenkins, "After Lynn White: Religious Ethics and Environmental Problems," *Journal of Religious Ethics* 37, no. 2 (2009).

33. Andrew Light, "The Case for a Practical Pluralism," in *Environmental Ethics: An Anthology*, Andrew Light and Holmes Rolston, eds. (Malden, MA: Blackwell, 2003), 235, 241. See the introduction to Andrew Light and Avner De-Shalit, *Moral and Political Reasoning in Environmental Practice* (Cambridge, MA: MIT Press, 2003).

34. Minteer and Manning, "Pragmatism in Environmental Ethics: Democracy, Pluralism, and the Management of Nature," 321.

35. Light, "The Case for a Practical Pluralism," 233.

36. Bryan G. Norton, *Toward Unity among Environmentalists* (New York: Oxford University Press, 1991).

37. Robyn Eckersley, "Enviromental Pragmatism, Ecocentrism, and Deliberative Democracy: Between Problem-Solving and Fundamental Critique," in *Democracy and the Claims of Nature*, Ben Minteer and Bob Pepperman Taylor, eds. (Lanham, MD: Rowman & Littlefield, 2002), 58.

38. Eckersley, "Environmental Pragmatism," 65.

39. Minteer and Manning, "Pragmatism in Environmental Ethics," 325.

40. Ben Minteer and Robert Manning, "Convergence in Environmental Values: An Empirical and Conceptual Defense," in *Nature in Common? Environmental Ethics and the Contested Foundations of Environmental Policy*, Ben Minteer and Robert Manning, eds. (Philadelphia: Temple University Press, 2009), 78.

41. See Micheal Zimmerman, "Ecofascism: A Threat to American Environmentalism?" in *The Ecological Community*, Roger Gottlieb, ed. (New York: Routledge, 1997).

42. Norton, *Sustainability: A Philosophy*, 334–38.

43. Norton, *Toward Unity among Environmentalists*.

44. Light, "The Case for a Practical Pluralism," 234.

45. Holmes Rolston, "Converging versus Reconstituting Environmental Ethics," in *Nature in Common? Environmental Ethics and the Contested Foundations of Environmental Policy*, Ben Minteer and Robert Manning, eds. (Philadelphia: Temple University Press, 2009).

46. John Dewey, *Democracy and Education* (New York: MacMillan, 1916).

47. Norton, *Sustainability: A Philosophy*, 151.

48. Ben Minteer, *The Landscape of Reform: Civic Pragmatism and Environmental Thought in America* (Cambridge, MA: MIT Press, 2006), 6.

49. C. S. Holling, ed. *Adaptive Environmental Assessment and Management* (New York: International Institute for Applied Systems Analysis, 1978).

50. Carl J. Walters and C. S. Holling, "Large-Scale Management Experiments and Learning by Doing," *Ecology* 71, no. 6 (1990).

51. Kai Lee, *Compass and Gyroscope: Integrating Science and Policy* (Washington, DC: Island Press, 1993), 7–13, 69–73.

52. C. S. Holling et al., "Science, Sustainability and Resource Management," in *Linking Social and Ecological Systems: Management Practices and Social Mechanisms for Building Resilience*, C. S. Holling et al., eds. (Cambridge: Cambridge University Press, 1998).

53. C. S. Holling, "What Barriers? What Bridges?" in *Barriers and Bridges to the Renewal of Ecosystems and Institutions*, Lance Gunderson et al., eds. (New York: Columbia University Press, 1995), 14.

54. K. N. Lee, "Appraising Adaptive Management," *Conservation Ecology* 3, no. 2 (1999).

55. Norton, *Sustainability: A Philosophy*, 120.

56. The allusion is to Cornel West, *The American Evasion of Philosophy: A Genealogy of Pragmatism* (Madison: University of Wisconsin Press, 1989).

57. It is useful to read Norton's methodological appendix in *Sustainability: A Philosophy* in company with the account of American pragmatism as "meliorist

transitionalism" in Colin Koopman, *Pragmatism as Transition: Historicity and Hope in James, Dewey, and Rorty* (New York: Columbia University Press, 2009).

58. C. Walters, "Challenges in Adaptive Management of Riparian and Coastal Ecosystems," *Conservation Ecology* 1, no. 2 (1997).

59. Norton, *Sustainability: A Philosophy*, 356.

60. F. Berkes et al., "Rediscovery of Traditional Ecological Knowledge as Adaptive Management," *Ecological Applications* 10, no. 5 (2000), 1252, 1260. See also Matthias Finger and Philomene Verlaan, "Learning Our Way Out: A Conceptual Framework for Social-Environmental Learning," *World Development* 23, no. 3 (1995).

61. Leopold, *A Sand County Almanac*, 225.

62. Bryan G. Norton, *The Search for Sustainability: Interdisciplinary Essays in the Philosophy of Conservation Biology* (Cambridge: University of Cambridge Press, 2003), 47–63; Minteer, *The Landscape of Reform: Civic Pragmatism and Environmental Thought in America*.

63. R. Gregory et al., "Deconstructing Adaptive Management: Criteria for Applications to Environmental Management," *Ecological Applications* 16, no. 6 (2006): 2424.

64. Oswald Schmitz, *Ecology and Ecosystem Conservation* (Washington, DC: Island Press, 2007), 126, 138.

65. Lee, *Compass and Gyroscope*, 185–87, 198.

66. Kai Lee, review of *Sustainability: A Philosophy of Adaptive Ecosystem Management*, by Bryan Norton, *Ecoscience* 13, no. 4 (2006): 565–66.

67. Leopold, *A Sand County Almanac*, 210.

68. The ecocentric Leopold is vigorously defended by J. Baird Callicott: Callicott et al., "Was Aldo Leopold a Pragmatist? Rescuing Leopold from the Imagination of Bryan Norton," *Environmental Values* 18 (2009): 453–86.

69. William James, *The Moral Equivalent of War* (New York: American Association for International Conciliation, 1910).

70. Louis Dupré, *Passage to Modernity: An Essay in the Hermeneutics of Nature and Culture* (New Haven, CT: Yale University Press, 1993): 73–74. For an account of pragmatism's evacuation of nature as a road to ethical nihilism, see Roger Lundin, *From Nature to Experience: The American Search for Cultural Authority* (Lanham, MD: Rowman and Littlefield, 2005).

71. As in Braden Allenby, *Reconstructing Earth: Technology and Environment in an Age of Humans* (Washington, DC: Island Press, 2005).

72. A. Davison, "Ruling the Future? Heretical Reflections on Technology and Other Secular Religions of Sustainability," *Worldviews: Global Religions, Culture, and Ecology* 12, no. 2–3 (2008).

73. William French, "With Radical Amazement: Ecology and the Recovery of Creation," in *Without Nature? A New Condition for Theology*, 54–79. On the importance of thinking with paradigms, see also William C. French, "Subject-Centered and Creation-Centered Paradigms in Recent Catholic Thought," *Journal of Religion* 70, no. 1 (1990).

74. Brian Swimme and Mary Evelyn Tucker, *Journey of the Universe* (New Haven, CT: Yale University Press, 2011).

75. Berkes et al., "Rediscovery of Traditional Ecological Knowledge as Adaptive Management." See Fikret Berkes, *Sacred Ecology: Traditional Ecological Knowledge and Resource Management* (Philadelphia: Taylor and Francis, 1999).

76. Lance Gunderson et al., *Barriers and Bridges to the Renewal of Ecosystems and Institutions* (New York: Columbia University Press, 1995).

77. Rasmussen, "Ecology and Morality," 266.

78. Holmes Rolston, "Value in Nature and the Nature of Value," in *Philosophy and the Natural Environment*, Robin Attfield and Andrew Belsey, eds. (New York: Cambridge University Press, 1994), 226.

79. See Willis Jenkins, "Assessing Metaphors of Agency: Intervention, Perfection, and Care as Models of Environmental Practice," *Environmental Ethics* 27, no. 2 (2005).

80. M. Sagoff, "Do Non-Native Species Threaten the Natural Environment?" *Journal of Agricultural and Environmental Ethics* 18, no. 3 (2005); D. Simberloff, "Non-Native Species Do Threaten the Natural Environment!" *Journal of Agricultural and Environmental Ethics* 18, no. 6 (2005). See also N. Hettinger, "Exotic Species, Naturalisation, and Biological Nativism," *Environmental Values* 19, no. 1 (2001): 193–224.

81. See Kate Rawles, "Biological Diversity and Conservation Policy," in *Philosophy and Biodiversity*, Markku Oksanen and Juhani Pietarinen, eds. (Cambridge: Cambridge University Press, 2004), 199–216.

82. D. M. Lodge and K. Shrader-Frechette, "Nonindigenous Species: Ecological Explanation, Environmental Ethics, and Public Policy," *Conservation Biology* 17, no. 1 (2003). See also J. M. Evans et al., "Adaptive Management of Nonnative Species: Moving beyond the 'Either-Or' through Experimental Pluralism," *Journal of Agricultural and Environmental Ethics* 21, no. 6 (2008).

83. Kristen Shrader-Frechette, "Practical Ecology and Foundations for Environmental Ethics," *The Journal of Philosophy* 12, no. 12 (1995).

84. B. A. Minteer and J. P. Collins, "Ecological Ethics: Building a New Tool Kit for Ecologists and Biodiversity Managers," *Conservation Biology* 19, no. 6 (2005): 1810.

85. B. A. Minteer et al., "Editors' Overview: The Emergence of Ecological Ethics," *Science and Engineering Ethics* 14, no. 4 (2008); B. A. Minteer and J. P. Collins, "From Environmental to Ecological Ethics: Toward a Practical Ethics for Ecologists and Conservationists," *Science and Engineering Ethics* 14, no. 4 (2008); Minteer and Collins, "Ecological Ethics"; B. A. Minteer and J. P. Collins, "Why We Need an 'Ecological Ethics'," *Frontiers in Ecology and the Environment* 3, no. 6 (2005).

86. See J. A. Vucetich and M. P. Nelson, "What Are 60 Warblers Worth? Killing in the Name of Conservation," *Oikos* 116, no. 8 (2007).

87. See Robert Hood, "The Role of Cases in Moral Reasoning: What Environmental Ethics Can Learn from Biomedical Ethics," in *Moral and Political Reasoning in Environmental Practice*, Andrew Light and Avner de-Shalit, eds. (Cambridge, MA: MIT Press, 2003), 239–58; Shrader-Frechette and McCoy, *Method in Ecology: Strategies for Conservation*: 101–2.

88. H. W. J. Rittel and M. M. Webber, "Dilemmas in a General Theory of Planning," *Policy Sciences* 4, no. 2 (1973).

89. Ludwig et al., "Ecology, Conservation, and Public Policy," 482.

90. Gregory et al., "Deconstructing Adaptive Management."

91. Ann Swidler, "Culture in Action: Symbols and Strategies," *American Sociological Review* 51 (1986): 273.

92. See R. Kemp et al., "Transition Management as a Model for Managing Processes of Co-Evolution towards Sustainable Development," *International Journal of Sustainable Development and World Ecology* 14, no. 1 (2007). D. R. Armitage et al., "Adaptive Co-Management for Social-Ecological Complexity," *Frontiers in Ecology and the Environment* 7, no. 2 (2008).

93. Susan Drake Emmerich, "The Declaration in Practice: Missionary Earthkeeping," in *The Care of Creation*, R. J. Berry, ed. (Downers Grove, IL: Inter-Varsity Press, 2000); *When Heaven Meets Earth*, directed by Jeffrey Pohorski, co-produced by Susan Drake Emmerich and Jeffrey Pohorski (Los Angeles: Skunkfilms Productions, 2007), DVD.

94. Emmerich, "The Declaration in Practice," 151.

95. See Ben Minteer, "Pragmatism, Piety, and Environmental Ethics," *Worldviews: Global Religions, Culture, Ecology* 12, no. 2–3 (2008): 179–96.

96. Andrew Light, "Taking Environmental Ethics Public," in *Environmental Ethics: What Really Matters, What Really Works*, D. Schmidtz and E. Willott, eds. (New York: Oxford, 2002).

97. B. G. Norton, "Beyond Positivist Ecology: Toward an Integrated Ecological Ethics," *Science and Engineering Ethics* 14, no. 4 (2008): 590–91.

98. Sarah McFarland Taylor, *Green Sisters* (Cambridge, MA: Harvard University Press, 2007).

99. B. A. Minteer, E. A. Corley, and R. E. Manning, "Environmental Ethics beyond Principle? The Case for a Pragmatic Contextualism," *Journal of Agricultural and Environmental Ethics* 17, no. 2 (2004): 134.

100. So observes John Hart, who was also on the drafting committee; John Hart, *What Are They Saying about Environmental Theology?* (New York: Paulist Press, 2004), 50.

101. *The Columbia River Watershed: Caring for Creation and the Common Good (TCRW)*, The Catholic Bishops of the Watershed Region (January 2001), quoted from Introduction and IV.2.

102. For elaboration, see John Hart, *Sacramental Commons: Christian Ecological Ethics* (Lanham, MD: Rowman and Littlefield, 2006).

103. *TCRW*, "Poetic Reflection" in the concluding appendix.

104. *TCRW*, section II.

105. Thomas Berry, "Management: The Managerial Ethos and the Future of Planet Earth," *Teilhard Studies* 3 (1980), 8.

106. Swimme and Tucker, *Journey of the Universe* 111, 128.

107. Thomas Berry, *The Great Work: Our Way into the Future* (New York: Bell Tower, 1999).

CHAPTER FIVE

Toxic Wombs and the Ecology of Justice

✦

The whole creation has been groaning in labor pains until now, and not only the creation but we ourselves . . . who wait for the redemption of our bodies.
(Rom 8:22–3)

New Haven, the city that my child breathes and drinks, is an "environmental justice community." That state designation means that its high levels of poverty and its history of racial discrimination require any action that would lead to further toxic exposures to meet extra legal review. Already this small city hosts two interstates, two rail lines, an oil port, a sewage incinerator, two power generators, and many relics of heavy industry. It is not coincidental that a poorer and browner city bears disproportionate hazards of the energy, transportation, and waste disposal of the wealthiest state in the country. Living in New Haven means living in an environmental sacrifice zone, which means letting others use our bodies to run an industrial experiment.

The last chapter showed how to integrate science and ethics in the management of wicked problems while criticizing adaptive management frameworks for their inattention to social power. This chapter focuses on a problem that is wicked in several senses. Environmental toxins prove difficult for science-based management because they involve complex uncertainties and because they involve unprecedented injustices. The complex uncertainty: every human body carries novel compounds that a few generations ago did not exist and whose risks remain unclear. We are all enfleshed in an unplanned biological experiment. The unprecedented injustices: that experiment runs more intensely in poorer and browner bodies. While exposure is pervasive because toxins disperse through ecological flows, it is also uneven, because ecological flows are shaped by social power.

The chemical experiment with the human body is a microcosm of the broader human experiment with earth. As tides of novel compounds circulate through ecological systems, they begin to remake the womb of life on earth, with uncertain influences on human health, evolutionary processes, and ecological systems. The United States alone produces trillions of pounds of some 80,000 chemicals, including 5,400 compounds that are each produced in quantities over 10,000 pounds per year.[1] The US Centers for Disease Control (CDC) currently tracks only about 150 chemicals. Within the American regulatory regime, chemicals are considered safe until proven otherwise—and proof is an arduous and expensive undertaking, as political as it is scientific. Of the 150 it does track, the CDC finds that every human body inhabiting the United States bears most of them, including persistent organic pollutants such as dioxins and pesticides.[2] What that means for our health or earth's future we do not know. From our ignorance about cumulative and combinatorial exposures and the long-term impact on ecological systems, writes risk expert John Wargo, we must "create an environmentally intelligent society that is self-conscious of the subtle ways that humanity is transforming the chemistry of the planet and our bodies."[3] How to turn an accidental experiment into social learning about sustainability?

The chemical experiment runs more acutely in certain kinds of bodies. Race remains the most statistically significant indicator of toxic waste sitings in the United States. Poverty increases likelihood of everyday exposures around the world. Children are disproportionately sensitive to chemical exposures. The womb is uniquely vulnerable and, as this chapter will show, a synecdoche of anthropocene human power interacting with life-sustaining systems. Using vulnerable bodies to run chemical experiments recalls infamous bioethics cases such as the Tuskegee syphilis experiment. The racism and misuse of science in the Tuskegee case illuminate dimensions of environmental injustice, even though the "experiment" of toxins is less intentionally designed. However, the problem of toxic exposures runs deeper because it challenges how ethics conceptualizes injustice. Confronting the problem of toxins requires following social power through ecological relations, interpreting ecosystems as political systems, and rethinking the subject of human rights. This chapter explains how environmental justice projects follow power through all its ecological relations, adapting the meaning of justice and expanding moral anthropology as they do.

Religious ethics has not always appreciated environmental justice projects as sites of moral adaptation, even though they represent some of the most creative and successful responses to sustainability problems. This chapter explores some explanations for the lack, which include obtuseness to white racism and social power within the field of religion and ecology, as well as obtuseness to religion in the social sciences that describe environmental justice projects. In ethics, the lack of attention to environmental justice projects also has to do with cosmological methods overly impressed by debate between ecocentric and anthropocentric worldviews. Preoccupation with developing an ecological worldview can suppress attention to community health projects and make their concerns seem unsuitably anthropocentric. That perception, I argue, misses how environmental justice projects contest the whiteness of mainstream environmental thought, make ecological relations into arenas of political struggle, and begin to expand justice toward the ecological embodiment of personhood. Struggling over relative priorities for "ecology" versus "justice" in a moral worldview obscures how struggles for survival politicize received concepts of "ecology" and ecologize received concepts of "justice."

Following leads in ecofeminist and womanist ethics, I argue that grassroots struggles against ecologically mediated threats to survival use concepts of justice in ways that begin to re-enflesh human personhood within ecological relations. I illustrate that trajectory by showing how practices born from "maternal resistance" to childhood toxic exposures now support projects to establish rights for Mother Earth. This chapter thus traces a movement from using rights to protect humans from ecologically mediated perils, to transforming the subject of rights, to establishing the rights of an ecological membership.

ECOLOGY IS POLITICAL

I begin from two cases in the United States that often serve as origin stories for the emergence of an environmental justice framework. These were hardly the first instances of communities recognizing injustice in their ecological relations. Struggle over environmental risks and resources is a basic feature of human history, which the fields of political ecology and environmental history have begun to recover. I begin with Love Canal and Warren County, the two standard North American stories, in order to illustrate what religious ethics has often missed in them: how environmental justice projects function as sites of ethical expansion and how they draw on religion and cosmology.

The lesson of these sections is not that synthetic chemicals are evil. I am looking for how communities can use practices of justice to develop the sort of adaptive intelligence that can interpret the increasing presence of chemicals in ecological systems. Synthetic chemicals help societies alleviate basic miseries, including food scarcity, energy lack, and treatable disease.

Assessing their use and production requires understanding their role within ecological systems. For perhaps the most famous example, the insecticide DDT allowed many countries to eradicate malaria. In some areas it opened possibilities of freedom where malarial parasites had beleaguered human development for most of history.[4] Its inventor received a Nobel prize in medicine because the chemical freed so many human bodies from parasite burdens. Yet DDT produces another kind of body burden: scientists discovered that it accumulates in biological tissue over time, magnifying as it moves up trophic levels in a food chain. Rachel Carson's 1962 *Silent Spring* brought this research to public attention, showing the mobility of chemicals along ecological flows and the permeability of human bodies to those flows. Disappearing songbirds were—to use a troubling metaphor that we will see again—the miner's canary.[5]

In North America, Carson's *Silent Spring* helped create public awareness of vulnerability to environmental toxins, but it was an upstate New York mother who mobilized a new kind of movement for social justice. Lois Gibbs started the Love Canal Parents Movement when she discovered that her child's chronic sickness likely had to do with the 21,000 tons of chemical waste over which their neighborhood school was built. Her white, working-class neighborhood had for years reported chemical odors and clusters of sickness, including excessive miscarriages, but their complaints had been dismissed by the state. Then in 1978, with new evidence about the health effects of dioxin and PCBs emerging, the New York Commission of Health decided to close the school and evacuate nearby families. Gibbs's family was not within the initial evacuation cordon and was told that they were safe. Distrustful of the information they were receiving, the neighborhood enlisted a nongovernment scientist and under her direction conducted its own health research, documenting abnormally high rates of miscarriage, birth defect, and respiratory illness. The newly formed Environmental Protection Agency (EPA) followed up with blood tests, which showed chromosome damage indicating that residents were at increased risk of cancer and reproductive problems.[6]

Angry and frightened at the results, a crowd of neighborhood mothers held two EPA agents hostage for five hours in order to demand a broader evacuation. Gibbs was their public spokesperson, insisting to the White House that their basic rights as citizens had been violated and that they should be moved. President Carter agreed. After the victory, Gibbs founded the Citizens Clearinghouse for Hazardous Waste (now the Center for Health, Environment, and Justice), which assists communities facing environmentally mediated harms.[7] The Love Canal protest concretized the idea that environments could mediate unseen violations of human dignity.

Subsequent struggles would protest "toxic trespass," referring to "the involuntary use of one's body for someone else's chemicals."[8] By making rights claims to interpret toxic risks, these struggles present human ecology as a condition of *political* vulnerability.

Do ecologically mediated hazards merit rights protections? As the Love Canal movement was asserting its rights, the international community was considering whether to articulate a new class of human rights. After the 1972 Stockholm Conference declared that humans have a right to "an environment of a quality that permits a life of dignity and well-being," the United Nations debated whether such an environmental right would conflict with other rights (especially a right to development).[9] A series of UN special reports made the case for recognizing a new environmental right by amassing evidence that political power serially deprives persons of their dignity by doing violence to the ecological relations on which they depend.[10] By the mid-1990s, however, the United States and other economic powers had quashed the inquiry because of worries that rights-based environmental protections would impede free market access to resources.[11] They preferred the more pliable discourse of "sustainable development," thus using the idea of sustainability to limit the ecological entailments of political justice. Sustainability and human rights appeared separate and rivalrous projects.

Yet environmental justice projects continue to make rights claims in situations where political powers unfairly control the ecological relations that sustain human dignity. Those rights claims depict ecology as a scene of political violence. By protesting unfair exposures to hazards of industrial society, protests like the one at Love Canal draw attention to the political production of environmental risks. Ulrich Beck argues that as movements use social norms (like rights) to interpret distribution of those risks, they force societies to recognize their responsibility for the organization and function of environmental systems. Protests like the one at Love Canal, Beck thinks, deepen the sort of ecological awareness opened by Carson into a form of critical reflection on industrial society as itself a kind of ecological system.[12] Deploying justice norms to interpret toxic risks lets rights practices drive critical learning about ecological systems.

It would be a mistake to think—as some sustainability theorists do— that environmental justice projects constrain their scope to anthropocentric welfare concerns of local constituencies.[13] On the contrary, using rights to interpret environmental hazards expands the scope of ecological thought to reckon with the way political power shapes ecological systems. The relative status of humans in a moral cosmology is not their point. "The environmentalism of the poor," argues Joan Martinez-Alier, works to show how ecological relations are political relations, and as such sites of political struggle and social violence.[14] The antitoxics campaign begun from Love Canal did more than represent an identity-driven protest of working-class white people. Theorists often think that way, suggests David Schlosberg, because of the primacy of distributive theories of political justice.[15] The initial claim of distributive fairness by the Love Canal parents initiated a process of community reflection on its chemical habitat, which opened criticism of how science and politics collude to keep vulnerable citizens uninformed about their own bodies, which pushed citizens toward rethinking their embodiment within a politically shaped ecology. Making rights claims traces human vulnerability through ecological space and expands the competency of justice to follow.

MOTHERS FOR JUSTICE

Environmental justice movements (EJM) arise from many different communities in response to various problems, but there is a striking demographic pattern: they are disproportionately led by women.[16] Gibbs entered activism as part of mothering a sick child, and the Parents Association she started quickly attracted other mothers concerned about miscarriages, birth deformities, and family health. "By and large it is women in their traditional role as mothers," says sociologist Celene Krauss, "who make the link between toxic wastes and their children's ill health." That is not to say there is an essential connection of women and nature or female identity and child-rearing. Krauss observes those leaders tactically deploying constructed gender roles and ideologies of motherhood as political sites "to initiate and justify their resistance."[17] In her maternal role as protective caregiver Gibbs could even be applauded for taking hostage EPA agents in order to safeguard her children. She was mobilizing what Sara Ruddick calls the "maternal politics" of movements that "deploy the symbols and passions of mothering" in struggles against political violence. (Not only females protecting biological offspring may deploy those symbols and passions; maternal politics might be mobilized from other caregiving relations with a political rather than biological account of mothering.)[18] How do practices of mothering construct environmental justice?

Leaders sometimes deploy tropes of motherhood to identify the specific relations threatened by environmental justice. Winona LaDuke thus frames the challenges of an Akwesasne Mohawk community located near industrial waste zones through the voice of an Akwesasne midwife, who says: "women are the first environment," because as "we accumulate toxic chemicals like PCBs . . . they are stored in our body fat and excreted primarily though breast milk." Reproductive mothering identifies the environment under toxic threat: the relations that sustain and birth the next generation. Those relations, and toxic threats to them, exist beyond the Akwesasne community and beyond the human community. The midwife's experience with repro- ductive trouble in the community led her to look for confirming research in whales in the nearby polluted St. Lawrence River. She discovered that they too had high toxic loads and poor reproductive success. That led her to initiate the Akwesasne Mother's Milk Project, studying bioaccumulation of chemicals within a central mothering relation. LaDuke sees their project connecting a toxic harm with the future of a people: "rebirthing their na- tion, from the first environment of the womb, to the community and future generations."[19] The project has even further implications: connecting whales and future generations in Akwesasne wombs illustrates how toxins pose threats to the processes through which life is made and sustained.

Wombs are particularly vulnerable to toxic trespass. Chemical expo- sures pose disproportionate risks for pregnant women, fetuses, and infants, especially when they accumulate in human milk or uterine tissues. Mercury and PCBs, which accumulate in many fish eaten for food, accumulate also in reproductive tissues where they pose exceptional hazards to healthy child- birth. Meanwhile research continues on the impact of the pesticides and flame retardants found in human breast milk.[20] Prenatal exposure to pesti- cides, which is more likely among socially disadvantaged mothers, appears to have significant negative impact on childhood brain development. Young children often have different patterns of exposure (crawling on carpets and licking toys in tactile exploration), higher proportional intakes of chemicals (small bodies with high energy circulation), and lower thresholds of risk during particular periods of development (early exposure to lead hinders brain development). Yet toxicity tests usually refer to a mature adult body and do not account for the intensity and combination of childhood expo- sures, so what little research is conducted on synthetic chemicals is method- ologically biased against children.[21] "We are by default conducting a massive clinical toxicological trial," say two pediatric research physicians; "and our children and their children are the experimental animals."[22]

Interpreting toxic risks within the relations of mothering interprets what industrial powers may be doing to the basic relations through which life is sustained. When an Akwesasne midwife finds that the same PCBs ac- cumulating in human mother's milk also hinder reproduction in whales, she identifies within mothering a form of ecological violence indifferent to species and deathly to the whole matrix of life. Giovanna Di Chiro thus sees EJM developing a reproductive expansion of justice. "All environmen- tal issues are reproductive issues," she writes, because "efforts to protect the health and integrity of natural systems . . . are struggles to sustain the

ecosystems that make all life possible." Resisting toxic threats to all reproduction, working for "the maintenance and sustainability of everyday life
and earthly survival," may then arise from everyday practices of mothering—from bearing, feeding, clothing, and protecting our children.[23]

Everyday acts of caring for children can give rise to a broader ethic
of care for all the relationships that sustain us. If cultivated as a moral and
political practice, writes Anna Peterson, caring for children can make parents respect and protect the sustaining relations that mother us all. By parenting "we experience, in the flesh . . . the concrete ways in which we are
constructed and constrained by our relationships." Parenting decenters us,
orients us to the bodily needs of others, and makes us recognize the fundamental dependency and relational character of human personhood.[24] It
might also make parents and caregivers identify with life-nurturing aspects
of earth. Peterson observes that connection in the Navajo world: "Not only
women who give birth biologically but also the earth, sheep, the cornfield,
and other entities in the Navajo world are literal, not metaphorical, mothers
because Navajo people rely on them for survival."[25] Struggles against toxic
threats may then lead caregivers to protect all those things upon which we
rely for survival, protecting the entire "ecology of mothering."[26] Of course,
the experience of caring for dependents does not automatically make a
person care for other creatures or connect political and ecological justice.
Parental devotion sometimes makes persons more insular and less socially
engaged. It takes a creative leader like Gibbs to make the connections from
her own experience of caregiving to a broader political struggle in which
sustaining values and relations are in peril.

Making those connections from within cultural practices of mothering
runs risks with gender. Consider LaDuke, here writing the foreword to an
anthology on gender and environmental justice: "Our bodies are a mirror
of our mother, and of Mother Earth. And so we walk, healthy, beautiful,
vibrant, voluptuous through the minefield of industrialism. It is a minefield
of toxic chemicals and of toxic sexual images that poison and entrap our
bodies."[27] LaDuke's imagery involves its own minefield of controversy as it
makes symbolic connections among embodiment, earth, women, and sexuality. Invoking "Mother Earth" also invokes essentialist notions of women,
romantic ideas of the "ecological Indian," and gendered constructs of nature.
Gendering the scene of environmental toxins this way allows for resonant
protest phrases like "rape of nature," but may reinforce cultural logics of
domination that license violence against women and exploitation of earth.[28]

Maternal politics thus invite ecofeminist criticism. The discussion in
religious thought is especially rich here, offering lines of critique and construction important to environmental justice. Since Rosemary Radford

Ruether's pathbreaking *New Woman New Earth* (1975), ecofeminist critics have confronted disembodying religious narratives that identify human personhood with an amaterial, other-worldly, masculine spirit. By typologically connecting and derogating embodiment, materiality, earth, women, and sexuality, those narratives underwrite several kinds of domination.[29] In response, ecofeminist theologies have reintegrated embodiment and creation into the experience of God and understandings of moral anthropology, often by reclaiming feminine, maternal, and ecological images of the divine.[30] In an incisive analysis relevant to protecting mothering systems, Catherine Keller argues that classical Christian doctrines of creation exhibit a fearful recoil from earth's reproductive agency. Her work suggests that when projects confront chemical experimentation with women's wombs they face cultural mimicry of a god who imposes his fiat in disregard of earth's creative wombs. Protecting ecological and maternal wombs from toxic violence may require recovering creation as "ocean of divinity, womb and place-holder of all beginnings."[31]

However, ecofeminist theologies reflect weak engagement with environmental justice struggles, which is typical of religious ethics in general. Tovis Page argues that the connection lags because scholarship in ecofeminism has tended to work with ideal worldviews rather than material practices, despite analyses that should bend methodological commitments in materialist directions.[32] That claim does not hold universally and Page observes important exceptions. It does, however, seem that ecofeminist scholarship has more often pursued broad claims about cultural cosmology than engaged the survival struggles of specific communities. Dorceta Taylor thinks that abstraction reflects a tendency for ecofeminism to think from experiences of white women—usually professional academics who understand their world through ideological contest. Environmental justice projects are predominately led by women of color, observes Taylor, and these leaders tend to understand their struggles for justice in ways at once more concrete and more complex.[33] They may also understand motherhood differently than white parents do. Patricia Collins has shown how black women receive a unique inheritance of diverse mothering roles, which they fashion in various ways to meet the specific challenges of their communities. Black mothering has sometimes been pathologized by white culture and exploited by black men. However, motherhood remains a symbol of power for black women, writes Collins, catalyzing many into political actions they might not otherwise have considered.[34] One surprising arena for black motherhood has been the democratic politics of waste management. While the concern of every mother, toxins show up in some communities more than others.

ENVIRONMENTAL RACISM

At the same time that the white residents of Love Canal were winning their battle over environmental toxins, the black residents of Warren County, North Carolina, were losing theirs. In 1978 a company trying to evade new toxic waste regulations dumped PCB-contaminated fluid along 240 miles of highway. The EPA approved a state cleanup plan that proposed to create a landfill for the waste in Warren County, whose residents were mostly poor and African American. Local protests followed and eventually involved national civil rights leaders. When protesters lay across a road to put their bodies in front of trucks bringing the contaminated soil, it led to over 500 arrests. It was "the first time anyone in the United States had been jailed trying to halt a toxic waste landfill," observes Robert Bullard, and it opened a new dimension in the civil rights movement. Twenty years after Martin Luther King was assassinated during a sanitation worker's strike in Memphis, his Southern Christian Leadership Council (SCLC) stood in front of waste trucks to dramatize a new front in the struggle against American racism.[35]

In Bullard's telling, at Warren County the civil rights movement discovered the environmental dimensions of social justice and, by framing them as matters of civil rights, made environmental problems matter to minority communities. Says Bullard, "blacks did not launch a frontal assault on environmental problems affecting their community until these issues were couched in a civil rights context," which made environmental issues part of "a struggle against institutionalized racism."[36] That story has become an important origin narrative for the emergence of EJM in the United States, often interpreting differences between justice movements and environmentalist movements. However, the history at Warren County is more complicated, and the complications point to overlooked expansions of justice. EJM do more than involve racial minorities in environmentalism; by using rights to contest ecologically mediated violence they open ecological dimensions of human liberation. That moral creativity can be missed when the story of Warren County is told as the emergence of an environmentalism that is distinct for being black and anthropocentric, and when the role of religion and spirituality in the story is overlooked. I address the first point in this section and turn to neglect of the role of religion in the next.

At first, racism was not the interpretive frame for local resistance to the Warren County hazardous waste facility. The Concerned Citizens group that first formed in opposition to the dump was in fact mostly Euro-American and Eileen McGurty thinks that their resistance was motivated by "the strong bonds to the land held by citizens in the rural south." She notes that the group initially sought help from Senator Jesse Helms.[37] In other words, some reason for opposition to dumping toxins in Warren County was rooted in the same agrarian ethos that in many parts of the south supported white *resistance* to civil rights. The initial justice claims at Warren Country were not antiracist; they were motivated by concern for local land rights, informed by emerging knowledge of environmental toxins. The controversy took place at a moment when the nation's consciousness of environmental toxins had been heightened by Love Canal, which was just concluding. When Lois Gibbs came to North Carolina to help rally opposition, citizens had already heard about PCBs in breast milk and already had reasons to distrust the science and governance of toxic containment.[38] The situation in Warren County at first seemed similar: chemical exposures were threatening the health of a relatively poor community.

Then one Warren County mother helped invent a new dimension of ecological politics. Dollie Burwell had helped lead a successful black voter registration effort and was thereby connected to the SCLC and the United Church of Christ Commission on Racial Justice. When she got involved with the toxins controversy, Burwell did so as a mother concerned for the whole community's health and as a black civil rights activist confronting white racism. Burwell's connections led to the involvement of Ben Chavis, who had recently been released from four years of wrongful imprisonment following a very public civil rights boycott. Their arrest in front of the trucks made the protest become a civil rights event and a confrontation with white power.[39]

Whether Burwell or Chavis first uttered the charge of "environmental racism" (it is attributed both ways), the idea dramatically shifted moral perceptions of the relation between environmental problems and social justice.[40] Within a year the NAACP passed a resolution on hazardous waste. Whereas previously it might have appeared that toxins posed a generally equal risk across communities, the charge of racism illuminated systemic unfairness in their spatial distribution. Black children are more likely to have toxins in their drinking water, and the strongest reason why is because they live in a predominately black community. A landmark 1987 report, "Toxic Waste and Race in America," established the initial evidence that race was the most significant statistical factor in the location of toxic waste sites.[41] (Twenty years later it still was.)[42] A 1992 report showed that EPA cleanups of Superfund sites were faster and the penalties higher in white areas, regardless of wealth.[43]

By showing that rights to equal protection under the law could be violated through mundane environmental management, like waste disposal decisions, the idea of environmental racism has become "one of the most influential ideas affecting modern environmental law's evolution." It stands with Aldo Leopold's "land ethic" and Garret Hardin's "tragedy of the commons" in shaping public perception of environmental problems, says legal scholar Richard Lazarus.[44] The idea illustrates how a society's environmental practices (both polluting and protecting) inevitably mediate its pathologies of power. Yet like the ideas of Leopold and Hardin, the phrase "environmental racism" is sometimes celebrated in ways that cripple critical investigation of underlying problems. When used to explain or refer to the demographic constituencies of those who participate, it can make environmental justice seem as if it were (merely) racial minority expressions of environmentalism. The success of Bullard's work on environmental activism in black communities has become so influential that in North America the term "environmental justice" is sometimes used to refer to any participation of racial minority communities in environmental activities. Calling something an "environmental justice event" sometimes makes a demographic description (nonwhite participants) rather than a practical one (focused on justice and power). If it functions as a term of demographic identity rather than as a critical resource for interpreting political ecologies, the idea of environmental justice distracts from how projects shift the meaning of justice.

With similar perversion, the idea of environmental racism can sometimes actually obscure the way white power flows through ecological relations. The idea of environmental racism should challenge received notions of what racism is and how it functions. The American imagination of racism often focuses on direct violence or discrimination between persons, but the racist landscape of toxic waste is the outcome of environmental management policies that explicitly aim to protect all citizens from toxic harm. "Our understanding of racism is . . . shaped by the most extreme expressions of individual bigotry, not by the way in which it functions naturally, almost invisibly (and sometimes with genuinely benign intent), when it is embedded in the structure of a social system." So writes Michelle Alexander in her account of mass incarceration as a "colorblind" system of racial control.[45] In the case of environmental toxins, economic efficiency often directs toxins to sacrifice zones created by processes blind to the race of nearby citizens, but also blind to inherited power over land resources and the subtle biases that depress the economic value of some communities into "rational" waste zones. When racism refers to deliberate discriminatory acts against discrete individuals or communities, it becomes nearly impossible to prove and only marginally relevant to ecological flows of political violence.

Treatments of environmental racism as intentional discrimination therefore undermine projects to confront toxic risks by focusing on "race-neutral" procedures of environmental decision making. When Bullard's 1990 *Dumping in Dixie* established nationwide evidence of racist distribution of toxins, it depicted the inevitable outcome of chemical production on the landscape of white power: most of the profits flow to white and wealthy citizens, while most of the hazards flow into black and poor citizens. Race-neutral decisions about waste disposal (Bullard agrees) cannot transform the racist ecology of chemical production because procedural discrimination does not fully explain how white power uses ecological space.

For example, geographer Laura Pulido shows that Los Angeles generated a racialized pattern of suburban expansion as white fears of nonwhite residents and urban development plans historically inflected each other. As white socioeconomic opportunity concentrated geographically and protected its privilege in plans for housing, education, and environmental quality, nonwhite neighborhoods lost in relative value, making them more cost-efficient for polluting industries to locate there. In order to confront toxic exposures in Los Angeles, says Pulido, justice-oriented projects must see how "space is a resource in the production of white privilege" and understand how the landscape of toxic distribution is a result of urban development processes working over time in a racialized society.[46] A "race-neutral" decision process thus permits a racist landscape to reproduce itself, only now with the cover of justice. The idea of environmental racism, then, goes beyond deliberate targeting of minority communities to illuminate the processes that sustain the ecology of white privilege, confronting what Rob Nixon calls "slow violence"—the "violence that occurs gradually and out of sight . . . an attritional violence that is typically not viewed as violence at all."[47]

The ecological implications of white power have usually remained invisible to dominant (white) streams of American environmental thought. However, the use of civil rights to confront the toxic landscape of white power helps establish something that ecological thinkers (including Leopold and Hardin) often want: expansion of ethics to an ecological membership. When projects protest ecologically mediated hazards, they imply political rights to live in a healthy ecological community, which makes implicit claims about the ecological vulnerability of human personhood and the membership conditions for protecting it. If persons have a right to protection from toxic trespass, it is because they have a claim to participate in ecological relations that sustain human embodiment. Unfortunately, a discursive divide between environmental justice and white/mainstream environmentalism sometimes obscures this contribution: environmental justice projects recover humanity's ecological body.

That divide emerged at Warren County when the Sierra Club saw the local protest as political resistance to a national environmental quality

initiative. The Sierra Club supported EPA regulations for managing hazardous wastes, which guided the procedure and assessment for the Warren
County decision. Civil rights challenges to the EPA confounded the Sierra
Club and they withdrew from the scene.[48] The absence of existing environmental organizations at the Warren County protests has come to represent a divide between justice-driven and conservation-driven approaches to
environmental problems. That divide led to the invention of "mainstream
environmentalism" as a name for conservation-focused organizations that
usually do not see their complicity with the landscapes of white power. For
decades, environmental justice movements around the world have defined
themselves against mainstream environmental organizations that ignore
how nature is a resource for social power. Conserving nature always simultaneously conserves a political order.

The key difference among movements is not their demographics nor
the degree of ecocentrism in their worldview; it is whether and how they
recognize ecological relations as political relations. Environmental justice
movements force environmental actions (of any sort) to take responsibility for how their perception of "the environment" participates in political
control of ecological systems. That includes taking responsibility for the
historical politics that produce their ecological imaginary and the contemporary social practices that it supports. North American conservation has
often sought to protect the places and species remembered in the narrative
of European conquest of a new, wild world. The idea of wilderness is part
of the ecological imaginary that supported white invasion by constructing
nature as pristine and empty, in need of the civilizing project of conquest.
If other people already lived there, then they too must be primitive and
wild, in need of conquest. Civilizing culture has a duty to clear them from
the land, whether by removal or annihilation.[49] Because wilderness was part
of an ecological imaginary supporting white superiority and human (i.e.,
European) colonization of nature, contemporary environmentalisms shaped
by concern for "pristine nature" must at least take responsibility for the history from which they emerge and the political landscapes that they sustain.
The logic of toxic "sacrifice zones," argues Charles Mills, still depends on
the ecological imaginary of white supremacy.[50] Conservation strategies that
(still) mandate state removal of indigenous people from "protected areas"
continue to draw on the logic of civilizing wild nature and wild savages.[51]

Even when modern cultural projects seek to protect "native" peoples
and care for "the environment," shows theologian Willie Jennings, they do
so from within the massive colonial displacement of identity from land that
gave rise to racialized perceptions of "native" and "nature." As constructs

of race constricted identity to bodies, argues Jennings, they generated a
new mode of encountering land and peoples that permits either romantic
care or exploitation without reciprocal influence over the agent. "With the
emergence of whiteness, identity was calibrated through possession of, not
possession by, specific land."[52] Racialized agency thus stands behind all the
possibilities of power over new spaces and peoples. The modern politics of
race and of environmentalism continue to reproduce a fundamental disconnection of identity formation from place inhabitation.

It makes sense, then, that environmental justice projects imagine "the
environment" differently, in support of a different politics. Dorceta Taylor's
research shows that participants in environmental justice movements tend
to imagine nature not as sublime and distant wilderness but in terms of
the everyday places where they live, work, play, and worship.[53] In order
to win attention to those places and their connection to political vulnerabilities, environmental justice projects must wrest discursive control away
from mainstream ecological imaginaries. Frustration with mainstream inat-
tentiveness to local struggles for environmental quality has sometimes led
leaders to disparage the value of other species as a way of discrediting the
ecological imaginary of mainstream environmentalism. Dollie Burwell once
said that "African Americans are not concerned with endangered species
because we are an endangered species."[54] Academic voices sometimes repeat
that disdain for other species. In an often-cited essay, James Cone exhibits
disaffection from whales and spotted owls in order to display disaffection
from white environmentalism.[55] The rhetorical point of those statements is
to force mainstream environmentalism to recognize its collusion with white
power and to acknowledge the environmental experiences of those struggling against it. Their anthropocentrism is not about a metaethical priority
for humans in general; it is an epistemic priority for those oppressed by
white power.

Environmental justice projects insist on beginning from experiences of
political violence, which ecocentric approaches tend to conceal and abet.
Paul Outka argues that the whiteness of ecocentric thought and the anthropocentrism of critical race theory trace to different fundamental experiences of union with nature (white sublimity and black trauma in his
analysis).[56] The ecological imaginary carried by Sierra Club calendars, with
their pictures of endangered species in sublime, people-less landscapes, thus
forms part of what Emilie Townes calls the fantastic hegemonic imagination
(see chapter 2). The material culture of environmentalism often imagines
"nature" in terms of the European experience with the New World, while
erasing the past and present traumas of the landscape. Those calendars become part of the cultural production of white power.

It distorts the conflict to suppose that the difference among environmentalisms traces to the relative anthropocentrism or ecocentrism of their worldviews. When environmental justice leaders contest the ecological imaginary of white power by disparaging other species, their protests unfortunately reinforce the appearance of human-centered justice movements opposing nature-centered environmental movements. It is more helpful, I think, to understand environmental justice projects as interpreting the meaning of nature from experiences of ecological violence. By emphasizing that environments are historically constructed and socially organized, they reframe environmental problems as political problems. By deploying rights concepts to protest the ecological flow of toxins into the bodies of disempowered citizens, they begin to interpret personhood in terms of its ecological relations. The moral choice here is not between nature and humans, but for or against ecologically embodied justice.[57]

Deploying justice to interpret environmental problems thus begins to change the subject of justice. Making human rights claims to confront ecological violence begins to ecologically expand human personhood. The anthropocentrism here does not work to exclude the interests of nonhumans but rather to reconstruct the "anthropos" in terms of its ecological relations. "This is not an attempt to make humans dominant over the rest of nature," explains Dorceta Taylor; "it is a way to say that humans . . . are a part of the ecosystem."[58] As it does, it connects the interests of whales and spotted owls to our own, for they also depend on the health of the environments made and managed by human powers. At its most basic level, says David Naguib Pellow, environmental justice stands for the "inextricable relationship between the degradation of people and their ecosystems," and the practices that disrupt that power. When those practices trace racism to its roots, thinks Pellow, they find a unified cultural practice of human and environmental domination.[59] Contesting racist distribution of toxins leads to questioning nearly everything about modern industrial culture, from its imagination of nature to its moral anthropology. Seeking justice on toxic landscapes leads toward a logic of integrated ecological and social membership.

My point in this section has been that as environmental justice projects deploy civil rights practices to confront racist distribution of toxins, they expand the basic notion of justice that those rights practices carry, in ways that begin to ecologically rethink the human person. Christian ethics chronically misses that moral creativity, in part because the role of religious practices and ideas within environmental justice movements is often overlooked. If theological scholars would treat environmental justice struggles as sites of interesting ethical and theological production, it could change the shape of liberation.

RELIGION AND ENVIRONMENTAL LIBERATION

The religious creativity of environmental justice movements is chronically overlooked by social scientists, by environmental pragmatists, and (oddly) by religious ethicists. Sociological observers of EJM have been eager to draw connections with the civil rights movement but they tend to skip associations with religion. When Warren County protesters marched to block the road, they marched out from a church.[60] The protests were initiated when a black church and a white church came together to organize a coalition and were organized in church-based mass meetings, which included preaching and prayer along with soil science and protest tactics. On the few occasions when Bullard mentions church involvement, he explains its significance as mobilization of an indigenous black institution.[61] But the black church is not *just* a social institution; it is also an interpretive theological community. When protesters sang hymns, preached sermons, and prayed publicly they were doing more than mobilizing an important local institution. They were also inculcating a spirituality of social justice that could integrate theological, scientific, and local knowledges to interpret their problems.

The writer of one of the few ethnographies of an environmental justice project observes that "every grassroots-led meeting that I attended during fourteen months of fieldwork began and ended with a prayer. . . . Christianity, specifically black Baptist faith, was an integral part of the grassroots environmental justice organizing." Yet she devotes only a few pages to religion, and those are marked mostly by her bemusement at its unfamiliar and quaint habits.[62] Her bemusement reflects a broader unease with religion in social science and in environmental thought, which leads to ignorance about how everyday communities interpret their problems. Reflecting that she too has never attended an environmental justice event that did not begin with prayer, Pulido says of her discipline that "geographers have been largely dismissive of the spirituality of the people we study."[63] The resulting accounts miss important dimensions of how communities experience their environments and how they go about working to change them.

The role of religion is also overlooked by a field that has even stronger reasons to attend to lived moralities. Environmental pragmatists share environmental justice commitments to begin moral thought from community experience and seek concrete responses to specific problems. However, as I observed in the last chapter, pragmatists rarely engage either environmental justice projects or religious communities. This may be because environmental justice movements are politically marginal, often questioning the fairness of democratic decision making within structures of unequal power or the function of adaptive management in landscapes of white supremacy.

Maybe their radical critiques or their public spirituality make environmental justice projects appear too "religious" for pragmatist sensibilities. In any case, the neglect is regrettable because antitoxic community movements create grassroots practices for developing the sort of adaptive environmental intelligence that pragmatists envision.

Religious practices can be a critical element in cultivating that environmental intelligence. Integrating confrontation with toxins into a faith community's witness to hope in the face of evil can mobilize expansions of social justice. For example, giving witness to one's experience in the face of trouble, observes Valeria Kaalund, is a traditional practice through which black churches interpret their reality. Witnessing in a mass meeting gives individuals opportunity to draw their everyday experience into the words of the biblical prophets and the movements of black militancy. Kaalund portrays Dollie Burwell doing this in womanist style by using scripture to face death threats and appropriating hostile culture to renarrate the Warren County situation in her own voice.[64]

Yet even religionists overlook the religious creativity of EJM. The distinctiveness of Burwell's voice, and of the many other female leaders of color (and of faith), has been overlooked within religion and ecology as well as within liberationist theological ethics. Within the field of religion and ecology, environmental justice projects may be overlooked because they seem too pragmatic and insufficiently cosmological. But interpreting them that way misses how grassroots movements work. In an important article on the significance of EJM for Christian ethics, Larry Rasmussen writes that "organizations addressing environmental racism do not begin, as ethicists are wont, with moral theory. . . . They work from concrete injuries of injustice and seek incremental remedies." The differences in method generate separate intellectual cultures: "many in the circle under the sway of Thomas Berry's singular influence, of John Cobb's, care deeply about justice . . . just as many EJ thinkers care about worldviews. . . . But with the exception of some ecofeminist and womanist work, these circles overlap little."[65] Rasmussen is politely saying that religion and ecology is so white in demographic because it has been so white in method. Its favored norm of "eco-justice" does not come close to meaning the same thing as "environmental justice" because they refer to two totally different uses of justice.[66] Until it sees and incorporates how communities use their religious and cultural inheritances to confront ecologies of racism, the field of religion and ecology colludes with white power.[67]

While some community leaders and pastors call for development of a "black environmental liberation theology," the project remains wanting.[68] That may be because black liberationist thought also has yet to fully engage

environmental justice projects. Consider how James Cone treats environmental racism (in the one place that he does). Cone rightly castigates white
ecotheologians for being methodologically racist by starting from worldviews of creation rather than experiences of oppression. In contrast, he cel-
ebrates the "group of black churchwomen in Warren County" who made
ecological issues into civil rights issues. Cone then complains that in ecotheology, "people of color are not treated *seriously*, that is, as if they have something *essential* to contribute to the conversation."[69] Yet Cone himself does
not seem to see any essential contribution from the black churchwomen,
because he moves on without notice of their creative expansion of justice—
or its implication for his own theology of liberation. Instead he gives a nod
to womanist writers.

Womanist writers have been among the few religious thinkers to see
how environmental justice projects inscribe freedom into holist cosmologies. For example, after calling environmental racism a form of collective
lynching, Townes writes that "the yoking of civil and environmental rights
is crucial to ontological wholeness." Connecting civil rights and ecological violence, she suggests, improves and maybe shifts the understanding of
persons protected by rights. Townes wants investigations into the concrete
realities of environmental racism to lead her toward an ontology that makes
better sense of all the injustices involved.[70] Alice Walker follows responses
to environmental racism into a wide moral membership. When she says
"everything is a human being," her statement is not anthropocentric but
anthropocosmic: she interprets earth's vulnerability to human power from
within the embodied vulnerability of human personhood, as experienced
by black women. Racist violence interprets ecological violence as Walker
writes that "the Earth itself has become the nigger of the world."[71] Delores
Williams deepens that connection by developing a theological relation between the defilement of female, black bodies and the defilement of earth.
Sin is not disembodied and notional; it seeps materially and ecologically, as
the evil of white violence accumulates as PCBs in wombs of black women.[72]
In response, writes Williams, womanist theologies develop "active opposition to all forms of violence against humans (male and female), against
nature (including nonhuman animals), against the environment and against
the land."[73]

Religious ethics still awaits a full account of justice generated from the
experience of black women struggling against ecological violence.[74] There
appear two broad theological categories for doing so: liberation and survival. For black women of faith, says Karen Baker-Fletcher, confronting
environmental racism should manifest an account of liberation in which

"hope and salvation are experienced in connection with God as Spirit within creation—in skies, trees, water, land, birds, family, friends, humanity, the body."[75] Cone's difficulty in hearing womanist voices as ecological theologians may be instructive of what would be needed for that account. Cone may not appreciate the expansion of liberation in environmental justice projects because following that trajectory would require his liberation theology to develop a cosmic christology similar to the sort found in the eco-theologies that he criticizes.

J. Kameron Carter's engagement with Cone's theology of race shows the deficit, as well as a way for black liberation theology to rethink freedom within the cosmic body of Christ. Carter worries that Cone's attempt to think with black freedom movements repeats a moral anthropology that works against the disruptive potential of those struggles. Specifically, Cone focuses so intently on the blackness of freedom that he seems at risk of essentializing race.[76] The subject of justice seems overdetermined by a naturalized identity. The subject of the Warren County freedom movement, I have been suggesting, is more porous. She is an ecologically embodied person, raced and gendered within the sustaining relations of a political ecology. Carter thinks that Cone's liberation falls short of the transformation anticipated in black freedom movements because the person of Christ, and so moral anthropology in general, seems disconnected from creation. The treatment of whiteness and the displacement in Willie Jennings's analysis of the origins of race supports the general point here, that to reach as far as the vulnerability of persons to ecological violence, it must recover connections of personhood and creation.

Some other recent work from black liberation theology recognizes that need by recovering cosmic christology on the notion that liberation can only be as ecological as the body of Christ. Dwight Hopkins writes that the crucial legacy of Warren County is the lesson that "holistic disease requires ecological justice, that is, holistic health and healing."[77] For black theology to take up that lesson and develop an environmental liberation theology, says Hopkins, then it would need a christology that can bear ecological justice. He suggests that black theology engage with cosmological scriptures such as all creation groaning for liberation (Romans 8). Thomas Hoyt reaches in a similar direction, moving from environmental racism to interpret humanity though a microcosmic account of the incarnation: "God thus united with the whole biophysical universe, which is micro-embodied in humans." For Hoyt that includes all our ecological relations, sustaining and toxic: "through the flora, fauna, minerals, chemicals, and radiation we imbibe by eating, drinking, breathing, and simply being, humans embody a representative sampling of all the elements of the ecosphere." Because "this totality is what God associated with in the incarnation," liberation must reach as far, through the body of Christ to the ecosphere.[78]

Perhaps, however, liberation is not the most apt category for describing the ecology of justice in antitoxics projects. Concerned that liberation has been an androcentric idea in black theology, concealing black female experience and creativity, Delores Williams identifies survival as a second African American tradition for interpreting struggles against injustice. Working from the Genesis story of Hagar, Williams sees God responding to Hagar's expulsion to the wilderness not with liberation, but with "new vision to see survival resources." When black women organize resistance to toxic neighborhoods, their action can be read within "a long tradition of black mothers and nurturers who were catalysts for social change in and beyond the African-American community." The struggles of black women caring for children and communities should be a key source, Williams argues, for how theologians interpret God's response to experiences of violation, exclusion, and oppression.[79]

Important to the critique of wilderness and ecocentrism by environmental justice thinkers, Williams shows that struggles for survival produce multivalent appreciations for creation. In Hagar's experience, what was at first experienced as a place of deathly ordeal became a place that sustained and nurtured her. Wilderness is not only important to colonial and nature-romantic imaginations, argues Williams; it has also been a sustaining friend and sacred space in black religious experience going back to slavery.[80] Struggles for survival need not silence the claims of other creatures, one could extend Williams to say; they may come to value and even include all earth.

Both categories, liberation and survival, have potential to think the ecology of justice carried by environmental justice projects, if they follow its arc of ecological membership. The cosmological ferment within environmental justice was made evident at the First National People of Color Environmental Leadership Summit in 1991, networking among African American, Latina, and Native American communities yielded a remarkable statement, which began: "We, The People of Color, gathered together at this multinational People of Color Environmental Leadership Summit, to begin to build a national and international movement of all peoples of color to fight the destruction and taking of our lands and communities, do hereby re-establish our spiritual interdependence to the sacredness of our Mother Earth."[81]

Thinking across different political violences led participants to find in humanity's ecological body a microcosm of political violence against earth itself. When PCBs accumulate in the wombs of brown women, it calls into question not only fairness in distribution of toxic risks, but the sort of culture that produces toxic threats to the womb of life. Affirming the sacredness of Mother Earth helped participants in the 1991 Summit illustrate a form of violence serially threatening the relations through which communities are sustained. Among the summit participants were Warren County protesters, some of whom had previously disdained "mainstream" pieties for nature. Reflecting with representatives from other vulnerable communities, especially Native Americans, they affirmed their interdependence in sacred Mother Earth in order to confront shared threats to survival.

MOTHER EARTH RIGHTS

The language of survival and genocide appears across environmental justice projects attempting to make the connections of human rights and ecological destruction. The witness of Ken Saro-Wiwa, executed by the state of Nigeria in 1995, helped establish those links. Where human rights groups had not recognized environmental destruction as a form of violence, Saro-Wiwa showed how his minority Ogoni people were being slowly killed through the death of their lands by destructive oil exploitation. Genocide can happen slowly and indirectly, he insisted, through the political weapon of ecological deprivation.[82] As toxins slowly disrupt reproductive capacities of communities, that interpretation appears widely across EJM. Charles Cobb calls the dumping of environmental toxins in black communities "attempted genocide," and Emilie Townes calls it "lynching a whole people."[83] Native American activists interpret toxic contamination as one aspect of genocide conducted through ecocide.[84] Especially for indigenous peoples whose way of life depends on the integrity of a bioregion, environmental destruction may be an assault on their existence, a foreclosing of their future.

Indigenous environmental justice struggles have made "Mother Earth" a strategic symbol for grassroots resistance to environmental injustice. Its rising importance was showcased at the World People's Conference on Climate Change, where a broad coalition of justice groups affirmed a "Universal Declaration of the Rights of Mother Earth." How should religious ethics interpret the emergence of a Mother Earth cosmology within environmental justice coalitions? The cultural scene here is complex, since nature-related goddesses appear in many ancient traditions and because Mother Earth also appears in many emergent forms of nature spirituality. Deployed by environmental justice coalitions, however, Mother Earth is used to interpret conjunctions of political violence and environmental destruction in order to generate corresponding ideas and practices of justice.

Genocide is the paradigm case in arguments for a human right held by a group, rather than by individuals, because it is violence directed against persons because of their membership in a specific group. In the case of indigenous peoples, human dignity is shaped by a cultural form of membership in an ecological community. Invoking genocide points to the need for rights that can protect indigenous peoples from indirect, environmentally mediated harms with accumulating potential to destroy the membership on which their existence depends.[85] Rights for Mother Earth recognize the genetic priority of ecological membership to cultural membership. All peoples come from the womb of earth and depend on her sustenance; some peoples are more vulnerable than others.

Mother Earth rights make the peril to endangered communities—especially those indigenous communities living in intimate relationship with an ecosystem—an indicator of peril to the sustaining womb of all people. Those communities whose ecological vulnerability is more immediate and precarious make rights claims on those whose consumptive violence affects the sustaining relations of every person and every culture.[86] Environmental justice communities sometimes refer to themselves as the "miner's canary," whose death is the first sign of poison.[87] The suffering of peoples who know their dignity through particular biocultural relations is a first sign of problems in the planetary experiments under way by dominant cultures.[88]

The claims of justice made by indigenous peoples in resistance to the political ecology of North Atlantic capitalism, says George Tinker, therefore represent a "gift we have to give back to our colonizer." For they show how a dominant culture's way of life is unsustainable, introducing "a new, critical paradigm that could generate a liberative force in the world today."[89] Affirming earth's sacredness disrupts white settler views of nature as a frontier of resources, free for the taking by right of the power to do so. By making those "resources" part of a sacred trust, rights-based resistance thickens the biocultural relations that market societies elide. Sacralizing ecological relations resists market practices that let dominant cultures assume they can exploit "resources" without review and permission from all concerned.[90]

Using rights to protect the ecological membership of life thus challenges the moral cosmology carried in conventional liberal uses of human rights. If liberal justice permits ecological death, it must get something wrong about reality. The expanded rights claims of indigenous peoples, including those that sacralize ecological relations, make justice rediscover humanity in its ecological memberships. As Tinker argues, those claims are not just self-protection, but witness: "Not only do Indians continue to tell the stories, sing the songs, speak the prayers, and perform the ceremonies that root themselves deeply in Mother Earth; they are actually audacious enough to think that their stories and their ways of reverencing creation will some day win over our White settler relatives and transform them."[91]

In this view, Mother Earth rights protect the possibility of a human future. The maternal symbol is significant: earth is mother to humanity, and so the sustaining matrix of human rights. The Bolivian declaration therefore states that "to guarantee human rights it is necessary to recognize and defend the rights of Mother Earth."[92] The 2008 Constitution of Ecuador established precedent for that connection. After recognizing human rights to a safe environment and the biocultural rights of indigenous peoples, the Constitution develops rights for nature in the figure of *Pachamama*: "Nature, or Pachamama . . . has the right to exist, persist, maintain and regenerate its vital cycles."[93] *Pachamama*, an indigenous Qechua term that may translate as "Mother Earth," and which functions in a similar pancontinental way, affirms direct moral respect owed the ecological womb of human dignity.

Can human rights and Mother Earth rights coexist? Panic among some North Atlantic Protestants would suggest that a goddess religion is re-emerging that, through rights constraints on economic activity, carries hints of human sacrifice to nature deities.[94] Some human rights advocates worry that recognizing direct rights for nature might carry antihumanist implications that begin to erode the basic moral vision of the UDHR. From the other side, some conservationists worry that recognizing rights for nature as a response to human vulnerability insufficiently protects nature for its own sake.

Environmental justice movements hybridize the discourses of human rights and ecological cosmology to open a third way. They deploy the most important moral idea of liberal culture (human rights) with the symbol of imperiled biocultural worlds (Mother Earth) in order to resist ecological destruction as political violence. By compelling attention to the ecological conditions of human dignity and extending rights to nature in order to protect the possibility of cultures shaped by intimate ecological membership, their resistance warns ecologically indifferent cultures of their imperiled future. As "miner's canaries" these vulnerable communities warn North Atlantic industrial cultures of their slow violence against the womb of all life.

Neither anthropocentric or ecocentric in the usual sense, asserting rights for Mother Earth is a way to recover the full dimensions of human personhood into its sustaining membership. Mother Earth rights might be described as "anthropocosmic," for they interpret their moral cosmos through the ecological vulnerability of human personhood.[95] Justice here does not focus on "nature" indifferently to the human presence, but on Mother Earth, known through our dependence on her as the womb of our existence. Specifying qualitative markers for direct obligations to nature is an elusive game. Are species, communities, or processes primary holders of value? In chapter 4 we saw how ecologists struggle to provide objective benchmarks of ecological "health" or "integrity." The concepts rely on supplementary evaluative judgments about what nature is and should be. Granting rights to Mother Earth constructs nature and its health in more definite terms, rooted in the relations, species, and processes that sustain the ecological embodiment of humanity.

That sort of reasoning appears close to what is sometimes called "weak anthropocentrism," but notice the expanding "anthropos" here. Justice for Mother Earth means sustaining conditions for humans capable of affirming the sacredness of Mother Earth. The human is the *interpretive center* of this cosmos, but because she is enfleshed in a wider membership in which she must recognize her contingency, on which she is dependent, and from which she understands her self and her purpose, the human is *not the moral center*. The health of the womb of earth is interpreted by the health of the human persons it births, whose flourishing lies in knowing and respecting earth as a sacred membership.

The adoption of Mother Earth rights in Latin American theological communities exhibits this anthropocosmic pattern. Christian indigenous theologians, who understand themselves as bearers of a double inheritance, have been especially active in developing this witness. A declaration of indigenous churches has called on other Christian churches to affirm rights to "all forms of life as well as Mother Earth."[96] A gathering of indigenous women theologians explains how a sacred performance of human trusteeship is at stake: "We recognize ourselves as being caretakers of the natural and ancestral seeds, cultivators of the earth and of the struggles of the excluded peoples . . . preservers of the balance and harmony of *Pachamama*."[97] Justice for the excluded means inclusion into an ecological membership possessed of its own sacred claims. Already their witness has begun to influence responses from nonindigenous theological communities. At the Bolivian People's Conference an ecumenical Christian statement opened by invoking "the cry of Mother Earth." Alluding to Romans 8:22, the statement hears that cry within Christian hope for liberation by hearing it as creation suffering birth pangs for a new life.[98] Theology can hear the cry of the earth and know it as a groan for liberation when it hears that cry through the voice of human suffering—and especially when it hears it in the voices of those who know themselves as caretakers of earth and whose suffering stems from ecological wounds.

South American theological communities have thus begun to articulate the cosmological dimensions of environmental justice still left mostly implicit in North American responses to environmental racism. They argue that protecting ecologically embodied persons requires recognizing that earth is an object of systemic violence and a subject in God's liberation. Much important theological work remains. South American theologians have yet to fully explain how to understand Mother Earth within biblical narratives and theological doctrine, and have yet to openly reckon with eco-feminist criticisms about associating gender and nature in a figure of the divine feminine.

The theological avenue of criticism here would entail demonstrating how to interpret Mother Earth within the political ecology of the body of Christ. Leonardo Boff has gone the furthest with this sort of project. His *Cry of the Earth, Cry of the Poor* makes crimes against Amazonian indigenous peoples the starting point for interpreting destruction against the forest it-self. "To hear these two interconnected cries and to see the same root cause that produces them is to carry out integral liberation." The "ultimate basis" of both violences, argues Boff, is an individualist, promethean anthropology that attempts to live humanity in disconnection from the universe. Inspired by Teilhard de Chardin and Thomas Berry, Boff attempts to renarrate libera-tion theology within a broader cosmology. The result bends liberation into divinization tropes of earth as macroanthropos and humanity as microcosm. Liberation theology "must comprehend the mission of human beings, man and woman, as expressions of Earth itself," manifesting and advancing the cosmic evolutionary process "in order to celebrate and glorify the Creator." The interpretive crux for Mother Earth, Boff rightly sees, lies in christol-ogy. Liberation theology, he sees, needs to be able to describe creation as "pregnant with Christ" and Jesus as the personal face of earth's liberation.[99]

In North America, Mark Wallace suggests similar ecotheological re-sources for environmental justice projects. Participating in antitoxic campaigns in Chester (Pennsylvania), Wallace recognizes the holistic im-plications of environmental justice and develops for it "a green spirituality" that sees all life as interdependent and laments all ecological decline. The political and religious practices in Chester need theologies that have recov-ered earth and embodiment into their spiritual center. When they do, they can interpret the waste trucks rumbling into Chester as a form of crucifix-ion, making their bodies into a sacrifice zone, which would invite them to understand their problems within God's suffering in and for creation. En-vironmental justice projects, argues Wallace, need the sort of cosmological spirituality that allows them to understand neighborhood survival efforts as participating in the resurrection hope for all creation.[100]

The suggestions of Boff and Wallace merit further development. Boff's christology is chronically unclear: sometimes he seems to conflate Christ's ecological body with evolutionary systems, to the danger of subsuming the voices of indigenous peoples into a cosmic process. At other points his account of ecology seems overdetermined by christology, as if Christ's human creativity is the natural telos of evolutionary systems. Wallace's account of Spirit, as one with earth and crucified as God, faces similar questions in thinking through the distinction of God and creation. Yet their work demonstrates the tensions that any theology of environmental justice faces as it interprets moral anthropology through respect for earth and interpreting nature through humanity's ecological body. They demonstrate and begin to meet the challenges to theological ethics posed by environmental justice projects, overcoming the disembodiment of liberation from the womb of creation.[101]

THE CHANGING ECOLOGY OF JUSTICE

I have been arguing that projects like the ones begun at Love Canal and Warren County shift the practical meaning of justice in ways that transform the ecological consciousness of their participants. As they protest unfair toxic exposure they begin to interpret their habitats as political ecologies. When they make rights claims in order to confront environmentally mediated harms they begin to recover their ecological embodiment. As the movement for Mother Earth rights shows, these projects may expand justice to protect an entire membership.

Some critics think that sort of view optimistically greenwashes environmental justice movements. "Imagine it," writes Andrew Dobson sarcastically; "what was in origin a campaign for compensation for the ill-effects of waste dumped in a small town in the United States becomes, in one direction, the force for the tying together of a whole range of other human justice issues . . . and, in the other direction, the spark that lights the fire of recognition that the effects of anthropogenic activity extend way beyond the human community into the realms of biodiversity."[102] A more sober look, says Dobson, shows that environmental justice projects constrain themselves to human welfare, never approaching the holistic ecological concerns of mainstream environmentalist movements. Sustainability and social justice are separate moral concerns, insists Dobson.

Dobson's criticism relies on a static and narrow concept of justice. It supposes that EJM apply a distributive principle of justice to protect a narrow set of welfare interests. I have been arguing that environmental justice projects use multiple ideas of justice, transforming them as they do, in order to meet a wide variety of problems. Schlosberg agrees, saying that EJM "offer a more expansive, plural, and pragmatic notion of justice."[103] As they work on various threats to humanity's ecological embodiment, EJM expand and reinterpret what justice entails. This is not to say that they apply a conceptual synthesis of ecology and justice. They rather deploy claims and practices of justice in new ways in order to meet new threats to human personhood. As they do, they expand the scope of what justice can address. Deploying rights to address toxins may make rights more competent to address biodiversity loss and climate change.

Developing an ethic of sustainability this way is not anthropocentric but anthropocosmic: norms of sustainability develop from confronting threats to human personhood mediated by violence against the ecological relations on which it depends. Justice to this broader, ecologically enfleshed human interprets what sustainability means. Human rights claims are thus important (but not exclusive) interpretive practices for deciding how to protect ecological systems. That generates a political ecology of justice in several directions. In one way, as seen at Warren County, using rights to interpret environmental problems prevents management of environmental risks from becoming another scene of domination. It refuses to let conservation or adaptive management conceal white power. Without rights claims interpreting sustainability, its norm could produce an apartheid planet of ecological reserves, gated enclaves of verdant security, and barren toxic settlements.

At the same time, using rights also expands justice along the relations of human vulnerability to include a wider membership in its protection. The important methodological claim here is about *how and where* justice is constructed, not *what* objects it includes. It means learning social and environmental ethics from struggles against ecologically mediated suffering. A charge of anthropocentrism misses the epistemological point: the ethics of justice must be learned from those communities struggling against ecological violence. When those communities come to include other species, a wider membership, and Mother Earth, justice is not fractured but deepened.

The latter inclusions seem surprising because environmental matters have normally been excluded from questions of social justice for two reasons: (1) environmental protections have not seemed basic to the political institutions protecting human dignity, and (2) nature lacks its own standing as a legal person. Environmental justice projects can defeat both exclusions.

The first is defeated by illustrating how ecological relations mediate political power. In John Rawls, environmental destruction may be wrong or lamentable for other moral reasons but it does not fall under the treatment of justice. Ecological protection is rather a good which citizens may privately pursue or for which they may publicly argue—as environmentalists do when they present conservation as part of a vision of the good life.[104] Love Canal and Warren County show, however, that as long as environmental harms and goods remain externalities of justice, then environmental management policies will continue to unfairly compound social privilege and exacerbate vulnerability. By showing that toxic waste distributes in racist patterns while control over nature accrues to the privileged, EJM begin to shift environmental issues from matters of the good to matters of the right.[105] When wealthy communities pay less for water than the poor, when dominant groups can appropriate the ethnobotanical knowledge of indigenous peoples while planting over their lands with commodity crops, when the wombs of the weak can be used by the powerful to dump their chemicals—then at least some forms of ecological protection become matters of basic justice.

Which forms of protection and how much are debates that interpret the ecological condition of human dignity. Because those debates are essential components of the political conversation over what is humanity, questions of environmental management entail forms of procedural and participatory justice. Guaranteeing those rights often supports the sort of ecological citizenship that effectively achieves a number of conservation goals. One of the most important is a right to information. Meaningful democratic participation depends on citizens having sufficient information about matters basic to their interests. Information about one's environment, argues Kristen Schrader-Frechette, is therefore a condition of "prima facie political equality."[106] Without reasonable intelligence about their exposure to chemicals, citizens cannot give informed consent to the risks.

Our de facto political condition is one of nonconsenting toxic trespass. Because industry may introduce new compounds without first establishing their toxicity, and because governments conduct insufficient research of their own, citizens must make decisions about zoning, employment, residency, and consumption with impossibly scanty information about chemical risks. One of the few sources of local information is the Toxic Release Inventory, where citizens can find disclosures from industry of spills and emissions. On the list for New Haven in 2010, for example, I find that someone released 6,844 pounds of tetrachloroethylene.[107] But how can I assess the significance of that risk for my child? And how can I understand that risk in combination with the 64 other chemicals on the 2010 inventory? Or make sense of the accumulating impact of releases over time?

More than information is required for informed consent; citizens must be able to make sense of information. A right to information implies a right to science. Because ecologies are political, ecological knowledge unavoidably shapes and serves political ends. Environmental justice projects have been skeptical of the function of scientific institutions. In the stories of Love Canal and Warren County, government science was implicated in the contradictions and injustices of political economies. So a right to participation may include a right to scientific data as well as a right to participate in the formation of research objectives. Crucially, the Love Canal and Warren County protests both involved scientists who could criticize the information they were being given by government and industry and help them demand the research they needed.

"Popular epidemiology" is one example of how those demands have already changed the shape of health research. Narratives of local health problems, of cancer clusters and abnormal miscarriage rates, are chronically dismissed by researchers as merely anecdotal or statistically insignificant. Environmental justice projects have led to community participation in the production of environment-related health research and, in consequence, to greater recognition of how social inequities produce illness, and finally to greater validation of neighborhood anecdotes.[108] Producing the environmental information needed for basic political participation has thus begun to overcome the disciplinary separation of medical problems from environmental problems, making the human body an integrating site of research for medical and environmental health.[109] Those who profit from disconnected information prefer that disciplinary separation. It is no accident that cancer research is overwhelmingly focused on treatment rather than causation, for much of it is funded by pharmaceutical companies with incentive to produce more chemicals, not question their long-term ecological function.

A right to information about basic political jeopardies thus may entail extensive environmental education, including a right of access to and participation in the relevant sciences. Simply meeting basic conditions of democratic participation provides conditions for broad social reflection on sustainability, and, insofar as producing the relevant information transforms a culture, may critically question the political ecology of human power.[110] When environmental justice projects push science to make connections of environmental and human health, they help produce the sort of environmental intelligence needed to understand the human experiment with its habitat.

So far we have "weak anthropocentric" claims of sustainability: reasons to protect ecological integrity by reason of the justice owed human persons. What sustainability means is interpreted through the environmental implications of human rights. Whether there is a right to fresh water, to a safe environment, or to biodiversity access, and whether future generations or indigenous peoples hold group rights with biological conditions—those arguments debate what must be sustained in order to protect conditions of human dignity. This approach is only as "weak," however, as its conception of the human is narrow. I have argued that recognition of human environmental rights steadily expands the underlying anthropology, in turn deepening the ecological extent of its justice.

A number of Christian theologians criticize the narrow accounts of human personhood carried by the justice of human rights. Alasdair MacIntyre, for example, thinks that rights are thin fictions for negotiating moral life without shared goods—a life of agonist, emotivist individualism.[111] Daniel Bell has criticized liberation theologies for using rights language that sets justice in opposition to the common good.[112] Bell and MacIntyre think that rights claims impoverish justice by treating individuals as if autonomous from their social relations and severed from the orientation of all creatures to love God as the highest good. Human rights, they think, carry a dystopic notion of human personhood sundered from its sustaining membership.

Deployment of rights within environmental justice projects, however, begins to displace the atomistic individual with persons who are constituted in their social and ecological embeddedness, who inhabit specific communities, and who depend on goods held in common with all living creatures. When environmental justice projects use rights to protest the social production of toxic bodies, they begin to reconstruct the ecological membership of humanity. By taking the human body as the site from which to interpret earth as a sustaining matrix, they reinterpret personhood in ecological context. Human environmental rights in this case work to overcome moral anthropocentrism precisely by focusing on the *anthropos* and protecting its habitat. In his theological account of the emergence of race, Willie Jennings writes that lost in colonial displacement—in European exit, African enslavement, indigenous genocide—was a way of becoming a person; "the loss here is of a life-giving collaboration of identity between places and bodies, people and animals."[113] Theology now tries to think the meaning of creation is a mistake so massive it has almost been forgotten. After Jennings, then, theologians might suppose that environmental rights carry a nearly utopic vision of human personhood restored to its sustaining membership.

An ecological anthropology of the sort defended by indigenous peoples in their rights claims need not be accepted by every culture in order to warrant extensive ecological protections. Just in order to avoid closing down this way of becoming a person, the possibility of concomitant ecological relations must be protected. That is the point behind claims of ecological genocide: with the disappearance of other species, the diminishment of migrations, the commodification of forests, and the destruction of landscapes, a way of being human is systematically extinguished. The justice that protects pluralist political societies thus has reason to adopt strong protection of environmental "goods" as a matter of protecting minority rights. That it must resort to rights of survival to do so implies a warning to the lived anthropology of dominant cultures. Perhaps an understanding of personhood so distant from its ecological womb that it seems invulnerable to environmental change is catastrophically mistaken. Perhaps moral methodologies that assume that most of life bears no claim on human respect lead to ruinous social stupidity.

Prima facie respect for nonhuman creatures may then be a biocultural condition for debate over what it means to be human. In the face of globalizing homogeneity, rights for nature may protect the space for cultural debate over possible ways of life. Recognizing legal rights for other species, for ecological processes, for forests, and for bioregions may be the most effective way to protect cultural possibilities other than living as if earth were but a storehouse of resources.

So far we have ground for respecting nonhuman life by two indirect ways. First, recovering their ecological embodiment may make moral agents more aware of shared perils with nonhumans and more sympathetic with their vulnerability.[114] Second, by bringing nature within the ecological body of humanity, it disrupts the logic of domination that depends on strong, hierarchical boundaries between subject and other by interpreting human subjectivity in terms of multiple ecological intimacies. It is important to note that justice is not here *extended* to nonhuman subjects as if honorary human individuals; all earth is rather *included* within the justice owed human persons. By following the respect owed human individuals, justice incorporates the social and ecological memberships that sustain a person.

That logic creates ground for more direct obligations of justice, overcoming the exclusion of other creatures from legal personhood. A moral anthropology that is realized through relations with nonhuman others needs to affirm the integrity and vulnerability of other species and of the entire world we share with them. That includes protecting earth from moralities that would entirely collapse it into some notion of the ecological self. Val Plumwood argues that constructing an ethic from a moral vision of the ecological self might not avoid selfish behavior. Including other species within the human self might, without sufficient recognition of their otherness, conflate them into humanity.[115] The sustaining paradox about other creatures, in other words, is that rightly valuing other creatures and systems for all the ways that they sustain our humanity requires recognizing that humans are not the reason for their existence or their value. In order to keep the *anthropos* fundamentally open to alterity and constructed by real relations, ethics needs those others to possess their own ground of respect. Rights for nature may be the best recourse for ethics to maintain the real alterity by which the human person is constituted and sustained.

To address the difficulty of interpreting those rights (what does a species want? what does an ecosystem deserve?), an anthropocosmic strategy makes a broad and deep account of human sustainability the specifying criteria. Mother Earth wants to give birth to human creatures that respect the wild diversity of her generative womb, who care for and protect other species, who participate in dynamic ecological communities as a caring keystone species. Organized by the symbol of Mother Earth, humanity's ecological embodiment grounds an account of justice that extends beyond humanity, recognizing that earth and her creatures have interests of their own. Protecting them is the only way to protect what sustains our humanity.

The logic of environmental justice projects, I am arguing, does not start from obligations of justice toward earth, but it does bend that way. To critics who object that responsibilities to nonhuman creatures should not come under the concept of justice, but rather under concepts of care or stewardship, the reply must worry for the softness of alternative concepts. Without capacity to make a claim on agents, nonhumans under our care or stewardship remain vulnerable to our self-serving conceits, the glosses we give our domination. Protection for the sustaining matrix of human flourishing must be strong enough to withstand the same "race-neutral" violence that produces a racist landscape of toxins. It must be justice rather than care, stewardship, or love, because it must confront power. Protecting the womb of life must include standing and legal review for species and systems, as well as provide for direct redress of injury. Those functions seem more likely by establishing legal guardians and trust funds for species and ecosystems, rather than by relying on humans to love their mother.[116] Recognizing those rights for Mother Earth does not require a final ontological description of nature or extending personhood to nature. It opens and protects interpretive space for understanding the womb of human life within political ecologies of unprecedented power.

CONCLUSION

In the last chapter I warned that a science-based ethic of adaptive management was naïve to social power, liable to exclusion of minority communities, and in need of a cosmological imagination. This chapter has shown how those three elements come together in environmental justice projects that confront violence suffered by disempowered communities, often by using religious and cultural inheritances in creative ways. I have argued that those creative trajectories need further recognition in the field of religion and ecology and further cultivation within religious ethics. Womanist, liberation, and indigenous theologies have resources for making fuller sense of environmental justice projects. The field of religion and ecology needs to cultivate such work in order to help overcome its methodological whiteness, and in order to understand how grassroots communities working for justice already make use of the ecological cosmologies that the field curates.

As everyday projects of communities like those at Love Canal, Warren County, and Cochabamba organize to protect the relations that sustain them, they expand capacities of justice. Participating in those projects creates an adaptive intelligence of sustainability alive to the ecological flows of political power. By expanding justice to meet the ecological vulnerability of human personhood, they also expand the subject of justice. Without necessarily beginning from an ecological worldview, they begin to cultivate a moral anthropology of ecological membership. They do so not to realize an ecological worldview, but to interpret and confront ecologies of power.

I began this chapter observing that my own city is an "environmental justice community." It is also a biotic community, lying at the confluence of three rivers flowing into a saltwater sound home to many fish species, and between two forested rock outcroppings that offer an important refuge to birds migrating up and down the east coast. Discovering what justice means for life in New Haven begins with breathing, smelling, and tasting this city, and following the political ecology of power into the landscapes of race, class, and gender. That movement cannot end until justice incorporates the entire membership of New Haven, until it can think of human vulnerability with the vulnerability of other bodies and of this womb of life.

I have argued that environmental justice projects begin to develop that capacity by constructing the ethics of sustainability through justice to embodied persons. To realize that trajectory, however, they need critical and creative theological engagement. Recently when a utility proposed opening an emergency power generator in the city, the New Haven Environmental Justice Network put up a fight and was able to negotiate a compromise that would lead to no net increase in air pollution. The utility provided funding for the city to purchase equipment that would reduce an amount of emissions equivalent to that likely to be released by the generator. That compromise shows how justice-focused arguments can accomplish political changes, but it also reveals the modesty of reforms typically won by community groups. Justice to the New Haven membership surely must mean more. It must begin to transform our industrial carapace, make the soil less deadly to life, the estuaries less sickening to fish, the noise and light less hostile to migrations. For environmental justice to become liberation, it must begin to break down ways of living that make us think we are impermeable to earth, not flesh of her flesh, born of her womb. Justice must restore flesh and spirit in a living membership.

The tension between overwhelming systems of power and practical possibilities of transformation is even stronger in consideration of global capitalism and the planetary size of the human economy. In the next chapter I treat the human economy in relation to its twin problems of impoverishment: human misery and biological loss.

NOTES

1. John Wargo, *Green Intelligence: Creating Environments That Protect Human Health* (New Haven, CT: Yale University Press, 2009), xi–xxii.

2. Centers for Disease Control and Prevention, "Third National Report on Human Exposure to Environmental Chemicals" (Atlanta: National Center for Environmental Health, 2005).

3. Wargo, *Green Intelligence*, 283.

4. Joachim Radkau, *Nature and Power: A Global History of the Environment*, Thomas Dunlap, trans. (Washington, DC: Cambridge University Press, 2008), 127–31.

5. Rachel Carson, *Silent Spring* (Boston: Houghton Mifflin, 1962).

6. B. Paigen, "Controversy at Love Canal," *The Hastings Center Report* 12, no. 3 (1982).

7. L. M. Gibbs and M. Levine, *Love Canal: My Story* (New York: SUNY Press, 1982).

8. Sandra Steingraber, *Living Downstream: An Ecologist's Personal Investigation of Cancer and the Environment*, 2nd ed. (Philadelphia: Da Capo Press, 2010), 279.

9. Stockholm Declaration, Principle 1.

10. These were known as the Ksentini Reports, after their lead researcher. See UN Doc. E/CN.4/Sub.2/1991/8.

11. The 1992 Rio Conference backed away from an explicit right with the vague statement: "humans are entitled to a healthy and productive life in harmony with nature." Declaration on Environment and Development, Principle 1. UN Doc. A/CONF. 151/26.

12. Ulrich Beck, *Risk Society: Towards a New Modernity* (London: Sage, 1992).

13. See Andrew Dobson, *Justice and the Environment: Conceptions of Environmental Sustainability and Dimensions of Social Justice* (Oxford: Oxford University Press, 1998); Robyn Eckersley, *Environmentalism and Political Theory: Toward an Ecocentric Approach* (New York: SUNY Press, 1992).

14. Juan Martinez-Alier, "Ecological Distribution Conflicts and Indicators of Sustainability," *International Journal of Political Economy* 34, no. 1 (2004); Juan Martínez Alier, *The Environmentalism of the Poor: A Study of Ecological Conflicts and Valuation* (Cheltenham, UK: Edward Elgar Publishing, 2002).

15. David Schlosberg, *Defining Environmental Justice: Theories, Movements, and Nature* (New York: Oxford University Press, 2007).

16. Giovanna Di Chiro, "Environmental Justice from the Grassroots: Reflections on History, Gender, and Expertise," in *The Struggle for Ecological Democracy*, Daniel

Faber, ed. (New York: Guilford Press, 1998); Dorceta Taylor, "American Environmentalism: The Role of Race, Class, and Gender in Shaping Activism 1820–1995," *Race, Gender and Class* 5, no. 1 (1997); Robert Bullard and Damu Smith, "Women Warriors of Color on the Front Line," in *The Quest for Environmental Justice: Human Rights and the Politics of Pollution*, Robert Bullard, ed. (San Francisco: Sierra Club Books, 2005).

17. C. Krauss, "Women and Toxic Waste Protests: Race, Class and Gender as Resources of Resistance," *Qualitative Sociology* 16, no. 3 (1993), quoted in Rachel Stein, "Introduction," in *New Perspectives on Environmental Justice; Gender, Sexuality, Activism*, Rachel Stein, ed. (New Brunswick, NJ: Rutgers University Press, 2004), 3.

18. Sara Ruddick, *Maternal Thinking: Toward a Politics of Peace* (Boston: Beacon Press, 1995), xx.

19. W. LaDuke, *All Our Relations: Native Struggles for Land and Life* (Cambridge, MA: South End Press, 1999), 16–23.

20. Cheston Berlin and Sam Kacew, "Environmental Chemicals in Human Milk," in *Environmental Toxicology and Pharmacology of Human Development*, Sam Kacew and George Lambert, eds. (Washington, DC: Taylor and Francis, 1997); J. L. Jacobson and S. W. Jacobson, "Intellectual Impairment in Children Exposed to Polychlorinated Biphenyls in Utero," *New England Journal of Medicine* 335, no. 11 (1996); P. J. Landrigan and A. Garg, "Chronic Effects of Toxic Environmental Exposures on Children's Health," *Clinical Toxicology* 40, no. 4 (2002).

21. D. T. Wigle, *Child Health and the Environment* (New York: Oxford University Press, 2003).

22. P. J. Landrigan et al., "Children's Health and the Environment: Public Health Issues and Challenges for Risk Assessment," *Environmental Health Perspectives* 112, no. 2 (2004), quoted in Philip Shabecoff and Alice Shabecoff, *Poisoned Profits: The Toxic Assault on Our Children* (New York: Random House, 2008), 20. In 2009 Landrigan started the National Children's Study, the first long-term research into environmental toxins and children's health.

23. G. Di Chiro, "Living Environmentalisms: Coalition Politics, Social Reproduction, and Environmental Justice," *Environmental Politics* 17, no. 2 (2008): 294.

24. Anna L. Peterson, *Everyday Ethics and Social Change: The Education of Desire* (New York: Columbia University Press, 2009), 61.

25. Anna Lisa Peterson, *Being Human: Ethics, Environment, and Our Place in the World* (Berkeley: University of California Press, 2001), 109.

26. I borrow the phrase "ecology of mothering" from Sarah Schroerlucke, who used it in a 2008 seminar paper.

27. Winona LaDuke, "Foreword," in *New Perspectives on Environmental Justice: Gender, Sexuality, Activism*, Rachel Stein, ed. (New Brunswick: Rutgers University Press, 2004), xiii.

28. See Catherine Roach, *Mother/Nature* (Indianapolis, IN: Indiana University Press, 2003); Karen Warren, ed., "The Power and Promise of Ecological Feminism," in *Ecological Feminist Philosophies* (Indianapolis, IN: Indiana University Press, 1996).

29. Rosemary Radford Ruether, *New Woman, New Earth: Sexist Ideologies and Human Liberation, with a New Preface* (Boston: Beacon Press, 1995).

30. For two examples, see Ivone Gebara, *Longing for Running Water: Ecofeminism and Liberation* (Minneapolis: Fortress Press, 1999); Sallie McFague, *The Body of God* (Minneapolis: Fortress Press, 1993). And see Heather Eaton, *Introducing Feminist Ecotheologies* (New York: T. and T. Clark, 2005).

31. Catherine Keller, *Face of the Deep: A Theology of Becoming* (New York: Routledge, 2003), 231.

32. Tovis Page, "Feminist, Gender, and Sexuality Studies in Religion and Ecology: Where We Have Been, Where We Are Now, and Where We Might Go," in *Inherited Land: The Changing Grounds of Religion and Ecology*, Whitney Bauman, Richard Bohannon, and Kevin O'Brien, eds. (Eugene, OR: Wipf and Stock, 2011), 102–24.

33. Dorceta Taylor, "Women of Color, Environmental Justice, and Ecofeminism," in *Ecofeminism: Women, Nature, Culture*, Karen Warren, ed. (Indianapolis, IN: Indiana University Press, 1997). Further agreement in Karen Baker-Fletcher, "Spirituality," in *Handbook of U. S. Theologies of Liberation*, Miguel de la Torre, ed. (St. Louis, MO: Chalice Press, 2004): 117–28.

34. Patricia Hill Collins, *Black Feminist Thought: Knowledge, Consciousness, and the Politics of Empowerment*, 2nd ed. (New York: Routledge Press, 2000), chap. 8.

35. Robert Bullard, *Dumping in Dixie: Race, Class, and Environmental Quality* (Boulder, CO: Westview Press, 2000), 31.

36. Bullard, *Dumping in Dixie*, 29. See also Bunyan Byrant and Elaine Hockman, "A Brief Comparison of the Civil Rights Movement and the Environmental Justice Movement," in *Power, Justice, and the Environment: A Critical Appraisal of the Environmental Justice Movement*, David Naguib Pellow and Robert J. Brulle, eds. (Cambridge, MA: MIT Press, 2005); Stephen Sandweiss, "The Social Construction of Environmental Justice," in *Environmental Injustices, Political Struggles: Race, Class, and the Environment*, David E. Camacho, ed. (Durham, NC: Duke University Press, 1998).

37. Eileen McGurty, *Transforming Environmentalism: Warren County, PCBs, and the Origins of Environmental Justice* (New Brunswick, NJ: Rutgers University Press, 2009), 73.

38. McGurty, *Transforming Environmentalism*, 40.

39. The civil rights leaders Joseph Lowery, Fred Taylor, and Walter Fauntroy were also arrested. See McGurty, *Transforming Environmentalism*, 92–99; Bullard, *Dumping in Dixie*, 29–36.

40. For the two attributions see Richard Lazarus, "'Environmental Racism! That's What It Is,'" *University of Illinois Law Review* (2000): 264n17; Valerie Ann Kaalund, "Witness to Truth: Black Women Heeding the Call for Environmental Justice," in *New Perspectives on Environmental Justice: Gender, Sexuality, and Activism*, Rachel Stein, ed. (New Brunswick, NJ: Rutgers University Press, 2004), 79.

41. United Church of Christ Commission for Racial Justice, "Toxic Wastes and Race in the United States: A National Report on the Racial and Socioeconomic Characteristics of Communities with Hazardous Waste Sites" (New York, 1987).

42. Robert Bullard et al., "Toxic Wastes and Race at Twenty: 1987–2007: Grassroots Struggles to Dismantle Environmental Racism in the United States" (Cleveland, OH: United Church of Christ Justice and Witness Ministries, 2007).

43. Marianne Lavelle and Marcia Coyle, "Unequal Protection: The Racial Divide in Environmental Law," *National Law Journal* 21, no. 3 (1992).

44. Lazarus, " 'Environmental Racism! That's What It Is,' " 273. For broader context, see Richard J. Lazarus, *The Making of Environmental Law* (Chicago: University of Chicago Press, 2004), 137–44.

45. Michelle Alexander, *The New Jim Cross: Mass Incarceration in the Age of Colorblindness*, revised edition (New York: The New Press, 2012), 184.

46. Laura Pulido, "Rethinking Environmental Racism: White Privilege and Urban Development in Southern California," *Annals of the Association of American Geographers* 90, no. 1 (2000): 25. See also Laura Pulido, "A Critical Review of the Methodology of Environmental Racism Research," *Antipode* 28, no. 2 (1996); Luke W. Cole and Sheila R. Foster, *From the Ground Up: Environmental Racism and the Rise of the Environmental Justice Movement* (New York: New York University Press, 2001), 54–72.

47. Rob Nixon, *Slow Violence and the Environmentalism of the Poor* (Cambridge, MA: Harvard Univeristy Press, 2011), 2.

48. McGurty, *Transforming Environmentalism,* 105–7, 125–27.

49. By "ecological imaginary" I mean a shared sense of inhabiting earth carried by the environmental practices that it makes possible, similar to the "social imaginary" of Charles Taylor, *A Secular Age* (Cambridge: Harvard University Press, 2007), 171–76. One way to interpret the practices of domination supported by a wilderness imaginary: read Charles Mills, *The Racial Contract* (Ithaca: Cornell University Press, 1997) with William Cronon, "The Trouble with Wilderness; or, Getting Back to the Wrong Nature," in *Uncommon Ground: Rethinking the Human Place in Nature*, William Cronon, ed. (New York: W. W. Norton, 1996).

50. Charles Mills, "Black Trash," in *Faces of Environmental Racism*, Laura Westra and Bill E. Lawson, eds. (Lanham, MD: Rowman and Littlefield, 2001). See Mills, *The Racial Contract*, chap. 2.

51. Mark Dowie, *Conservation Refugees: The Hundred-Year Conflict between Global Conservation and Native Peoples* (Cambridge, MA: MIT Press, 2009); W. M. Adams and J. Hutton, "People, Parks and Poverty: Political Ecology and Biodiversity Conservation," *Conservation and Society* 5, no. 2 (2007); Thomas H. Birch, "The Incarceration of Wilderness," in *Postmodern Environmental Ethics*, Max Oelschlaeger, ed. (Albany: SUNY Press, 1995).

52. Willie James Jennings, *The Christian Imagination: Theology and the Origins of Race* (New Haven, CT: Yale University Press, 2010), 59.

53. Taylor, "Women of Color, Environmental Justice, and Ecofeminism," 55. See also Martin Melosi, "Environmental Justice, Ecoracism, and Environmental History," in *"To Love the Wind and the Rain": African Americans and Enviromental History*, Dianne Glave and Mark Stoll, eds. (Pittsburgh, PA: University of Pittsburgh Press, 2006).

54. Burwell quoted in McGurty, *Transforming Environmentalism*, 104.

55. James Cone, "Whose Earth Is It Anyway?," in *Earth Habitat: Eco-Injustice and the Church's Response*, Dieter Hessel and Larry Rasmussen, eds. (Minneapolis: Fortress Press, 2007), 30.

56. P. Outka, *Race and Nature from Transcendentalism to the Harlem Renaissance* (Basingstoke, UK: Palgrave MacMillan, 2008).

57. See J. Myers, *Converging Stories: Race, Ecology, and Environmental Justice in American Literature* (University of Georgia Press, 2005); David E. Camacho, "The Environmental Justice Movement: A Political Framework," in *Environmental Injustices, Political Struggles: Race, Class, and the Environment*, David E. Camacho, ed. (Durham, NC: Duke University Press, 1998).

58. Taylor, "Women of Color, Environmental Justice, and Ecofeminism," 54.

59. D. N. Pellow, *Resisting Global Toxics: Transnational Movements for Environmental Justice* (Cambridge, MA: MIT Press, 2007), 67.

60. McGurty, *Transforming Environmentalism*, 81.

61. Bullard, *Dumping in Dixie*, 31, 93–95.

62. Melissa Checker, *Polluted Promises: Environmental Racism and the Search for Justice in a Southern Town* (New York: NYU Press, 2005), 167.

63. Laura Pulido, "The Sacredness of 'Mother Earth': Spirituality, Activism, and Social Justice," *Annals of the Association of American Geographers* 88, no. 4 (1998): 719.

64. Kaalund, "Witness to Truth," 80–81. See also, Dana Alston, *We Speak for Ourselves: Social Justice, Race, and Environment* (Washington, DC: Panos Institute, 1990).

65. Larry Rasmussen, "Environmental Racism and Environmental Justice: Moral Theory in the Making?" *Journal of the Society of Christian Ethics* 24, no. 1 (2004): 4, 22–23.

66. See Richard Bohannon and Kevin O'Brien, "Saving the World (and the People in It, Too): Religion in Eco-Justice and Environmental Justice," in *Inherited Land: The Changing Grounds of Religion and Ecology,* Whitney Baumanet et al., eds. (Eugene, OR: Pickwick Publications, 2011).

67. See Elonda Clay, "How Does It Feel to Be an Environmental Problem? Studying Religion and Ecology in the African Diaspora," in *Inherited Land: The Changing Grounds of Religion and Ecology*, Whitney Bauman et al., eds. (Eugene, OR: Pickwick Publications, 2011).

68. Dianne Glave, "Black Environmental Liberation Theology," in *"To Love the Wind and the Rain."* See also Dianne Glave, *Rooted in the Earth: Reclaiming an African American Environmental Heritage* (Chicago: Lawrence Hill Books, 2010), chap. 10.

69. Cone, "Whose Earth Is It Anyway?," 30.

70. Emilie M. Townes, *In a Blaze of Glory: Womanist Spirituality as Social Witness* (Nashville, TN: Abingdon Press, 1995), 55, 60.

71. Alice Walker, *Living by the Word: Selected Writings, 1973–1987* (San Diego, CA: Harcourt Brace Jovanovich, 1988), 142, 147.

72. Delores Williams, "Sin, Nature, and Black Women's Bodies," in *Ecofeminism and the Sacred*, Carol Adams, ed. (New York: Continuum, 1993).

73. Delores Williams, "Straight Talk, Plain Talk: Womanist Words about Salvation," in *Embracing the Spirit: Womanist Perspectives on Hope, Salvation, and Transformation*, Emilie M. Townes, ed. (Maryknoll, NY: Orbis Books, 1997), 118–19.

74. Ecowomanism is under rapid development; see forthcoming work from Melanie Harris and from the authors in a special edition of the journal *Worldviews*.

75. Karen Baker-Fletcher, *Sisters of Dust, Sisters of Spirit: Womanist Wordings on God and Creation* (Minneapolis: Fortress Press, 1998), 63, 115.

76. J. Kameron Carter, *Race: A Theological Accent* (New York: Oxford University Press, 2008), 157–93.

77. Dwight Hopkins, "Holistic Health and Healing: Environmental Racism and Ecological Justice," in *Faith, Health, and Healing in African American Life*, Stephanie Mitchem and Emilie Townes, eds. (Westport, CT: Praeger, 2008), 17.

78. Thomas Hoyt, "Environmental Justice and Black Theology," in *Theology for Earth Community: A Field Guide*, Dieter Hessel, ed. (Maryknoll, NY: Orbis, 1996), 171.

79. Delores Williams, *Sisters in the Wilderness: The Challenge of Womanist God-Talk* (New York: Orbis, 1993), 5, 58.

80. Williams, *Sisters in the Wilderness*, 110–20, 159–61.

81. "Principles of Environmental Justice," First National People of Color Environmental Leadership Summit, Washington, D.C., October 27, 1991, last modified April 6, 1996, http://www.ejnet.org/ej/principles.html.

82. See Nixon, *Slow Violence*, chap. 3.

83. Cobb quoted in Bullard, *Dumping in Dixie*, 31; Townes, *In a Blaze of Glory*, 55.

84. Schlosberg, *Defining Environmental Justice*, 63; George Tinker, "An American Indian Theological Response to Ecojustice," in *Defending Mother Earth: Native American Perspectives on Environmental Justice*, Jace Weaver, ed. (Maryknoll, NY: Orbis, 1996).

85. See Patrick Thornberry, *Indigenous Peoples and Human Rights* (Manchester, UK: Manchester University Press, 2002).

86. Ramachandra Guha and Joan Martinez-Alier, *The Varieties of Environmentalism: Essays North and South* (New York: Routledge, 1997), 12.

87. Jace Weaver, "Introduction: Notes from a Miner's Canary," in *Defending Mother Earth*; Pellow, *Resisting Global Toxics*, 45–49. See L. Guinier and G. Torres, *The Miner's Canary: Enlisting Race, Resisting Power, Transforming Democracy* (Cambridge, MA: Harvard University Press, 2003).

88. "Study on the Need to Recognize and Respect the Rights of Mother Earth," UN Doc E/C.19/2010/4 (Permanent Forum on Indigenous Issues).

89. George Tinker, *American Indian Liberation: A Theology of Sovereignty* (Maryknoll, NY: Orbis, 2008), 19, 35.

90. J. D. Forbes, "Indigenous Americans: Spirituality and Ecos," *Daedalus* 130, no. 4 (2001): 292.

91. Tinker, *American Indian Liberation*, 56.

92. "Universal Declaration of the Rights of Mother Earth," World People's Conference on Climate Change and Mother Earth, Cochabamba, 2010.

93. Constituciones de 2008, Republica del Ecuador, Articles 71–72 (my translation).

94. For running examples of panic, see the "Secondhand Smoke" blog of Wesley J. Smith in *First Things*.

95. See S. Mickey, "Contributions to Anthropocosmic Environmental Ethics," *Worldviews: Global Religions, Culture, and Ecology* 11, no. 2 (2007).

96. "Joint Declaration of Indigenous Churches," World Council of Churches, May 21, 2009.

97. "Indigenous Women Form the First Community of Abya Yala Theologians," Latin America and Caribbean Communication Agency, January 6, 2010.

98. "Cambio Climatico: Declaracion ecumenica," Cochabamba, April 22, 2010. Signed by the Latin American Council of Churches, the Ecumenical Association of Third World Theologians, the Higher Andean Ecumenical Institute of Theology, among others.

99. Leonardo Boff, *Cry of the Earth, Cry of the Poor* (Maryknoll, NY: Orbis, 1997), 84, 112, 182.

100. Mark I. Wallace, *Finding God in the Singing River* (Minneapolis, MN: Augsburg Fortress, 2005); Mark Wallace, "The Spirit of Environmental Justice: Resurrection Hope in Urban America," *Worldviews: Global Religions, Culture, and Ecology* 12, no. 2–3 (2008): 197–220.

101. Eastern Orthodox sophiology offers symbol and logic for incorporating Mother Earth within Christian theology; see Jenkins, *Ecologies of Grace*, chaps 10–11.

102. Dobson, *Justice and the Environment: Conceptions of Environmental Sustainability and Dimensions of Social Justice*, 23–24.

103. Schlosberg, *Defining Environmental Justice*, 45.

104. John Rawls, *Political Liberalism*, 2nd ed. (New York: Columbia University Press, 1996), 245–47.

105. Schlosberg, *Defining Environmental Justice*, 104–7.

106. K. S. Shrader-Frechette, *Environmental Justice: Creating Equality, Reclaiming Democracy* (New York: Oxford University Press, 2002), chap. 2.

107. See the website of the Environmental Protection Agency; www.epa/gov/tri.

108. J. Corburn, "Community Knowledge in Environmental Health Science: Co-Producing Policy Expertise," *Environmental Science and Policy* 10, no. 2 (2007); P. Brown, "Popular Epidemiology and Toxic Waste Contamination: Lay and Professional Ways of Knowing," *Journal of Health and Social Behavior* 33, no. 3 (1992).

109. Patrick Novotny, "Popular Epidemiology and the Struggle for Community Health in the Environmental Justice Movement," in *The Struggle for Ecological Democracy: Environmental Justice Movements in the United States*, Daniel Faber, ed. (New York: Guilford Press, 1998); N. Krieger, "Theories for Social Epidemiology in the 21st Century: An Ecosocial Perspective," *International Journal of Epidemiology* 30, no. 4 (2001).

110. See Daniel Faber and Deborah McCarthy, "Neo-Liberalism, Globalization, and the Struggle for Ecological Democracy: Linking Sustainability and Environmental

Justice," in *Just Sustainabilities: Development in an Unequal World*, Julian Agyemanet et al., eds. (London: Earthscan Publications, 2003), 58. See also Daniel Faber, "The Struggle for Ecological Democracy and Environmental Justice," in *The Struggle for Ecological Democracy: Environmental Justice Movements in the United States*, Daniel Faber, ed. (New York: Guilford Press, 1998).

111. Alasdair MacIntyre, *After Virtue*, 2nd. ed. (Notre Dame, IN: University of Notre Dame Press, 1984), 66–70.

112. Daniel Bell, *Liberation Theology after the End of History* (New York: Routledge, 2001), chap. 3.

113. Jennings, *The Christian Imagination: Theology and the Origins of Race*, 63.

114. Schlosberg, *Defining Environmental Justice*, 133–42.

115. Val Plumwood, *Environmental Culture* (London: Routledge, 2002).

116. See Christopher Stone, *Should Trees Have Standing? Toward Legal Rights for Natural Objects* (Los Altos, CA: William Kaufmann, 1974).

CHAPTER SIX

Impoverishment and the Economy of Desire

✦

Be fruitful and multiply, and fill the earth and subdue it; and have domin-
ion over the fish of the sea and over the birds of the air and over every living
thing.

Genesis 1:28

[Israel] said: "I will follow other lovers, for they give me what I desire, my oil
and my drink.". . . Now the land mourns, and all who live in it languish,
together with the wild animals and the birds of the air. Even the fish of the
sea are disappearing.

Hosea 2:5, 4:3

Over the last two centuries of industrial expansion the human economy
appropriated unprecedented scales of earth's economy while generating
prosperity for unprecedented human populations. That growth was accompanied by two new forms of poverty: human destitution became a political
choice rather than a natural fact, and biological diminishment became a
planetary event. Making sense of the expanding size of humanity requires
interpreting the changing economy of human desire within the larger economy of earth. Does human dominion impoverish people and planet, or can
humans "be fruitful and multiply" in ways that sustain real wealth?

The question seems to resist pragmatic inquiry because any first step
seems caught between ideologies of limit and of growth. According to one
model of reality, the human economy has already met the limits of earth's
ecological capacity and must contract, while according to the other markets
will keep innovating ways for societies to grow. The debate often takes shape
along disciplinary lines between economics and the ecological science,
and many contestants in the debate say that their differences derive from

different worldviews. If disagreement is essentially "religious" in that way, rooted in different worldviews, then that points to one way for Christian ethics to enter the debate. Theologian John Cobb and economist Herman Daly open their theory of the sustainable economy in a religious critique of neoliberal economics and ground it in an alternative moral anthropology.[1] Yet I have tried in this book to confront problems without starting from metaethical foundations. Instead of building an economic ethic from an argument for a certain worldview, this chapter concentrates on understanding two practical problems of poverty: human destitution and biodiversity loss. Its first section explains human and biological impoverishment on their own terms, and then three successive sections interpret the relation of those two forms of poverty within three key aspects of the global economy: reproduction, consumption, and development. Each represents a different economy of desire, and within each, I argue, Christian ethics can develop practices for learning to desire real wealth through efforts to overcome impoverishment.

To help the reader mark how the argument flows I keep referring to one specific reform project throughout the chapter. In the mid-1980s the growing population of Ecuador had strained its resources. Food prices were high, some communities were hungry, and the state was borrowing money. The conventional economic therapy, pressed by its North Atlantic creditors, was growth-focused development. "Structural adjustment" to the global market included modernizing its agriculture for commodity export, which the state did because it needed hard currency in order to service its loans. The promise of a growth strategy for the hungry was that eventually an expanding economy would expand incomes and thus increase purchasing power. For many poor people, however, economic growth was experienced as further impoverishment. Nutritious food became more expensive while agricultural land was turned to monoculture commodity crops, increasing hunger and food insecurity. In response, a base ecclesial community in the small city of Riobamba began rethinking economic possibilities. While development experts readied more loans to subsidize food imports, the base community entered a process of reflection on scripture and economic analysis. Their reflections led them to condemn the debt-driven export/import scheme of global agricultural trade, which they saw as exploiting the poor for the profit of the wealthy. Watching poor farmers dispossessed of land by distant investors, who then proposed to sell back to them discounted foodstuffs from different land, they decided that the community needed an alternative model of development.

Now on Saturday mornings in Riobamba a side street is taken over by what appears to be an open market for vegetables: potatoes, corn, beans, radishes, cabbages, and tomatoes overflow from large sacks, and people move about sorting, weighing, and packing. Yet none of it is for sale; the workers are members of a regional food cooperative, dividing bulk produce among a hundred families. The community decided that it could address both the problem of hunger and monoculturing of land by networking families to purchase food in bulk from farmers directly. Called the Canasta Communitaria Utopia, the cooperative purchases and divides a food share based on principles of food sovereignty. Satisfying hunger, they insist, is not just about delivering a certain quantity of calories, but about satisfying the desire to participate in a culturally meaningful table and to live in an ecologically healthy land. Potatoes and quinoa represent not simply calories, but a set of social, economic, and ecological relations. Riobamba Utopia supports a diverse agricultural landscape by purchasing from small-scale producers, emphasizing indigenous and traditional foods, and trying to favor organic produce. Over the years its experiment has used the food economy to cultivate a different economic spirituality. As it feeds its members, it trains their desire to hunger for justice.[2]

This chapter considers the relation of religious ethics and global capitalism within changing ecological systems by examining what desire-shaping practices should learn from practical projects to overcome impoverishment. At several points I claim that Christian practices can learn how to reject the unthinking piety toward growth on which a global plutocracy depends for the spell of its power. But, wary of abstract portraits of the relation between religion and capitalism, grand critique is not my main point. I focus on trying to understand two different kinds of impoverishment and what they mean for the relation of the market economy to earth's economy. Christian practices offer a unique angle of interpretation because they intentionally seek to cultivate excessive desires. Whether it is practically possible to desire both the liberation of the poor and the conservation of life depends on practices that teach agents how to desire the infinite within the limits of creation.

IMPOVERISHMENT

The expansion of the human economy during the twenty-first century was nearly mythic in scale. Between 1900 and 2000 the world's gross product increased thirty times over, while population quadrupled, fed by a grain harvest that quintupled and powered by a sixteen-fold increase in energy availability. Yet the growth has also been accompanied by diminishments. After the world's marine fish catch increased by an absurd multiple of 35, many stocks collapsed, and with them entire marine communities. Bird and mammal species across the planet declined as the human economy encroached and then overtook other creaturely economies.[3] Human activity came to dominate nearly all earth's ecosystems, appropriating as much as half of the photosynthetic capacity of all terrestrial life.[4]

Meanwhile, despite the aggregate expansion of the human economy, many persons still live in chronic hunger, suffer sickness without health care, and are trapped below subsistence living. The ugly achievement of maintaining destitution in the midst of great wealth has been made possible by unprecedented inequalities. Since 1900, the divide between rich and poor also grew by an order of magnitude, so that by the end of the century just 1 percent of the population controlled 40 percent of the world's wealth, while the bottom *half* of the population shared 1 percent of the wealth.[5] Evaluating the human economy thus requires looking carefully at the relation between growth and two basic problems of impoverishment— human misery and biological loss. This section briefly describes those problems independently and assesses initial claims of moral obligation.

Human Poverty

Twentieth-century economic growth made it possible to imagine that we may not, as Jesus seemed to say, always have the poor with us.[6] Economic expansion made overcoming absolute destitution a plausible policy goal. A shared economy of sufficient wealth implies that destitution endures only because society permits it. So already "the poor" who suffer lack by nature and chance are no longer with us; we live with "the impoverished," whose lack is produced by a shared economy and permitted by those who have means to assist. The emergence of a globalized economy changes poverty from a tragic occasion for elective acts of charity into an unjust condition created by shared economic relations. How Christian ethics interprets love and justice within the global market thus depends on how it interprets the last century's experience of economic growth in relation to persistent impoverishment.

What is poverty?
In order to count extreme poverty, the World Bank uses the mean national poverty lines of the fifteen poorest countries, which most recently was $1.25/day (of purchasing power parity). In 2005 there were 1.4 billion people below this most basic threshold of subsistence—which is to say, about one quarter of humanity barely lives. But as the world economy has grown, fewer people suffer this deprivation, both in real numbers (500 million less than in 1980) and as a percentage of the population (down from nearly half the population only 25 years ago). In general, extreme poverty has declined about one percentage point (of total population) per

year while world gross domestic product (GDP) has grown about three percent per year.[7]

Because human poverty has declined as the world economy has expanded it might seem that the moral project of overcoming poverty reduces to the economic project of growing GDP. However, the relation between economic growth and poverty reduction is neither proportional nor automatic. Growth has been regionally concentrated, with China's development accounting for much of the decline in poverty. Extreme poverty in sub-Saharan Africa remains stubbornly high—over 50% in many nations. Moreover, economic growth has fueled a rise in inequality much more efficiently than it has a decline in real destitution. Which is to say, the wealthy have benefited much more from expanded GDP than have the poor. Globalization of growth, Paul Collier has shown, does little to help the poorest billion persons, whose economic exclusion is often worsened by globalization dynamics.[8] The wealthy are benefitting by sustaining structures of impoverishment.

Focusing on growth distorts other important causes of impoverishment. Income is not a good proxy for measuring poverty because political and social conditions determine what income can do for a person. For the past two decades the United Nations Development Programme (UNDP) has used a Human Development Index to combine other variables with income, starting with life expectancy and education. The first sentence of its groundbreaking 1990 Human Development Report announced a correction to the growth-focused legacy of Adam Smith by saying: "People are the real wealth of a nation."[9] Development should not then be measured solely by the obtuse proxy of GDP growth; economic health should be measured with indicators more closely connected to the lived desires of human persons. Amartya Sen, leading architect of the Human Development Index, argues that poverty is deprivation of the basic capabilities necessary to lead a life one values.[10] The "capabilities approach" stimulated new interpretations of poverty in economic and political context.[11] In 2010 the UNDP introduced its Multidimensional Poverty Indicator to better track lack of basic capabilities, and finds about one-third of humanity living in destitution—significantly more than the World Bank number.[12]

Overcoming impoverishment depends on social, cultural, and political conditions. Making the economy bigger does not necessarily make humanity less poor. During the worldwide recession of 2008–10, extreme poverty kept declining such that the world met its first Millennium Development Goal (halving extreme poverty from 1990 levels) ahead of schedule.[13] That does not mean that economic vitality is unimportant; it rather suggests that political, social, and cultural dynamics shape the chances people have for participating in economic relations. It suggests that, as Abhijit Banerjee and Esther Duflo argue in *Poor Economics*, ideological commitments to growth or development aid as the general solution can lead to lazy economic thinking. Poverty should rather be understood from within the practices that work to overcome it.[14]

What is owed the poor?

If economic growth, development aid, and poverty reduction name three different social projects, why are they so often conflated? Arturo Escobar argues that the North Atlantic world uses discourse about world poverty to justify its continued neocolonial expansion.[15] Maybe perverse dominions use poverty as an excuse for the projection of power. Development aid has come in for criticism by others who hold that it is counterproductive of the social and cultural conditions needed to develop wealth.[16] Skeptical and neocolonial criticism of development is of course its own kind of discursive production, good for academic critics who are not struggling for their next meal. (Even Escobar notices "a certain materiality of life conditions that is extremely preoccupying." Preoccupying indeed.)[17] Yet criticism of how economic ideologies use poverty to moralize power raises important questions about the practices through which we conceive and satisfy obligations to the impoverished.

Philosopher Peter Singer points to a direct opportunity for overcoming impoverishment: the beneficiaries of world economic growth have at their disposal sufficient resources to alleviate the worst suffering. (Thomas Pogge calculates that the collective shortfall from the poverty threshold amounts to only 2 percent of global household income.)[18] Yet those who could help, Singer observes, chronically overinvest in themselves, choosing small pleasures over opportunities to eradicate huge suffering.[19] Singer therefore thinks that the major obstacles to overcoming world poverty are psychological and philosophical, and seeks to cultivate a "culture of giving" to overcome irrational preferences for oneself and near neighbors. This should be a strong point for Christian ethics, since the tradition's resources for appealing to love of the poor are immense. Ancient and contemporary voices renew the tradition's memory of Jesus's teaching to the rich: if you wish to be good, then love your neighbors by selling your possessions and giving them to the poor. The scandal of "rich Christians in an age of hunger" is the scandal of Jesus betrayed by love denied.[20]

The chief difficulty with Singer's model of benevolence holds also for Christian responses to poverty centered around love, as it appears to rely on personal giving to address a structural problem of maldistribution. Love may be good for the salvation of the rich, but does it really overcome the causes of impoverishment? Aside from the meager chances of convincing enough individuals to be less selfish, such appeals seem to ignore social, cultural, and economic processes that make poverty. Aid that fails to generate lasting economic participation and to change political and cultural relations may in fact impede the long-term transformations needed to overcome poverty. Cultures of giving sometimes produce cultures of dependency, and may perpetuate feelings of inferiority and helplessness among the impoverished while feeding a god-complex among the wealthy.[21]

Conceiving obligations in terms of charity or benevolence, moreover, can obscure the causal responsibility of the economically powerful for systemic impoverishment. In an economically integrated world of sufficient wealth and yet such inequality, argues Pogge, those who live in need suffer not from neglected assistance but causal harm. "By shaping and enforcing the social conditions that foreseeably and avoidably cause the monumental suffering of global poverty, we are harming the global poor."[22] This is, says Pogge, the largest crime against humanity ever committed. Poverty projects should not plead for more aid; they should demand different institutions.[23] Transnational corporations take advantage of the desperate neediness of poor laborers, to the advantage of wealthier shareholders and consumers, because of massive economic inequalities subsidized by policies. Powerful nations restrict economic migration while imposing unfair trade terms through political bullying, thus trapping poor labor in a situation of exploitable vulnerability. Overcoming their impoverishment requires constraining the ability of the powerful to harm the weak.[24]

A long line of theological criticism, from Christian socialism through liberation theologies to alternative globalization efforts, agrees that what is first owed the poor is justice. From the early emergence of market societies, Christian socialisms have argued for more democratic economies. As that reform project waned, South American liberation theologies intensified criticism of economic violence by condemning structural sin in market relations that hurt the poor and favor the powerful. Liberationist projects address the economy as a scene of social violence, demanding that justice reorder economic relations to vindicate the poor and hold the wealthy accountable. In the current hegemony of neoliberal market capitalism, theological demands for justice for the impoverished can be heard as nearly treasonous (especially in the United States)—suggesting that the prophetic task increasingly encounters an entangled idolatry of nation and market.

However, Christian ethics sometimes focuses so intently on prophetic critique that it obscures the historical success of markets in creating income growth that has been important, even if not determinative, for reducing poverty. Some Christian social thought of recent decades uses existing poverty to leverage its denunciation of market globalization, ignoring the role that markets have played in reducing impoverishment. Absolute and relative rates of poverty have declined as more people participated in the global market. The decline was not nearly as much as wealth would allow, and market globalization continues to harm and entrap many people. Neither a salvific process nor the beast of Babylon, the market is an ambivalent institution. It generates wealth and it also impoverishes. How far it helps overcome impoverishment seems to depend (among other things) on whether political communities use market participation as one part of a strategy focused on individual needs and capabilities; whether unfair exploitation of global markets by the powerful can be constrained by justice; and whether cultures of trust and freedom emerge where histories of exploitation corrupt social relations.

What is owed the impoverished, I am arguing, are creative and persistent attempts to make economic relations work to overcome impoverishment. Christian ethics should resist general arguments for or against economic growth. The more important question is practical and contextual: how can markets be used to create real wealth for the poor and where do current market arrangements produce impoverishment? Answers should arise from the practices interpreting and confronting impoverishment.

Those practices should include personal giving. If nothing else, charity refuses indifference to the needs of others and lets the needs of the impoverished shape one's own economic spirituality. They should include development aid directed toward realizing basic capabilities of persons. They should include neocolonial criticism of charitable giving and development, which keep those practices accountable to their function in broader flows of power. They should include empowering the impoverished to confront economic problems on their own, through both microeconomic programs and macroeconomic representation. Impoverishment must not be permitted to deprive some persons of the capability to hold others accountable. Some aspect of engagement with poverty must include prophetic critique of the economic ideas of the powerful, at least to make visible a basic divergence in political economies of desire: the wealthy want more growth, while the poor want justice.

That conflict points to a final ambivalence about the relation of market capitalism and impoverishment. The cultural ethos of the market can itself impoverish. Markets not only allow persons to pursue what they desire; they also shape perceptions of what we *should* desire and how we should evaluate our lives. Our willingness to sacrifice the interests of the impoverished for the sake of economic growth that favors the wealthy suggests declining value for justice among affluent consumers.[25] Contrary to what economists often claim, markets are not indifferent to preferences; they shape human desire and a consumer growth economy produces the insatiability of desire it needs. The poor remain always with us in another sense, then: participants in a consumer market are never sated. They always consider themselves poor in relation to some further object of desire. Using markets to overcome impoverishment, then, will need economic practices that satisfy desires for deeper forms of wealth.

Biological Impoverishment

Humanity's economic expansion has been unambivalently bad for biological diversity. The two chief drivers of biodiversity loss, land use and climate change, are directly related to economic appropriation of ecological space.[26] Where humans have not directly displaced the habitat of other species, resource exploitation has degraded ecological communities. Overfishing has caused trophic collapse in marine communities.[27] Even where forests remain standing, overharvesting animals for meat has led to "empty forest syndrome."[28] As seas and forests become part of the human economy, their ecological membership thins. Altogether the human economy has become earth's sixth great extinction event. Species extinctions now occur two to three orders of magnitude (100 to 1,000 times) faster than the natural background rate.[29] That loss represents not only the disappearance of individual kinds of life; it represents diminishment of the processes that generate life. The Millennium Ecosystem Assessment Report uses an economic metaphor to summarize the problem: humanity is "running down natural capital" and so "living beyond our means."[30] If so, the human economy has become irrational, for its growth depends on a fundamental impoverishment.

What is biological impoverishment?
The term "biodiversity" covers a great range of differences, including number of species, genetic variation within species, populations within communities, kinds of ecological communities, complexity of ecosystem interactions, and the multiple ecological functions produced from those interactions. Scientists sometimes use the term to refer to one or several of those precise meanings, and sometimes they use it in a more encompassing sense to refer to nature's value.[31] Understanding how biological impoverishment is a moral problem thus requires clarity about the phenomena in question.

The extinction event currently under way should arrest moral attention, but the numbers of species lost do not fully capture biological impoverishment. Where a few numbers of an endangered species are protected in zoos or preserves, they still exist but they no longer meaningfully participate in earth's economy. Moreover, the human economy is running an "extinction debt," as many existing populations will not survive the ecological changes already set in motion by humanity.[32] Diversity of existing creatures is not the most important good at sake here. What matters is how various kinds of diversity play roles to support the productivity and function of ecological systems. Biodiversity loss degrades the resilience and generativity of nature's economy.[33] Overcoming biological impoverishment thus entails more than collecting and saving a number of specimens. It requires making the human economy work to sustain the biological diversity necessary to the resilience and functioning of ecological systems.

Why does lost functioning count as impoverishment? After all, trophic collapses and system flips do not indicate the end of ecological functioning but rather the emergence of a different ecological regime. Species extinctions are but a temporary problem in a geological perspective. From each of the last mass extinctions, life came roaring back—but very differently each time. The ecological functions on which human life depends are not necessary to earth. Those functions are emergent properties of complex adaptive systems that "permit our survival but do not exist by virtue of permitting it."[34] The possibility of a different ecological regime points to what Simon Levin calls the fragility of human dominion. Biological impoverishment means degradation of the systems that make earth a habitat for humanity. That may seem narrowly anthropocentric, but consider the scope of obligations created by treating humanity as the keystone species in a fragile ecological community. When biodiversity refers to "the functional relationship between the diversity of organisms and the set of ecological services on which humanity depends," then conservation must go beyond saving species and protecting reserves. Conservation must qualify the entire economy of human action in order to protect the common wealth of all earth.[35]

How should societies value biodiversity?

There are two controversial proposals for evaluating biological impoverishment. One way describes the relevant diversity in relation to properties that support human habitat, measuring biological impoverishment as loss to conditions that support human life. A second works the other way, considering the human species as one participant in an ecological community, and seeking to measure how this species sustains or destroys habitat and systems that matter for the whole membership. Holding the tension of those two proposals can help situate the current debate over "ecological services" and inquire into the real wealth of earth.

A major reason that economic activities—from fishing to agriculture to manufacturing to book writing—impoverish earth is because none of those actions pays the true costs of the ecological resources and services it uses. That leaves the value of biodiversity and the costs of its loss outside the market's communication of information through prices. Call it a market externality or simple plunder; either way, social behavior does not adequately respond to biological impoverishment because the human economy fails to value the biodiversity it uses. The inevitable consequence is overuse and encroachment to the point of collapse. Markets can help solve this valuation problem insofar as they can accurately price the ecological services used by various activities—but that is a difficult condition. Some crucial services, like wild pollination, might be valued with current commercial alternatives. Most services require indirect or contingent valuation, which makes accurate pricing dependent on dubiously informed and uncertainly rational consumers. Some of the most important services, like the function of genetic diversity to the resilience of complex adaptive systems, are the most difficult to value.[36] If economists create ways to capture the costs involved in biological impoverishment, they can use markets to cue human behavior and social policy to biological limits.[37]

Once again, however, a market approach proves ambivalent. The very act of attempting to value ecosystems services might further impoverish biodiversity by making it seem that the human economy can escape its consequences through extending market exchanges even further. So biological impoverishment becomes reason to consummate "the great transformation" of modern political economy by making market relations reshape not only human society but the economy of all earth.[38] Valuing nature's services may encourage humans to commodify ecological relations, to think of earth's variety as a portfolio of fungible stocks—as if one might literally trade blue whale stocks against Toyota holdings. Some things cannot be priced, as Michael Sandel argues, without corrupting their real value, as well as the persons doing the pricing.[39] Biodiversity loss should not be understood as depleted "natural capital," argues Holmes Rolston; it represents the loss of a different species of value—of intrinsic value. Deploying "natural capital" metaphors rather than intrinsic value to describe biological impoverishment weakens the case for responsibility and our moral perspective of the world. Species value themselves by creating adaptive organismic responses to their world, argues Rolston. Their value goes beyond whatever services they provide humanity, as do our duties of respect for them. We have even stronger duties to the evolutionary ecological systems that produce those self-valuing lines.[40] The problem with the human economy, then, is not merely that it is irrationally spending down a resource endowment, but that hegemony of its valuation corrupts our ability to recognize the real wealth of earth.

Recognizing the intrinsic value of biodiversity hedges against the corrosive effect of economic rationality even while using market devices to protect biodiversity. Our minds need intrinsic value, in other words, in order to value earth properly. Consider that the human mind evolved through millennia of intimate evaluative associations with nature, while market rationality has developed through just two centuries of trying to ignore nature's value.[41] Our biophilic minds hunger for another kind of growth, writes biologist E. O. Wilson: "The living world is the natural domain of the most restless and paradoxical part of the human spirit. Our sense of wonder grows exponentially."[42] Biological impoverishment represents an impoverishment of the human soul, which—paradoxically—cannot be overcome without learning to appreciate nonhuman intrinsic values in the variety of life. Christian conservation projects sometimes articulate a version of that view when they present experience of biodiversity as a kind of sacrament. Kevin O'Brien argues that biodiversity has sacramental value because it connects humans to the workings of God. Biological loss, therefore, is "the dangerous destruction of our ability to know and respond to God."[43] Creaturely diversity reflects in knowable ways the unknowable Creator, who makes humans capable of union with the infinite by uniting their minds with the diversity of the finite. So biological loss impoverishes the human ability to know God, which Christians hold as humanity's deepest desire.[44] The point: within the right sort of practices, earth can teach humans how to value it and perhaps even offer a taste of infinite wonder.

Ethics does not need a theological account of sacramental value in order to hold that biodiversity should be protected on grounds stronger than the cash value of the ecological services it provides. It need only recognize how biodiversity plays a role in educating moral perception and desire. Earth's variety, and the ecological economy that produces it, are important to humans for reflecting on the character of value, of real wealth and real poverty. Biological impoverishment represents loss of earth's capacity to transform our poor desires and incompetent perceptions of value.[45] Again, that is a paradoxically anthropocentric approach to learning nonhuman values. And again, as with human poverty, markets seem an ambivalent institution, at once powerful in their potential to end impoverishment but corrupting in their effect on moral agents and often perverse in the outcomes they produce.

The Limits of Desire?

How far is it possible to desire the liberation of the poor and the conservation of all life? The global human economy produces two different kinds of impoverishment, and an apparent conflict between them. Slowing biological impoverishment seems likely to exclude resources from those who most need them. A population moving toward ten billion wants ever more from its economy, yet expanding desires for more may impoverish people and the planet. So how should an ethics of economy interpret the relation of human desire and ecological limits?

One tack of theological ethics argues that both forms of impoverishment have the same cause: the worldview of industrial capitalism. Leonardo Boff argues that "the cry of the poor" and "the cry of the earth" arise from a logic of domination in modern economic development. Economics needs a new cosmology, thinks Boff: until an individualist and violent self-understanding is replaced with a self in communion with creation, economic development will continue to mean destruction for all creatures, especially the poor and nonhuman life.[46] Boff's approach avoids conflicts between ecological conservation and human development by conflating two kinds of impoverishment into a critique of the moral cosmology of capitalism. That evades the question about the practical limits of desire with a protest against all available economic relations. If effective response to poverty requires economic revolution and spiritual transformation, then practical attempts to use existing economic and political relations to overcome impoverishment seem pathetic and complicit. But the promise of what is happening among the liberationist community in Riobamba, and many other sustainable economy projects like it, seems to demonstrate a more pragmatic utopianism. Their way into a sustaining economy involves decisions about how to use existing food markets, how to cultivate landscapes, and what specific things they should produce, use, and desire.

Theological ethics needs a finer grain of criticism than broad anticapitalist critique because the relationships of human desire, economic practices, and ecological limits are more various. The next three sections of this chapter explore three aspects of humanity's expanding ecological size: population, consumption, and development. Each represents a particular economy of desire and the debates within each have shaped central metaphors and ideas of sustainability. It is important to understand those debates in order to see how theological practices might shape desire differently, and so differently imagine the sustaining economy.

POPULATION AND THE LIBERATION OF DESIRE

When Thomas Malthus wrote *The Principle of Population*, he turned perception of population growth from social boon into economic problem by taking a biological view of the human species. Poverty, explained Malthus, is caused by an unequal relation between growth in population and growth in

food supplies. Excessive sexual desire drives human numbers past the limited supply of resources. Poverty was biologically inevitable, created by "the
constant tendency in all animated life to increase beyond the nourishment
provided for it."[47] It was also politically tragic, for aid to the poor would
only exacerbate the underlying cause by enabling further fertility and thus
increasing the number of suffering persons.

Humans numbered about a billion when Malthus wrote. It had taken
tens of thousands of years for our species to reach that number, but then
our population doubled in only another a century, and then doubled again
in about half a century. By 1950 there were four billion of us, and renewed
warnings that Malthusian collapse was imminent. Yet sixty years later, with
seven billion of us and more food than ever before, the impact of population
growth on sustaining systems remains uncertain. For 2050, estimates range
between eight and eleven billion; each one an individual person seeking the
resources to lead a life of dignity, many desiring to have children of their
own, and all desiring more and better.[48] How should ethics interpret the
intersections of desire, growth, and impoverishment?

By introducing a biological limit into political economy and drawing
policy conclusions about reproduction and poverty, Malthus started a debate that continues in contemporary arguments over sustainability. Does
holistic ecological thinking generate an imperative to sacrifice the poor for
the greater good? If natural scarcity made by the conflict of sexual desire
and biological limits is the primary cause of poverty, then indifference to the
needy becomes ecologically enlightened morality. Malthus was not indifferent to suffering but his notions of natural limits and sexual desire led him to
a bleak conclusion: since few restrain sexual desire, societies must restrict
the resources that enable the poor to reproduce. Within a few decades, Malthusian ideas stiffened the resolve of the upper classes to watch Irish peas-
ants starve. It was, after all, their own fault, breeding past nature's limits,
and the check on population now would be better for everyone in the long
run. Those ideas reappeared with every subsequent famine, until Amartya
Sen finally put to rest the biological myth of famine with evidence that famines are nearly always due to political failure rather than natural scarcity.[49]

The fearful legacy of Malthusian connections of desire, limit, and poverty illustrates the broader portraits of humanity drawn when trying to rethink political economy within nature's economy. Thinking of sustainability
from irrepressible sexuality and immovable natural limits makes humanity appear a cancer in the body of earth, reproducing senselessly until it
kills its host. The excessive growth appears, of course, among the suspect:
poor women from "other" races, nations, and religions. Influential concepts

that still shape ideas of sustainability—including "tragedy of the commons," "carrying capacity," and the IPAT equation (Impact = Population × Affluence × Technology)—were initially developed to construct an ecological ethic of reproductive sex. In order to understand the role of those ideas in a broader economic ethic, we need to see how they emerged from fears about natural limits and reproductive sexuality.

Sex and Sustainability

The view that sexual freedom leads to procreative disaster delayed by a century the recognition that securing reproductive freedom for poor women generally leads to fewer births, not more. Malthus could have heard that alternative perspective from Mary Wollstonecraft, author of *A Vindication of the Rights of Women* and spouse of the political idealist William Godwin, against whom the biological materialist Malthus was arguing.[50] Wollstonecraft argued for women to have more control over the spacing of children. Were women to have greater reproductive freedom, she held, they would choose fewer children. (Wollstonecraft herself died in childbirth, as do still about one thousand women each day.)[51] It took more than a century for sustainability thinkers to begin to appreciate her view, as Malthusian fears fed classist and patriarchal perceptions of poor women as sexually uncontrollable and politically degenerative.

At first feminists saw an opportunity in population concerns. Between 1900 and 1950 feminists advocating reproductive freedom forged an uneasy alliance with neo-Malthusians and eugenicists.[52] However, by conceding female sexuality as the source of a population problem, the neo-Malthusian feminists made women vulnerable to social control in a different way. Overpopulation discourses made women appear as "breeders of both environmental destruction and violence."[53] Women, especially the poor women who supposedly desired so many babies, were the target community for programs limiting the ecological scale of humanity. Contraception was welcomed by early feminists and population critics for quite different reasons. The revolution of effective contraception was to make reproduction an optional choice in sexual relationships. Feminists wanted that choice as a way to realize individual freedom; neo-Malthusians wanted it in order reduce aggregate births. It was inevitable that the logic of freedom would conflict with the logic of limit.

In the 1960s, in the midst of the highest population growth rate humanity has ever seen, two essays from biologists put Malthusian ideas at the center of emerging concerns about ecological decline. In 1968 Paul Ehrlich's book, *The Population Bomb*, posited that earth's agricultural capacity had been exhausted, while population would continue its massive rise, raising the prospect of mass starvations.[54] That same year Garrett Hardin published "The Tragedy of the Commons," a now famous essay used to conceptualize many public goods problems. It is often forgotten that the problem Hardin originally had in mind was "the free commons in breeding." Hardin explains the dilemma with the thought experiment of a public pasture on which it is privately rational for every herder to add an extra animal. Because each herder shares only a fraction of the loss incurred by overgrazing, each has an incentive to overuse it and eventually the commons must collapse. Reproductive decisions are similar, thought Hardin: reproducers get the full benefit of an extra child but incur only a fraction of that child's cost to public goods.[55]

Hardin's "tragedy of the commons" held that human behavior must be considered collectively and in relation to the ecological systems upon which it relies. "The morality of an act is a function of the system at the time it is performed."[56] Private reproductive decisions become immoral in a biological system overburdened by humans. Yet morality motivates only a few individuals so the public needs some form of mutual coercion. Hardin argues that the good of sustaining the commons justifies overriding individual rights to coerce lower fertility rates, to bring the population within the carrying capacity of ecological systems.

"Carrying capacity" was a term already in use by biologists to assess the maximum plant or animal population that a habitat could sustain. By applying it to the human species, Hardin presses his readers to consider human behavior in relation to the limits of a biological system. Once established, those limits must curtail excessive reproductive desires. So, what are those limits? Joel Cohen's exhaustive study, *How Many People Can the Earth Support?,* finally cannot answer his title question. His survey shows the range of answers, and finds not only lack of consensus but that in fact the *range* of estimates increases with time. The most recent estimations of earth's human carrying capacity are the most divergent, from one billion to one hundred billion. So Cohen must content himself with observing that increasing numbers continue to force further adaptation from human societies, whose potential to expand earth's carrying capacity cannot be infinite but nevertheless seems indeterminate.[57]

That indeterminacy makes Hardin's moral dictum (that the morality of an act is a function of the system in which it occurs) difficult to apply. Carrying capacity does not provide ethics with definite limits that could then determine reproductive responsibilities. A concept created for biological studies of ruminant populations does not seem well suited to humans because cultural capacities are more flexible than Hardin's disciplinary training in biology allowed him to imagine. When a society suffers deprivation, especially hunger, it does not necessarily indicate an oversupply of humans; it more likely indicates a failure of political organization. Admitting that the limits change with economic and social organization does not mean that there are no biophysical limits. It just means that limits are difficult to set for innovative and adaptive societies. Mere recognition of finitude does not yield any definite responsibilities.

Given an uncertain limit and cultural flexibility, the question becomes how humanity might arrive at a settled equilibrium of size that reflects its values, rather than a number established through chance and misery.[58] Like reproductive decisions about family size, the maximum is not likely the optimum. Bringing about the maximum number of humans the earth could support could well make for the worst welfare outcome. Derek Parfit calls this the "repugnant conclusion" of standard utilitarian logic: the total sum happiness of 20 billion people barely living might be greater than that of 10 billion with a high standard of living.[59] So whether and how human reproduction represents a commons problem first requires a global conversation about optimum human population size. Once that optimum goal is established, this way of thinking goes, then reproductive choices can be coerced, either by enclosing the commons or by policy regulation. The first defeats the commons tragedy by transforming its public space into private property. Birthing rights might be assigned per capita, and tradable like other forms of property. The second might take the form of a law against birthing more children, such as China's 1979 introduction of a one-child policy. Regulatory coercion could take the somewhat softer form of incentives, perhaps through tax arrangements that remove relief for children or by offering incentives for sterilization, which India tried for a while.

Those hardly represent the sort of policies early feminists had in mind when endorsing contraception. What was for them a matter of reproductive freedom became reason for further social control of reproduction. "The use of alarmist population arguments that identify poor women's fertility as the major ecological threat to the planet," writes Giovanna di Chiro, led to policies that make the wombs of poor women the object of political intervention.[60] Response in Christian ethics from both left and right has intensified that concern. It was not because Hardin was unclear about the extent to which his sustainability logic should trump individual rights. Like Malthus, Hardin warned against food aid on the grounds that biological systems cannot afford such misguided moralism. His "lifeboat ethics" holds that when sustaining systems are overburdened, societies cannot rescue individuals without eventually causing the demise of everyone.[61] James Gustafson agrees that in a limited biological system, love for those in need may destroy the systems on which everyone depends. Christian ethics must acknowledge that "God has not so ordered the world that even the minimal provisions for survival and health can be made available to many persons." Population control for the common good, Gustafson follows the logic, warrants teaching contraception as "little short of an imperative" and, under certain conditions, coercively imposing it.[62] John Cobb and Herman Daly think markets might achieve reproductive control more peacefully and endorse the idea of tradable birthing rights.[63]

Of course some theologians resisted the logic of population control on the grounds that contraception is immoral. Pope Paul VI's *Humanae vitae* made it clear that appeal to the public commons could not justify the use of contraceptive or abortive technologies.[64] Magisterial social teaching has maintained that reproduction is the proper end of sexuality, and that when sexuality is sundered from that end its desire becomes disordered and excessive. That stance has made the Vatican reluctant to recognize population as a social problem, interpreting ecological impacts instead as a symptom of what happens when humans act against the moral order of nature.[65]

So far this is a sorry showing for Christian ethics of reproduction. On one side are ethicists ready to let a view of biological impoverishment justify sexual control of the disempowered; on the other are those whose teachings on sex determine their view of whether and how biological impoverishment happens. On both sides, male moralists use theological arguments to control female sexuality, treating the reproductive desire of women as a threat to the order of nature. However, another line of theological ethics has argued that promoting freedom is intrinsically right and, happily, a more effective way of protecting the common good.[66]

Liberating Desire

What if the deepest desire of poor women is for something else besides birthing more children? The theory of "demographic transition" holds that as societies develop modern economic systems they move from a near equilibrium rate of high birth and death rates to a period in which death rates move lower but birth rates remain high. In that period, the growth rate increases and population may rise dramatically. But as modernization continues, the birth rates lower and with them the overall growth rate, until a society achieves a new equilibrium with low birth and death rates.[67] The idea that economic growth can lead to lower growth rates led to the slogan "development is the best contraceptive."[68]

Some demographic and ecological thinkers worry that the turn toward development has more to do with relief from the difficult ethical questions about conflicts between reproductive freedom and biological limits.[69] Even if the rate of growth is falling, total population is still growing, adding the equivalent of another Mexico City every six months. The UN projects that the human population will stabilize at around ten billion on the statistical assumption that fertility rates will continually fall toward replacement levels.[70] With so much at stake for earth and humanity, what permits that assumption? Clearly in some contexts demographic transition has stalled: in Nigeria falling death rates without other significant human development may keep fertility rates from falling in tandem.[71] One reason may be development programs focused more on "cheap death control" (e.g., immunizations) rather than on the integrated economic development and political freedom needed by persons to have the opportunity to move themselves out of destitution.[72] Another may be that falling fertility is itself a contributing factor to development.[73]

The geographic distribution in growth rates is instructive. The global population growth rate peaked at 2.2 percent around 1970 and has been slowly declining since. For centuries the global average was five births per woman, then in a few decades it was halved to about 2.6 per woman.[74] The decline is not uniformly distributed: growth rates are generally higher among poorer populations and generally lower among wealthier populations. Inequality in growth rates seems to roughly track with inequality in wealth—and the range in both is historically unprecedented.[75] There is more to the situation than wealth and poverty, however. High fertility rates show up in contexts of female disempowerment (e.g., Saudi Arabia) and where mothers have poor prospects for maternal health and child mortality (e.g., Nigeria). Where women have greater enjoyment of human rights, including access to contraception, fertility rates trend lower. Where women have the most capability to realize their desires, it seems, they generally choose to have fewer children.

That includes being able to expect their children to survive. The replacement rate for the population of Japan, where childhood deaths are rare, is 2.06 children per woman. But in Nigeria, where childhood mortality is high, it takes nearly 3 children per woman to replace the population. Those replacement rates essentially "quantify the failure to survive among the youngest," and so give an indication of contextual reason for parents to seek more or less children. In Japan parents may choose fewer children because they can expect those they do have to survive.[76]

Reproduction is finally a matter of individual choices—choices intimate to each human parent's self-understanding, made within a complex of intuitions, expectations, and reasons. But this much is clear: when women have real choices, birth rates tend to fall. For whatever intimate reasons, having fewer children "is what people do when they have some basic education, know about family planning methods and have access to them, do not readily accept a life of persistent drudgery, and are not deeply anxious about their economic security . . . [and] are not forced by high infant and child mortality rates to be so worried that no child will survive."[77] Humans may have an insatiable desire for more, but it is not necessarily more children that they want. So the assumptions of Malthus and Hardin are precisely reversed: sustainability is threatened not by development aid and sexual autonomy but by their lack. The real moral problem represented by fast population growth is not how to constrain reproductive freedom but how to liberate it.[78]

That forces confrontation with uncomfortable cultural and religious dimensions to reproductive decisions. Political and economic development may not be sufficient to create conditions that allow women to choose to bear children on their own terms. Without attention to cultures of gender and sexuality, development processes may in fact weaken the freedom of women. Vandana Shiva draws the connections even more insidiously, arguing that modern agriculture dispossessed poor women of their control over ecological productivity at the same time that modern states sought control over women's reproductivity.[79] Modernizing development does not necessarily realize freedom for women; without changes in patriarchal moralities it may allow greater control over reproduction.[80]

The tension with Christian traditions is nowhere greater in sustainability ethics than with the fate of patriarchal sexual moralities. Traditional associations of "fill the earth and subdue it" with sexualized dominion of male over female makes for a natalist reproductive ethic. (Patristic dissent on the latter should be noted: Tertullian, Augustine, and John Chrysostom each argued that Christians were free to pursue celibacy because already the world was full to the limits.)[81] The difficulty here runs deeper than changing pastoral teachings against using contraception because Christian teachings on sexuality and reproduction carry gendered imaginaries of the human role in creation—for better or worse. Part of the horror of the European witch hunts likely had to do with attempts by ecclesial institutions to control female sexuality, in league with nationalist interests to promote reproduction. Midwives, who curated and communicated knowledge about reproductive control, were especially vulnerable to being lynched as witches. (At least one Inquisition handbook explained how midwifery was a likely vehicle of the evil crafts.)[82] Rosemary Radford Reuther thus argues that a global Catholic "crusade" to prevent policies of reproductive freedom is rooted in deep theological inheritances of misogyny and sexual dominion.[83]

Those inheritances carry imaginaries of the role of humanity in creation. Christian traditions often depicted creation as typologically feminine
and God as typologically masculine, so that creation was passive and receptive to God's active and fructifying agency. Human economic creativity then
takes a masculine role to earth's feminine passivity.[84] Christian marriage
practices enact that gendered cosmos when their disciplines include female
passivity to male authority, and when reproduction becomes its legitimating
purpose. Christian marriage models human dominion. While few couples
think of their relationship this way, marriage enacts the ecological form of
human economy.

Sexual ethics usually treats the morality of discrete acts or relations
rather than interpretations of how human action participates in the economy of creation. Yet the latter may animate resistance to change in sexual
teachings, for an entire moral cosmology may seem at stake for a theological
community. The magisterial teachings on sexual ethics attempt to protect an
interpretation of how human development participates in God's intentions
for creation. By protecting an account of how God realizes human dignity
within the limits of created life, it protects a model of dominion.[85] People
naturally and rightfully desire "to do more, know more, and have more in
order to be more," wrote Paul VI.[86] By insisting that those desires find their
only possible satisfaction in God, the magisterial teachings on the natural
order of sexual relations understand themselves to offer counsel on how
to desire the infinite within and through nature's limits. In the Protestant
world as well, shows a skeptical Amy Laura Hall, a "spirit of reproduction"
shapes how members understand their role in natural orders.[87] The practice
of faith within everyday family relationship thus enacts the satisfaction of
sexual desire within a finite creation. Critics of patriarchal sexual theologies
counsel different everyday practices, but they too must account for how
they enact the relation of desire and limit within the relation between the
human economy, earth's economy, and God's economy.

That cosmic question was in fact the theological topic most discussed
in ancient interpretations of the Genesis dominion passage. Jeremy Cohen
has shown that for most of its history, rabbinic and ecclesial commentators understood those verses as commentary on human personhood rather
than sexual or ecological mandates. Genesis 1:28 shows humans on a cosmic frontier, participating in the dominion of God yet connatural with the
wild fertility of earth. The same blessing given birds and sea creatures to
be fertile and increase is given to humanity. When ancient Christians used
the Genesis mandate to argue about sexuality, they did so to integrate the
cosmological vocation of humanity with whatever intuitions about sex and
morality were current.[88]

The connections among sexuality, reproduction, and cosmology sug- gest that rethinking the ethics of sexuality and marriage, as many Christian communities have been doing in recent decades, bears significance for how Christian communities interpret dominion. Contraceptive sex has forced Christian communities to reckon with nonreproductive ends of sexual re- lationships, and same-sex unions have pressed theological communities to reexamine how Christian marriage witnesses to the relationship of God and creatures. The theological controversies, while acrimonious, have been helpful for all parties to rethink how Christian marriage practice is a train- ing in desire. How and why we marry implicitly interprets the meaning and purpose of the economy.

A neglected but ancient strand in the tradition may help tutor the con- troversies. Nonnatalist and ascetic in ethos, it holds that marriage is first a practice of self-giving to another through which God orients the human desire to its true end in God. Sexual relationships might include the rearing of children but that is not their legitimating purpose. Marriage participates in God's way with creation through its covenant of mutual service. Couples enact God's dominion in ways other than making babies.[89]

Discriminating the ultimate end of sex and marriage from reproduc- tion does not diminish the value of rearing children. On the contrary, it better establishes that children should always be received as gifts, not made as products. In a world in which children are too often made for instru- mental reasons—to have laborers or caretakers, to perpetuate one's genetic survival or personal legacy, to display social status—Christian practice can stand for receiving children (by birth or adoption) as an elective choice to open oneself to gift and devote oneself to hospitality. Christian hope does not rest its future in making children for ourselves, but rather in becoming children of God. So child-rearing becomes a spiritual practice in which care for a creature becomes a way of receiving God's gifts.

The basic point of this section is that scaling the human economy to earth's economy should lead not to controlling reproductive desire but rather to liberating it. Essential to being able to receive children as gifts are the cultural, political, health, and economic conditions that permit women the freedom to choose whether and when to bear children. Demographic changes matter within a broader human economy of consumption and de- velopment, and the best way to manage the contribution of population growth to the overall dominion of the human economy is to start from both impoverishments: make women less poor and biodiversity more pro- tected. Yet that only starts the task of transforming the human economy, for the liberation of desire in reproduction needs the discipline of desire in consumption.

CONSUMPTION AND THE DISCIPLINE OF DESIRE

Human impact on ecological systems is less a product of how many persons exist than what those people do. If the average United States citizen uses twenty times more of earth's resources and services than the average Nigerian, then US practices of consumption matter more to the whole economy than Nigerian practices of reproduction. Observing similar tensions between individual freedom and common goods, as well as the imperative for two billion poor people to increase their consumption, how should ethics treat the economy of consumption?

Concepts developed in the population debates in fact help shift moral perception toward excessive consumption. In addition to his blunt metaphor of a "bomb," Ehrlich offered the equation I=PAT, where T stands for technology, A for affluence, P for population, and I for the total impact of humanity on ecological systems. Ehrlich intended the formula to express how population growth multiplies the destructive impact of economic and technological development. In subsequent decades, however, others have used the formula to shift attention toward reducing consumption or greening technology.[90]

One of the most successful impact metaphors illustrates why. "Ecological footprint" represents human appropriation of earth's economy on the premise that every human use takes up the biological capacity of a definite area of land or water. It then assesses the consumption impact of individuals, groups, or all humanity as a spatial measure by tallying the area of land and water that their energy, resource use, and waste require. The footprint represents excessive consumption in three ways. First, it depicts the threshold at which human appropriation exceeds the "natural income" of the biosphere. When the cumulative area of humanity's footprint exceeds the productive area of the earth, the human economy runs an "ecological deficit" that begins to erode the resource base on which it depends.[91] Second, because the footprint also represents the relative share of earth's capacity appropriated by individuals and groups, it illustrates unfair appropriations of capacity. Wealthy countries usually use an area of capacity that exceeds their territory; in the case of Holland, by fourteen times. Third, by using a land-area indicator to represent the size of humanity, footprint raises a question about how much economic space humanity should leave for non-symbiotic species. Or, since it is planetary in size, how to make space for other species within the human footprint.[92]

The footprint model thus shifts the economic geography of suspect desires from poor persons to wealthy persons, from global South to global North. It makes the most important driver of human impact not the babies of those living below the poverty line, but the consumption of those living above the "greed line."[93] By illustrating that the desires of a wealthy minority fuel the outsized economy of humanity as a species, it makes blaming the ecological consequences of economic growth on the children of poor persons excluded from consumption, rather than on the excessive resource appropriation of the economically powerful, an outrageous irony.

Religious ethics may have unique capacities for articulating that outrage and for transforming patterns of consumption. Sociologists note two difficulties in changing consumption. First, the easy target of conspicuous excess (private jets) is less ecologically important than the infrastructure of households (urban planning and food provision), but changing everyday infrastructures involves transforming cultural understandings of our economic life.[94] In turn, focusing on cultures of consumption creates tension with values of economic freedom and with the ethos of global market capitalism. Making consumption a central factor in overcoming impoverishment makes changing the exercise of consumer freedom a central economic task.[95] Yet consumer economies are organized around maximizing choice, not constraining or questioning it.

Christian ethics finds itself on more comfortable theological ground with those tasks, although it must reclaim forgotten practices to meet them. Ron Sider's *Rich Christians in an Age of Hunger*, first published in 1977 and reprinted many times since, argues that as the human economy reaches limits of resource production wealthy Christians have an obligation to reduce their own consumption. The needs of the poor condemn the affluence of rich Christians, argues Sider, who instead must begin by recovering contentment with simplicity.[96] Sider's outrage recalls early church critiques of wealth amid poverty, such as that in the sarcasm of Basil of Caesarea: "Those who love their neighbor as themselves possess nothing more than their neighbor; yet, surely, you seem to have great possessions! How else can this be but that you have preferred your own enjoyment to the consolation of the many?"[97] Other lapses in memory are more recent: Christina Hinze remembers that "just consumption" was originally part of the "just wage" teaching in early Catholic social thought. Social ethicists seemed to forget that teaching over the subsequent century of consumption-driven economic growth.[98] With finitude on the horizon again, James Nash calls for the recovery of another forgotten virtue—frugality—as a practice for respecting the needs of nonhuman creatures.[99] Catherine Keller reclaims asceticism for retraining desire away from destructive forms of consumption.[100] As they become aware of the role of consumption in driving social injustice and ecological impoverishment, Christian social thinkers across traditions and schools are remembering practices that discipline desire, reforming it into countercultural images of flourishing and freedom.[101]

Reforming Desire

How do Christian practices of desire relate to the productions of desire within the global consumer economy? Consider two options, one focused on reclaiming faith as its own economy of desire and one focused on transforming the ethos of consumer capitalism. The options are not exclusive but the tensions between them help interpret the possibilities of faithful response to impoverishment within economies of consumption.

The strongest theological criticism of consumer capitalism treats it as a religious belief system. Theologians associated with the school of "radical orthodoxy" critique market capitalism as a false church because it disciplines desire to want false wealth and seek false gods. The deep dysfunction of consumer capitalism, in this view, is not that it is ecologically unsustainable but that it makes persons into "consumers." It makes the exercise of competitive freedom an end in itself and treats the pursuit of finite goods as the chief end of life. Market capitalism works religiously because it shapes the desires that shape souls. It is ecologically dysfunctional because it models economic dominion as sheer projection of power over creation rather than participation within God's economy.[102] If it makes dark theological sense to say, as William Cavanaugh does, that humans are "being consumed" by consumer capitalism, then Christianity offers salvation: being consumed by God through learning how to desire and consume God's body.[103]

For the theologians of radical critique, a consumer economy fixated on unending expansions is symptomatic of a deeper error with worse theological consequences than mere ecological collapse. It is right that humans always want to have more and be more, but that restless insatiability needs an insatiable object. That is a basic Augustinian point: human desire is restless and insatiable because humans seek an infinite good. Trying to satisfy desire for God by enjoying more commodities is worse than a mere transactional error, as if selecting an inferior item to purchase; it is a devastating existential error that orients desire toward death by curving desire in on itself. When vain cupidity becomes a political commitment and global project, it disciplines whole societies to desire what will surely destroy them. When growth of consumer economies becomes a goal unmoored from the common good, the very figure of sin—desire curved in on itself—becomes economic policy. One consequence is a global market recklessly devouring earth, in order to feed all the insane wishes it has incited in persons whom it has made captive to a vicious ideology. Another is impoverishment of the human soul.

However, insofar as the reform of desire supports an interpretation of market consumerism as a rival religious system, it can make concrete economic reforms appear less meaningful, perhaps even complicit. Radical critiques of consumer economy make the practice of reforming desire a way of waiting on an utterly different economy of grace. That view is pessimistic that movements like the Riobamba food cooperative can make the global economy less dysfunctional or any more worth sustaining. Yet participants in Riobamba Utopia reflect on their practices differently. Enacting food sovereignty uses market relations in unexpected ways in order to open possibilities of civic friendship, economic justice, and landscape membership within a dominating political economy. They do not withdraw from market exchange and attempt to realize an alternative gift economy; they open alternative economic possibilities by using market relations for their own ends.

Consider a second view of reforming desire. Vincent Miller argues that consumerism should not be understood in terms of false belief and intellectual mistakes. That overplays the importance of belief and underplays the material structures and cultural habits that channel agency. Miller is struck by how many Christians profess beliefs in tension with consumerist excess, yet seem not to pursue practices in which to enact simplicity and social justice. Theologians should therefore pay more attention to the structures that frustrate the desire of the faithful to live differently. For example, the single-family house (and the institutions, incentives, and ideologies that support it) organizes interests and desires in ways at odds with what people profess they want to pursue and desire. That makes the question of reforming desire a problem of opening and deepening possibilities of agency.[104]

Luke Bretherton concentrates theological engagement with consumer capitalism on that problem. Christian practices of desire should seek concrete ways of using economic relations for their own political and moral ends. Forms of what Bretherton calls "political consumerism" use market exchanges in odd ways. The Riobamba food cooperative would count as one example; fair trade and farmers' markets as others. Faith communities often generate such initiatives, notices Bretherton, yet theological analysis tends to overlook them; "what theological analysis there is of the relationship between capitalism, consumerism, and Christian witness tends to be wholly negative and undermines any possibility of constructive forms of engagement." Christian ethics should pay more attention to how "capillaries of friendship and forms of faithful witness can be forged and sustained within any hegemonic system." Undertaken as practices of faith, those initiatives bear transformative potential for Christians and may open cultural space for political alternatives.[105]

This second approach supports alternative Christian disciplines of economic desire while maintaining that they can play a constructive role in transforming the ethos of dominant market arrangements. Max Weber showed how Calvinism cultivated an economic asceticism that made capitalism possible by supplying the cultural conditions, the "spirit," it needed to emerge.[106] That does not mean that theological beliefs simply translate into economic practices but it does suggest that consumer capitalism depends on cultivating a compatible spirit. William Connolly argues that the current "assemblage" of capitalism depends on an ethos (or "spirituality") of economic practice drawn from participation in markets and media as well as religious and political communities. Consumer capitalism and its spirituality reflexively reinforce one another as neoclassical theories about market freedom shape how citizens understand their own freedom and the meaning of its pursuits.[107] Connolly seems right: wealthy consumers crave ideologies that allow them to think that unfettered freedom provides them what they really want while at the same time driving growth that provides for the poor tomorrow.

Practices that slow the metabolism of consumption can begin to nurture a different economic ethos. Disciplines of desire refuse a bad utopianism: the sort that imagines an infinite world and assumes an unfettered economy populated by affluent consumers chasing selfish dreams somehow helps the poor and earth.[108] An ascetic spirituality shapes its practitioners by realities our economy trains us to forget: the limits of ecological systems, the needs of other persons, and our own selfish irrationality.

Disciplines of desire do not necessarily carry negative views of humanity and desire. On the contrary, ascetic practices vindicate hope that the economy of humanity can cultivate beauty and goodness. As a practice of dying to the spirituality of consumerism, neoasceticisms practice a critical suspicion toward our hungers, impulses, and wishes in order to ask what sort of imaginary has produced those desires.[109] Consumption is not intrinsically bad or impoverishing, but it is always morally and theologically significant. As Laura Hartman has shown, theological styles of consumption allow agents to reflect on how the world is presented to them within everyday choices, thus opening more space to use creation faithfully.[110] Making practices of desire accountable to what we believe we most deeply want refuses to let consumption or growth stand as unquestioned ends in themselves. Without the theological frame, that seems the basic point of Juliet Schor's argument for adopting "plenitude" lifestyles that recover personal fulfillment through practices that sustain social and ecological functioning.[111]

Schor's pivot away from sacrifice toward self-fulfillment should raise a worry at this point: might alternative uses of "asceticism" just give theological gloss to "green consumerism"? Purchasing fair-trade bananas easily becomes the performance of just another consumer style, barely different in its selfishness from others. However, Bretherton makes a distinction between "consumerism as a habitus or regime of life, and political consumerism as a nonrevolutionary attempt to restructure this regime by utilizing what is to hand."[112] Collectively purchasing local foods as a practice of faith shapes participants into a different economic rationality while utilizing an available agricultural market, national currency, and legal contracts. Because it is situated within efforts to be faithful, using market devices to purchase food cultivates a unique economic spirituality, in which desire and wealth are reinterpreted within God's self-giving. Consumer markets and their underwriting ideologies are hegemonic but they do not utterly defeat the possibilities of faithful agency. Withdrawal is not the only or best option for those who seek the economy of grace. Kathryn Tanner puts it this way: "theological economy encroaches on and enters within the territory of the economy it opposes for the purpose of transforming the operations of that field. . . . [It] works from within it, to turn or convert it to different principles of operation." Using market relations for the odd purposes of faith begins to create the alternative economy envisioned by the Christian utopia of grace. "It comes to life from within the belly of the beast."[113]

Christian practices can reform desire by using economic structures in unexpected ways in order to orient them anew toward overcoming impoverishment. Connolly thus holds hope for "eco-egalitarianism" in "microeconomic experiments" like the Bruderhof communities. "This Christian minority challenges the dominant spirituality of American capitalism with an ethos that turns and twists the capitalist assemblage in a distinctive direction."[114] Other ways of reorienting consumer capitalism could include fair trade, microlending, farmer's markets, carbon offsets, and community-based ecotourism. Each initiative turns participants' focus from objects of desire to practices of desire by teaching participants what to value in one another and earth. It is not irrelevant that each of those initiatives has made a real difference in market structures. Fair trade has registered protest of exploitative commodity production and created markets that support living wages. Microcredit has opened greater economic participation to the very poor. Farmer's markets have made responsible relations among producers, consumers, and their shared land part of the value of food. Carbon offsets show a desire by energy users to recognize and the pay the costs of their use. Community-based ecotourism has made conservation more profitable and encouraged nonconsumptive uses of biodiversity. As practices of faith, those forms of political consumerism become forms of "playing with creation . . . in disciplined and generative ways, ways that seek to love one's neighbor and that are open to the healing and perfection of the *saeculum*"— which is to say, to seeking the well-being of Babylon or the transformation of "the beast."[115]

The moral hazard of celebrating capillaries of friendship and alternative economic tactics is that economic justice can seem to become just a strange religious performance or the odd dissent of odd consumers. Celebrating possibilities for odd (faithful) forms of moral agency within hegemonic consumer capitalism may weaken the case for structural changes. If the presence of fair-trade bananas in the grocery mollifies Christian consumers, who can now suppose they act in expectation of the economy of grace while doing little to change basic unfairness and violence in global trade, then those bananas are a morally toxic commodity. For buying them might substitute for witness against the trade policies that hurt the poor and degrade earth, and might conceal how consumer capitalism determines what choices are available.[116]

In contrast, the Riobamba Utopia food cooperative supports a strong neocolonial critique, informed by a broadly Marxist analysis. It presents its practices as resistance to North Atlantic control over Ecuadoran peoples and lands, and argues that the global commodity market impoverishes both because it is the mechanism used by a "civilization of wealth" to capture resources from poorer peoples and lands. Participants in Riobamba Utopia criticize "ecological debt" (the debt owed by the North to the South for uncompensated capture of its resources) and call for "Northern structural adjustment" toward an ecosocialist revolution. The Utopia food cooperative thus engages in utopian economics to drive a strong critique of global capitalism. On its account the food cooperative redirects economic channels in order to open utopian space for a "civilization of poverty" in which God's desire for the poor takes center stage.[117]

The prophetic utopian elements in the Riobamba cooperative add an important counterpoint to Bretherton's and Connolly's insistence that radical critique cannot substitute for concrete action: it cannot only because concrete economic action is the condition for deep economic transformation. Against Bretherton's "non-revolutionary" tone, participants in the Riobamba cooperative do describe their initiative as a revolutionary project. Opening capillaries of friendship within markets must become ways to protest the "open veins of Latin America."[118] Practices must help prepare for life in an economy restructured around the priority of ending impoverishment rather than the freedom of the powerful. The liberationist perspectives of

Riobamba Utopia go beyond criticizing consumerism as a discipline of desire to criticizing the discipline of peoples and lands. The greatest sin of the global consumer market is not that it impoverishes the souls of the wealthy but that it steals food from the poor. The reformation of desire by Utopia Riobamba therefore shapes its participants to desire justice and revolution by desiring native quinoa and potatoes.

This approach differs from the radical theological critiques by shifting from visions of God's excessive plenitude toward practices that acknowledge dependence on God, on one another, and on earth. Embracing poverty, in that sense, is the condition for pragmatic utopianism. Dependency is the condition for knowing and receiving grace. From within practices that do justice to mutual dependency, the basic dysfunction in consumer capitalism is that it lets the powerful shape market structures and cultural spiritualities to support their own pursuit of more power. Alternative uses of markets to pursue alternative desires show that markets could work differently, and could do so without establishing an utterly different ecclesial economy. The Utopia food cooperative is not a gift economy; its members do not obtain and distribute food through circulation that gives no thought to rights or scarcity (as it can appear in the visions of the radical orthodoxy theologians). Nor does it represent a rival religious system. Utopia is a membership economy that uses market exchange to make efficient purchasing decisions, that attends constantly to fairness in distribution of labor and produce, and seeks to reform political institutions to better overcome scarcity. It represents a theological and social use of markets to achieve ends worth desiring. It is revolutionary because that use of market exchange is so different from its usual function that it anticipates an entirely different set of economic institutions and cultivates a different economic spirituality.

Desiring More

All of these theologians—the radical orthodox, the liberationists, and the pragmatists—agree that if consumption is the real problem of the human economy, then forming desire by the right practices is the central economic task. Because that task lies at the heart of Christian practice, the countercultural economic projects of faith communities can play a creative role in resituating markets within broader social and ecological purposes. In particular, Christian projects can affirm that the insatiable desire for more is proper to the human creature. The question for its economic life is finding the right mode of "more." What we desire, proclaims the gospel of Riobamba, is more justice, more beauty, more dignity. We overcome impoverishment by putting poverty at the center of the economy and learning to desire real wealth, which may include learning to desire revolution.

When turned toward a revolutionary project, peculiar market relations can transform a Riobamba street into a colorful pageant of civic and environmental cooperation. That is not just a side-street spectacle, dismissible as a private religious performance. Basic reforms on a broader scale are possible, and they do not require miraculous transfiguration to make the market work for ends other than its own growth. For example, two quite modest and feasible political interventions would make a great difference in constraining the most reckless aspects of the global growth economy and making it more responsive to impoverishment. (1) A tiny transaction charge on stock and currency trades would disincentivize the high volume of short-term betting that has taken over financial markets. A widely supported global campaign calls this a "Robin Hood Tax" because it would generate funds from activities that enrich the already wealthy, which could be used to combat impoverishment.[119] Even stalwart neoclassical economists can agree that disentangling short-term betting from long-term investing would make markets better able to discriminate between speculation and real enterprise.[120] (2) A carbon pollution tax would internalize the social and ecological costs of fossil fuel into energy costs. By finally getting human use of the atmosphere as a waste sink into a price signal, it would allow markets to do what they do best: drive creativity and invent new possibilities. A carbon tax would leverage consumer activity to drive the sort of pervasive cultural creativity that can create structural shifts in energy consumption. The funds it generates could be used for conservation and restoration efforts that begin to slow biological diminishment.[121] Both policies would constrain the short-term thinking that causes long-term impoverishments and both would generate public funds that could be used to protect the poorest persons, and biodiversity, from economic jeopardy.

Critics object that such modest reform tools cannot fix systemic market failures such as those at the root of problems like anthropogenic climate change. In cases where the economy encroaches too far on biophysical systems or valued social goods, the critics say, market exchanges simply must be limited by appeal to other norms.[122] Establishing those limits, however, seems to involve political contests that can only be resolved by appeal to fundamental beliefs. Better, I think, to see how far market devices can be used to make human behavior respond to impoverishment. The chief obstacle to setting impoverishment at the center of metrics of economic performance seems merely "spiritual:" the ethos of market consumerism makes modest anti-impoverishment reforms appear implausible and radical. The economic ethos cultivated in microeconomic projects like fair trade and food sovereignty makes such reforms possible. Projects that put poverty at the center focus attention on the real economy by measuring what markets do by their value for the lives of the poor and for the ecological membership on which all life depends.

DEVELOPMENT AND THE SATISFACTION OF DESIRE

Perhaps as important as what humans desire is how economic production satisfies those desires. If technological systems better mimicked ecological systems—as industrial ecology attempts to do—then the human economy might learn to work more as a productive participant within earth's economy, and less as a consumptive exploiter of found wealth. Consumption might not inevitably mean zero-sum appropriation. Focusing on development also restores a focus on human poverty that can be missed by focusing on excessive consumption: even if the wealthy discipline their desires it will not necessarily help the poor to satisfy theirs. A basic goal for development must be to help the poorest consume more. Can development satisfy justified human desires for more without impoverishing earth?

Economic Agnosticism

In 1970 the agronomist Norman Borlaug won the Nobel Peace Prize for breeding high-yield, disease-resistant varieties of cereals. The resulting "green revolution," supported by aggressive modernization of agricultural practices, led to a rise in world food supply and a drop in prices. Once worried about overpopulation, by the end of his life Borlaug was confident that, so long as agricultural research was adequately supported, earth could sustainably feed billions more. Despite population rising faster than ever during the period of Borlaug's research, per capita food supply actually increased.[123] Agricultural development could also help conserve biodiversity, argued Borlaug, because more efficient food production systems could spare biological capacity for other species and processes, even while feeding more people. The green revolution made agriculture a model for economic development, in this view, satisfying the hunger of the poor while reducing ecological impact by learning how to integrate human innovation and earth's productivity.[124]

Participants in Riobamba Utopia would ridicule notions that development saves biodiversity and that modernizing agriculture better feeds the poor. Their entire project mobilizes in response to green revolution and modernizing projects that, in their view, produced more impoverishment than wealth. The neoagrarian thinkers Vandana Shiva and Wendell Berry have been two of the most searing critics of this style of development. Shiva argues that the green revolution was really about transferring control of land from powerless farmers to industrial capitalists. Development was the ideology used to justify dispossession of land in the name of the poor, but its real effect was to suppress nonmonetary forms of productivity. In particular, argues Shiva, the productivity of women and the productivity of earth are chronically ignored by a development ideology that sees poverty wherever it sees resources that the global market would like to control. The green revolution impoverished communities of cultural and biological diversity, and made them dependent on the monoculture of the market.[125] Development, in this view, is simply another episode of colonialism, as Berry writes: "the same story of the gathering of an exploitative economic power into the hands of a few people who are alien to the places and the people they exploit. . . . It impoverishes one place in order to be extravagant in another, true to its colonialist ambition."[126] The agrarian counterpoint thus appears stark: development impoverishes.

Yet agrarians hold a remarkably optimistic view of a certain manner of development. The base ecclesial community at Riobamba decided that growth in commodity agriculture appears as development only by excluding ecological losses and counting impoverishment of food cultures as structural adjustment. Their response was to create an alternative model of food production, a form of development that satisfies the needs of its members while better realizing earth's creativity. The lesson that Shiva and Berry draw from experiences like those of the Riobamba community is not that human development always degrades ecological memberships. On the contrary, they hold that economies shaped by wise and skilled communities can elevate nature, improve a landscape, and satisfy the desire of people. They think development impoverishes when it focuses narrowly on growth. That sort of development is bound to destroy communities adapted to membership in a place because its logic depends on its ignorance of earth's wealth. "A part of the function of industrial education is to preserve and protect this ignorance," writes Berry.[127]

The field of ecological economics presses the case that mainstream economic devotion to growth and efficiency supplies the industrial education that preserves ignorance. The ignorance of neoclassical economics is built into its primary device for measuring development: gross domestic product. Failing to measure losses to ecological wealth or capability of the poor to meet their needs, GDP is, as Herman Daly puts it, "a reflection of the interests of a limited subset of the Great Economy (primarily the interests of those connected with the management of financial capital), whereas what may be valuable to the poor (clean water and air) and other organisms (healthy habitats) hardly registers at all."[128] A nation can clear-cut forest for lumber export and count it as productivity, despite immiserating the people and other creatures who depended on the forest and despite the loss of ecological services. In many cases GDP is an index of ruin, not wealth.

Adding to the outrage, the ideology of growth promises amelioration of those (uncounted) losses with the notion that, after initial increases in inequality and degradation, more growth reduces both.[129] Leaving aside whether inequality and pollution should be welcomed as signs of economic vitality, the growth-focused model of development has no sane reason to exclude ecological resources and services from its reckoning of wealth, nor to treat the ability of individual persons to meet their needs as secondary to the function of an economy. Refusing to accept such ignorance does not, however, impugn all human development. It simply refuses to conflate development with growth. Ecological economics aims for a more inclusive account of the relation between human and ecological systems in order to develop better measures of economic health. Doing so would force cultural consideration of the meaning and purpose of economy.[130]

Agrarianism and ecological economics sometimes present themselves as alternative worldviews in order to contest the hegemony of growth-focused development. Drawing a contrast to a worldview bent on maximizing plunder of resources and overcoming biological limits, they call for a new vision organized around respect for limits. The pieties of growth, they say, obscure losses to the real wealth of earth and distract citizens from considering the real meaning of an economy. Religious tropes help emphasize the hegemony of neoliberal economics. Sociologist Daniel Bell describes faith in economic growth as a "secular religion" due to its power in organizing society around a common purpose.[131] Historian J. R. McNeill calls economic growth the "state religion" of globalization, directed by clerics who spread a gospel that takes nature out of economics.[132] Economist Robert Nelson agrees, interpreting neoclassical economics as a religion and its experts as priests touting a kind of salvation.[133] Anthropologist Alf Hornborg sees behind global finances mythic cosmology and religious fetish that blind citizens to the interests of power driving cultures toward collapse.[134] In his textbook on ecological economics, Daly criticizes devotion to growth-focused development as "idolatrous, worshipping a false god."[135] It makes sense, then, that Daly collaborates with a theologian, John Cobb, in order to propose an alternative economic cosmology. They describe the difference as a religious conflict between "alternative biospheric visions."[136]

However, making the question of development *initially* a religious question can obscure possibilities for constructing practical alliances and distract from more important moments for religious thought. Mainstream economists are happy to concede to agrarians and ecological economists that their differences are religious because that allows them to dismiss criticisms as private beliefs. Nelson observes the frustration of attempting to conduct religious arguments with those who do not think they are religious.[137] Most neoclassical economists think they merely describe how reality works. The most effective way to contest their account is not, I think, with an alternative set of assumptions but with proposals for what it looks like for markets to "work." Theologians and other critics should object that, in its current configuration, global capitalism is organized to solve the wrong economic problem.[138] Growing financial profitability may matter for the wealthy but is at best subsidiary to the real economic problem: overcoming impoverishment. When agrarians and ecological economists criticize current development trajectories by trying to establish an alternative worldview, they lose leverage to make practical problems of impoverishment reshape how development could function. They introduce theological consideration at the wrong point and in an unhelpful way.

I have observed how Amartya Sen's *Development as Freedom* helped achieve a major turn in economics, from focusing on domestic product to enabling human capabilities, by questioning what growth-focused development really achieved for the poor. Income, posited Sen, is a means to satisfying a more fundamental desire: the freedom to live lives that we value. Sen's way of refocusing development on the problem of human poverty informed a major reorientation in the "human development" framework of the United Nations Development Programme, and has become influential for many antipoverty initiatives.[139] Sen did not argue for a different moral cosmology; he asked whether growth-focused economic development focused on the right problem and whether it was in fact solving it.

Pragmatic attention to the problem of biological impoverishment can shift development thinking as well. Conservation strategies have often focused on protecting nature from the human economy by setting aside protected areas. But it might be more useful to think, as do some economists, that "the problem is not that markets are so pervasive, but that they are not pervasive enough."[140] When public goods can be used without reflecting their true value, the incompleteness of the market makes for distorted incentives. Markets organize social behavior through incentives, so when goods or costs are incompletely accounted within a market economy, distorted incentives make for dysfunctional social action. Ecologists and economists of nearly every worldview can agree on this: if societies internalized all the costs of land use and ended free rent for resource exploitation, then markets would significantly reshape social behavior in ways that protect biological diversity. Conserving biological wealth cannot entirely rely on protecting land areas from all forms of human development. It needs to internalize the value of biodiversity within social and political processes in order to build cultures of conservation.[141]

Neither percentage growth of GDP nor percentage size of protected areas is an adequate proxy for sustaining wealth. We think so only when we accept economic ideologies that either obscure the relation of human economy to ecological systems or restore the relation in tragically oppositional terms. It does not require a religious position to insist on indices that make a better accounting. The Human Development Index, I argued earlier, is a much more important economic indicator than GDP. For biodiversity we still need a good index. Valuing of ecological services is important but seems too pliant to the logic of fungibility and commodification, while the Living Planet Index seems too focused on counting specimens rather than measuring the health of ecological processes. Yet those are important starts to making biological impoverishment matter to economic development.

My basic point here is that the meaning of economy is shaped less by the ideological worldviews created to explain it than by the problems it organizes social behavior to resolve. Most of the information we currently receive about the global economy makes it seem that the planet's most important problem is producing financial growth in the form of "gross product." Letting the daily stock tickers captivate attention organizes political discussion of economic health around irrelevant issues while distracting attention from the problems that do matter. The homepages of major newspapers do the world a disservice in that regard. The pernicious effect of those misleading indices of wealth is that they subtly reinforce attention on problems of financial capitalism that only matter to the wealthy. Making growth our basic economic problem—especially growth in the short term of daily stock tickers—allows a global plutocracy to continue profiting from the plunder of people and land, with the promise that eventually the poor and earth also benefit. It does not take religious belief to insist that impoverishment is the basic problem around which to organize and evaluate an economy—although it may take religious imagination and analysis to break the spell of growth ideologies. Unthinking piety toward growth is the spirituality that a global plutocracy depends on to sustain its power and its plunder.

Transforming Dominion

Christian ethics, I am arguing, should remain impious and agnostic about both growth and limits in the midterm and should be pragmatically ambivalent about markets over the long term, in order to insist on commitments to overcome impoverishment. Christian theology does not have an economic system. Theology should be economically atheistic by refusing to believe in any financial gods and pragmatically materialist by refusing to abstract from the problems of human and biological impoverishment. Prospects for a less impoverishing economy do not depend on establishing an alternative belief system; they start from creating effective ways to forge coalitions around problems that matter to all creatures. Attempting to establish a more comprehensive vision and waiting on the collapse of capitalism would just allow those most invested in the present to continue to control its structures and incentives, so perpetuating the relations that conceal impoverishment and cultivate bad pieties.[142]

Here lies the most helpful role for theological contributions. Renegotiating the meaning of the economy needs communities that demonstrate how to make existing economic assemblages work against impoverishment. As they meet real needs, they begin to transform the ethos of a political economy by orienting it toward real wealth. At their best, theological enactments of economy can model the possibility of nonviolent human dominion, in which the human economy does not inevitably destroy earth and oppress the poor, but creates ways to bless both. The development practice of Riobamba Utopia is not only about realizing individual capabilities, and not only about cultivating agro-ecological diversity, but about valuing cultural health and land health, about enabling membership in a broader community, and about satisfying the desire of creation itself. Its food economy does more than supply a certain quantity of calories at a certain price: it preserves the cultural memory of potatoes and quinoa, prepared in recipes that give expression to a long membership in the land, served at tables grateful to earth and Creator. When those practices are understood as care for earth's creativity, a midwifing of what *Pachamama* births, the end of economy becomes opening participation in the deepest mystery of life. It is no accident that the byproduct is beauty: carefully tended, family scaled, diversely planted farms; a colorful street cornucopia; creative table fare. So Riobamba Utopia cultivates a different economic spirit through the pragmatic ways it renegotiates a local food economy to overcome impoverishment.

Christian agrarian writers explain how projects like the one at Riobamba focus on the real problems of economy and turn them into occasions for satisfying the deepest desire of humanity. What Wendell Berry admires in the skills, self-limitation, and cultural memory involved in local food production are the virtues learned from adaptive membership in a place. They look different on every farm and in every community, but the general pattern of adaptive virtues takes the form of obligation to received gifts. The viciousness of industrial capitalism lies in its arrogant insistence on making all the world a commodity from which nothing can be learned except an aggregate bottom line. It sustains its ignorance by refusing to acknowledge that what we produce is always also a gift. If more communities shaped their productive activity as gestures of return, writes Berry, "the economy would have to accommodate the need to be worthy of the gifts we receive and use."[143] The economy would need to satisfy desires to be transformed by our uses of earth, to be made capable of seeing and working with its gifts.

In the agrarian view, human uses of earth do not inevitably impoverish. Violence and immiseration result from development practices that train us to satisfy our desires as if doing so were not also the primary way we receive and care for sacred gifts. Economic activity is, in other words, the material way of living out the human purpose in creation, and that is finally the meaning by which it should be measured. Global industrial capitalism impoverishes communities and lands not because of too much dominion, but precisely because of its lack. Dominion need not mean monarchy and monoculture; it could mean membership learned within particular land communities. Modern monoculture represents neither dominion nor real development but simply a form of plunder by the powerful few who profit from it, justified by what Shiva calls a "monoculture of the mind."[144] Real economic development, says Berry, involves "the arts of adapting kindly the many human households to the earth's many ecosystems and human neighborhoods." Real economic development thus looks like good farming, learned through care and gratitude, in settled commitment to a wide membership of accountability. "This is the economy that the most public and influential economists never talk about, the economy that is the primary vocation and responsibility of every one of us."[145]

Some critics worry that any notion of positive economic activity, however critical of industrial capitalism, underwrites continued human domination of earth. Romantic ideas of stewardship, argues Clare Palmer, let destructive humans imagine themselves as benign masters, thus warranting the conversion of a wild and diverse planet into one giant farm serving the needs of the master's house.[146] That worry, the agrarians would reply, rests in a poor view of farming and a tragic view of humanity. Good farming, explains Norman Wirzba, enacts a kind of dominion that subverts the industrial logic of domination. Good farming is learned through humble service, and so puts humans in their place by letting creation teach them both *how* to satisfy their desires and *that* their highest desire is to make a fitting and grateful return. "Unlike versions of development and progress that are premised on the destruction of the sources of life for humanity's 'improvement,' service promotes . . . an existence in which the elements of creation are enabled to maximally be as their Creator intended them to be."[147] By arguing that good farming is not about mastery but about tending the diversity of land to cultivate real wealth for an entire membership, human and nonhuman, the agrarians offer hope that the human economy need not curse the land. Humanity might bless earth—if we work with and for creation, if we master our selfishness in service to all our neighbors, if we cultivate wildness as a kind of wealth. The sustainable economy, then, is one that conserves the ecological and cultural conditions for earth to teach us gracefulness. It cultivates biodiversity and wildness, plants many hedges against our ignorance, and puts more faith in regenerative soil than depletable oil.

The agrarian theologians display the sort of creative economic ambivalence for which I have been arguing. Their nostalgia for household communitarianism and their rural romanticism can sometimes overdetermine their criticism of industrial capitalism—downplaying the gender, race, and class captivities once supported by ideologies of the happy peasant. They chronically fail to appreciate why cosmopolitan markets and urban life would appeal to those long in bondage to field labor. Yet they overstate their criticism, I think, because agrarianism is so fundamentally positive toward economics. They are disgusted by the impoverishment wrought by globalizing capitalism precisely because they reject the idea that human development must inevitably "encroach" on ecology and exploit the poor. They refuse the logic of sacrificing ecological integrity and the needs of the poor for economic growth because they refuse the underlying logic of trade-offs.[148] Economic reasoning is not about making choices among rivalrous goods to maximize benefit, but about cultivating forms of wealth that satisfy an entire membership. An economy could develop differently, producing habitat for others while producing food for humans. Economy should be the skillful art of blessing, not the dismal math of scarcity.

When development projects demonstrate how to satisfy the desire for bread through practices that nurture a commonwealth, they let us hope that the human economy can do better than limit its impact. They become icons of hope that humanity can in fact bless creation. Blessing God "is something we learn to do, and by doing it we are formed," writes Ellen Davis. Economy is always moral formation. A theological account of economy holds that "development" and "productivity" can work as practices by which we learn to bless one another with real wealth. "Blessing is essentially the transformative experience of knowing and honoring God as the Giver; it means valuing the steady flow that sustains the world even above the gift of life that each of us receives."[149] The theological measure of economy is finally liturgical, then, holding that in worship humanity's deepest desires are met. Right human use of earth has its end in uniting earth's people and creatures in thanksgiving. In its attempts to worship God, the human economy can be ugly, self-serving, dispiriting, exclusionary, and more impoverishing than its worth. Christian churches prove that every Sunday. But economy, like worship, also has the potential to be glorious, bringing forth the real wealth of earth by gathering all creatures into a cosmic liturgy.[150]

Lest this now seem theological abstraction glossing a utopian vision, remember how practical and mundane is the biweekly exchange of Riobamba Utopia. Blessing happens by hauling 100 kilo sacks and dividing potatoes, by contracting with farmers for tomato crops and teaching young people to cook Andean soups. Economic icons are also made in efforts to construct buildings that breathe air and convert sunlight, to plan cities as both humane habitats for democracy and functioning forests, to manufacture electronics from "cradle to cradle" on the resource recapture model of industrial ecology. Even a road—that asphalt ribbon of roadkill and alienating speed—can help nurture and satisfy the desire for membership in place, as the Flathead Indian Reservation has recently shown.[151] Realistic interim measures are ready to hand. Simply internalizing the real costs of our present global market, through measures like a financial transactions tax and a carbon tax, would reduce some impoverishing effects of the global economy. Requiring corporations to release triple bottom line accounting and publicizing what national economies really accomplish through indices like the Human Development Index and the Living Planet Index would help orient political attention to the real meaning of economy. The worldwide proliferation of projects like fair-trade networks, micro-lending, food cooperatives, and so on shows the hunger humanity has for our economy to be and do more. Christian practices must deepen and feed those hungers for the true bread of life.

Projects like Riobamba Utopia show that such practices happen not only around altars and fonts. They also happen by redeploying market relations in order to make kitchen tables and watersheds into sacraments. Our greatest worry about the dominion of an impoverishing economy that disappears life and excludes the poor should not be that it will collapse. We should rather fear that plutocratic capitalism will continue to find ways to sustain itself. Faith in the economy of grace needs tactics to resist the pieties that conceal impoverishment and disorient desire. "Practice resurrection," writes Wendell Berry in the close to his poem, "The Mad Farmer Liberation Front." Good farming in a world of false dominions requires cultivating madness and liberating love. "Love the lord. Love the world . . . Take all that you have and be poor."[152] The tactics of faith take shape as a willingness to be poor in a world of false wealth.

CONCLUSION

This chapter has argued that the global economy should be evaluated by its relation to two fundamental problems of impoverishment. Human poverty and biological loss are the twin measures of whether and how the economy of human dominion works violence or cultivates wealth. I have argued that Christian projects should avoid deploying theology in support of abstract ideological contests and instead focus on creating concrete possibilities for overcoming impoverishment. In response to the planetary size of human desire, I focused on how practices of faith might work oddly within three different economies of desire. In regard of population growth, reproductive desire needs liberation. In regard of consumption, consumer desire needs discipline. In regard of development, we need economies that satisfy desires for real wealth. Those three sets of practices refuse to accept the problems of plutocratic capitalism and break faith with its obsession with growth. Faith-based projects, like the Utopia begun by the Riobamba base ecclesial community, demonstrate how faith in the economy of grace can drive a pragmatic utopianism that seeks to let God liberate, discipline, and satisfy our desire through creation.

The fundamental economic problem from a theological perspective is not that humans desire too much, but that we do not desire enough. We are all responsible for the economies in which we participate and complicit in habits by which they form our hearts and minds. Devotion to the pursuit of riches requires certain pieties of indifference to human suffering and ecological destruction. Pious about growth, we look away from human needs and gravely accept the destruction of biological life. If that is the way of wealth, we cannot afford it. We must find ways to divest from this economy of misery and invest in real wealth. The returns are much better.

It seems unlikely that humanity will soon learn that economic lesson. Anthropocene earth hardly looks like a mosaic of lovely farms with margins of thick forest and green cities. Its oceans have rather been filled with engine noise and trash gyres. As humanity has multiplied, forests have been thinned of life. Cities are built as habitat for automobiles, to which the harvest is fed while children go hungry. This economy of misery must not be sustained, and in the long run it cannot last. But meanwhile plutocratic powers keep seeking their own dominion. This chapter has tried to show that prophetic anger need not turn to despair, that if communities keep inventing ways to open economic spaces for the pursuit of real wealth, the hope of a peaceful dominion is possible. However, if the human empire continues to expand as it has, impoverishing people and planet, then the future of hope depends on nurturing the moral capabilities of future generations to inherit this ugly dominion. I turn in the next chapter to intergenerational ethics.

NOTES

1. Herman E. Daly, John B. Cobb, and Clifford W. Cobb, *For the Common Good: Redirecting the Economy toward Community, the Environment, and a Sustainable Future*, 2nd ed. (Boston: Beacon Press, 1994).

2. I visited the cooperative in January 2010 through a seminar organized by the Latin American Council of Churches. My thanks to Christopher Morck for organizing the seminar and for comments on this chapter.

3. Statistics from A. Maddison, *The World Economy: A Millennial Perspective* (New Delhi: OECD, 2007); J. R. McNeill, *Something New under the Sun: An Environmental History of the Twentieth-Century World* (New York: W. W. Norton, 2000). For perspective on the statistics see Joel Cohen "Linking Human and Natural History: A Review Essay," *Population and Development Review* 27, no. 3 (2001): 273–84.

4. J. Rockström et al., "A Safe Operating Space for Humanity," *Nature* 461, no. 7263 (2009); P. M. Vitousek et al., "Human Appropriation of the Products of Photosynthesis," *BioScience* 36, no. 6 (1986); Peter M. Vitousek et al., "Human Domination of Earth's Ecosystems," *Science* 277, no. 5325 (1997).

5. See Gerald Meler and James Rauch, *Leading Issues in Economic Development*, 8th ed. (New York: Oxford University Press, 2005), 127–31.

6. Matt. 26:11.

7. S. Chen and M. Ravallion, "The Developing World Is Poorer Than We Thought, but No Less Successful in the Fight against Poverty," *The Quarterly Journal of Economics* 125, no. 4 (2010).

8. Paul Collier, *The Bottom Billion* (New York: Oxford University Press, 2007).

9. UNDP, *Human Development Report 1990* (New York: Oxford University Press, 1990), 1.

10. Amartya Kumar Sen, *Development as Freedom* (New York: Knopf, 1999).

11. Martha C. Nussbaum, *Women and Human Development: The Capabilities Approach* (New York: Cambridge University Press, 2000).

12. UNDP, *Human Development Report 2010* (New York: Palgrave MacMillan, 2010).

13. Shaohua Chen and Martin Ravallion, "An Update to the World Bank's Estimates of Consumption Poverty in the Developing World," World Bank Development Research Group, March 1, 2012. But see the searing skepticism about MDG measurements in Thomas Pogge, *Politics as Usual: What Lies behind the Pro-Poor Rhetoric* (Cambridge: Polity Press, 2010), chap. 3.

14. Abhijit Banerjee and Esther Duflo, *Poor Economics: A Radical Rethinking of the Way to Fight Global Poverty* (New York: Public Affairs, 2011).

15. Arturo Escobar, *Encountering Development: The Making and Unmaking of the Third World* (Princeton, NJ: Princeton University Press, 1995).

16. William Easterly, *The White Man's Burden: Why the West's Efforts to Aid the Rest Have Done So Much Ill and So Little Good* (New York: Penguin, 2006).

17. Escobar, *Encountering Development,* 53.

18. Pogge, *Politics as Usual:What Lies behind the Pro-Poor Rhetoric,* 12.

19. Peter Singer, *The Life You Can Save: Acting Now to End World Poverty* (New York: Random House, 2009).

20. Ronald Sider, *Rich Christians in an Age of Hunger: Moving from Affluence to Generosity,* 5th ed. (Nashville, TN: Thomas Nelson, 2005).

21. Steve Corbett and Brian Fikert, *When Helping Hurts* (Chicago: Moody Publishers, 2009); Bryant Myers, *Walking the Poor: Principles and Practices of Transformational Development* (Maryknoll, NY: Orbis, 1999).

22. Thomas Pogge, "Real World Justice," in *Current Debates in Global Justice*, Gillian Brock and Darrel Moellendorf, eds. (Dordrecht, Netherlands: Springer, 2005), 33.

23. Thomas Pogge, "The Ethics of Assistance," in *The Ethics of Assistance*, Deen K. Chatterjee, ed. (New York: Cambridge University Press, 2004). Thomas Pogge, "Severe Poverty as a Human Rights Violation," in *Freedom from Poverty as a Human Right: Who Owes What to the Very Poor*, Thomas Pogge, ed. (New York: Oxford University Press, 2007).

24. Richard W. Miller, *Globalizing Justice: The Ethics of Poverty and Power* (New York: Oxford University Press, 2010).

25. For the opposite view, that economic growth is condition for liberal justice, see Benjamin Friedman, *The Moral Consequences of Economic Growth* (New York: Knopf, 2005).

26. O. E. Sala et al., "Global Biodiversity Scenarios for the Year 2100," *Science* 287, no. 5459 (2000).

27. J. B. C. Jackson et al., "Historical Overfishing and the Recent Collapse of Coastal Ecosystems," *Science* 293, no. 5530 (2001).

28. E. L. Bennett et al., "Why Is Eating Bushmeat a Biodiversity Crisis?", *Conservation Biology in Practice* 3, no. 1 (2002).

29. R. Leakey and R. Lewin, *The Sixth Extinction: Patterns of Life and the Future of Humankind* (New York: Doubleday, 1992); D. B. Wake and V. T. Vredenburg, "Are We in the Midst of the Sixth Mass Extinction? A View from the World of Amphibians," *Proceedings of the National Academy of Sciences* 105, no. Supplement 1 (2008); J. B. C. Jackson, "Ecological Extinction and Evolution in the Brave New Ocean," *Proceedings of the National Academy of Sciences* 105, no. Supplement 1 (2008).

30. The Board of the Millennium Ecosystem Assessment, "Living beyond Our Means" (Washington, DC: World Resources Institute, 2005), 5.

31. D. Takacs, *The Idea of Biodiversity: Philosophies of Paradise* (Baltimore, MD: Johns Hopkins University Press, 1996).

32. D. Tilman et al., "Habitat Destruction and the Extinction Debt," *Nature* 371, no. 6492 (1994).

33. Kate Rawles, "Biological Diversity and Conservation Policy," in *Philosophy and Biodiversity*, Marku Oksanen and Juhani Pietarinen, eds. (Cambridge: Cambridge

University Press, 2004); D. Tilman, "Causes, Consequences and Ethics of Biodiversity," *Nature* 405, no. 6783 (2000).

34. Simon Levin, *Fragile Dominion: Complexity and the Commons* (New York: Basic Books, 1999), 15.

35. C. Folke et al., "Biological Diversity, Ecosystems, and the Human Scale," *Ecological Applications* (1996): 1019.

36. Economic metaphors, such as "insurance" against catastrophes, can suggest policy analogues; Folke, "Biological Diversity," 1021.

37. R. Costanza et al., "The Value of the World's Ecosystem Services and Natural Capital," *Nature* 387, no. 6630 (1997); Gretchen Daily, ed., *Nature's Services: Societal Dependence on Natural Ecosystems* (Washington, DC: Island Press, 1997).

38. Karl Polanyi, *The Great Transformation: The Political and Economic Origins of Our Time*, 2nd ed. (Boston: Beacon Press, 2001).

39. Michael Sandel, *What Money Can't Buy: The Moral Limits of Markets* (New York: Farrar, Straus, and Giroux, 2012).

40. Holmes Rolston, *Conserving Natural Value* (New York: Columbia University Press, 1994).

41. Stephen Kellert, ed., "The Biological Basis for Human Values of Nature," in *The Biophilia Hypothesis* (Washington, DC: Island Press, 1993).

42. E. O. Wilson, *Biophilia* (Cambridge: Harvard University Press, 1984), 10.

43. Kevin O'Brien, *An Ethics of Biodiversity* (Washington, DC: Georgetown University Press, 2010), 61.

44. See Willis Jenkins, *Ecologies of Grace: Environmental Ethics and Christian Theology* (Oxford: Oxford University Press, 2008), chaps. 6–7.

45. On the pedagogical and transformative values of biodiversity, see Bryan Norton, *Why Preserve Natural Variety?* (Princeton, NJ: Princeton University Press, 1987); Sahotra Sarkar, *Biodiversity and Environmental Philosophy: An Introduction* (Cambridge: Cambridge University Press, 2005).

46. Leonardo Boff, *Cry of the Earth, Cry of the Poor* (Maryknoll, NY: Orbis Books, 1997).

47. Thomas Malthus, *An Essay on the Principle of Population*, 6th ed. (London: John Murray, 1826), bk. 1, chap. 1.

48. *World Population to 2300*, United Nations Department of Economic and Social Affairs (New York, 2004), ST/ESA/SER.A/236.

49. Amartya Sen, *Poverty and Famines: An Essay on Entitlement and Deprivation* (Oxford: Oxford University Press, 1982).

50. Mary Wollstonecraft, *A Vindication of the Rights of Women* (Boston: Peter Edes, 1792). On the arguments among Malthus and Godwin, see Clark Wolf, "Population," in *A Companion to Environmental Philosophy*, Dale Jamieson, ed. (Malden, MA: Blackwell, 2003).

51. Margaret C. Hogan et al., "Maternal Mortality for 181 Countries, 1980–2008: A Systematic Analysis of Progress towards Millennium Development Goal 5," *The Lancet* 375, no. 9726 (2010).

52. Dennis Hodgson and Susan Cotts Watkins, "Feminists and Neo-Malthusians: Past and Present Alliances," *Population and Development Review* 23, no. 3 (1997).

53. Betsy Hartmann, "Population, Environment, and Security: A New Trinity," in *Dangerous Intersections: Feminist Perspectives on Population, Environment, and Development*, Jael Silliman and Ynestra King, eds. (Cambridge, MA: South End Press, 1999), 8.

54. Paul Ehrlich, *The Population Bomb* (New York: Ballantine Books, 1968).

55. Garrett Hardin, "The Tragedy of the Commons," *Science* 162, no. 3859 (1968).

56. Hardin, "The Tragedy of the Commons," 1245.

57. Cohen gives the median range as 7.7 to 12 billion. Joel E. Cohen, *How Many People Can the Earth Support?* (New York: Norton, 1995), 210–39, 368–69.

58. Massimo Livi-Bacci, *A Concise History of World Population*, 3rd ed. (Malden, MA: Blackwell, 2001), 204.

59. Derek Parfit, *Reasons and Persons* (Oxford: Oxford University Press, 1984), 387–90.

60. G. Di Chiro, "Living Environmentalisms: Coalition Politics, Social Reproduction, and Environmental Justice," *Environmental Politics* 17, no. 2 (2008): 283.

61. Garrett Hardin, "Living on a Lifeboat," *Bioscience* 24, no. 10 (1974): 561–68.

62. James Gustafson, *Ethics from a Theocentric Perspective: Ethics and Theology*, vol. 2 (Chicago: University of Chicago Press, 1984), 219, 246.

63. To those who fear dystopic scenarios in a market for rights to bear children, Daly and Cobb note that it would not appear much odder than our current private market in reproductive technologies. Daly, Cobb, and Cobb, *For the Common Good*: 243–46.

64. Paul VI, *Humanae vitae* (1968).

65. Benedict XVI, *Caritas en veritate* (2009).

66. See James Martin-Schramm, "Population, Consumption, and Eco-Justice: A Moral Assessment of the 1994 United Nations International Conference on Population and Development," in *Consumption, Population, and Sustainability*, Audrey Chapman et al., eds. (Washington, DC: Island Press, 2000). S. Bok, "Population and Ethics: Expanding the Moral Space," in *Population Policies Reconsidered: Health, Empowerment, and Rights*, Gita Sen et al., eds. (Boston: Harvard School of Public Health, 1994).

67. Frank Notestein, "Population: The Long View," in *Food for Thought*, T. W. Schultz, ed. (Chicago: University of Chicago Press, 1945).

68. The phrase has been attributed both to Indira Gandhi and to John D. Rockefeller III. See it elaborated into a call for more robust efforts to combat poverty in Peter Unger, *Living High and Letting Die: Our Illusion of Innocence* (New York: Cambridge University Press, 1996).

69. M. Campbell, "Why the Silence on Population?", *Population and Environment* 28, no. 4 (2007). Similarly, ecofeminist theologian Catherine Keller worries about a "liberal conspiracy of silence" on population growth; Catherine Keller, "A Christian Response to the Population Apocalypse," in *Population, Consumption, and the Environment*, Harold Coward, ed. (Albany: SUNY Press, 2005), 110.

70. "World Population to Reach 10 Billion by 2100 if Fertility in All Countries Converges to Replacement Level," UN Department of Economic and Social Affairs (NewYork, May 3, 2011).

71. M. King, "Demographic Entrapment," *Transactions of the Royal Society of Tropical Medicine and Hygiene* 87, Supplement 1 (1993).

72. Cohen, *How Many People Can the Earth Support?*, 49–50.

73. On contraception as the primary factor in demographic transition, see M. Potts, "Population and Environment in the Twenty-first Century," *Population and Environment* 28, no. 4 (2007).

74. Robert Engelman, *More: Population, Nature, and What Women Want* (Washington, DC: Island Press, 2008), 14.

75. Livi-Bacci, *A Concise History of World Population,* 19–20.

76. Engelman, *More,* 14.

77. Amartya Sen, "Population: Delusion and Reality," *NewYork Review of Books* 41, no. 15 (1994).

78. On the shift from population control to reproductive health, see C. Garcia-Moreno andT.Turmen, "International Perspectives onWomen's Reproductive Health," *Science* 269, no. 5225 (1995).

79. Vandana Shiva, *Staying Alive* (London: Zed Books, 1988).

80. See FatimaVianna Mello, "Sustainable Development by and forWhom?" in *Beyond the Numbers:A Reader on Population, Consumption, and the Environment*, Laurie Mazur, ed. (Washington, DC: Island Press, 1994); PaigeWhaley Eager, *Global Population Policy: From Population Control to Reproductive Rights* (Burlington,VT: Ashgate, 2004), 108–10.

81. Patristic population quotations are gathered in Susan Bratton, *Six Billion and More: Human Population Regulation and Christian Ethics* (Louisville, KY.: Westminster John Knox Press, 1992), 75–78.

82. Engelman, *More,* 144–54; Rosemary Radford Ruether, *NewWoman, New Earth: Sexist Ideologies and Human Liberation, with a New Preface* (Boston: Beacon Press, 1995), chap. 4.

83. Rosemary Radford Ruether, "Women, Reproductive Rights and the Catholic Church," *Feminist Theology* 16, no. 2 (2008).

84. See Catherine Keller, *Face of the Deep:A Theology of Becoming* (NewYork: Routledge, 2003).

85. David Matzko McCarthy, "Procreation, the Development of Peoples, and the Final Destiny of Humanity," *Communio* 26, no. 4 (1999).

86. Paul VI, *Populorum progressio*, article 6.

87. Amy Laura Hall, *Conceiving Parenthood: American Protestantism and the Spirit of Reproduction* (Grand Rapids, MI: Eerdmans, 2008).

88. J. Cohen, *"Be Fertile and Increase, Fill the Earth and Master It": The Ancient and Medieval Career of a BiblicalText* (Ithaca, NY: Cornell University Press, 1989).

89. See Eugene Rogers, "Sanctified Unions: An Argument for Gay Marriage," *The Christian Century*, vol. 121, no. 4 (2004).

90. P. Ehrlich and J. Holdren, "Impact of Population Growth," *Science* 171, no. 3977 (1971): 1212–17. See M. R. Chertow, "The IPAT Equation and Its Variants," *Journal of Industrial Ecology* 4, no. 4 (2000).

91. M. Wackernagel and W. E. Rees, *Our Ecological Footprint: Reducing Human Impact on the Earth* (Gabriola Island, BC: New Society Pub, 1996), 51–60.

92. Paul E. Waggoner, "How Much Land Can Ten Billion People Spare for Nature?" *Daedalus* 125, no. 3 (1996); Eric Sanderson et al., "The Human Footprint and the Last of the Wild," *Bioscience* 62, no. 10 (2012): 891–904.

93. The concept of a "greed line" is being developed in the World Council of Churches; see Rogate Mshana, "Poverty, Wealth, and Ecology: The Impact of Economic Globalization" (Geneva: World Council of Churches, 2008), and a special issue of *The Ecumenical Review* 63, no. 3 (2011).

94. S. R. Curran and A. de Sherbinin, "Completing the Picture: The Challenges of Bringing 'Consumption' into the Population-Environment Equation," *Population and Environment* 26, no. 2 (2004).

95. Juliet Schor, "Toward a New Politics of Consumption," in *The Consumer Society Reader*, Juliet Schor and Douglas Holdt, eds. (New York: W. W. Norton, 2000).

96. Sider, *Rich Christians in an Age of Hunger.*

97. Basil the Great, *On Social Justice,* Paul Schroeder, trans. (Crestwood, NY: St. Vladimir's Seminary Press, 2009), 43.

98. Christina Firer Hinze, "What Is Enough? Catholic Social Thought, Consumption, and Material Sufficiency," in *Having: Property and Possession in Religious and Social Life,* William Schweiker and Charles Matthewes, eds. (Grand Rapids, MI: Eerdmans, 2004).

99. James Nash, "Toward the Revival and Reform of the Subversive Virtue: Frugality," in *Consumption, Population, and Sustainability: Perspectives from Science and Religion*, Audrey Chapman et al., eds. (Washington, DC: Island Press, 2000).

100. Keller, "A Christian Response to the Population Apocalypse."

101. Maria Antonaccio, "Asceticism and the Ethics of Consumption," *Journal of the Society of Christian Ethics* 26, no. 1 (2006): 80, 90.

102. Stephen Long, *Divine Economy: Theology and the Market* (New York: Routledge, 2000); John Milbank, *Theology and Social Theory: Beyond Secular Reason* (Oxford: Blackwell, 1993); Daniel Bell Jr., *Liberation Theology after the End of History: The Refusal to Cease Suffering* (New York: Routledge, 2001).

103. William Cavanaugh, *Being Consumed: Economics and Christian Desire* (Grand Rapids, MI: Eerdmans, 2008).

104. Vincent Miller, *Consuming Religion: Christian Faith and Practice in a Consumer Culture* (New York: Continuum, 2009).

105. Luke Bretherton, *Christianity and Contemporary Politics: The Conditions of Faithful Witness* (Oxford: Wiley-Blackwell, 2010), 176, 187.

106. Max Weber, *The Protestant Ethic and the 'Spirit' of Capitalism*, Peter Baehr and Gordon C. Wells, eds. (New York: Penguin, 2002).

107. William Connolly, *Capitalism and Christianity, American Style* (Durham, NC: Duke University Press, 2008).

108. John Casidy depicts neoclassical theory as utopian economics and blames it for the major market failures of recent decades; John Casidy, *How Markets Fail: The Logic of Economic Calamities* (New York: Picador, 2010).

109. Elizabeth Theokritoff, *Living in God's Creation: Orthodox Perspectives on Ecology* (Crestwood, NY: St. Vladimir's Press, 2009), 115.

110. Laura Hartman, *The Christian Consumer: Living Faithfully in a Fragile World* (New York: Oxford University Press, 2011).

111. Juliet Schor, *True Wealth: How and Why Millions of Americans Are Creating a Time-Rich, Ecologically-Light, High-Satisfaction Economy* (New York: Penguin Books, 2011).

112. Bretherton, *Christianity and Contemporary Politics*, 178.

113. Kathryn Tanner, *Economy of Grace* (Minneapolis: Fortress Press, 2005), 89.

114. Connolly, *Capitalism and Christianity, American Style*, 111.

115. Bretherton, *Christianity and Contemporary Politics*, 197.

116. Anna L. Peterson, *Everyday Ethics and Social Change: The Education of Desire* (New York: Columbia University Press, 2009), 114–26.

117. Ignacio Ellacuria, "Utopia and Prophecy in Latin America," in *Towards a Society That Serves Its People* (Washington, DC: Georgetown University Press, 1991), 44–88; Jon Sobrino, *No Salvation Outside the Poor* (Maryknoll, NY: Orbis, 2008).

118. Eduardo Galleano, *Open Veins of Latin America: Five Centuries of Pillage*, Cedric Belfrage, trans., (New York: Monthly Review Press, 1973).

119. See RobinHoodTax.org.

120. L. H. Summers and V. P. Summers, "When Financial Markets Work too Well: A Cautious Case for a Securities Transactions Tax," *Journal of Financial Services Research* 3, no. 2 (1989). For endorsement on theological grounds, see Tanner, *Economy of Grace*, 128.

121. Shi-Ling Hsu, *The Case for a Carbon Tax: Getting Past Our Hang-Ups to Effective Climate Policy* (Washington, DC: Island Press, 2012).

122. For criticism of deploying tools like carbon taxes to achieve sustainable economic scale see Daly and Cobb, *For the Common Good*, ch. 7; for criticism of market approaches to valued social goods like distributive fairness, see Sandel, *What Money Can't Buy*.

123. L. T. Evans, *Feeding the Ten Billion: Plants and Population Growth* (New York: Cambridge University Press, 1998), 165–78.

124. See Paul B. Thompson, *The Spirit of the Soil: Agriculture and Environmental Ethics* (New York: Routledge, 1995).

125. Vandana Shiva, *Staying Alive: Women, Ecology, and Development* (London: Zed Books, 1988); Vandana Shiva, *Earth Democracy: Justice, Sustainability, and Peace* (Cambridge, MA: South End Press, 2005).

126. Wendell Berry, "The Agrarian Standard," in *The Essential Agrarian Reader*, Norman Wirzba, ed. (Washington, DC: Shoemaker and Hoard, 2003), 24. For his reckoning the toll of modern agricultural development in the United States, see Wendell Berry, *The Unsettling of America* (San Francisco: Sierra Club Books, 1977).

127. Berry, "The Agrarian Standard," 25.

128. Herman Daly, "Sustainable Economic Development: Definitions, Principles, Policies," in *The Essential Agrarian Reader*, Norman Wirzba, ed. (Washington, D.: Shoemaker and Hoard, 2003), 65.

129. In relation to both inequality and environmental degradation, this promise takes shape along a "Kuznets curve." See Jeffrey Frankel, "The Environment and Globalization," in *Economics of the Environment*, Robert Stavins, ed. (New York: W. W. Norton, 2005); K. Arrow et al., "Economic Growth, Carrying Capacity, and the Environment," *Science* 268, no. 5210 (1995).

130. See Robert Costanza, "Ecological Economics: Reintegrating the Study of Humans and Nature," *Ecological Applications* 6, no. 4 (1996).

131. Daniel Bell, *The Cultural Contradictions of Capitalism* (New York: Basic Books, 1996), 237.

132. McNeill, *Something New under the Sun: An Environmental History of the Twentieth-Century World*: 335–36.

133. Robert H. Nelson, *Economics as Religion: From Samuelson to Chicago and Beyond* (University Park: Pennsylvania State University Press, 2001).

134. Alf Hornborg, *Global Ecology and Unequal Exchange: Fetishism in a Zero-Sum World* (Oxford: Routledge, 2013).

135. Herman Daly and Joshua Farley, *Ecological Economics: Principles and Applications*, 2nd ed. (Washington, DC: Island Press, 2011), 49.

136. Daly, Cobb, and Cobb, *For the Common Good*, 380–85.

137. Nelson, *Economics as Religion*, 313. See R. C. Foltz, "The Religion of the Market: Reflections on a Decade of Discussion," *Worldviews* 11 (2007).

138. See Tanner, *Economy of Grace*, 119.

139. Sen, *Development as Freedom*.

140. N. O. Keohane and S. M. Olmstead, *Markets and the Environment* (Washington, DC: Island Press, 2007), 3.

141. S. R. Brechin et al., "Beyond the Square Wheel: Toward a More Comprehensive Understanding of Biodiversity Conservation as Social and Political Process," *Society and Natural Resources* 15, no. 1 (2002).

142. Connolly, *Capitalism and Christianity, American Style*, 14.

143. Berry, "The Agrarian Standard," 27.

144. V. Shiva, *Monocultures of the Mind: Perspectives on Biodiversity and Biotechnology* (London: Zed Books, 1993).

145. Wendell Berry, "It All Turns on Affection" (Jefferson Lecture in the Humanities, National Endowment for the Humanities, Washington, DC, April 23, 2012).

146. Clare Palmer, "Stewardship: A Case Study in Environmental Ethics," in *Environmental Stewardship: Critical Perspectives—Past and Present*, R. J. Berry, ed. (London: T. and T. Clark, 2006).

147. Norman Wirzba, *The Paradise of God: Renewing Religion in an Ecological Age* (New York: Oxford University Press, 2003), 148.

148. On the logic of trade-offs, see Alan Holland, "Are Choices Tradeoffs?" in *Economics, Ethics, and Environmental Policy*, D. W. Bromley and Jouni Paavola, eds. (Oxford: Blackwell, 2002).

149. Ellen F. Davis, *Scripture, Culture, and Agriculture* (New York: Oxford University Press, 2009), 164.

150. For more on cosmic liturgy, see Jenkins, *Ecologies of Grace*, chaps. 10–11.

151. See peopleswaywildlifecrossings.org.

152. Wendell Berry, *The Mad Farmer Poems* (Berkeley, CA: Counterpoint, 2008), 12.

CHAPTER SEVEN

Intergenerational Risk and the Future of Love

✦

Much more important than burnt sacrifices is to love God with all one's heart and to love one's neighbor as oneself.

Mark 12:33

At the Church of St. Paul & St. James in New Haven, the liturgy begins with procession that starts from a columbarium in which lie ashes of the community's ancestors and moves toward a table that feeds its hope in the future. The columbarium is the most striking inheritance of a building with many layers of history: a meeting hall overlays the trappings of a gym, itself overlaying the remnants of a dance hall; three floors of meeting spaces (now dilapidated); two kitchens (no longer up to code); beautiful stained-glass windows (in need of repair), and a hand-carved vaulted ceiling. Constructed during a wealthier era when industrial manufacturing thrived, energy was cheap, and church attendance was a social convention, the building now saddles its congregation with unsupportable costs. Its future depends on structural change, but what to do with sacred infrastructure that is the inherited trust and actual bodies of previous generations? Meanwhile, in a basement room beneath the sanctuary, the community has been feeding people every Saturday for decades. With what resources it has, its Loaves & Fishes food ministry strives to be uncommonly hospitable to those living at the edge of hunger. Hundreds come each week and everyone receives a bag of groceries, can eat breakfast, shop for free clothes, see a physician, and let their children play.

At the outset of this book I observed that the intergenerational dimensions of climate change pose some of the most daunting ethical difficulties. Greenhouse gas emissions of previous generations have already made our grandchildren's biosphere different than it would have been. How this generation acknowledges responsibility for that fact will shape the lifeworld that future generations inherit. It will also shape how future generations interpret how well we lived our lives. The degree to which their judgment matters to us and how we frame our responsibilities to the future is crucial to climate action, because even with rising emissions the impacts of climate change are likely to remain relatively modest for years. Impacts grow severe by 2050 and quite dire by 2100, but by then it will already be decades too late to avert them. Which species and processes of life survive into the next century depends on actions taken in the first quarter of this one. Costly decisions to change our energy infrastructures, and perhaps our ways of life, depend on how we conceive obligations to the future.

One aspect of the climate challenge is therefore similar to that facing St. Paul & St. James: industrial cultures know their future must look different but they have inherited infrastructure and traditions that many hold sacred. Meanwhile, the constant claim of today's needs makes it tempting to defer costly changes to the next generation. Because the most serious risks accumulate over time, action to confront climate change hinges on how cultures understand their obligations to the future. How they undertake those obligations determines opportunities for today's poor.

This chapter considers four major models of intergenerational ethics by testing them through the field's most difficult question: how to consider risks to future generations against claims of the present poor? Attempts to motivate robust climate action sometimes elide that tension. For example, a UN Development Programme (UNDP) report says: "Climate change demands urgent action now to address a threat to two constituencies with little or no political voice: the world's poor and future generations."[1] Those two constituencies, however, do not share exactly the same interests in how the world takes action for climate change. For while the poor hunger today, future generations stand vulnerable to how the world satisfies its hunger. In regard to climate policy, today's poor need policies of immediate adaptation while future generations need mitigation of emissions. The choice is not exclusive and obviously the reason for climate inaction is hardly that societies are paralyzed between strong commitments to the poor and the future. However, despite the political hazard of making too much of the question, considering conceptual tensions between today's need and tomorrow's risks can surface moral tensions that run right to the heart of what sustainability means.

Christian ethics has been oddly quiet about intergenerational obligations. Its silence may have to do with uneasiness about entertaining a test question that could trouble methodological priorities for the poor. Or it may be because discussion of the future in Christian theology approaches eschatology, which, in a time of misappropriated and macabre apocalypticisms, has sometimes been an embarrassing genre for Christian communities. Yet both those reasons—the potential trouble to a central commitment and the popular interest in religious and environmental apocalypticism—indicates the importance for intergenerational ethics for the future of Christian ethics. "Future generations will pass a harsh judgment on a generation that looked at the evidence on climate change," continues the UNDP report, "and then continued on a path that consigned millions of the world's most vulnerable people to poverty."[2] Judgment may indeed be coming, but how this generation will be judged depends on how it makes practical sense of the relation between those two constituencies—the poor and future generations. So where might Christian ethicists find reform projects enacting responsibilities for the future?

The method of this concluding chapter differs from the others because it works in the absence of a practical reform project. Instead it works implicitly, taking Christian liturgy as formation into a temporal imaginary and then developing constructive suggestions for how its practice might meet intergenerational problems. The Church of St. Paul & St. James does not explicitly try to bear responsibility for intergenerational risk, so I draw out the implications of its liturgical practices and imagine how they might adapt to answer the tensions of intergenerational ethics represented in its own building. By working in the absence of a project, this chapter also tests the limits of a pragmatic strategy. How to do ethics when there do not appear to be any relevant projects?

I close the book this way in order to offer a reflection on sustaining ethics amid pervasive irresponsibility. An important part of what we owe future generations is the skill to rightly judge what they inherit from us, including our notions of intergenerational obligation. A fate worse than their harsh judgment on us would be a future that had lost the concepts to recognize our failures. Ethics depends on sustaining capacities of judgment, which, I argue, requires sustaining evaluative practices over and across time. The future of ethics depends on nurturing the ability of future generations to judge and (perhaps) forgive us for what they inherit.

INTERGENERATIONAL ETHICS

Intergenerational thinking is not new. Obligations to ancestors and descendants often turn the screws of Greek tragedies and charge the genealogies of the Hebrew scriptures with reflection on inherited sins, family curses, and bloodlines of justice. What is new are patterns of technological agency that foreseeably alter the material conditions of life for future generations. Ernest Partridge observes that responsibility to the future was not even recognized as an issue for normative ethics until the 1970s.[3] In a 1981 anthology Partridge could include or summarize nearly every extant work on the subject.[4] With technological power over the future "the nature of human action has changed," wrote Hans Jonas in 1984, but ethics then had yet to develop concepts of responsibility for the future.[5] Perhaps Christian ethics, with its ancient traditions of generational thinking, could help?

The challenges to Christian ethics in offering practical help illustrate six difficulties for any intergenerational ethic. The first is the central conflict for the field: ethicists must find a way to develop obligations to the future that do not weaken commitments to presently vulnerable persons. Sometimes Christian ethicists so fear the weakening of presentist commitments that they work to suppress appearances of intergenerational tension. Telling here are the early contributions from Thomas Derr and Daniel Callahan, whose work in Protestant and Catholic traditions (respectively) agrees on finding theological reasons to care about the future while refusing the conflict with the present. Derr argues that the intuition that humans must answer to some future for their life work "may be strengthened considerably where people view their lives in the transcendent perspective which the religious imagination affords," but he warns against letting that imagination permit harms to the present for the sake of the future.[6] Callahan pursues a characteristically Catholic insistence on the enduring order of human nature, but diminishes intertemporal claims on present needs by placing them within an ambiguous natal metaphor: "the nothingness of future generations is a pregnant nothingness." Risks to the future should matter to our moral horizon but not as real conflicts among actual persons.[7] So even when Christian ethicists want to develop obligations to future generations they have an impulse to save presentist moral priorities.

That impulse may explain a second difficulty: risks to future generations sit outside the time of the Christian temporal imagination.[8] They appear beyond the lifespan of agents embodied in presence to another (the typical arena of love and justice), yet "before" the coming end-times (the typical register of the future). The temporal expanse of humanity's power thus sits between the two dominant temporalities of theological ethics. Religious eschatologies do not help an intergenerational ethic, argues Jonas, because they prepare an agent for a transhistorical moment by reorienting her to the immediacy of the present. Religious futurity does not temporally expand responsibility; it participates in another time altogether. Intergenerational ethics needs to generate actions for the sake of a future that the agent will not herself enjoy. Marxist utopianism, economic development, and liberal progressivism produce that kind of temporal imagination, thinks Jonas, but they each depend on a narrative of progress. The basic problem of technology is that its progress accumulates catastrophic risks to the tomorrow it incrementally improves. We do not need a temporal imaginary that sustains action for the future, thinks Jonas, for the ideologies of industrial modernity already offer us that. We need an ethic of responsibility that constrains the risks our actions serially pose to the future worlds they are making.[9] The possibility of intergenerational ethics thus depends on inventing a dimension of moral time that interrupts the implicit temporality carried in today's patterns of economic life. The answer to present poverty has been a promise of tomorrow's growth, conveniently fed by present consumption by the currently wealthy. The future is what the poor have been offered. Now even that thin promise seems uncertain, as economic growth threatens basic conditions of tomorrow's life.

A third difficulty militates against making that interruption: the chronic incentive to defer action and discount the interests of the future corrupts ethical reasoning. Stephen Gardiner observes that the asymmetric separation of cost and benefit across time suppresses development of intergenerational responsibility. Costs to action are "front-loaded" (must be paid now) while the most valued or costly consequences are "back-loaded" (appearing later). Moreover, as each generation arises into agency it inherits not only the irresponsibility of the previous generation but increased disincentive to do any better. As climate risks grow, agents face a temporal prisoner's dilemma with declining prospects for resolution because inaction now makes action in the future ever more costly.[10] Adequate responsibility for climate change depends on some present generation interrupting this cycle of moral corruption.

A key way that Christian ethics has confronted the incentive to defer ethical thinking encounters a fourth difficulty. Sometimes theologians depict members of future generations as victims in order to bring them under the protection of a theological priority for the poor. Doing so, however, raises conceptual problems about the personhood of those being harmed. Emmanuel Agius observes recent Catholic social thought developing a theme of solidarity with future generations. John Paul II invokes "a grave responsibility to preserve this order for the well-being of future generations."[11] The United States Conference of Catholic Bishops draws the moral connection most closely, invoking a single human family in its response to climate change: "Our obligations to the one human family stretch across space and time. They tie us to the poor in our midst and across the globe, as well as to future generations."[12] Whether the victims of atmospheric powers live now or in the future should be as insignificant as whether they live in the northern or southern hemisphere.[13] Such temporally indifferent solidarity may authorize rights protections for future persons.[14] That allows Catholic social thought to link advocacy for the rights of the unborn with advocacy for future persons, since both share vulnerability to decisions made by present persons.[15]

Drawing the analogy with unborn infants suggests the conceptual difficulty here: if a fetus invites controversy over its status of moral personhood, the personhood of those who do not exist for decades is even more tenuous. How can we have obligations to persons who do not yet exist? The problem is not simply that we cannot know the specific needs and interests of future persons. Those might be established through a durable moral anthropology and represented by proxy. The difficulty rather lies in Derek Parfit's objection that specific future persons will exist only because of decisions made by the present generation. "Parfit's Paradox" stalls harm-based forms of obligations, because the very actions that seem to pose risks to future persons are also those responsible for bringing about their existence. If the world chooses an austere climate policy for the sake of avoiding harm to future persons, those measures would, by affecting reproductive decisions, affect the number and identity of future persons. If, on the other hand, it chooses no policy, those measures would lead to a different number and identity of future persons. The latter group would inhabit a world with worse conditions than those of the former group would have, but they cannot claim that they have thereby been harmed, for they would not exist at all except for those world-worsening decisions. Parfit concludes that "person-affecting" models of ethics, which focus on harm to future persons, cannot help intergenerational ethics. (He finds so regrettable the damage this does to intuitive obligations that he suggests concealing the difficulty from policy makers!)[16]

Parfit's Paradox illuminates the peculiar kind of moral relation that present agents have with future persons. Temporal distance is not like spatial distance, and justice cannot cover it in the same way. Obligations across time have a natal quality, in that they help bring about the persons to whom they would be responsible. Later in the chapter I consider how ethics might develop a parental model of obligation, one that reflects the reproductive generativity through which new generations of life come into existence through the body of the present. However, attempting to escape the paradox by appealing to a reproductive relation encounters a fifth kind of difficulty: the narrowness and weakness of parental sentiment. If concern for future generations is really concern for one's *own* descendants, then wealthy agents in powerful societies may care less about reducing emissions on the supposition that at least their descendants will be able to adapt to difficult conditions. Moreover, parental sentiment dissipates with temporal distance; we might make sacrifices for our grandchildren but not for their grandchildren. Yet the temporal delays amid emissions activity and climatic feedback make the world of the fifth and sixth generation crucial to deciding present responsibilities. Shall we leave responsibility for those risks to mere sentiments of love?[17] To resist the corrupting incentives and interrupt inertial presentism, intergenerational ethics seems to need stronger concepts.

Attempting to depart from person-affecting models of ethics, Parfit tries an impersonal principle of beneficence that would permit comparison among alternative scenarios. Possible worlds, rather than specific persons, are then the subject of ethical evaluation. Parfit's own efforts, organized around overall welfare, cannot avoid leading to repugnant conclusions. He cannot justify why he prefers a world with fewer people and a high quality of life rather than one with many persons and a low quality of life.[18] Nonetheless, his attempt recognizes the role that scenarios may play in moral reasoning about the social reproduction of future worlds. Imagining possible futures can help agents reflect on the worlds being made by current practices, values, and powers.

Science fiction can sometimes play this role. In the case of climate change, science nonfiction stimulates reflection on the worlds we may make. The Intergovernmental Panel on Climate Change (IPCC) develops climate scenarios with several storylines of plausible atmospheric feedback from human action. "Each storyline is basically a short 'history' of a possible future development."[19] Presenting plausible future scenarios invites a global public to consider risks and responsibilities, to think with the future. Christian ethicist Carol Robb treats the IPCC scenarios as ethical alternatives for comparative preference, evaluating various paths as future worlds more and less compatible with theological values. In her approach, ethics can help agents reflect on the worlds their choices are making by reading them against the sort of world envisioned by scripture.[20] The Great Transition Initiative cultivates a similar mode of reflection with more dramatic scenarios, with the view that the exercise of considering what worlds we make can itself instill deeper moral investment in the future.[21]

Thinking with scenarios can be useful for reflecting on the trajectory of current practices but it encounters a sixth and final challenge to the field of intergenerational ethics: to what extent can the present anticipate how future generations will judge the world that they inherit from us? Making choices among possible future worlds forces present agents to offer values and reasons for their choice, but how can they be sure that future persons will hold those same values and reasons? Making a choice seems to imply supplementary obligations to ensure that future persons will share commitments held in the present. The present is responsible not only for the kind of world that future persons will inhabit but for the kind of agent who will interpret it as a more or less just inheritance. Our responsibility to future generations must be intelligible to them when they rise into agency, which means that the present must strive to also transmit possibilities of evaluating our decisions. Intergenerational ethics depends on some intergenerational practices of moral formation.

Major models of intergenerational ethics meet some of those challenges to the field while foundering on others. The argument within and about each illustrates difficulties that a theological ethic of intergenerational obligation must answer. I eventually suggest Christian liturgical practices might shape participants in transgenerational moral practices. However, each model I examine beforehand establishes aspects of the temporal imaginary still undeveloped in Christian ethics. The first insists directly on what Christian ethics has largely tried to evade: assessing risks to future generations against present sacrifices.

INVESTMENT

Investment is the dominant model for shaping intergenerational fairness, conforming agents into its temporal imaginary and largely setting the terms for how societies interpret risk to future generations. Yet it often attempts to conceal its moral assumptions. This section therefore takes time to understand how the model works and where it begs for further deliberation. An ethic of intergenerational risk should know the concepts and practices that already determine responsibilities to the future.

An investment model acknowledges an obligation to provide fair savings to the future, which includes considering cost and risk over time. Investment does not choose for a particular world, but rather seeks to maintain a continuous capacity for successive generations to pursue their own interests. Its aspiration is fair balancing: "development that meets the needs of the present without compromising the ability of future generations to meet their own needs."[22] In order to do so it must find a rational method for measuring present needs against future abilities, which requires making commensurable costs and benefits separated over time. The model compels societies to see trade-offs among rivalrous goals: overcoming present poverty, growing wealth for tomorrow, satisfying immediate consumption desires, conserving natural resources for future generations, and protecting ecological systems for the future of life. Its method frames those decisions within a single currency of comparison for those different goods and an assumption about how time depreciates that currency. The rationality of an investment model thus depends on a series of moral commitments, begging for a recovery of ethics that many economists would rather suppress.

The basic problematic of sustainability, explains Robert Solow, is that societies act unfairly toward the future when they discount the future too steeply. It is unfair for the present generation to profit from consuming the atmosphere's carbon sink while highly discounting the costs of that consumption to societies fifty years from now. Doing so takes a free ride on the future. If the market sets discount rates that allow business as usual to deplete resources without supplying a substitute, and to do so as if it were rational, then—says the economist Solow—moral intervention is needed. The public should establish more fair investment policies.[23]

I will return to discounting but let us first ask: what principles should guide fair investing? The American forester Gifford Pinchot famously defined conservation by expanding the utilitarian dictum: "the greatest good to the greatest number *for the longest time*."[24] That captures the intuition of an investment model, but if the social math of maximizing two variables was already controversial then adding a third begs for supplemental norms. Without a limiting generational horizon, investment responsibility becomes absurd. (Does it include the interests of whatever post-human civilization lives 250,000 years from now?) Without discounting, obligations to the future could tyrannize the present, for future benefits would justify massive present sacrifices. Now, limiting overdeveloped senses of obligation to the future is hardly the major challenge for intergenerational ethics. Current policies run on election cycles and "investment banks" can hardly think past the day's stock market close. Without losing sight of the extraordinarily narrow temporality in capitalist democracies, let us consider how to construct principles of fairness for investing over time.

An investment model does not necessarily imply utilitarianism. John Rawls, recognizing that intergenerational relations challenge his contractual account of justice, develops a "just savings principle." The principle establishes an obligation to do well for successive generations while avoiding the implications of a time-neutral partnership across all generations that could dictate severe austerities. Rawls stipulates that parties in his "original position" do not know their position in time. Ignorant of one's generation, the parties specify the procedure by which they would want all previous generations to determine the savings rate.[25] The result, argues Rawls, would correlate rates of saving with the achievements of a civilization and its level of wealth. When relatively poorer, the savings rate may be lower (because resources are needed more); when more developed, it may be higher (because they can afford to save). The savings rate may then fall to zero once a civilization has created just and effective institutions. At that point, its duty to the future only includes maintaining the institutions and preserving their capital base. A schedule of just saving thus determines the most fair path of developing the just society. That political goal constrains the "difference principle," which holds that (present) inequality must be warranted by benefits it creates for the (presently) least advantaged. The just savings principle implies that present inequalities may also be permitted for the sake of investing resources to construct and maintain institutions of justice, and to safeguard economic processes of accumulation that realize them.[26]

Rawls's model of fairness to the future is structurally similar to Solow's. Both use an investment model and both agree that choosing a savings rate amounts to choosing a notion of fairness to the future in tension with obligations to the least advantaged of the present. Their difference lies in the substance of *what* must be sustained, which informs principles for determining the rate. Solow thinks societies have an obligation to leave the future the capacity to be "as well off" as the present, which for him means maintaining fungible capital. Rawls holds that societies must sustain institutions and commitments to political justice. In effect, Rawls holds a "strong" view of sustainability (he names specific goods to be sustained) while Solow holds a "weak" one (he thinks that goods are fungible). The difference between them represents a critical argument over the extent to which the investment model may fairly refashion the world it inherits and passes on. To the extent that a society decides that various goods of earth are fungible resources it interprets risk and opportunity by a universal currency of value. Yet even if its investments succeed, generating wealth and welfare for future generations, a person in the future might read histories of forests alive with the sounds of birds and monkeys and think that, despite her wealth, she has been impoverished of something invaluable. In that case, her complaint would hold that the investment strategy wrongly decided *how* she would value. How can present investors ensure the acceptability across time of their logic of obligation to the future?

That point comes up in a different way with regard to discounting, which is an especially crucial device for interpreting climate responsibilities. Discounting permits comparison of costs and values separated by time by offering a practical device to take account, in the present, of the odd economic fact that future values do not yet exist. However, because the device is so influential in determining the rationality of economic behavior over time, small variations in the rate have a massive impact on what the responsibility entails. It is important to illustrate this point because the choice of discount rate can effectively mean the difference between the future mattering to present decisions or not.

With a high discount rate of ten percent, avoiding eight million dollars' worth of damage ten years from now would be measured at about $3.1 million of present value. Beyond fifty years, however, the damage would count for almost nothing. With a low discount rate of one percent, damage ten years out is valued at $7.2 million, and—crucially—damage fifty years from now is counted as $4.9 million in present value.[27] Why does that matter? Consider that the US Environmental Protection Agency uses a value of about eight million dollars to weight the cost of a human life. With a high discount rate, the risk of millions of human deaths in two generations counts as almost nothing to our present responsibilities, making costs to mitigate emissions always seem like a bad investment. Societies can keep deferring serious energy policy changes and, with convenient rate selection, call their irresponsibility a good investment. That explains why Herman Daly and John Cobb suspect that the point of discounting "is simply to convert 'a very large number' into a very small number under the cover of numerological darkness."[28] Perhaps ethics should simply reject discounting then?

Precisely because discounting makes such a massive difference it seems better to open its assumptions to public debate in order to argue for a more responsible rate. For example, calling climate change "the greatest and widest-ranging market failure ever seen," the Stern Review focuses on discounting as a key point of leverage. Stern's crucial intervention—and its most controversial contention among economists—was to argue for an ethical revaluation of discount rates.[29] Stern thinks that predominate rates (4–10%) do not fulfill commitments to future generations that most citizens take themselves to have. That means that the investment model has been consistently guiding societies away from making climate choices in line with their actual sense of obligation to future generations. If so, then, an investment model with a high discount rate it forces political societies to impoverish the future against their own commitments.

The exercise of setting discount rates thus becomes a principled site of struggle against incentives to presentist moral corruption. It forces societies to reckon with a gap between obligations they take themselves to hold to future generations and presentist economic behavior that belies those obligations. In the midst of collective economic behavior that warrants a free ride on the future under the cover of rational efficiency, introducing ethical consideration at least makes selection of the rate an open political deliberation. Uncovering the moral assumptions built into rates at least allows political societies the opportunity to protest against policies that compel them to tyrannize future generations.[30]

Understanding how to navigate the ethical choices here requires understanding two different kinds of discount and their odd relation: pure time preference and social rate of time preference.[31] A pure time preference for the present is the rarely defended position that the welfare of those in the future is less important than the welfare of those currently alive. That position holds that the temporal position of suffering affects its disvalue (that suffering in 1650 weighs differently from suffering in 2050 just because of its position in time), implying ethical inequality between persons of different generations. One of the first economists to treat discounting, Frank Ramsey, is often quoted for saying that a pure time preference for the present "is ethically indefensible and arises merely from the weakness of the imagination." A social rate of time preference, on the other hand, tutors the weak temporal imaginary of mortal, impatient creatures so that investment is not entirely determined by preferences for our own generation and immediate descendants. When another economist pans pure time preference as "a polite expression for rapacity and the conquest of reason by passion," he describes everyday behavior in the consumer economy.[32] Our practical reasoning seem susceptible to being free riders on the future, especially with regard to behaviors that cause problems after the agent's own death. How should mortal persons think about a proper relation between present consumption of atmospheric space and the needs of future generations?

The social rate of time preference (or "social discount rate") is a moral and political choice about how we should answer that question. Those who dismiss all discounting, like Daly and Cobb, seem to miss the difference.[33] Discounting is the policy expression of what we think about equity among generations. The most important question is not whether it should be done (all who save or borrow participate in it), but whether the rate can represent a moral choice that criticizes the implied temporality of everyday economic behavior.

The key point, then, is whether or not moral reasoning may factor the social discount rate. Economists usually rely on discount rates set by bond market behavior. Effectively, that leaves our central practice of intergenerational obligation to the behavior of investment bankers—a group infamous for short-term thinking, not to mention rapacity. To set a rate by political decision, perhaps in the way that Rawls suggests, depends on whether principled considerations can depress the discount rate in the view that financial behavior seems more presentist than we actually think fair. It depends, in other words, on whether we think obligations to future generations should emerge from principles of justice or financial investment behavior.

The consequence of that question shows up in the different climate policies supported by Stern and William Nordhaus. The two economists share very similar assumptions about average economic growth and near-zero pure time preference, but Stern's social discount rate of one percent supports an aggressive mitigation policy, while the four percent rate used by Nordhaus makes mitigation seem less efficient than other strategies and social investments.[34] The massive policy difference reflects two different schools of thought on how to set discount rates—and two different relations between ethics and economics. Nordhaus wants to set the social discount rate from observed market behavior, thus making the discount rate a democratic outcome of actual preferences. Stern takes a prescriptivist approach, incorporating considerations of moral principle in order to lower the rate in view of intuitive obligations not to imperil conditions of life for future generations—perils for which Stern thinks present economic behavior poorly accounts. Stern's discount rate thus proposes that societies should use ethics to criticize their economic behavior. Nordhaus's rate treats economic behavior as itself the relevant intergenerational ethic.

What an investment model of obligation to the future means for climate change hinges on the outcome of that controversy. A robust mitigation policy needs Stern's approach: moral intervention in rate setting. Exposing discount rates as political choices removes obligations to the future from market-determined rationality and makes them matters of open political debate. It makes the practical way we measure risks to the future directly accountable to our ideas of intergenerational justice rather than our consumer behavior, and frees an investment model from the assumptions of investment banking.

One of those assumptions is that markets will continue to generate more wealth than loss. However, sustainability problems raise concerns about the long-term health of the human economy and in the last chapter we saw multiple reasons to doubt the promise of everlasting growth. It is at least plausible that the accumulating consequences of fossil-fueled capitalism could destabilize the global economy while deteriorating ecological conditions. With such decline in mind, Henry Shue argues that the ethical question pivots away from a just savings rate. "The specter of climate change means, by contrast, that we may be confronting the issue of the just-deterioration rate. How much worse off than the previous generation can we permit the next to be?"[35]

As each assumption of an investment model is uncovered and questioned, Christian ethicists might welcome the opening of economics to moral deliberation. However, it is not obvious that theological accounts of social justice would generate more robust commitments to future generations.

An ethic of neighbor love might in fact confirm the presentist priority that an account of responsibility for climate change must overcome. In the theological case it is not the selfish, rapacious sort of priority for today, but an other-regarding love for the hungry that would seem to demand that societies focus attention on today. It would seem that the Christian temporal imaginary of pro-poor theological communities concentrates on the suffering of today and specifically diminishes the importance of "storing up treasure in worry for tomorrow."[36] If the body of Christ stands before us hungry and thirsty today, what Christian ethic can hold resources in reserve to wait on tomorrow? Perhaps, then, a Christian account of justice would support *higher* rates of social discounting in order to steer resources away from alleviating the worries of tomorrow and toward alleviating poverty? Of course, present economic policy is hardly paralyzed between concern for the poor and future generations. The plutocratic presentism in actual economic behavior is manifestly indifferent both to the impoverished and to future generations. However, the conceptual dilemma about relative priorities between the present poor and future generations raises a question about the capacity of Christian ethics to contribute to the debates. Theological communities that claim to understand justice through a preferential option for the poor seem to have a narrow temporal imaginary. Simply adding future generations into that preferential option leaves Christian ethics within an imaginary that cannot receive concrete questions about how risks to the future should reshape present behavior. So while an investment model of obligation can open space for critical ethical revision, Christian ethics needs a model that reframes the temporal tensions.

INTERGENERATIONAL MEMBERSHIPS

A second model of obligation considers fairness within an intergenerational membership rather than between generations separated by time. That reframes intergenerational problems by making temporal distance among persons less significant. The model appears in communitarian and stewardship forms. Both describe duties owed to a membership that includes ancestors and descendants.

Communitarian approaches sometimes develop a rights-based approach from the views of a theorist suspicious of rights. Edmund Burke wrote against the French revolution that it offended "a partnership not only between those who are living, but between those who are living, those who are dead, and those who are to be born."[37] In opposing Thomas Paine, who appealed to rights in order to nullify obligations to oppressive memberships, Burke argues that there is a temporality to moral personhood. His famous argument displays some of the tensions in using the idea of an intergenerational membership to generate duties of justice. Contemporary ethicists sometimes use the temporal conception of Burke to further pursue the rights politics of Paine. For example, Avner de-Shalit argues that moral agents should understand themselves as part of a "transgenerational community" because this best reflects the constitution of personhood. We do not exist as isolated individuals but within communities made up of past, present, and future members. There must be a temporality to the justice of rights, then, then because there is a temporality to personhood. Obligations may be owed directly to future generations as members of the community by which we have and understand our own moral personhood.[38]

A communitarian approach thus incorporates relations to future generations into an account of human dignity. Like the ecologically expanded account of dignity that we saw in the environmental justice projects of chapter 5, this model temporally expands human dignity in an attempt to meet the structure of problems like climate change. If human dignity is constituted within a membership that exists across time, then protecting the interests of all persons includes protecting a decent future. Richard Hiskes makes that argument by adopting the ecological account of human dignity found in environmental justice and adding to it a temporal expansion, so that personhood includes intergenerational as well as ecological relations. This approach offers a less controversial way of establishing strong sustainability guidelines, for if justice already recognizes ecological dimensions of human dignity, those dimensions hold for the entire temporal membership in which dignity is realized.[39]

The membership model avoids Parfit's nonidentity problem since justice resides in a group right rather than an individual right. Rights for future individuals seem unintelligible since they would involve a right that could not be claimed, held by those who owe their existence to the agents from whom the right is supposed to protect them. A group right, however, held by a moral membership existing over time, can protect the basic interests that any member possesses in virtue of membership. Because the membership crosses generations, Edward Page argues, "future persons will possess interests broadly comparable to our own when they come into existence and at least some of these interests will be vulnerable, either individually or collectively, to the behavior of prior generations."[40] So this model does not recognize rights held *by* future generations or persons; the rights are held by a transgenerational membership.

That argument approximates what indigenous peoples movements have claimed in their appeals to group rights. Insofar as peoples understand their identity as a membership shaped by long living in one place, their appeal to a group right carries a combined temporal and bioregional dimension. Accumulating threats to those conditions mediate threats to the future of a cultural membership, so the future risks of climate change fall under concepts of harm to the transgenerational membership within which a people holds its right and by which it understands its identity. For example, the Anchorage Declaration, made by a global gathering of indigenous representatives discussing climate change, appeals to "our rights as intergenerational guardians" of cultural knowledge (a trust of wisdom, it notes, for which other peoples now have need). Recognizing the rights of indigenous peoples, the Anchorage Declaration claims, includes protecting their capacity to guard a transgenerational community's way of life.[41] When that community holds a cyclical view of time, moreover, it folds the linear alienations of risk and value, of the sort found in an investment model, into the affections and disturbances of a near membership.

The chief difficulty for any communitarianism is that its obligations appear contingent on a shared membership or cultural identity. How does a people know that its membership is a good or just one? Bryan Norton's account of sustainability describes a society's future-involving decisions as a "community performative act." The meaning of such acts, says Norton, is grounded in "the communal values that constitute a place and create an identity for a people in their place," which they implicitly ask subsequent generations to protect. Norton goes on to argue for strengthening the communitarianism of Burke by a "stronger sense of human territoriality" and a stronger connection of cultural identities with natural history.[42] However, moral bonds made by territorial defense of naturalized identities are more likely to haunt the future than help it. Grounding intergenerational obligations in the dominant identities of a landscape could possibly be helpful to indigenous peoples (who Norton does not have in mind), but would more likely mean that obligations to the future would sustain landscapes of white power and support xenophobic exclusions.

A stewardship approach to the membership model preserves the basic logic while loosening its dependence on a particular identity. The idea of intergenerational stewardship, observes Page, works from a sense that each generation has inherited from the past a trust, for which it has an obligation of indirect reciprocity: in recognition of received benefits, an obligation to make a fitting gesture of return by improving (or at least not degrading) the inheritance for the future.[43] This duty is not based in the survival of any particular people or way of life; it arises from recognition of a received gift and the implicit obligation of any gift to make some fitting, nonidentical return.

The relevant membership here is the community of those who have received the inheritance and its implicit, open-ended obligation to the future.

The basic point of the membership model holds in the stewardship
form: personhood is constituted by temporal relations and those relations
generate specific intergenerational obligations. Risks to the future of life
pose risks to the integrity of present moral agents because they threaten
the integrity of a trusteeship responsible for earth's future. For example,
extinction for up to one half of the kinds of life due to climate change not
only impoverishes earth; it impoverishes humanity of an intergenerational
role. Closing down the processes of creation closes down human self-
understanding as guardians of an inherited river of life.

Theocentric accounts of stewardship work differently: by that logic,
agents owe a return directly to God, from whom the trust is received and
on behalf of whom it is administered. It is possible to combine theocentric
and intergenerational accounts of stewardship, if the direct obligation to
God is understood as a practical command to care for a trust for the sake of
future generations. Theological ethicists have not yet developed stewardship
in that way, but Michael Northcott has suggested that Christian ethics could
contribute to a membership model by developing its understanding of the
communion of saints. "In this doctrine Christians affirm that their sociality
is not confined to those who live now but that they inhabit a story that they
receive from the dead, and especially from those martyrs and saints who
suffered innocently for their refusal to claim any dominion other than the
Lordship of the crucified and risen Christ."[44] Christianity as an intergenerational membership here keeps a trust of faith that is disruptively suspicious
of human claims to exercise stewardship. The communion of saints supplies
two things missing in neoliberal individualism, argues Northcott: a sense of
connection among generations and an accountability to Christ that refuses
to let apparent demands of power trump the imperative of love.

Leaving aside the return of particularist identity issues, accountability
to love offers a norm for evaluating the integrity of a membership. It also
suggests a possibility for approaching the tension between today's hungry
and tomorrow's harms: doing theology from the place of the vulnerable
might include developing an account of love from within the perspective of
an intergenerational membership threatened by climate change. That helps
warrant indigenous communitarian strategies. Note that this approach does
not try to overcome presentist priorities by including future persons as
honorary members of "the poor," but rather seeks solidarity with the present poor as members of an intergenerational membership of love in which
they have their dignity. That implies that meeting present needs must, at
least, not undermine the intergenerational membership that constitutes the

dignity of all persons. Preserving the membership of love, which entails some future-oriented obligations, becomes a component of justice.

A difficulty with this approach is that it may justify significant sacrifices from today's poor individuals for the sake of an imagined membership in which their dignity consists. That repeats the problem of Paine's fear of an intergenerational partnership, but with an added economic twist. If the global economy does expand such that future generations enjoy greater welfare than the present, then the membership model may implicitly demand more from weaker (present) members than from wealthier (future) members—which is precisely the unfairness that an investment model attempts to prevent. Simultaneous appeals to the plight of the poor and future generations in a common membership must not elide their different vulnerabilities. Page acknowledges the odd turn of his account of intergenerational justice here: "There might be victim-involving acts that do not in fact diminish well-being, but are nevertheless interest-violating." The relatively wealthier residents of the world resulting from lax climate policy could still be frustrated with their ancestors, as Page says, for "robbing them of their dignity by giving them the gift of blighted life rather than giving another set of people the gift of a much better life."[45] A lax climate policy might be unjust even if the world resulting from it is much wealthier than the present one because justice respects the integrity of relations rather than overall welfare.

We return, then, to the chief difficulty for Christian ethics: can intergenerational justice require sacrifice from the present poor for the sake of the membership to which they belong? In the face of significant and defeasible human suffering today, do such sacrifices amount to what one critic calls "inverted ancestor worship"?[46] I later turn to the way ancestors actually show up in Christian worship and how that relates to sacrifice, but first I want to point out one more difficulty with the membership model, which lies in its chief strength. Appealing to the way intergenerational membership constitutes human personhood recognizes that moral agency is maternal in that it is always mothering a future. "We do not tell the truth about flesh," writes Muers, "unless we talk about how it is inherited and passed on." Personhood is not simply "placed" in time, as debates over a just savings rate can make it seem; it is exercised processively and generatively, making the very world to which it imagines obligations. In the membership model, the task of justice is not to cross temporal distance; "it is from the pregnant or maternal body that it becomes most obvious that future generations are not originally separate from 'us'." We need not choose for Burke or for Paine, for communitarian partnership or revolutionary rights. Ethics can instead work from the processes of generation by which humans mother the future. The maternal self models a concept of the social maternal: "we are part of a social ecology that endures across generations, and of social 'bodies' in and from which future generations are formed."[47]

Here is the difficulty: mothering the future could become an imperious act of self-reproduction. Even without the communitarian appeal to common identity with a shared territory, a sense of maternal agency gestating culture over time raises questions about the sort of "mothers" we should be. How far may we attempt to make our descendants interpret their memberships and obligations identically to how we have? To what extent does our own identity and integrity depend on the sort of persons that our "children" become? I will soon turn to the way that Muers begins developing a liturgical model that helps answer those questions, but first turn to a precautionary model because it develops a line of obligation that seems to satisfy important intuitions while raising even more troubling questions.

PRECAUTION

A precautionary model starts from a rather thin duty: do not cause catastrophe. Moral agents must, at the least, protect the minimal conditions of survival. In Jonas's imperative of responsibility, that means protecting the ongoing exercise of moral agency from plausible, even if low-probability, risks of destruction. So what are those minimal conditions of agency and from what sorts of destruction do they require protection? A precautionary model asks societies to identify conditional goods—goods that permit the pursuit and realization of all other goods. Conditional goods cannot be made commensurable in the same way as other forms of capital, for they are the ground of social value and the possibility of a decent future. They are goods without which a society can no longer recognize itself. Uncertainties in long-range economic and ecological forecasting make an investment model unreliable for assessing risks to conditional goods.[48] A precautionary model warrants taking action to prevent great harm even when forecasting makes the harm seem distant or unlikely.

Precaution thus shifts the politics of uncertainty. If climate change creates plausible long-term risks, even if their probability is low or uncertain, then expensive action now to reduce or avoid those risks becomes more rational. Uncertainty about disaster is a reason to take action, not to defer it. Precaution also shifts the ethics of research method: whereas research usually focuses on avoiding false positives of a hypothesis of harm, in regard to irreversible or catastrophic lines of causation it should seek to avoid false negatives. In regard of very serious harms, better to err in supposing that the risk is real than in supposing it is not.[49] That warrants research into

uncertain possibilities of abrupt "tipping point" changes, like a sudden decline in Atlantic thermohaline circulation, which seems unlikely but would
be catastrophic. It suggests that significant policy action need not await certainty that an atmosphere with 700ppm CO_2e would be devastating to Asian
water supplies; action may be justified even if research shows the harm is
merely possible.

Critics of the precautionary model object that unlikely catastrophes become too visible in the mind of fear-ridden publics. Cass Sunstein protests
that precaution makes economically prudent decision making susceptible
to the irrationalities of human cognition. Dispositions to focus on potential
losses (rather than potential gains), and on those risks most visible in the
fears of public culture, could lead to social paralysis as multiple claims of
precaution oppose every important project.[50] If a society becomes overly
fascinated by scenarios of collapse, precaution would lead to unfair over-
investment in security to the detriment of other important social projects.

Can justice inform how we should think about averting possible catastrophes? Rawls offers a "maximin" thought experiment: in conditions of
uncertainty, one should consider alternatives according to their worst possible outcomes and then select the scenario with the least worst outcome.
That is the rule, suggests Rawls, that we would want an enemy to use if she
were making decisions about the world in which we would live.[51] Gardiner
adopts that approach in regard to the most perilous long-term outcomes of
climate change. When there is a scientifically plausible threat to conditional
goods, precaution interrupts the corrupting propensity of each generation
to shift risk to the next by making each accountable to the worst possible
outcome of the risks they take.[52] Sunstein himself admits that appeals to
precaution may be needed when societies irrationally disregard catastrophic
risks—and climate failure is his example.[53] A precautionary model is warranted when other political factors suppress attention to conditional goods
in jeopardy.

How do we know which possible harms bear such basic significance?
What are conditional goods? Precaution is not a calculating device like discounting; it rather initiates iterative reflection on the goods necessary for
human personhood and on the threats to them. Those goods might be political institutions, economic conditions, or ecological relations. Precaution
obtains when those goods seem imperiled by long-term risks of ordinary
structures of cultural action. It is the stance of a society wary of overcon-
fidence in its own stability or progress and the counsel to hedge our social bets. Consider evolution, writes Jonas: nature's inventions never risk
everything at once but rather experiment in incremental steps. Insofar as
our technological powers compress evolutionary time, we accumulate risks

that begin to wager human existence. Jonas's warning: "Never must the existence or the essence of man as a whole be made a stake in the hazards of action."[54]

In what does "the existence or the essence" of humanity consist? For Jonas, it is the act of taking responsibility. As humans act across time, they have obligation to the future of human agency to preserve the possibility of responsibility because it is the condition for moral agency. For Jonas that includes "care for the future of all nature on this planet as a necessary condition of man's own." Attention to imperiled ecological conditions of moral agency therefore alters the dominant temporal imaginary in western ethics, making for an "an ethics of preservation and prevention, not of progress and perfection."[55] By making us accountable to possible catastrophes, a precautionary model suspends faith in economic and technological progress as guarantors of a decent human future. Fossil-fuel culture is beginning to look like it has risk margins akin to those run by the financial houses betting on mortgages.

Precaution offers a middle way between the "weak sustainability" view, in which the conditional good is capital, and the "strong sustainability" view in which conditional goods include many specific and nonsubstitutable goods. Brian Barry cleverly argues that because that debate matters for how humans understand themselves, fairness to future generations requires protecting conditions for ongoing debate. "One of the defining characteristics of human beings is their ability to form their own conceptions of the good life." The good we must protect for future generations, then, is "the opportunity to live good lives according to their conception of what constitutes a good life." Corollary to that obligation, "conditions must be such as to sustain a range of possible conceptions of the good life."[56] The implication of Barry's position is a relatively strong version of sustainability, but on pragmatic rather than ontological grounds. It recognizes no obligations to nature itself or to the intrinsic values of species and creatures, but seeks to protect ecological (and other) systems as conditions important for holding open the question of which conception of the good human life is best.

Barry's approach begins to thicken the commitments of a precautionary model because it implies an obligation to nurture respect for the importance of pluralist debate. Future generations will think fair the inheritance of apt conditions for debate only if they agree that argument over conceptions of the good life forms an important part of being human. They will think fair their inheritance from us, that is, only if they also consider themselves as participants in intergenerational deliberation over the conditional goods of human life. Protecting the conditions of argument thus implies a

maternal responsibility to nurture the next generation to appreciate deliberation over conditional goods.

As it accrues obligations to help future generations appreciate what
we protect, a precautionary model begins to conform to some aspects of a
membership model. Norton's pragmatist account displays the similarity.[57]
The obligation may be agnostic about which options future generations
will want, but it is not disinterested in what sort of moral agents they will
become. Communities that work to preserve environmental goods for the
future, observes Norton, also work to create and protect the moral culture
that will keep valuing such goods. "Successful protection of wilderness . . .
requires not only protection of the physical aspects of the places, but also
the successful transmission of an attitude of love, respect and caring for
these places."[58] Setting aside wilderness areas for the sake of the future is
not an austerely ignorant act, done to offer the future one option among
others. It makes a claim on those who come after us, that they too should
value the protection of at least some wilderness. So too for protecting
institutions of justice. Protecting a "safe minimum standard" for things of
great value transmits not only the good itself, but a proposal to keep valuing it.[59]

How we think about the long-term risks of climate change therefore
makes a long-term proposition about what humans should value. If we are
willing to discount catastrophic risks for the sake of preserving wealth accumulation, we do better to admit that we hold accumulation as a basic
good whose moral culture we hope to perpetuate, rather than to insist that
we discount risks out of fairness to the poor or to future generations. Or,
if societies are willing to move social spending from relief of malnutrition
to emissions abatement in order to avoid the worst risks of climate change
(supposing that we were willing in the first place to devote meaningful
spending toward overcoming hunger), we should admit that doing so makes
a moral proposal to our descendants about which project matters more.
This interpretive variant of the precautionary model offers a way of understanding strong concern for the welfare of future generations among those
with weaker commitments to the present poor. Partha Dasgupta thinks that
today's rich know that they are responsible for climate change but do not
think that they are for poverty.[60] They may be wrong about their actual responsibilities for impoverishment but their intuition to bear responsibility
for problems they know themselves to be causing affirms for their descendants something basic to being a moral agent: one is accountable to fore-
seeable effects of one's actions. Acting to protect the future against risks
imposed by present action acknowledges that the integrity of present agents

will be judged by future generations. Instead we maintain an ecologically dangerous, economically uncertain, and morally corrupting fossil-fuel way of life that, in cumulative effect, is already constraining the range of freedom our descendants will have. So at present humanity is failing to maintain that basic gesture of responsibility.[61]

We compound our failure on climate change if we also induct our descendants into patterns of chronic irresponsibility. We do even worse if future generations fail to judge those actions as irresponsible. The success of defending conditional goods depends not only on reducing catastrophic threats to those goods, but on nurturing a future that agrees that its ancestors protected the right goods. We could fail our responsibilities, John O'Neill observes, if we fail to raise up generations capable of appreciating how responsibility counts as an achievement. "Our primary responsibility," O'Neill writes, "is to attempt . . . to ensure that future generations do belong to a community with ourselves." We do that by passing on "an ongoing argument concerning what those values are to be."[62] In the case of failed climate responsibilities, our ironic duty is to ensure that future generations inherit the capacity to properly judge our failures. Cultivating their capacity to judge us is how we cultivate their interpretive capacity to recognize the same basic goods that we hold important.

That ironic duty points to the darker mood of a precautionary model. Whereas an investment model usually accommodates an optimistic attitude toward economic progress, and a membership model anticipates the continuance of its community, precaution cultivates anxiety that a way of life contains seeds of its demise. Precaution, suggest two theorists of trauma, is the temporal attitude of a civilization traumatized by its own violence and losing confidence in its future. With its faith in progress weakened, precaution is the attitude of a civilization that has begun to think of itself as tragic.[63] Perhaps progress is the catastrophe, and precaution our preparation for the coming reckoning.

In its darkest moment, a precautionary model may ask the question that Jonathan Lear asks in his reading of the Crow (Native American) genocide: how might one prepare for the collapse of a way of life? Insofar as a meaningful life depends on the concepts and subjectivities made by culture, it is vulnerable to that culture's demise. Cultures do not normally train members to endure their own breakdown; a culture's concepts and virtues assume the endurance of the field that makes them possible. A precautionary model usually asks how to avoid catastrophic blows to society, but if one foresees unavoidable breakdown of a cultural way of life, then the precautionary question changes: how to nurture hope in the face of catastrophe? In that case, it asks how to prepare coming generations for a future whose integrity we cannot secure. Within a culture's own terms of goodness and justice, the only options would seem to lie in giving witness to the end of goodness and justice with the end of a way of life—that is, in despair or martyrdom.

However, observes Lear, belief in a transcendent good would allow one to anticipate a new field of possibilities that would allow a different, albeit unforeseeable, way of living the good. Even after it is lost, persons in the future might find a way to poetically redeploy a tradition in a way that creates integrity with its past. Living a recognizable Crow life was a possibility destroyed by European invasion and genocide. "After that, nothing happened," said a Crow chief who had in fact survived for decades longer. He meant, suggests Lear, that the possibility for events to happen for a Crow person had been obliterated when the goods conditional for a Crow life were destroyed. Yet the chief lived in hope that a recognizably Crow life might be given back one day, on the new and unknown terms made by survivors developing new fields of possibility to be Crow. Faith in a good beyond the conditional goods allows that radical hope. However, in the period of genocide, cultivating hope in a Crow future required odd virtues: not those that defend a way of life against all odds, but those that prepare one to abandon a conception of the good life, in hope that it shall, in some unknowable way, come back to life again. In catastrophe, responsibility to the future means sustaining a faith that life can be given back to us, even if we lack the concepts for imagining what that could mean.[64]

Those are bleak meditations. They illustrate how persons should undertake obligations to future generations when they see their way of life collapsing in insurmountable catastrophe. In that case we must cultivate odd virtues in ourselves and our descendents, including the courage to abandon the concepts of goodness and justice supported by a passing way of life, even when we lack the concepts to supply alternatives. In that period of discontinuity, as an intelligible future closes down, responsibility to the future reduces to sustaining hope for a future whose goods it can no longer foresee or understand.

The basic point in this section is that a precautionary model needs elements of the membership model, because sustaining conditions of responsibility requires care for interpretive practices of evaluating and transmitting inherited moral proposals. That entails maternal obligations to nurture cultural capacities for receiving ambiguous inheritances. In relation to climate change, we must prepare our grandchildren to reckon with our failure and properly judge our irresponsibility, that they might resist corrupting intergenerational incentives to deferral and take up the debts of repair and restoration that they will inherit from us.

Religious ethics seems promising here because religious traditions function as transgenerational arguments that cultivate accounts of right and wrong and maintain the practices that keep interpreting those capacities of judgment. Christian ethics, however, faces a difficulty insofar as its practices of love take priority in interpreting right and wrong. For the two central practices of love seem to disjoint time: responding to the needs of one's neighbors as immediately as to one's own and worshiping God above all else. Those two practices invest every present moment with a divine significance that prepares the faithful for a coming transformation—not for the next generation, but for another kind of time altogether. Do practices of love sacrifice the future?

CHILD SACRIFICE

Noting theological silence about contemporary anxieties over risks to the future, Rachel Muers argues that theological ethics should revisit the eschatological expectations of the future formed in Christian worship. Pregnant herself while writing, Muers asks: in a world with a threatened future, "what does it mean that we can bear and raise children?"[65] Despite how widely that concern is felt by contemporary parents, the question is rarely asked in Christian ethics. In a series of articles and an important book, *Living for the Future*, Muers shows how to receive the question within the practices by which Christian memberships already mother the future.[66] She starts from a basic frustration: why, in the face of evidence that our actions sacrifice our children's world, do we keep acting in the same ways? What should ethics make of this chronic failure of responsibility? "The problem," she supposes, "is at least in part anthropological, requiring some discussion of who *we* are as the subjects of ethics."[67] How do moral agents become parents who sacrifice their children this way?

Muers starts by claiming maternal images of Christ and the church in order to "re-imagine the social existence of Christianity as itself a maternal body."[68] That establishes the temporally expanded anthropology accomplished by a membership model and offers a metaphor for reconceiving tensions between the needs of today and of tomorrow: a pregnant woman cares for the coming child by caring for her own body, for from her flesh the future bodies forth. Perhaps the immediate loves of the church body prepare an analogous way of loving the future. Where might an ethicist look to find the church actively mothering the future?

Muers turns to worship as a practice that nurtures agents into responsibility for the future by interrupting the relationships through which we sacrifice the future. "Enacting love of God—as in worship—is a primary exercise of intergenerational responsibility." That seems an odd way of establishing responsibility since liturgical love intensifies a disjoint between present and future. In worship, Muers affirms, Christians practice the difficult insistence that God must be loved above any love of this world or tomorrow's security. We owe our children training in this exercise of refusing to love a way of life more than love itself. "The worship of this particular form of existence and the will to maintain it at any cost is not part of what is owed to future generations. There is an apophatic or anti-idolatrous aspect to recognizing God—rather than anyone or anything else—as the establisher and guarantor of connections between generations."[69]

Practicing the love of God in worship allows agents to imagine and participate in God's judgment on a way of life that makes such sacrifices to itself. Preparation for an eschatological future does not then, as Jonas fears of religious ethics, diminish intergenerational responsibility; it opens freedom for the future. That is how social ethics should hear the apocalyptic teachings of Jesus, writes Muers; not as stripping away the temporality of personhood but as confronting bad inheritances and thereby reopening the future. The eschatological Jesus does not abrogate the intergenerational ethos found in the Hebrew Scriptures, says Muers, he rather restores it by rescuing the future from human attempts to control and colonize it. Christ is "a fulfilling interruption of generational succession," the gathering of all generations into a membership of freedom.[70] The Jesus who teaches against taking care for tomorrow restores intergenerational solidarity by undoing idolatry.

In a provocative reading of the child sacrifice cult of Molech (which appears in Leviticus and Jeremiah), Muers interprets intergenerational irresponsibility as a paradoxical willingness to make sacrifices to secure the future. The Molech cult involved the burnt sacrifice of children in ritual attempt to stave off misfortune and protect posterity. Muers follows early rabbinic commentary on the prohibition of Molech as a condemnation of idolatry. Molech was not just one idol among others, in this interpretation, but a horrifying image of how idolatry functions in general. "Everyone is liable to worship Molech," exegetes Muers, participating in the horror by attempting "to control their future and their posterity by perpetuating deathly patterns of existence."[71] Notice how the logic of child sacrifice comes near some logics of sustainability: "it is a survival strategy; a temporary adherence to falsehood for the sake of a greater good." It excludes the present cry of the child in order to secure a future for the community. As "a system of bringing both past and future generations under the control of some powerful subgroup of the present . . . The Molech cult recognizes the inevitable consequences of generational succession . . . but responds to them by trying to gain control over the process."[72] Both the refusals to address climate change and some policies to confront it may be a contemporary form of child sacrifice—not because we refuse to make sacrifices, but because we refuse to stop sacrificing.

The vicious paradox is that this sacrifice *for* the future occurs as sacrifice *of* the future in the bodies of children. That is what societies are asked to accept when they are told to suppress the cries of hungry neighbors to protect a way of life for future generations—a way of life that at the same time consumes the ecological womb of tomorrow. Sacrifice becomes the social logic of sustainability, a norm of "responsibility" and a secular liturgy that teaches persons what to love above all else. The burning of children, or their perpetual hunger, symbolizes the dedication of the future to the same fires, the same hunger. Responsibility for mothering the future begins, then, by confronting the worship of sacrifice itself. Muers thus turns the usual ethical question about what sacrifices we should make for the future into one more daunting: how to prepare the future to forgive us for horrifying sacrifices? Practicing worship of the one who identifies with sacrificial victims rather than power-seeking priests makes participants capable of resisting their idolatrous inheritances. A Christian's obligation to the future, in this view, is to pass on liturgical practices that school agents in the capacity to recognize false sacrifice and refuse inherited patterns of seeking security at the cost of justice.

This liturgical model of obligation to the future is structurally similar to the precautionary models of Norton and O'Neill, which sustain the deliberative processes through which future generations will learn how to value. It differs in that liturgy is less like a philosophical argument; liturgy shapes the imaginations and dispositions of agents by inducting them into the interior and exterior habits of love. In a eucharistic liturgy, agents inhabit the body of God's sacrifice-ending love and learn the moves of responding to the world with grace rather than sacrifice. Liturgy teaches how to judge what we inherit from previous generations by inducting participants in interpretive practices that unmask and resist idolatries. By passing on those practices, along with the idolatries that we inevitably transmit as well, we help the future respond with grace to the accumulated debts and destruction our ways of life are making. Liturgy mothers the future by sustaining a practice for judging inheritances rightly and then still finding hope, even amid chronic failures to stop oppressing its poor and disappearing creatures.

In recent decades, Christian ethics across an ecumenical range has been recovering liturgy as a site of Christian moral formation. Often inspired by Alexander Schmemann's exposition of desire, power, and embodiment, these recoveries interpret the formation of moral agents through a liturgical anthropology.[73] For example, informed by Schmemann, James K. A. Smith interprets everyday cultural practices as quasi liturgies, similar in formative impact. These "cultural liturgies," from shopping malls to football games, function as pedagogies of desire, writes Smith, for they are sites where a social imaginary is produced. The Christian practice of liturgy implies the sort of anthropology that makes persons susceptible to imaginative productions of desire. Humans are "liturgical animals," whose imagination of what to love and how to desire it is learned through embodied performances. Amid the liturgies of spectacle and consumption that shape persons by pitiable desires, Smith wants Christian worship to function as a "contemporary apocalyptic," unmasking the idolatrous character of contemporary institutions by offering an alternative drama of formation.[74]

Nowhere has liturgical resistance appeared more powerfully than in William Cavanaugh's interpretation of torture as perverted liturgy, and his account of eucharistic practice as political resistance and counter imagination. For him, the church's liturgy thus performs a therapeutic disruption of time; "the feast of the last day irrupts into earthly time and the future breaks in to the present." Here again, eschatological permeations of time sustain the church's "subversive imagination."[75] Whereas Jonas thinks that eschatology impoverishes moral formation, Cavanaugh and Smith intensify the eschatological dimension of liturgy in order to make it sufficiently disruptive from present practices of everyday life.

While interpretively powerful, however, liturgical therapy threatens to undermine real responsibilities for the definite risks of climate change. By making worship the content of practical obligation to the future, the model can diminish the significance of practical policies to protect the future of life from climate risks. Especially in the face of claims from today's hungry neighbors, those policies may appear as a temptation to false sacrifice—which is exactly what climate denialists claim. Muers does not shy from the presentist and anthropocentric implications. Running against usual notions of what an ethic of sustainability should say, Muers insists that enacting the love of God follows the pattern of "Jesus Christ the unsustainable." His "refusal to defer an act of healing, to wait for a proper season, to ignore a present demand, all place over against the 'sustainability' of a system the 'sustaining' of this or that person."[76] That is not a policy prescription; it is a refusal to sacrifice this particular person on a logic for a system that promises justice and life tomorrow. It is an insistence that the conditional good that the future most needs is the sort of love taught by Jesus: a love that attends to immediate neighbors and God above all else.

Muers is powerful in her insistence that the obligation of sustainability is to hold open the future against life-defeating ideologies, but her dialectical presentism seems too easily appropriated by religious and political appeals to the poor crafted to deny concrete responsibilities for climate change. Appeals to love might well leave the material structure of the fossil-fuel economy unchanged, with the irresponsibility moralized as a doing our best by our children in the knowledge that God brings a better future. Some North American Christian rhetoric on climate change makes exactly those points to reestablish a temporal imaginary in which future risks do not matter: love the present poor and wait on God's future. While Muers's whole account resists the sort of interpretation that would leave life untouched, her liturgical model needs two points of supplementation.

First, it must disentangle two kinds of presentism: between a chosen priority for today's hungry poor and the mesmerized selfishness of moment-to-moment consumerism. Smith sees that liturgical resistance includes "resisting a presentism that can only imagine 'living for the moment,'" thereby reorienting participants to the future.[77] Muers implies (but does not quite say) that loving solidarity with the hungry poor becomes training in living for the future. How does neighbor love reshape the temporal imaginary produced by consumerist impatience? Second, in order to offer an account of responsibility for climate powers, Christian ethics needs its intergenerational membership to include ecological membership. Can liturgies of eschatological expectation involve all creatures in waiting on the future?

PRACTICING THE FUTURE OF FORGIVENESS

Apocalyptic interruption seems a dangerous strategy of intergenerational ethics. In North American Christianity, fantasies of rapture deflect attention from responsibilities for the future and some pastors use eschatological visions to intentionally suppress climate risks. The *Left Behind* book series tutors a macabre reveling in the catastrophes awaiting those on the wrong side of Christ's return, supporting the sort of temporal imaginary that permits climate denialism. Environmentalist apocalypticism functions no better, as catastrophist fantasies of abrupt climate change on *The Day after Tomorrow* seem to counsel fatalist despair at doing anything. Or they fund zealous calls for vigilante destruction of industrial civilization.[78] Yet the very fact that popular apocalypticisms—religious and secular—function so badly for securing practical obligations to the future just underscores the need for ethics to engage eschatology.[79]

Christian liturgies do practice a kind of apocalyptic interruption, but they practice that interruption within long-cultivated traditions of waiting on the future. The Church of St. Paul & St. James inherited its liturgical practice from previous generations and holds itself accountable for passing them on to future generations. Even (especially) through its jazz improvisa-tion on the form, the church performs rites from its *Book of Common Prayer*, which preserves ancient forms of Christian worship shared across genera-tions. While the community does not explicitly reflect on its obligations to future generations, the practice of worship received from ancestors and carefully nurtured for the next generation cultivates an ethic of respon-sibility for the future. The act of liturgy is itself a transgenerational ethic, performing the communion of saints with inherited forms of interruption and anticipation.

What happens in worship shapes how participants inhabit time. If the meaning of its practice seems unclear or inadequate for inhabiting the tem-porality of climate change—as it does at St. Paul & St. James—then cul-tivating interruption and anticipation in an era of climate change begs for some liturgical changes. At least, Christians must ask whether their worship transforms the popular apocalypticisms carried in the everyday political and economic liturgies in which they participate. As atmospheric powers pro-ject human agency across new dimensions of time, creating fears about clos-ing horizons and specters of collapse, liturgists must find new ways to create the fulfilling interruptions that produce faithful openness to the future.

Meditating on the eschatological drama of Christian worship, theologian Hans Urs von Balthasar summarizes the way liturgy should transform cul-tural apocalypticism: "Christian hope changes this one-sided movement to-ward the future into a hope for something that is present and final, although it still waits for its fulfillment."[80] To help criticize Christian dramatization of the future, von Balthasar revisits two great twentieth century theologians of the future, Teilhard de Chardin and Jurgen Moltmann. Moltmann's theol-ogy of the cross makes political solidarity a theological practice that keeps history open to the change that God would work in it. Christians practice the future, writes Moltmann, by creating solidarity with those liberation projects that history would ignore, forget, and leave behind.[81] Teilhard con-nects Christian practice of the future with earth's evolutionary unfolding of the form of Christ. His notion of an emerging "noosphere," correspon-dent to humanity's growing powers over the planet's evolution, continues to attract public attention as a concept apt for thinking about anthropocene responsibility.[82]

Moltmann and Teilhard thus propose two practical conditions for wor-ship in the time of uncertain futures. Moltmann emphasizes solidarity with the poor as a way of keeping the powers of political history open to the future God brings. Teilhard emphasizes the involvement of earth's own time in the coming of Christ. Von Balthasar worries that in both the content of their hope is not as clear as it should be because the reality of the person of

Christ is not as definite as it should be. Without the real body of Christ present and open to participants, the future of political history and earth's evolutionary seems vague and unavailable in worship.[83] Von Balthasar illustrates two concrete points for liturgical reform in the time of climate change: liturgical practices need to more fully incorporate embodied solidarity with the poor (Moltmann) and cocreative celebration with all earth (Teilhard) in order to keep performing the fulfilling interruptions that reopen creation to its future in God (Muers after von Balthasar). Participating in the present body of Christ in worship must be experienced as also participating in the future body of Christ.

Loving God in worship does not magically rescue the future from violent powers; it opens hope from amid overwhelming failure and defeating violence. In the weekly services of St. Paul & St. James, shaping participants into a love that opens such hope requires reclaiming and reconnecting two ancient ways of worshiping: "the liturgy of the poor" and "cosmic liturgy." In the rest of this section I explain why recovering those two ways of worship could begin to make everyday liturgical life more competent to intergenerational risk.

Patristics scholar Susan Holman argues that the contemporary church has forgotten (for reasons easily guessed) its ancient "liturgy of the poor." Early authorities such as John Chrysostom, Jacob of Sarug, and the Cappadocians described receiving the poor as a form of liturgy because it was a way of commemorating the body of Christ. Feeding the poor is sacramental, they held, because Christ comes in the body of the hungry and suffering. Feeding the hungry was more than an expression of Christian charity, then; it was God's self-offering. Says Sarug, when you come across a beggar, recognize that "the Creator, to whom the entire creation belongs, has abased Himself so as to borrow from you."[84] Charity was Eucharist: a practice by which the faithful were habituated into the love needed for a future with God. Service to the bodily needs of the poor was more than an expression of liturgy; it *was* liturgical practice.

Charity on its own is no sufficient response to poverty but incorporating its practice into liturgy could help churches claim the importance that caring for needy persons exercises their way of caring for the future. At St. Paul & St. James, the exercise of distributing groceries on Saturday morning remains disconnected from the eucharistic table of Sunday morning. While a treasured and enduring social commitment, treated by many volunteers as their most important (and for some, only) religious ritual, the church has yet to make receiving the hungry a visible part of its liturgy.[85] Until we learn how to better welcome our Saturday visitors as occasions of transforming grace, as the real presence of the hungry body of Jesus, the parish's practice of the future remains thin and disincarnate. For the problem of climate change, when caring for the poor is part of the liturgical practice by which a church waits for the coming Christ, then it can credibly claim that it refuses to sacrifice the poor for the sake of the future by showing how it opens itself to the future from solidarity with the poor. Following Molt-mann, it practices the coming of God through solidarity with the crucified in history. Practicing hospitality to the presence of God as a form of liturgy helps drive moral discernment between two kinds of presentism: receiving each individual person's immediate need as a sacrament can be a practice that helps interrupt the selfishness of consumerist life and teach us to wait on the real bread of life.

The second liturgical change also reclaims an ancient and forgotten drama of Christ's body. Schmemann writes that "it is only because the Church's *leitourgia* is always cosmic, i.e., assumes into Christ all creation, and is always historical, i.e., assumes into Christ all time, that it can there-fore become eschatological, i.e., make us true participants of the Kingdom to come."[86] Schmemann there glosses a theological tradition with roots in Maximus the Confessor, who described all creatures as *logoi* in the *Logos*, and who understood liturgy as a cosmic event in which every creature finds its voice and role in the glorified body of Christ.[87] Yet, across communions, most Christian liturgies rarely make visible the presence of creatures other than humans. Most worship practices remain focused on a God-human dyad that seems naked of creation, garmented only by symbolic allusions to the rest of the cosmos. Nonhuman creatures rarely come to voice in church and rarely appear as tangible mysteries through which to find the glory of Christ. Participants in monoculture liturgies are shaped for a future inhab-ited only by humans—a future that anthropocene powers are doing their best to bring about.

In an era of biodiversity loss, the absence of nonhuman creatures from regular worship allows Christians to remain oblivious to what E. O. Wilson calls "the folly our descendants are least likely to forgive us."[88] Amid biologi-cal disappearances, worshiping without other creatures makes congregants supine to the powers that disappear creatures. Restoring diverse creaturely voices and earth's creativity into everyday presents a difficult challenge to the liturgical arts. The reform here requires much more than celebrating Earth Day or blessing pets on the Feast of St. Francis. The exceptionality and awkwardness of those days just underscores a fundamental ecological illiteracy in Christian worship.

Recovering creation into liturgy does not imply that worship must lose its otherworldliness. On the contrary, if disappearing life is the normal con-sequence of the world in which we live, then otherworldliness in worship may be needed to reconnect participants to earth. Christian indigenous councils have been asking other churches to recover that theological capacity to break from dominant cultural cosmologies. Lutheran liturgist Gordon Lathrop attempts to learn from indigenous cosmologies how to recover the subversive role of worship. In order to craft the poetics of antinarrative in a "sarcophobic" world, Lathrop argues that churches should learn from indigenous rituals how to teach love for creation.[89] Not all liturgies function equally well in shaping persons for resistance to the idolatries of a warming world; disrupting the logics of sacrifice requires churches to reverse the suppression of earth's flesh in worship, and encounter anew the goodness of creation. Indigenous peoples' churches challenge the worship of the wider Christian body to resist sacrifice of the future by bringing other creatures to voice within worship—including the groaning of Mother Earth and the polyphonous wisdom of God within creation.[90]

Recovering earth in theological symbol and giving voice to the praise of other creatures would be almost apocalyptically disruptive in the austerity of many churches. Paul Santmire agrees that it should be, opening his book on *Renewing Christian Liturgy in a Time of Crisis* by making his own connection of climate change and the Molech cult. Santmire agrees with Muers that liturgy overturns rituals of sacrifice, and with Smith, Cavanaugh, and Lathrop that it offers countercultural moral formation. In a time of climate change, he writes, liturgy is an eschatological practice, "a witness to the future arrival of the consummated creation."[91] Learning to worship God with other creatures is good apocalyptic, opening a community to the future of creation.

Christian worship thus has potential for teaching its participants how to inhabit the temporality of climate change and how to bear risks across generations as a practice of faith. I have argued that, in order to realize its potential as a practice of intergenerational responsibility, liturgists need to reclaim two dimensions of Christ's sacramental body: receiving the poor as the body of God, and worshiping with all creation to clothe the body of God. Those two ancient dimensions of liturgy once stood connected. Writes Holman, "'liturgies' to the needy were also understood on a suprahuman level, as action that contributed to the remaking and healing of the whole cosmic order."[92] Performed in a cultural time compressed by high-speed trading and "spent" in consumerist mania, liturgies must find a way to heal and redeem time. If sufficiently creative, they can reorient participants to the time of earth's evolutionary unfolding by teaching them how to wait on its future through acts of solidarity with today's poor.

A liturgical approach does not resolve the practical tensions of intergenerational ethics. It inducts participants into a transgenerational practice for bearing responsibility for the future before God. It makes our first obligation to future generations to sustain the interpretive practices through which the church names and bears how contemporary action risks the future. From their ancient ancestors, Christians receive liturgy as a practice that can unmask a bad logic of sustainability: sacrifice that promises to secure the future through the consuming fires of the present. Action that silences the poor and disappears other creatures, both in the name of securing tomorrow's growth, makes false sacrifice.

A liturgical approach does not suppose that a religiously pluralist world must come into Christian churches in order to interpret obligations to future generations. By nurturing its own interpretive practices for its particular transgenerational membership, Christian worship may help foster wider cultural debate over how societies enact obligations to the future. Liturgy illustrates one way to transmit the capacity of humans to live in conditions of human power by judging the temporal imaginaries of everyday life. Making explicit that function of liturgy and attempting to improve it, as this chapter has done, makes room for exploration of how other cultural practices transmit capacity for future generations to judge the practices of temporal responsibility that they inherit.

Religious worship of God (in whatever tradition) does, however, play a unique cultural role. This chapter had to work in the absence of any definite project, appealing to implicit and prospective aspects of liturgy. It can be depressing to do ethics in response to overwhelming problems, before ominous horizons, in the absence of meaningful responses. Worship is finally an act of hope that the future remains God's. Worship sustains hope that, even should this way of life collapse, God will act to open a new way of life. In his meditation on the Crow genocide, Lear writes that "radical hope anticipates a good for which those who have the hope as yet lack the appropriate concepts with which to understand it."[93] Worship is a way to hope even when nothing is happening. That kind of worship is not the hope that God will, just in time, rescue humans from their folly and sustain their way of life. On the contrary, worship prepares moral agents for a future they cannot understand or even imagine, for which they yet lack the concepts and practices.

Meanwhile, Christian liturgy works to sustain a thicker hope in the future of love. I have argued that Christian liturgy should incorporate theological projects often considered secondary to worship: sacramental hospitality to the hungry and sacramental celebration with all creatures. Those moments of worship happen in all the projects by which churches attempt to enact the body of Christ, and so (as Graham Ward puts it) "practice the future like a foreign tongue."[94] If undertaken as a liturgy, those projects become part of transgenerational practices that sustain the commitments to love through which Christians participate in God's judgment and redemption of all time. Liturgy then becomes a practice of confessing false sacrifices, bearing responsibility for the catastrophes they cause, and yet holding hope in the liturgy itself as the future of love. There are many sins and follies for which future generations may not forgive us. The hope that they will be able both to rightly judge us and, perhaps, to forgive us depends on passing on the interpretive practices that sustain love. We sustain hope by nurturing the capacity of the future to forgive us.

CONCLUSION

In the silence of theological ethics on intergenerational obligations, this chapter has treated liturgical practices as formation into an odd participation of time. It has explained major models of obligation to the future, including investment, membership, and precautionary models, and has argued for a liturgical model that focuses on preparing the future to evaluate what they inherit from us. By seeking to pass on the capacity of future generations to forgive us, this model offers a minimal way of bearing responsibility for the risks our actions pose to the future. For Christian worship to accomplish that training, churches need to better dramatize how loving solidarity with the poor and singing with all creation are sacramental acts. Our greatest intergenerational obligation, then, is to sustain love, for so we prepare future generations to judge us and, we hope, to forgive us.

Incense billows from the doors of St. Paul & St. James on All Saints Day. Members gather at the back of the church, circled around the baptismal font that holds the waters of future members, just in front of the columbarium that holds the ashes of deceased members. As the fragrant smoke rises into the church and out the doors into the sky, a cantor sings out the honored martyrs in the communion of saints: *Martin Luther King, shot down in Memphis . . . Oscar Romero, killed in El Salvador . . . Perpetua, torn by beasts in Carthage . . . Thomas Cranmer, burned in Oxford . . . Edith Stein, killed in Auschwitz. . . .* The smoke of execution pyres, of holocaust furnaces—these are the most abominable offerings that could be made to gods. By praying with those sacrificed for some idol of a human future, the church seeks God's way of opening a future where none seemed possible. The smoke of abominable sacrifices is, in worship, redeemed into the incense of prayer. The self-offering of Jesus ends the logic of sacrifice, opening a future made instead by love.

The membership of St. Paul and St. James waits on that future in its worship, which is where we experience God's judgment of the smoke and stench of humanity's incessant sacrifice, as well as God's way of forgiveness. Enough of your burnt sacrifices, says the prophet Isaiah; turn from evil, and begin learning justice by feeding the hungry children.[95] The pleasing offering is a contrite heart, ready to be converted anew to God and neighbor and so find love's way into the future. As the congregation turns from the smoky font to process toward the eucharistic table, it does not leave inherited evils behind nor rescue the future from their consequence. Blood is still spilled and burned in the name of gods. Pious indifference still sacrifices children, disappears species, haunts my child's future. Yet as it processes, its act of the congregation liturgy maintains the practice that teaches our children how to forgive us, how to sustain hope in a future we lacked the concepts to teach them, and how to begin practicing the future like a foreign tongue.

NOTES

1. United Nations Development Programme, *Fighting Climate Change: Human Solidarity in a Divided World* (New York: United Nations, 2008), 2.

2. United Nations Development Programme, *Fighting Climate Change*, 2.

3. Ernest Partridge, "Future Generations," in *A Companion to Environmental Philosophy*, Dale Jamieson, ed. (Oxford: Blackwell, 2003), 377–90.

4. Ernest Partridge, ed. *Responsibilities to Future Generations* (Buffalo, NY: Prometheus Books, 1981).

5. Hans Jonas, *The Imperative of Responsibility: In Search of an Ethics for the Technological Age* (Chicago: University of Chicago Press, 1984), 1.

6. Thomas Derr, "The Obligation to the Future," in Ernest Partridge, ed., *Responsibilities to Future Generations*, 40–41.

7. Daniel Callahan, "What Obligations Do We Have to Future Generations?" in *Responsibilities to Future Generations*, 73.

8. I use "temporal imaginary" in a way similar to the "social imaginary" of Charles Taylor: as a commonly shared sense of inhabiting time that makes possible the shared practices by which we orient ourselves to the future. Those practices may be financial (borrowing and saving), planning (insurance and trusts), as well as shared expectations in the way we explain personal and corporate acts in unfolding histories. See Charles Taylor, *A Secular Age* (Cambridge, MA: Belknap Press of Harvard University Press, 2007), 171–76.

9. Jonas, *Imperative of Responsibility*, 13–23, 123–28.

10. Stephen Gardiner, "A Perfect Moral Storm: Climate Change, Intergenerational Ethics, and the Problem of Corruption," *Environmental Values* 15 (2006).

11. Quoted in Emmanuel Agius, "The Earth Belongs to All Generations: Moral Challenges of Sustainable Development," in *Caring for Future Generations: Jewish, Christian, and Islamic Perspectives*, Emmanuel Agius and Lionel Chircop, eds. (Westport, CT: Praeger, 1998), 107.

12. United States Conference of Catholic Bishops, *Global Climate Change: A Plea for Dialogue* (2001).

13. Emmanuel Agius, "Intergenerational Justice," in *Handbook of Intergenerational Justice*, Joerg Chet Tremmel, ed. (Northampton, MA: Edward Elgar, 2006).

14. For example, Kristen Shrader-Frechette argues "that all persons in all generations have an equal, prima facie right to life and therefore to bodily security"; Shrader-Frechette, *Environmental Justice: Creating Equality, Reclaiming Democracy* (New York: Oxford University Press, 2002), 95–96. See also Edith Brown Weiss, "In Fairness to Future Generations and Sustainable Development," *American University Journal of International Law and Policy* 8, no. 1 (1992).

15. Laura Westra, *Environmental Justice and the Rights of Unborn and Future Generations* (London: Earthscan, 2006), 137.

16. Derek Parfit, *Reasons and Persons* (Oxford: Oxford University Press, 1984), 372–73.

17. See Richard Hiskes, *The Human Right to a Green Future: Environmental Rights and Intergenerational Justice* (New York: Cambridge University Press, 2009), 12–14.

18. Parfit, *Reasons and Persons*, 369–90.

19. IPCC 2007 Assessment Report, Section 4.1. See R. Swart et al., "The Problem of the Future: Sustainability Science and Scenario Analysis," *Global Environmental Change* 14 (2004).

20. Carol S. Robb, *Wind, Sun, Soil, Spirit: Biblical Ethics and Climate Change* (Minneapolis: Fortress, 2010).

21. P. Raskin et al., *Great Transition: The Promise and Lure of the Times Ahead* (Boston: Stockholm Environment Institute, 2002).

22. World Commission on Environment and Development, *Our Common Future* (New York: Oxford University Press, 1987), 43.

23. Robert Solow, "Sustainability: An Economist's Perspective," in *Economics of the Environment: Selected Readings*, Robert Dorfman and Nancy Dorfman, eds. (New York: W. W. Norton, 1993).

24. Gifford Pinchot, *The Fight for Conservation* (New York: Doubleday, 1910), 48 (my emphasis).

25. John Rawls, *Political Liberalism* (New York: Columbia University Press, 1996), 273–74. Rawls abandons his earlier stance in which parties in the original position are contemporaries representing family lines; see John Rawls, *A Theory of Justice* (Cambridge, MA: Belknap Press of Harvard University Press, 1971), 251–59.

26. For a development of Rawls in support of an intergenerational sustainability theory, see Marcel Wissenburg, "An Extension of the Rawlsian Savings Principle to Liberal Theories of Justice in General," in *Fairness and Futurity: Essays on Environmental Sustainability and Social Justice*, Andrew Dobson, ed. (Oxford: Oxford University Press, 1999). Also Clark Wolf, "Intergenerational Justice, Human Needs, and Climate Policy," in *Intergenerational Justice*, Axel Grosseries and Lukas Meyer, eds. (Oxford: Oxford University Press, 2009).

27. To calculate the present value of future costs, multiply cost by the discount factor yielded by this equation: $1/(1 + r)t$, where r is the discount rate and t is years from now.

28. Herman E. Daly et al., *For the Common Good: Redirecting the Economy toward Community, the Environment, and a Sustainable Future*, 2nd ed. (Boston: Beacon Press, 1994), 154.

29. Nicholas Stern, *The Economics of Climate Change: The Stern Review* (Cambridge: Cambridge University Press, 2006), i.

30. D. Pearce et al., "Valuing the Future," *World Economics* 4, no. 2 (2003).

31. There are different ways of explaining these two basic kinds of time preference. My terminology follows that of the IPCC's Second Assessment Report: K. J. Arrow et al., "Intertemporal Equity, Discounting, and Economic Efficiency," in *Climate Change 1995: Economic and Social Dimensions of Climate Change: Contribution of Working Group III to the Second Assessment Report of the Intergovernmental Panel on Climate Change*, James Bruce et al., eds. (IPCC, 1996). See also John Broome, "Discounting the Future," *Philosophy and Public Affairs* 23, no. 2 (1994).

32. Both Frank Ramsey and R. F. Harrod are quoted in Stern, *The Economics of Climate Change*, 31. (The Stern Review sets the pure time preference just above zero to account for the possibility that future generations might be eliminated by some catastrophic event.)

33. Arrow et al. in *Economic and Social Dimensions of Climate Change* think that Daly and Cobb are confused about the difference of the two kinds. See also P. Dasgupta, "Discounting Climate Change," *Journal of Risk and Uncertainty* 37, no. 2 (2008).

34. William D. Nordhaus, *A Question of Balance: Weighing the Options on Global Warming Policies* (New Haven, CT: Yale University Press, 2008).

35. Henry Shue, "Deadly Delays, Saving Opportunities: Creating a More Dangerous World?" in *Climate Ethics: Essential Readings*, Stephen Gardiner et al., eds. (New York: Oxford University Press, 2010), 157.

36. Matt. 6:19–34.

37. Edmund Burke, *Reflections on the Revolution in France* (Oxford: Oxford University Press, 1993), 96.

38. Avner de-Shalit, *Why Posterity Matters: Environmental Politics and Future Generations* (London: Routledge, 1995).

39. Hiskes, *The Human Right to a Green Future: Environmental Rights and Intergenerational Justice*.

40. Edward Page, *Climate Change, Justice and Future Generations* (Northampton, MA: Edward Elgar Publishing, 2006).

41. "The Anchorage Declaration," Indigenous Peoples' Global Summit on Climate Change, Anchorage, Alaska, April 24, 2009.

42. Bryan G. Norton, *Sustainability: A Philosophy of Adaptive Ecosystem Management* (Chicago: University of Chicago Press, 2005), 335–38.

43. E. A. Page, "Fairness on the Day after Tomorrow: Justice, Reciprocity and Global Climate Change," *Political Studies* 55, no. 1 (2007).

44. Michael Northcott, "Anthropogenic Climate Change, Political Liberalism and the Communion of Saints," *Studies in Christian Ethics* 24, no. 1 (2011): 44.

45. Page, *Climate Change, Justice, and Future Generations*, 149.

46. Wilfred Beckerman, *A Poverty of Reason: Sustainable Development and Economic Growth* (Oakland, CA: Independent Institute, 2002), 40.

47. Rachel Muers, *Living for the Future: Theological Ethics for Coming Generations* (New York: T. and T. Clark, 2008), 4, 127, 8–9. See also Rachel Muers, "The Gender of Generations: Future Generations and the Social Maternal," *Ecotheology* 11, no. 3 (2006).

48. On long-range uncertainties, see note 35, Dasgupta, "Discounting Climate Change," and John Broome, "Discounting the Future."

49. J. Lemons et al., "The Precautionary Principle: Scientific Uncertainty and Type I and Type II Errors," *Foundations of Science* 2, no. 2 (1997).

50. C. R. Sunstein, "Beyond the Precautionary Principle," *University of Pennsylvania Law Review* 151, no. 3 (2003).

51. Rawls, *A Theory of Justice,* 131–33.

52. Stephen Gardiner, "Protecting Future Generations: Intergenerational Buck-Passing, Theoretical Ineptitude, and a Brief for a Global Core Precautionary Principle," in *Handbook of Intergenerational Justice*, Joerg Chet Tremmel, ed. (Northampton, MA: Edward Elgar, 2006).

53. Sunstein, "Beyond the Precautionary Principle," 1016–18.

54. Jonas, *Imperative of Responsibility,* 37.

55. Jonas, *Imperative of Responsibility,* 118, 136, 139.

56. Brian Barry, "Sustainability and Intergenerational Justice," in *Environmental Ethics: An Anthology,* Andrew Light and Holmes Rolston, eds. (Oxford: Blackwell, 2003), 492–93.

57. Norton does not recognize his similarity with Barry, whose position he seems to misunderstand; see Norton, *Sustainability: A Philosophy,* 315–25.

58. Norton, *Sustainability: A Philosophy*, 328.

59. "Safe minimum standard" is Norton's version of precaution; Norton, *Sustainability: A Philosophy,* 346–48.

60. "Dasgupta, "Discounting Climate Change."

61. See Shue, "Deadly Delays, Saving Opportunities: Creating a More Dangerous World?", 157.

62. John O'Neill, "Future Generations: Present Harms," *Philosophy* 68, no. 263 (1993), 42.

63. Didier Fassin and Richard Rechtman, *The Empire of Trauma: An Inquiry into the Condition of Victimhood*, Rachel Gomme, trans. (Princeton, NJ: Princeton University Press, 2009), 275.

64. Jonathan Lear, *Radical Hope: Ethics in the Face of Cultural Devastation* (Cambridge: Harvard University Press, 2006).

65. Muers, *Living For the Future*, 2.

66. Rachel Muers, "Pushing the Limit: Theology and Responsibility to Future Generations," *Studies in Christian Ethics* 16, no. 2 (2003); Rachel Muers, "Idolatry and Future Generations: The Persistence of Molech," *Modern Theology* 19, no. 4 (2003); Muers, "The Gender of Generations: Future Generations and the Social Maternal"; Rachel Muers, "Feminist Theology as Practice of the Future," *Feminist Theology* 16, no. 1 (2007).

67. Muers, *Living for the Future,* 151.

68. Muers, *Living for the Future*, 143.

69. Muers, *Living for the Future*, 50, 197.

70. Muers, *Living for the Future*, 33.

71. Muers, "Idolatry and Future Generations," 555.

72. Muers, *Living for the Future*, 67, 70.

73. Alexander Schmemann, *For the Life of the World* (Crestwood, NY: St. Vladimir's Seminar Press, 1973).

74. James K. A. Smith, *Desiring the Kingdom: Worship, Worldview, and Cultural Formation* (Grand Rapids, MI: Baker Academic, 2009), 92.

75. William Cavanaugh, *Torture and Eucharist* (Oxford: Blackwell, 1998), 223, 226.

76. Muers, *Living for the Future,* 160.

77. Smith, *Desiring the Kingdom*, 157.

78. Tim Lahaye and Terry Jenkins, *Left Behind: A Novel of the Earth's Last Days* (Wheaton, IL: Tyndale House, 1996); *The Day after Tomorrow*, directed by Roland Emmerich (Los Angeles, CA: Twentieth Century Fox, 2004), DVD. On violent resistance, see Derrick Jensen, *Endgame: The End of Civilization* (New York: Seven Stories Press, 2006).

79. That is a key point in Barbara Rossing, *The Rapture Exposed: The Message of Hope in the Book of Revelation* (New York: Basic Books, 2005.) See also Barbara Rossing, "River of Life in God's New Jerusalem: An Eschatological Vision for Earth's Future," in *Christianity and Ecology: Seeking the Well-Being of Earth and Humans*, Dieter T. Hessel and Rosemary Radford Ruether, eds. (Cambridge, MA: Harvard University Press, 2000).

80. Hans Urs von Balthasar, *Theo-Drama: The Last Act*, vol. 5 (San Francisco: Ignatius Press, 1998), 152.

81. Gustavo Gutierrez asks "what will become of those favored by God in the world that is to come?" Gustavo Gutierrez, "Liberation Theology and the Future of the Poor," in *Liberating the Future: God, Mammon, and Theology*, Joerg Rieger, ed. (Minneapolis: Fortress, 1998), 104.

82. Described in von Balthasar, *Theo-Drama*, 152–80. See Pierre Teilhard de Chardin, *Le Phenomene Humain* (Paris: Editions de Seuil, 1955).

83. Von Balthasar died before he could read Moltmann's mature eschatology in Jürgen Moltmann, *The Coming of God: Christian Eschatology*, Margaret Kohl, trans. (Minneapolis: Fortress, 1996).

84. Sarug is quoted in Susan Holman, *God Knows There's Need: Christian Responses to Poverty* (New York: Oxford University Press, 2009), 49.

85. For provocative suggestions on how to integrate a food pantry and eucharistic liturgy, see Sara Miles, *Take This Bread: A Radical Conversion* (New York: Ballantine Books, 2008).

86. Schmemann, *For the Life of the World,* 123.

87. Willis Jenkins, *Ecologies of Grace: Environmental and Christian Theology* (New York: Oxford University Press, 2008), chaps. 10–11.

88. E. O. Wilson, *Biophilia* (Cambridge, MA: Harvard University, 1984), 121.

89. Gordon Lathrop, *Holy Ground: A Liturgical Cosmology* (Minneapolis: Fortress, 2003), 127.

90. "Joint Declaration of Indigenous Churches," World Council of Churches, May 21, 2009; "Cambio Climatico: Declaracion ecumenica," Latin American Council of Churches, April 22, 2010.

91. Paul Santmire, *Ritualizing Nature: Renewing Christian Liturgy in a Time of Crisis* (Minneapolis: Fortress Press, 2008), xiii, 39–45.

92. Holman, *God Knows There's Need*, 157.

93. Lear, *Radical Hope*, 103.

94. Graham Ward, *Cultural Transformation and Religious Practice* (Cambridge: Cambridge University Press, 2005), 170.

95. Paraphrase of Isaiah 1.

AFTERWORD

Sustaining Grace

✦

The last chapter concluded on a bleak note: perhaps the future of Christian ethics lies in sustaining the practices through which future generations might forgive us. Yet this book opened in the irenic, open spirit of pragmatism. Has its hope faded through wearying engagement with overwhelming problems and moral incompetencies? I have argued in each chapter that hope must be hard won; in the face of problems that defeat moral agency and social cooperation, hope is vindicated through projects that adapt, invent, and expand the practices that open new possibilities of cultural action. The pragmatist experiment of this book only works insofar as the problems it addresses are received as transforming judgments on our moral traditions and cultural ways of life. Christian faith offers no promise that we will succeed or that God will rescue our ways of life. Faith struggles to find how God is opening new ways from the midst of no way.

This book also concluded on a distinctly theological note—on forgiveness and grace. The experiment of this book has been methodologically pluralist, with Christian ethics playing host to many disciplines by serving as the running example of a tradition under strain. I have shown how overwhelming problems stress moral traditions by examining their difficulty for Christian life in particular. Whether Christian life can be sustained with integrity in the midst of these problems depends on whether and how communities of faith invent ways to keep loving neighbors, doing justice, and walking humbly with their God. Analogous demands hold for other traditions: their future depends on how their members generate new competencies of responsibility in the practices that sustain the tradition's meaning. Their religious creativity looks different because it is generated from different internal anxieties and logics, but it can play a similar sustaining role.

If, however, our cultures are already too corrupt or our traditions too incompetent to sustain their meaning amidst new problems, then the experiment of this book is damning. I have tried to create a generative tension between prophetic imagination and practical realism. John Dewey saw the liability to that pragmatist combination: "We thus tend to combine a loose and ineffective optimism with assent to the doctrine of take who take can: a deification of power." Dewey's answer, however, seems weak and cheaply religious: "faith in the power of intelligence to imagine a future which is the projection of the desirable in the present, and to invent the instrumentalities of its realization, is our salvation."[1] Ethics in the anthropocene era needs less confidence in our ability to save ourselves and less pious certainty about what is desirable about the present. To confront deifications and speak about salvation, the pragmatist could use a word from a theologian. Joseph Sittler once wrote that "light is not squeezed out of darkness by virtue of determination to transform darkness into light by the sheer alchemy of aspiration and felt need. But darkness realized is creative of a receptive theater for the drama of God's salvatory action in Christ; there is a *dynamics* of damnation."[2] My prophetic pragmatism supposes that we live in a time of gathering darkness and asks ethics to work with the dynamics of damnation. When reform projects interpret the problems we face as damning of the traditions they have inherited and of the futures our powers are making, they open space for moral transformation.

Something analogous holds, I think, for all moral traditions. One need not be Christian to think that hope for some kind of salvation from ourselves waits on something beyond what we can make or change, or even expect. Hope lives in wait upon something like grace—on goods that we cannot take or make on our own, that come only as gift. Meditating on the future of Crow culture after genocide, the philosopher Jonathan Lear writes that "radical hope anticipates a good for which those who have the hope as yet lack the appropriate concepts with which to understand it."[3] Industrial civilization has not yet collapsed and it is likely to keep inventing ever more destructive instrumentalities to sustain its powers. The projects that I described generating an ecology of justice, an economy of desire, and the future of love do not seek a sustainability of the same violence and ugliness. They anticipate goods for which they still lack concepts and do not yet fully understand. Because it is not reproduction of the same, not mere extension of this way of life into the future, hope is both an arduous practical task and a form of waiting for transformation.

Sustaining hope lies finally not in adaptively managing environments, nor in greening economies, protecting rights, ending poverty, or saving biodiversity. It certainly depends on creative efforts to do those things but it will be vindicated by something we do not yet possess. We are sustained, finally, by grace. In the practical problems, especially overwhelming and wicked problems, we are confronted by mysteries that we cannot solve but must learn to live. Facing those problems we face anew a mystery of human life: how to see ourselves as evolutionary products and yet somehow capable of transcending it? How to see ourselves as planetary managers and yet fragile creatures? This book has argued that learning from our problems is a way of learning aspects of the mystery in which we live. Through discovering what practices of love can mean for climate change or what we can make justice do in the ecology of toxins, we let earth teach us what story to tell about ourselves. What must we sustain? Not our power or our way of life; not even human survival. We are sustained by grace, and so we must sustain our openness to being transformed by graces not our own.

NOTES

1. John Dewey, *The Political Writings*, Debra Morris and Ian Shapiro, eds. (Indianapolis, IN: Hackett Publishing, 1993), 9.

2. Joseph Sittler, "A Theology for Earth," *The Christian Scholar* vol. 37, no. 3 (1954): 369.

3. Jonathan Lear, *Radical Hope: Ethics in the Face of Cultural Devastation* (Cambridge, MA: Harvard University Press, 2006), 103.

Index

CPSIA information can be obtained
at www.ICGtesting.com
Printed in the USA
BVOW08s0146180118
505449BV00002B/109/P